BECOMING ROMAN, BEING GALLIC, STAYING BRITISH

BECOMING ROMAN, BEING GALLIC, STAYING BRITISH

Research and Excavations at Ditches 'Hillfort' and Villa 1984–2006

Stephen Trow, Simon James and Tom Moore

Oxbow Books

First published in the United Kingdom in 2009. Reprinted in 2017 by
OXBOW BOOKS
The Old Music Hall, 106–108 Cowley Road, Oxford OX4 1JE

and in the United States by
OXBOW BOOKS
1950 Lawrence Road, Havertown, PA 19083

Paperback Edition: ISBN 978-1-84217-336-7
Digital Edition: ISBN 978-1-78297-532-8 (epub)

A CIP record for this book is available from the British Library

For a complete list of Oxbow titles, please contact:

UNITED KINGDOM
Oxbow Books
Telephone (01865) 241249
Email: oxbow@oxbowbooks.com
www.oxbowbooks.com

UNITED STATES OF AMERICA
Oxbow Books
Telephone (800) 791-9354, Fax (610) 853-9146
Email: queries@casemateacademic.com
www.casemateacademic.com/oxbow

Oxbow Books is part of the Casemate Group

Front cover: Excavation of the villa in 1985
Back cover: Aerial photograph of Ditches enclosure in 1985 (NMR copyright)

CONTENTS

LIST OF FIGURES

LIST OF TABLES

PREFACE

Ditches lies in the Gloucestershire Cotswolds. The site takes its name from the now-slighted earthworks of an Iron Age enclosure, or small hillfort, covering 4ha/10 acres occupied in the later Iron Age. This was apparently directly succeeded by a startlingly early 'Roman villa' located within the Iron Age earthwork. These remains overlook the valley of the Bagendon brook, flowing southwards to pass through the massive Bagendon Dykes just above its confluence with the Churn, which then carries its waters southwards through Cirencester, Roman *Corinium,* on its way to join the Upper Thames.

The history of this exceptional site spans the transition from Iron Age to Roman Britain. What might continuity of occupation here between the two periods tell us about that process in the Cotswolds? How does Ditches relate to the contemporaneous and more famous site a few kilometres downstream, the so-called *oppidum* at Bagendon, and its great earthworks flanking the entrance to the valley?

Including recent additional field-work by Tom Moore and interpretations of the site in the context of current understandings of Iron Age and Roman Britain, the present volume reports primarily on a project which was part of a wider campaign of research excavation and field survey conducted in the environs of Bagendon during the early 1980s by staff and graduate students from the University of London Institute of Archaeology (now part of University College London), assisted by a group of enthusiastic and highly skilled local volunteers. This programme was concentrated on two projects: renewed, small-scale excavation at Bagendon, building on the work of Elsie Clifford (1961), led by Dr Richard Reece (Moore, Reece and Trow forthcoming), followed by fieldwork further up the valley at Ditches.

In 1980 the Ditches site had been included in a list of sites meriting urgent rescue excavation as a result of a survey of plough damaged sites in the Gloucestershire Cotswolds (Saville 1980), one of a series of similar prioritisation exercises undertaken in key areas of arable cultivation. Sadly, these strategic surveys delivered comparatively limited results, partially because the resultant lists of threatened sites massively outstripped the resources available for rescue archaeology and partially because, by the 1980s, the emphasis of state-funded archaeology was turning to other threats, particularly destruction caused by development and aggregate extraction and the loss of wetlands.

Notwithstanding this, the proposal of the site as a candidate for rescue excavation, coupled with the results of local amateur archaeologist Will Saunder's fieldwalking – which drew attention to the site's potential links with Bagendon – stimulated the interest of Stephen Trow and Simon James, leading them to undertake excavations between 1982 and 1985.

The results of the 1982–3 work were published in the *Transactions of the Bristol and Gloucestershire Archaeological Society*

(Trow 1988a), and partial post-excavation analysis was undertaken for the 1984–5 seasons. Sadly, shortage of funds and the demands of paid employment in archaeology prevented the completion of post excavation work. Consequently the project languished, although the resultant recognition of the site's importance ensured that it was scheduled by the Secretary of State in 1988 and had already been taken out of cultivation in 1986 by its owner, Henry Robinson, with grant-aid provided through the Cotswold Environmentally Sensitive Area Scheme in 2005. The excavation work at Ditches, although limited in scale and delayed in final publication, has nevertheless averted the threat initially recognised by Alan Saville.

Simon James's return to the university sector in the late 1990s (first at Durham, now at Leicester) offered the renewed possibility of progress. Fundamental to this was the interest and willingness of Dr Tom Moore to bring the publication to fruition, in collaboration with the original excavators. Cirencester-bred himself, and now a lecturer at Durham University, an Iron Age archaeologist with the local knowledge and enthusiasm required for the task, Tom Moore was the ideal researcher to complete this work. We are both very grateful to him for taking this on and bringing it to a successful conclusion.

It may be asked, what is the value of publishing this relatively old excavation now? Our justification is simple. The implications of the data from Ditches were of national significance in 1985, but are of even greater relevance and topicality now, since they contribute directly to one of the most prominent themes in contemporary archaeological research: the nature of the Iron Age to Roman transition in southern Britain. Our understanding of this is being revolutionised, not least by the work of John Creighton (2000; 2006). New conceptions are challenging the significance of the Claudian invasion of AD 43, suggesting that Roman political influence in southern Britain was much more important than commonly thought decades before this. Instead of a sudden dramatic event, the Roman take-over was a long drawn-out process, which began especially with intimate links between Caesar and his successors the Julio-Claudian emperors on one side, and the dynasts they supported or implanted in Britain on the other. High status archaeological sites central to these relations, including the so-called *oppida,* developed in southern Britain in the decades between Caesar's raids and the Claudian occupation. Those at Colchester, Silchester and Verulamium subsequently developed into Roman cities, but there were other such centres of late Iron Age and earliest Roman-period royal power, and alternative trajectories of development. The Ditches–Bagendon–Cirencester complex surely represents one such centre, although the limited scale of investigation to date makes its story less certain. The potential significance of Ditches in the light of these initial investigations is explored in the present volume, and will be considered further in subsequent publications.

Stephen Trow and Simon James

SUMMARY

Excavations at Ditches, Gloucestershire during the 1980s investigated a large late Iron Age enclosure which proved to contain a remarkably early Roman villa. Excavation of the enclosure ditch and internal features, including storage pits and an occupation layer indicated occupation from the late Iron Age into the Roman period. Several phases of Romano-British building were uncovered revealing an unusual sequence of development for a villa in the region and representing an exceptionally early villa beyond south east England. Discoveries included a well-preserved cellar and a range of finds, including Gallo-Belgic wares, Iron Age coins, coin moulds, Venus figurines and brooches indicating high-status occupation in the late Iron Age and early Roman period. The site appears to have been part of a larger complex, which included the dykes of the '*oppidum*' at Bagendon, the relationship between these elements enabling a new perspective on the late Iron Age–Roman transition in southern Britain. The form and date of the villa also sheds light on the relationships between the late Iron Age elites and communities of southern England and Gaul. Further evidence suggests the villa was abandoned in the later second century AD, emphasising the unusual sequence of the site.

The excavations of 1984–5 have been augmented by further work, including a new geophysical survey and reassessment of the finds, providing further evidence of the nature of Iron Age and Roman activity. Alongside re-appraisal of much of the 1980s evidence, this analysis allows the earlier material to be compared with more recent studies of the late Iron Age–Roman transition contributing to debates over processes of 'Romanization', questions of social and political continuity and the nature of villa development in Britain.

RESUMÉ

Les fouilles menées durant les années 1980 à Ditches, dans le comté du Gloucester, mirent au jour un vaste enclos remontant à la fin de l'âge du fer et dans lequel s'est développée une remarquable villa gallo-romaine précoce. La fouille de cet enclos et des structures internes, en particulier de silos et d'une couche d'occupation, indiquait que l'occupation était continue de l'âge du fer à l'époque gallo-romaine. Plusieurs phases de constructions romano-britanniques ont été identifiées, témoins d'une rare séquence de développement de ce genre de site pour cette région du sud-est de l'Angleterre. Il convient de noter la découverte d'un cellier remarquablement conservé et d'une série de mobilier incluant des céramiques gallo-belges, des monnaies moules de monnaies de l'âge du Fer, des statuettes de Vénus et des fibules plaçant cet établissement à un niveau élevé de la hiérarchie à la fin de l'âge du Fer et à la période romaine précoce. Il semble cependant s'intégrer dans un ensemble plus vaste, qui incluait le barrage de l'« oppidum » de Bagendon, les relations entre ces deux éléments entrouvrant de nouvelles pistes de recherches pour cette période charnière dans le sud de la Grande Bretagne.

La reprise des prospections géophysiques et une nouvelle étude du mobilier a permis de compléter les travaux remontant aux années 1984–1985, confirmant la nature des activités à l'âge du fer et à l'époque gallo-romaine alors entrevues. La réévaluation de ce site et de ce mobilier permet ainsi de fournir de nouveaux éléments au débat en cours sur le processus et les vecteurs de la « romanisation », concernant en particulier la pérennité des structures sociales et politiques et le rôle de la villa dans le développement de la Grande Bretagne romaine.

Traduction: Pierre Nouvel

ZUSAMMENFASSUNG

Im Rahmen der Ausgrabungen in Ditches, Gloucestershire, in den 1980er Jahren wurde eine große Befestigungsanlage der späten Eisenzeit untersucht, in deren Innern die Überreste einer bemerkenswert frühen römischen Villa zutage kamen. Befunde aus dem Bereich des Grabens und Strukturen aus der Innenfläche, wie Speichergruben und eine Siedlungsschicht, deuten auf eine Nutzung der Anlage von der späten Eisen- bis in die frühe Römerzeit. Darüber hinaus konnten anhand von Gebäuderesten mehrere Phasen romano-britischer Siedlungsaktivität erfasst werden, die auf eine, für diese Region unübliche Entwicklungssequenz deuten und die außerhalb von Südostengland sehr frühe Zeitstellung der Villa unterstreichen. Neben einem gut erhaltenen Keller kam auch eine große Zahl von Funden zutage, darunter Belgische Ware, eisenzeitliche Münzen sowie Gussformen derselben, Venus-Figuren und Fibeln, die auf die Anwesenheit einer Oberschicht in der späten Eisen-, wie auch der frühen Römerzeit schließen lassen. Die Fundstelle dürfte als Teil eines größeren Komplexes anzusehen sein, zu dem auch die Wälle des Oppidums von Bagendon gehören, wobei die Beziehung zwischen diesen einzelnen Strukturen schlaglichtartig neue Einblicke in den Übergang von der späten Eisen- zur frühen Römerzeit in Südengland erlaubt. Formale Charakteristika und Datierung der Villa sind auch im Hinblick auf die Kontakte zwischen späteisenzeitlichen Eliten bzw. Gesellschaften Südenglands und Galliens von Bedeutung. Die Villa scheint schließlich im späten zweiten Jahrhundert n. Chr. verlassen worden zu sein, was erneut die ungewöhnliche chronologische Stellung dieses Komplexes in der Region unterstreicht.

Die Ausgrabungen der Jahre 1984/85 wurden durch weiterführende Untersuchungen ergänzt, darunter neue geophysikalische Prospektionen sowie eine Neubearbeitung des Fundmaterials, um auf diese Weise den Charakter eisenzeitlicher und römischer Aktivitäten in der Region erfassen zu können. Über eine Neubeurteilung der in den 1980er Jahren zusammengetragenen Informationen hinaus, konnte im Rahmen dieser Analyse das frühe Fundmaterial mit jüngsten Studien zum Übergang von der späten Eisen- zur frühen Römerzeit verglichen werden, um somit einen Beitrag zur Diskussion um den Romanisierungsprozeß selbst, wie auch zur Frage sozialer und politischer Kontinuitäten sowie der Entwicklung römischer Villen in Britannien zu leisten.

Übersetzung: Sabine Hornung

ACKNOWLEDGEMENTS

All three authors would like to express their gratitude to Henry Robinson, the owner of the Ditches site, for the considerable help and encouragement he provided during the original work and with the 2006 geophysical survey. His continued commitment to the future preservation of the monument is especially welcome. Thanks must also go to the many archaeologists and interested amateurs who freely gave up their time to work on the site. There are too many to mention individually but special thanks must go to Will and Fran Saunders, our local helpers, without whom the project would not have been possible; to those volunteers who helped over a period of years notably Catherine Roberts, Roland Smith, Simon Smith, Justin James, Bobby Entwhistle and Danny Merceron; to Sue Trow who provided invaluable help with the post-excavation work; and to Lyndon Trow for help with the preparation of interim reports. We would also like to thank Peter Horne, then of RCHME (now EH) air photographic unit, for tipping us off that new air photos of Ditches showed the hitherto unsuspected villa. The 2006 geophysical survey was undertaken by Tom Moore with assistance from Claire Nesbitt, Akira Nishitani and Adam Rogers. Thanks are due to English Heritage for granting a Section 42 licence for this work. We would also like to express our gratitude to the staff of Moorwood farm, Paula Gentil at Corinium Museum, Cotswold District Council, the Cirencester Excavation Committee and HGM Leighton for their assistance. We would like to thank all the authors of the specialist reports who kindly revised their contributions, 15 years after the originals, in a speedy and understanding way and for new specialist reports from Steven Willis and Fiona Roe. Thanks also to Annette Hancocks for identification of the kiln evidence. The illustrations are by Joe Skinner, Claire Thorne, Tom Moore and Deborah Miles.

Financial support for the work was provided by the Bristol and Gloucestershire Archaeological Society, Cotswold District Council, the Council for British Archaeology, the Institute of Archaeology Gordon Childe Bequest Fund, the Robert Kiln Charitable Trust, the Roman Society, the Royal Archaeological Institute, and The Society of Antiquaries of London. In 2004, the Headley Trust and The Society of Antiquaries of London provided a grant to enable the writing up and publication of the excavation and we would like to express our gratitude for their support. We would particularly like to thank Martin Millett for his help and advice. Finally, we are grateful to Richard Hingley, Steven Willis and Richard Reece for reading and commenting on earlier drafts of the text, to Roy Friendship-Taylor for information on Piddington and Sarah Monks for her work on the final edit. The views expressed, and any errors, remain the responsibility of the authors.

INTRODUCTION

Site location

Ditches enclosure (SO 996095) is situated 8km north-north-west of Cirencester in the parish of North Cerney, some 500m west of the modern hamlet of Woodmancote (Fig. 1). The site lies 220m above sea level on the western shoulder of a south-facing spur of Great Oolite limestone defined by the Bagendon Brook and the River Churn. To the north and east, the site is surrounded by very gently rising land; to the south and west it is flanked by shallow dry valleys and overlooks the Bagendon valley. Southwards, the site has extensive views as far as the Marlborough Downs. The Bagendon valley is cut through the Great Oolite and the underlying Fuller's Earth and from the interface of these deposits, immediately south of the site, several springs emerge and drain into the brook.

The site and its previous archaeological investigation

The site comprises an Iron Age enclosure superseded by a Romano-British villa complex (GSMR 4684). Frequently described as a 'hillfort' (e.g. RCHME 1976), as will be discussed later, the form and date of the enclosure suggest it may be better regarded as a 'large enclosure'. It occupies part of two modern arable fields, 'Ditches' to the north and 'Barley Slad' to the south, and is bisected by a farm trackway. Plough damage to the site is severe and few features surviving as earthworks are obvious at ground-level. On drawings made for the first Ordnance Survey *c.* 1815, the perimeter of the enclosure is visible in the pattern of field boundaries, one of which still survives. The site was first recorded from the air by W. A. Baker in 1959 and subsequently visited as part of the RCHME Cotswold survey (RCHME 1976, 85). An assessment of plough-damage was also carried out by CRAAGS (Saville 1980).

Aerial photography and a partial geophysical survey (Trow 1988a, 21–24) revealed that the site comprises a double-ditched oval enclosure, with its southern and eastern sides slightly 'flattened' (Figs 3 & 4). A pair of ditches defining a trackway leads from an entrance at the north-eastern corner of the enclosure into a dry valley east of the site. To the south-west a curving 'antenna' ditch runs from a second entrance into a second dry valley to the west. Within the enclosure a ditched trackway, abruptly changing direction twice, joins the north-eastern and south-western entrances. Other features within the enclosure include lengths of ditch and a variety of pit-like features.

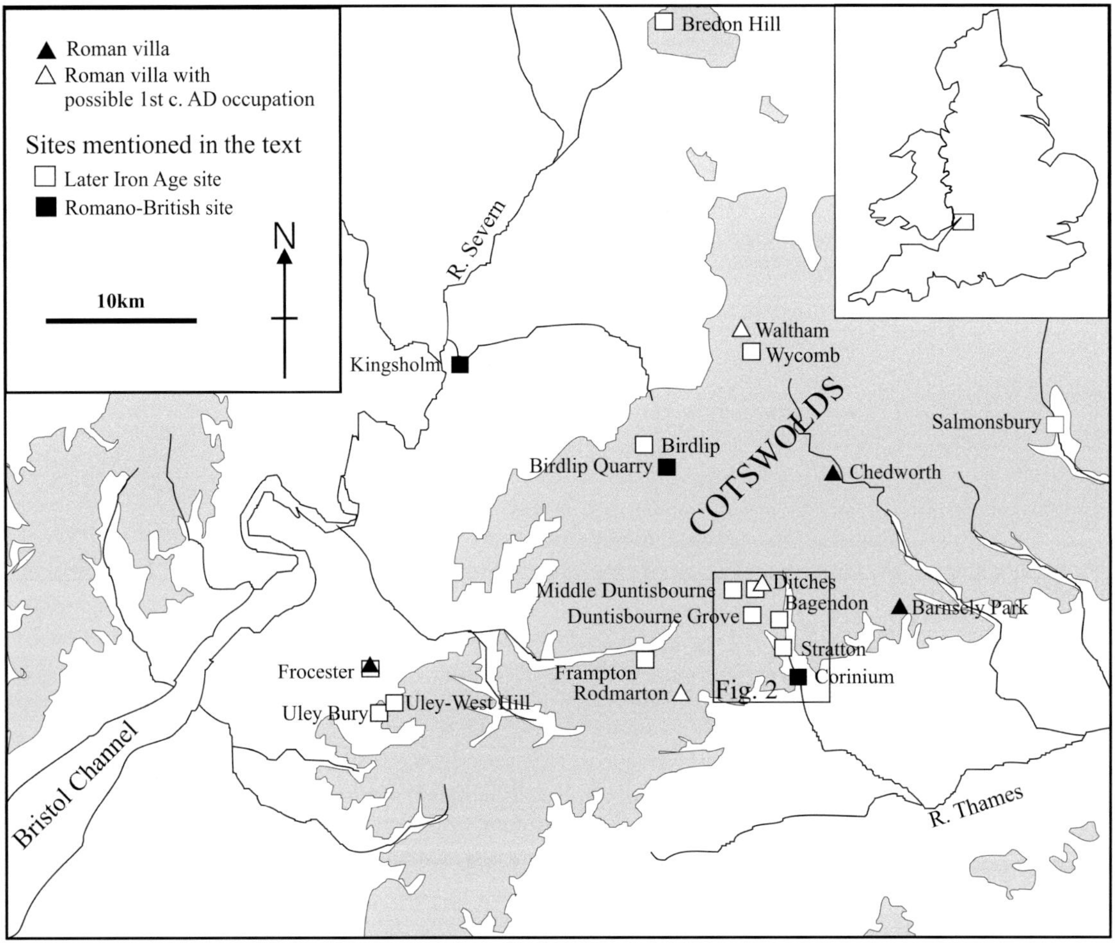

Fig. 1. Location of Ditches enclosure in relation to selected Late Iron Age and Roman sites in the region.

The RCHME survey recorded the presence of Romano-British material in the ploughsoil of the site and suggested the presence of a Roman building in the south-eastern corner of the enclosure (RCHME 1976, 85). It was not until 1984, after several episodes of aerial reconnaissance, that the position of Romano-British buildings within the enclosure was finally confirmed by the RCHME Air Photographic Unit (Fig. 3, NMR SQ 9909/23/3209-3213 to 33/1254-1255). These images revealed the presence of a masonry-built Romano-British structure, apparently a villa building, in the north-western quadrant of the enclosure. The building appeared as a main block of six rooms oriented east–west with a corridor to the north, south, and west. Fieldwalking of the interior of the enclosure confirmed the presence of a widespread scatter of Romano-British occupation debris with a concentration of third and fourth century AD pottery in the south west quadrant. Amongst the material recovered were two fine intaglios (Trow 1982). Between 1982 and 1985 excavations were carried out to examine the date of the enclosure and contemporary occupation and the

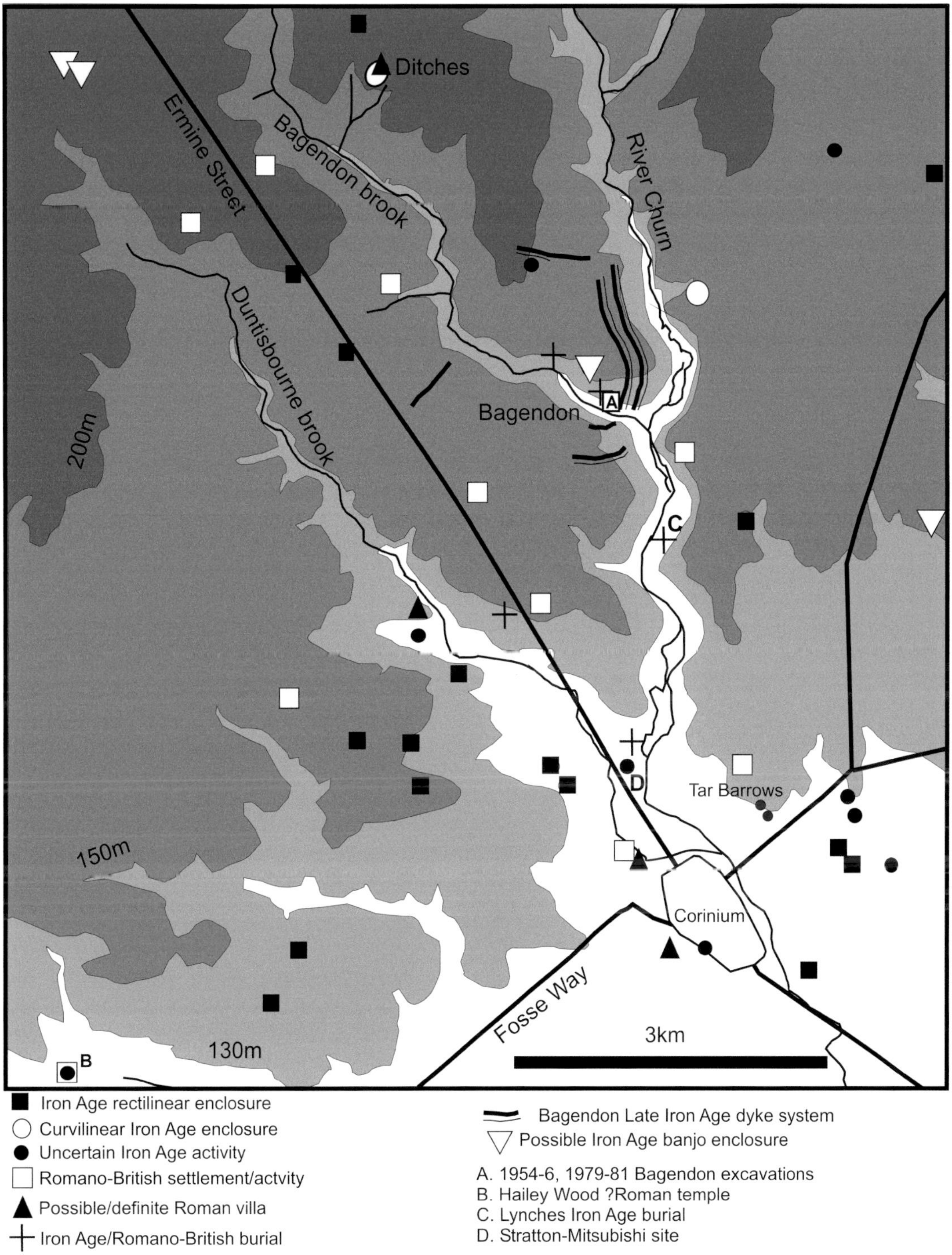

Fig. 2. Ditches and the Bagendon environs.

Fig. 3. Air photograph of Ditches enclosure taken in 1984, looking east, showing the villa as a cropmark.

nature and date of the Roman villa. A dark area visible on the geophysical survey undertaken in 1982 (Trow 1988a, 25) was also examined. The 1982–3 excavations (Figs 5 & 6), trenches A, B, C and D, focused on the nature and date of the Iron Age enclosure and have already been published (Trow 1988a). The 1984–5 excavations form the basis of this report.

Regional settlement pattern (Figs 1 & 2)

Little fieldwork has been carried out in the area immediately north of Cirencester. Known Iron Age sites are relatively rare, represented mainly by upstanding monuments such as hillforts and a number of cropmark enclosures (Moore 2006b; RCHME 1976). Since the excavation of Ditches a number of rescue excavations have provided broader evidence for the context of the site. Of particular importance has been the excavation of two probable enclosures at Middle Duntisbourne and Duntisbourne Grove *c.* 2.5km to the south of Ditches. These contain similar assemblages of late

Iron Age/early Roman material dating to the early first century AD and are seemingly provided with a terminus ante quem by the building of Ermin Street which overlies both (Mudd *et al.* 1999, 95). More recently, isolated pits containing late Iron Age and early Roman material have been revealed at Stratton, near Cirencester and may suggest another, as yet uninvestigated, late Iron Age site in the area (Wymark 2003). In addition, to the south of Bagendon an isolated burial at Baunton/Lynches has been radiocarbon dated to approximately the first century BC (Mudd *et al.* 1999, 76). Elsewhere on the Cotswolds Iron Age and early Roman enclosures at Birdlip (Parry 1998) and The Bowsings, Guiting Power (Marshall 1995), both occupied in the first century AD, indicate the nature of late Iron Age settlement in the region. To the east an enclosure at Winson was excavated in the 1980s (Cox 1985) and, although not fully published, appears to date to the early or middle Iron Age. Late Iron Age activity has also been identified at Wycomb near Cheltenham (Timby 1998) and at Frocester in the Severn

Fig. 4. Aerial photograph, looking north east, of enclosure showing the outer antenna ditch.

Valley (Price 2000). Limited evidence also suggests possible late Iron Age activity at the site of the potential Roman Temple complex at Hailey Wood (Moore 2001). Ditches has also been included amongst a group of enclosures defined as small 'hillforts' which are scattered across the Cotswolds dipslope, with its nearest known neighbours at Pinbury and Norbury (RCHME 1976), although whether these enclosures have any functional or chronological similarities is uncertain.

The pattern of late Iron Age settlement in the immediate area of Ditches is dominated by the Bagendon '*oppidum*', an area of between 80–200 hectares centred on the Bagendon Brook, a tributary of the River Churn, and partially enclosed by a system of dykes. Limited excavation here in the 1950s (Clifford 1961) led to the identification of Bagendon as the tribal centre and mint of the Dobunni. A reassessment of Clifford's work (Swan 1975, 59–61) questioned the late Iron Age dating applied to the occupation of the excavated area at Bagendon and proposed an alternative dating in the early years of the Roman occupation. Excavations adjacent to Clifford's trenches in the 1980s (Moore *et al.* forthcoming) have added some support to this proposal although there may be evidence of occupation prior to the conquest.

The Romano-British settlement pattern in this area comprises a mixture of minor farmsteads and probable villa sites. On the same ridge as the Ditches site, some 2km to the north west is the settlement at Combend (RCHME 1976, 35–6), while 2km to the south, on the opposite side of the valley is another Romano-British site at Stancombe (RCHM 1976, 49–50). Both settlements include several masonry structures and, unlike the Ditches site, they are situated in sheltered valley-side positions straddling the spring-line. Some 1.5km to the west on the ridge opposite Ditches, is a complex of cropmark enclosures apparently linked to a Romano-British masonry-built building by a trackway (RCHME 1976, 48). Within a radius of 10km of Ditches there are at least 13 known settlements which can be classified as villas including the extensively excavated establishments at Barnsley Park and Chedworth (RCHME 1976, 26; Webster 1981a). The context of Ditches and Bagendon in the Iron Age and early Roman landscape of the region is the subject of a further review in a subsequent article (Moore *et al.* in prep.).

THE 1984–5 EXCAVATIONS

The site (Fig. 5)

The 1982–3 seasons of excavations at the site have been fully published elsewhere (Trow 1988a) and this discussion will concentrate solely on the results of the 1984–5 seasons. Continuing the practice of the 1982–3 seasons, the latter two campaigns each comprised the work of a small team of excavators (mostly students and local volunteers) over several weeks, in September 1984 and July–August 1985. Four trenches, E, F, G, and H, were excavated during the two seasons. Trenches E and H (Fig. 5) were positioned immediately south-west of Trench D, the North-East gate area of the Iron Age enclosure, excavated in 1983 (Trow 1988a, fig. 14), while trenches F and G were positioned in order to locate and examine the villa building (Structure 1: Fig. 5 and 16). In trenches E and F the topsoil was removed using a Massey Ferguson 20H tractor although final stripping was carried out by hand in order to minimise damage to underlying contexts. In trenches G and H topsoil stripping was carried out manually and, apart from surface cleaning in order to study features in plan, no contexts were excavated.

The aims of the excavation

Trenches E and H, excavated during 1984 (Fig. 6), were intended to explore features on the eastern perimeter of the site in order to assess the implications of a possible hedgerow removal operation. As such the 1984 work was complementary to the work of the previous two seasons (Trow 1988a, 24). Geophysical survey in 1983 suggested the presence of pit-like features in the area south-west of Trench D and it was hoped that sampling of these features would determine their relationship to the previously sampled inner perimeter ditch of the Iron Age enclosure and provide evidence for the nature of the pre-conquest occupation within the enclosure (Trow 1988a).

In 1984 and 1985, the purpose of trenches F and G was to locate on the ground the masonry-built structure revealed by aerial photography (Fig. 5). To this end, Trench F originally took the form of a hand-dug area 2m wide and 14.4m long north–south designed to determine the position and dimensions of the building and Trench G was positioned in order to locate its north-western corner.

The aims of the 1985 season were to determine the plan and dimensions of the building, its date of construction and developmental history, its state of

Fig. 5. Plan of Ditches enclosure based on aerial photographs with location of 1982–5 trenches.

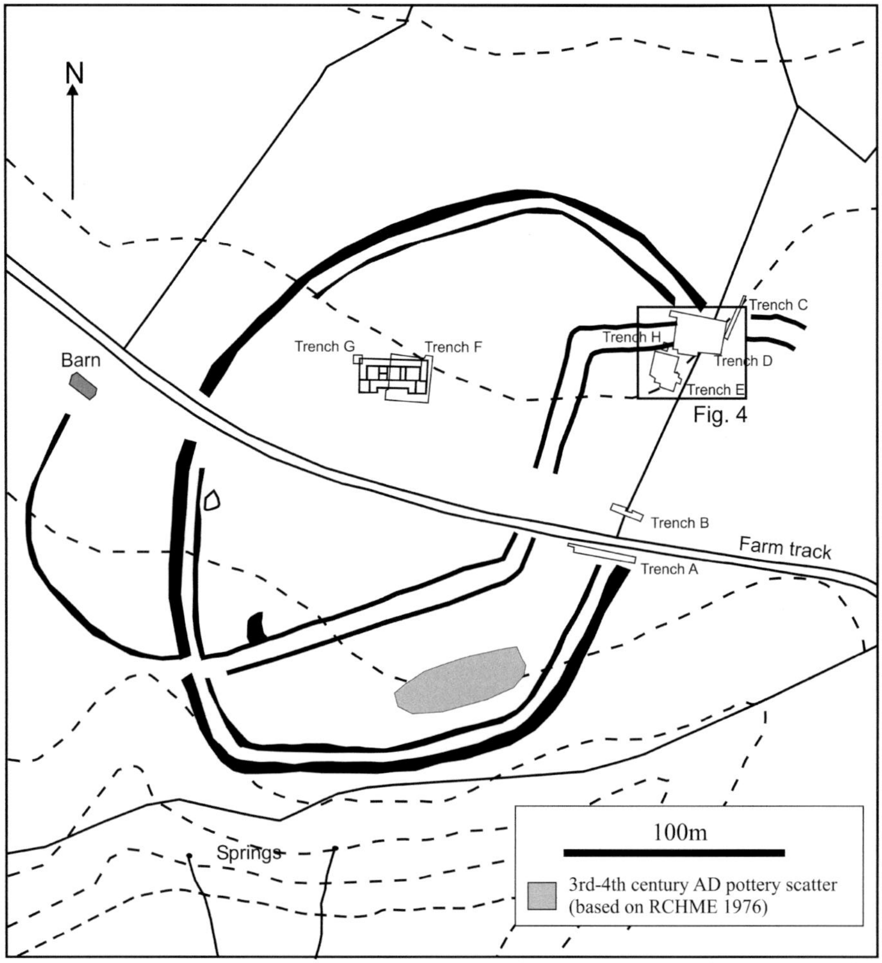

preservation, and its susceptibility to plough-damage. The purpose of the work was to establish whether the building was eligible for statutory protection or whether, if damage to the site was very severe, further large-scale excavation work was a more suitable response.

The apparent lack of cropmark definition at the eastern end of the building indicated that the destruction caused by cultivation might be particularly advanced here. Accordingly, this area was chosen for excavation and in 1985 Trench F was expanded to include the eastern half of the building. Trenches F and G were intended to meet the aims set out above by means of the sampling of preserved contexts rather than by total excavation.

The excavations defined archaeological features by trench name and individual context numbers to define both fills ( ) and cuts/features [ ]: e.g.. *F[400]*, *E(320)*. Throughout small finds are identified by *s.f.* followed by the number. The s.f. from contexts associated with a particular phase of activity are listed and can be found in the catalogues of specialist reports.

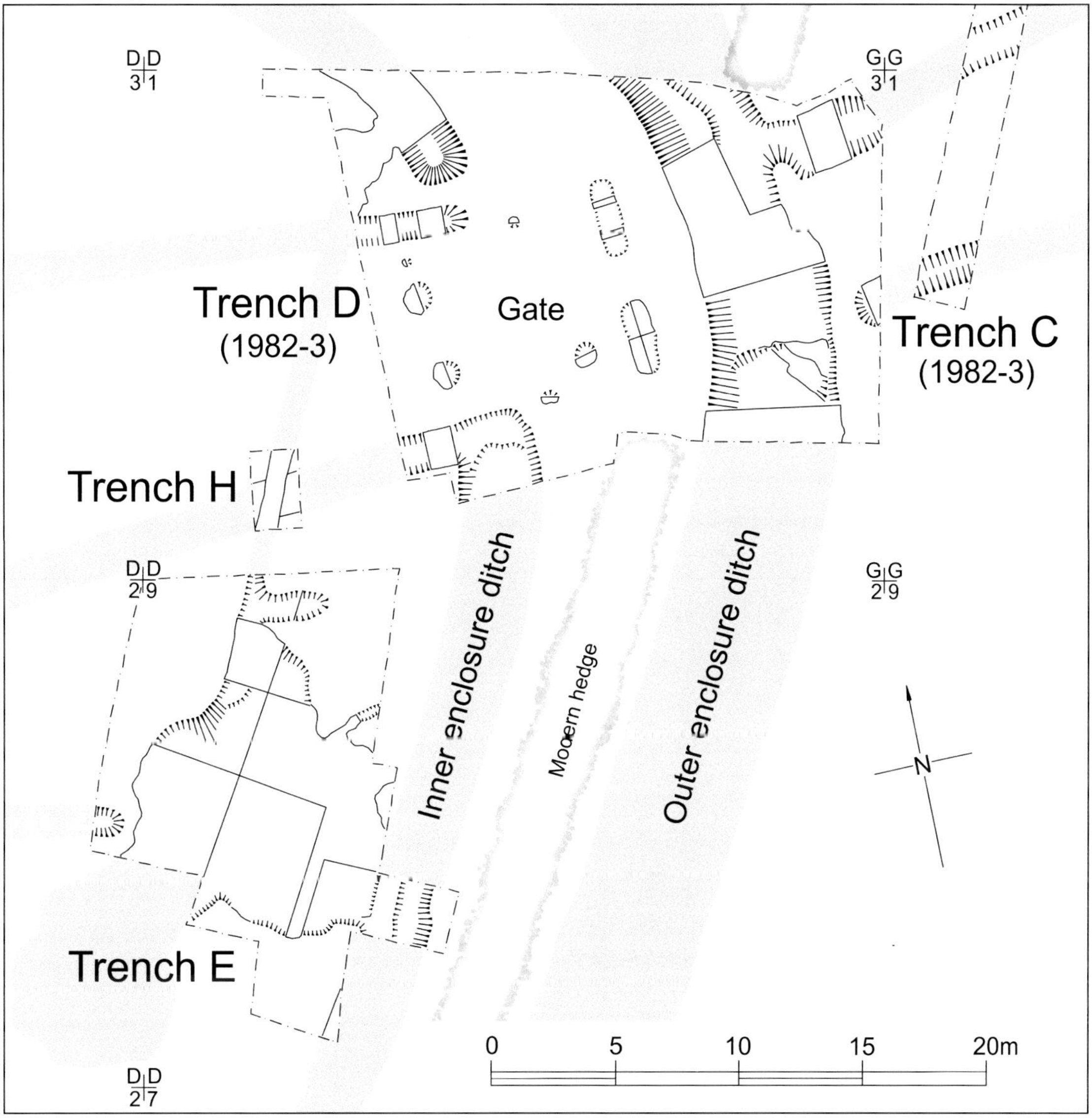

Fig. 6. Plan of Trench E in relation to trenches excavated in 1982–3 (after Trow 1988a).

Trenches E and H: quarry complex near north-east enclosure gate

Trench E comprised a rectangular area with extensions to the south and east and a total area of 175 square metres located immediately south-east of Trench D (Figs 6, 7 and 8; Trow 1988a). The trench was located immediately west of the Inner Enclosure Ditch as indicated by geophysical survey. The ditch was located in plan in the south-eastern corner of the trench and in its eastward extension, while the central area of the trench was occupied by a large pit-type feature. Plough erosion had destroyed any horizontal stratigraphy and surviving layers were confined to the rock-cut features. Trench H comprised a six square

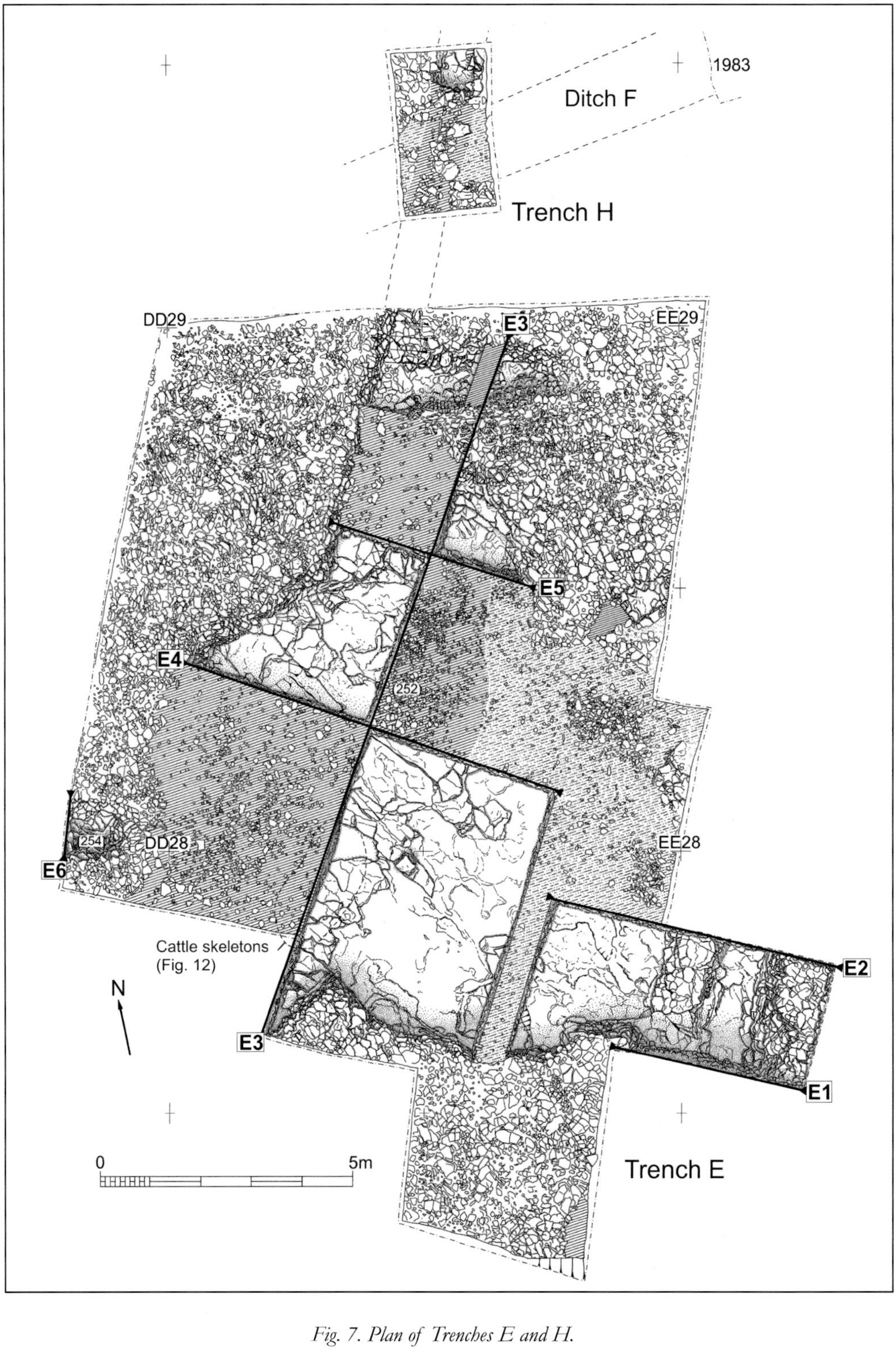

Fig. 7. Plan of Trenches E and H.

Fig. 8. View of Trench E, looking north, after excavation.

metre box intended solely to examine the relationship of the two features.

The principal features recorded in Trenches E and H can be assigned to eight phases of activity and are described below in chronological order. The description of each phase is concluded by a summary of the principal finds and a discussion of dating evidence.

Several additional features within Trench E cannot confidently be ascribed to a phase. These include a shallow curving gully on the western edge of the trench, which contained no finds and whose relationship to the large pit could not be demonstrated. Some 4m north-west a cigar-shaped feature E[305] 3m long and 1m wide cannot be dated other than by its being cut by ditch E/H[255]. The feature produced no finds and its bland fill of clean orange clay was unlike that of any other excavated feature. Immediately south of the cut was E[259] an area of disturbed limestone bedrock including many vertically-pitched slabs. Together E[259] and E[305] appeared to be a periglacial feature.

Phases 1 and 2: ditch F dug and backfilled

Excavation of Trench H revealed trackway ditch F, the terminal of which was excavated in 1983 some 4m to the north-east (Trow 1988a, 29). The ditch was recorded in plan but not excavated.

Finds

None

Dating evidence

No evidence for the date of the digging of ditch F was recovered. Excavation in 1983 demonstrated that the backfilling of the terminal of ditch F predated the cutting of the Inner Enclosure Ditch (Trow 1988a, 37 and fig. 15 section D5) and is therefore late Iron Age or earlier.

Phase 3 and 4: Inner Enclosure Ditch dug and backfilled (Fig. 9)

Where sectioned, the Inner Enclosure Ditch had a "U-shaped" profile with the western (inner) edge stepped. The cut of the ditch E[322] had a maximum depth of 2.1m below the modern ground surface and a maximum width of 3.2m. The presence of a Claudian coin and

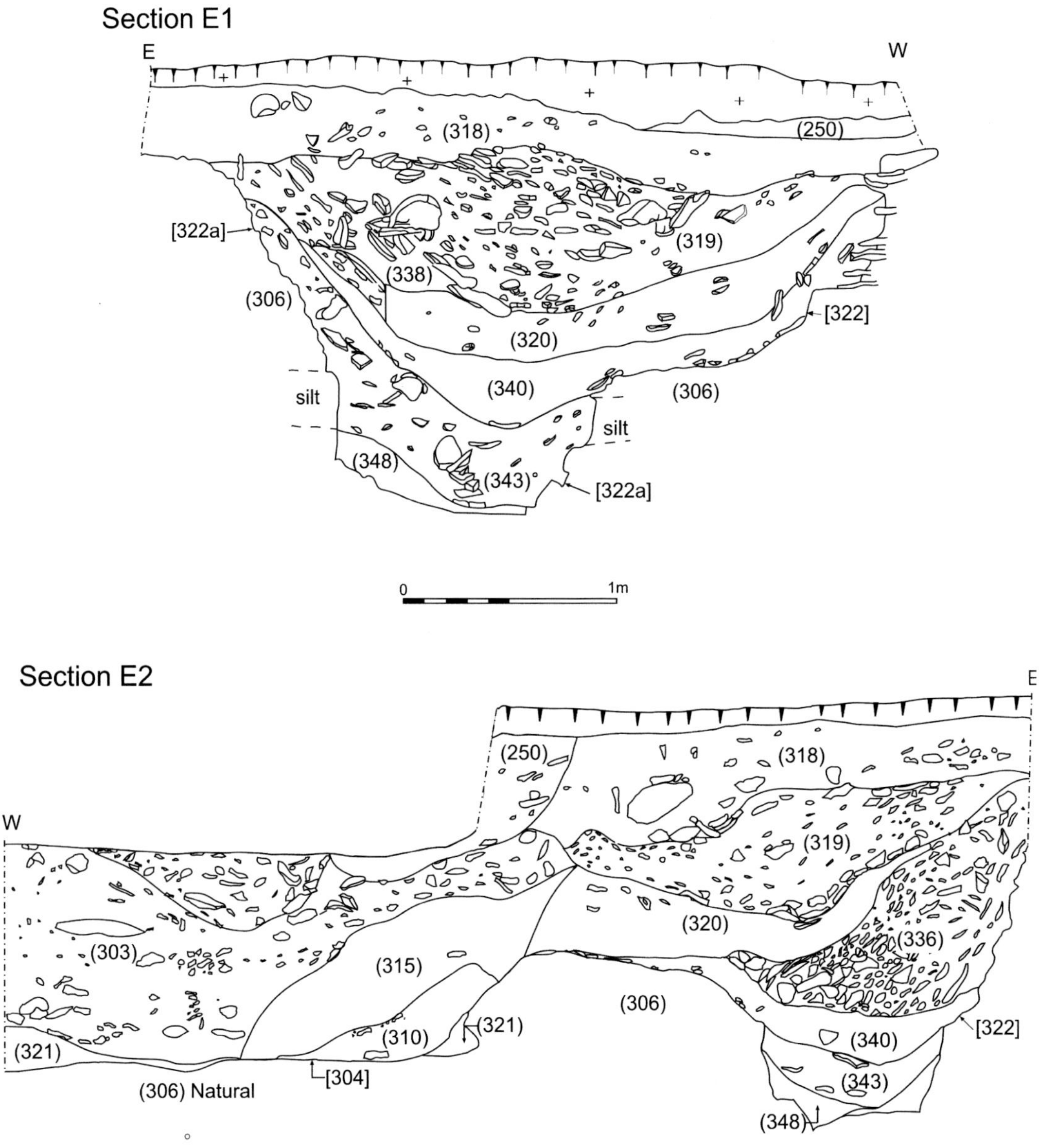

Fig. 9. Sections of the Inner enclosure ditch E[322].

Claudian finewares in the backfills may suggest that the ditch was dug sometime prior to AD 45. This ditch may be a recut of an earlier Inner Enclosure Ditch E[322a], the fills below being notably sterile of finds, potentially suggesting a pre-conquest date. It is possible therefore that the original ditch is somewhat earlier and may suggest the recut ditch was backfilled relatively soon after it was dug. It is noticeable, however, that no such recut is visible in the section of Inner Enclosure Ditch excavated in 1982 (Trow 1988a, 32) and it is possible these layers instead represent earlier slumping. It is also somewhat unlikely that a limestone ditch would be 'recut' as such, and instead may have been 'cleaned out' on a regular basis. This being the case, the original digging of the ditch could be much earlier than the first century BC.

Around the mid first century AD, probably between AD 45–55, the ditch was deliberately backfilled. The ditch fill comprised a sequence of rubble and domestic rubbish deposits comparable to those recorded in previously excavated sections (Trow 1988a). From the lowest deposit upwards, the fills included E(348) a primary silting composed of redeposited natural golden-yellow clay outwash from the ditch sides, E(343) a secondary silting of orange-brown clay and limestone rubble, E(340) a fill of grey "humic" silt with a high charcoal content and quantities of animal bone and pottery, E(336/337/338) a lens of limestone rubble in a yellow clay matrix, E(320) a dark grey-brown "humic" layer with much charcoal, and domestic rubbish, and E(319) a thick dump of limestone rubble in an intermittent brown clay matrix or largely soil-free. These layers showed considerable signs of having "slumped" into the ditch, presumably due to the considerable compaction of layers E(340) and E(320). The ditch was sealed by E(318) a layer of plough-disturbed subsoil.

Finds

Ceramic key group A
Brooches: s.f. 177, 179, 184, 185, 187
Iron Age Coin: s.f. 178
Roman Coin: s.f. 175
Copper Alloy: s.f.181, 182
Baked clay: s.f. 194; kiln fragments
Glass: s.f. 190

Dating evidence

The manufacture of the three most closely datable brooches probably pre-dates AD 50 (Mackreth below). Ceramic key group A includes Claudian or Claudio-Neronian samian and Claudio-Neronian/pre-Flavian Gaulish wares (Gallo-Belgic) whilst the coarsewares includes Savernake wares, early Severn Valley wares and Iron Age tradition material consistent with a mid first century AD date. Coin s.f. 175 from E(310), probably a local Claudian copy (see Kenyon below), has been suggested as having a mid-Claudian to mid-Neronian date which matches the ceramic evidence. The coin exhibits little wear suggesting it was probably deposited within or close to this date range. The dating evidence from 1984–5 concurs well with the excavation of the Inner Enclosure Ditch in 1982–3 (Trow 1988a, 37) and shows a similar sequence of apparently relatively rapid backfilling around the AD 50s. However, the date of the initial digging of the Inner Enclosure Ditch (and the outer ditch, see Trow 1988a, 37) is still difficult to establish with any certainty. The lack of pottery from primary silting E(348), in contrast with the density of finds of mid first century AD date in upper layers, alongside the possible evidence of a recut, tends to support the theory that the initial ditch was dug in the pre-conquest period and was possibly recut somewhat later, although how much earlier the ditch was originally dug is difficult to determine.

Phase 5: Quarry pit and east–west ditch dug (Figs 10 & 11)

Subsequent to the backfilling of the Inner Enclosure Ditch, its fills were partly truncated by the cutting of a wide, shallow pit immediately to its west (Fig. 9, Section E2). The pit was visible on aerial photographs and the 1980s geophysical survey (Trow 1988a, fig. 4) as a large irregular anomaly. Excavation revealed the pit to consist of a four-lobed cut E[304], the southernmost lobe of which was

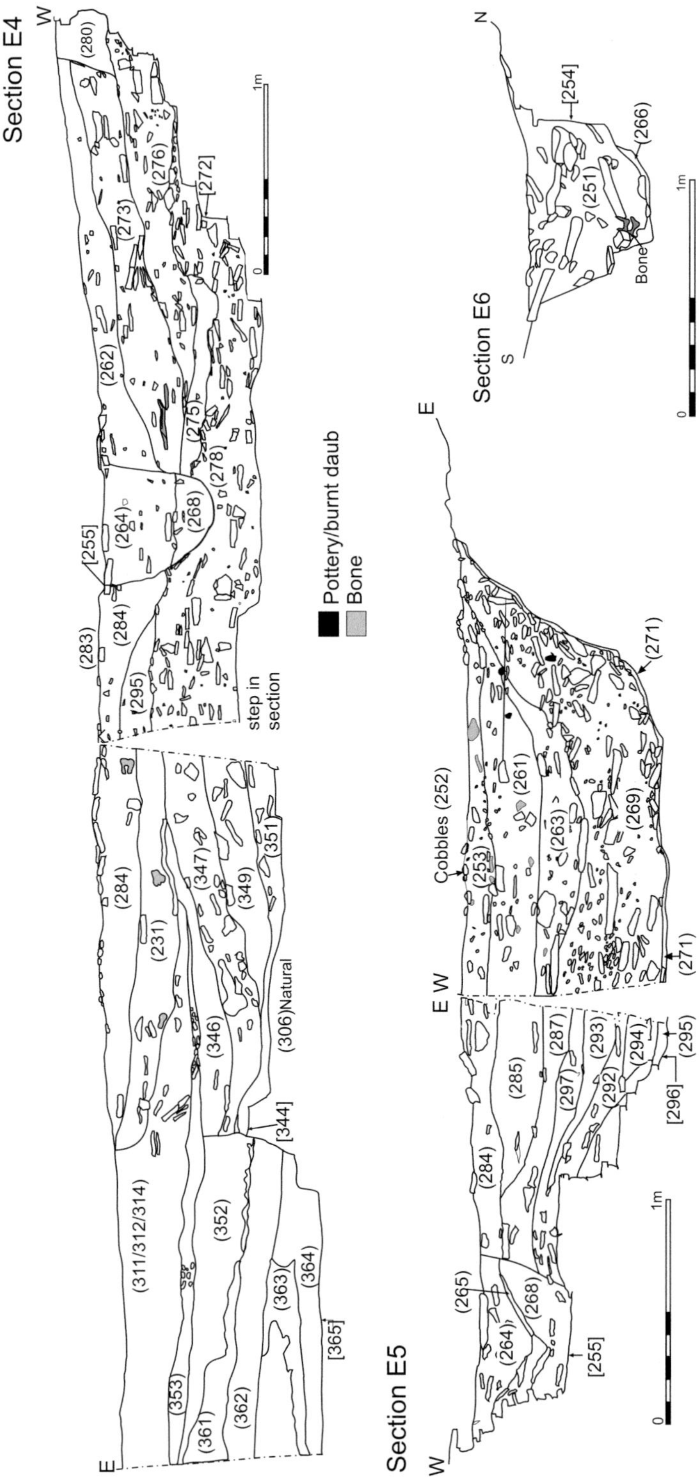

Fig. 10. Sections of quarry pit in Trench E, North-South ditch E[255] and east–west ditch E[254].

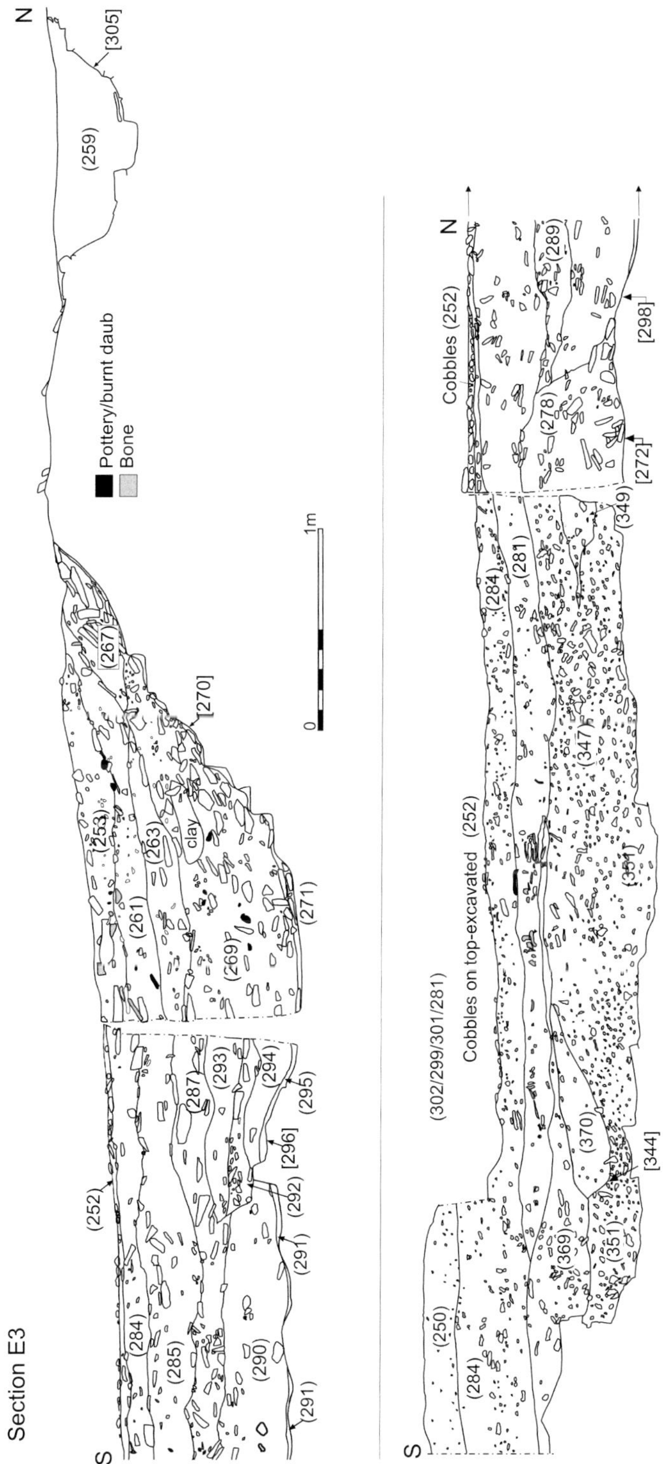

Fig. 11. Sections of Quarry pit in Trench E.

not excavated, with vertical, shelving or even undercutting edges and a maximum depth of *c.* 1.20m. At surface level, the pit gave the impression of having been created as a series of independent sub-circular cuts, although analysis of the pattern of fills did not support this. The pit cut through the upper frost-shattered limestone bedrock into the freestone below and is interpreted as a quarry for building-quality limestone.

Immediately west of the pit, in the south-western corner of Trench E was the terminal of a ditch E[254] (Fig. 10, section E6). The remainder of the ditch was located by geophysical survey (Trow 1988a, fig. 4, anomaly E) and can be identified from aerial photographs and the 2006 geophysical survey anomaly Y-P (Fig. 27). This evidence demonstrates that E[254] continues westwards for at least 70m.

Finds
None

Dating evidence
A terminus post quem of AD 45–55 is provided by the stratigraphic relationship of the pit and the Inner Enclosure Ditch. Ditch E[254] is assigned to this phase because its termination appears to respect the position of the Quarry pit suggesting that both features were open at the same time.

Phase 6: Quarry pit and east–west ditch backfilled; cattle burials inserted into Quarry pit (Figs 10–13)

The majority of the backfill of the pit is a confused series of tips, layers, and lenses of redeposited natural limestone brash, redeposited natural orange-brown clay, and limestone rubble. Despite being carefully excavated in plan, no coherent pattern of tipping was discerned and only occasional hints of cuts were recorded in the fill of the pit. No definite arrangement of cuts, interpretable in terms of the lobular cuts into the limestone natural, could be reconstructed. The pit fills were sterile in terms of artefacts, apart from one undiagnostic (possibly Iron Age?) sherd. It seems probable, considering the nature of the fills and the lack of incorporated finds, that quarrying activity was accompanied by the simultaneous dumping of surplus substandard limestone, brash, and topsoil into worked-out parts of the quarry rather than being moved to a formal spoilheap.

Two types of pit fill stand out from this general pattern. Firstly, fill E(310), laid directly on the shelving eastern side of the pit where it cut the fills of the Inner Enclosure Ditch, and secondly fills E(273) and E(262), sealing the fills on the western side of the Quarry pit. E(310) comprised a 0.2m thick layer of dark grey-brown silt derived directly from E(320), a fill in the Inner Enclosure Ditch and sealed by the more typical pit fills. E(310) contained various finds derived from this layer including the Claudian coin noted earlier (see Kenyon below).

Sealing the heterogeneous mix of brash, clay and rubble composing the fills of the western half of the Quarry pit, are two superimposed fills with a greater "humic" content. The lower layer E(273) (alternatively numbered E(261), E(281), E(285), E(286), and E(299)) comprises a dark-grey clay-silt with a high charcoal content and considerable quantities of animal bone, oyster and ceramics. This fill is partly sealed by E(262) (alternatively numbered E(253) and E(284)) a layer of mid-dark brown loam. Although limited by a clearly defined "edge" on their eastern side, the fills cannot be linked to a well defined cut in the underlying layers (see above) and may, therefore, represent the surviving extent, protected by subsidence into the underlying pit, of more extensive layers now truncated by cultivation. (The finds from these layers are similar in character and date to those from the Inner Enclosure Ditch and they may comprise the redeposited fills of the inner ditch back-shovelled as the Quarry pit was excavated into the side of the backfilled ditch).

Incorporated within layer E(273) and sealed by layer E(262) were the skeletons of at least five articulated cattle (see Rielly below) possibly representing the disposal of several diseased animals (Figs 12 & 13). However, excavations at Roman Fields, Abbeymead near Gloucester (Atkin 1987, 16) and The Bowsings, Gloucestershire (Marshall 1991) have revealed similar cattle burials in enclosure ditches both of apparently similar date,

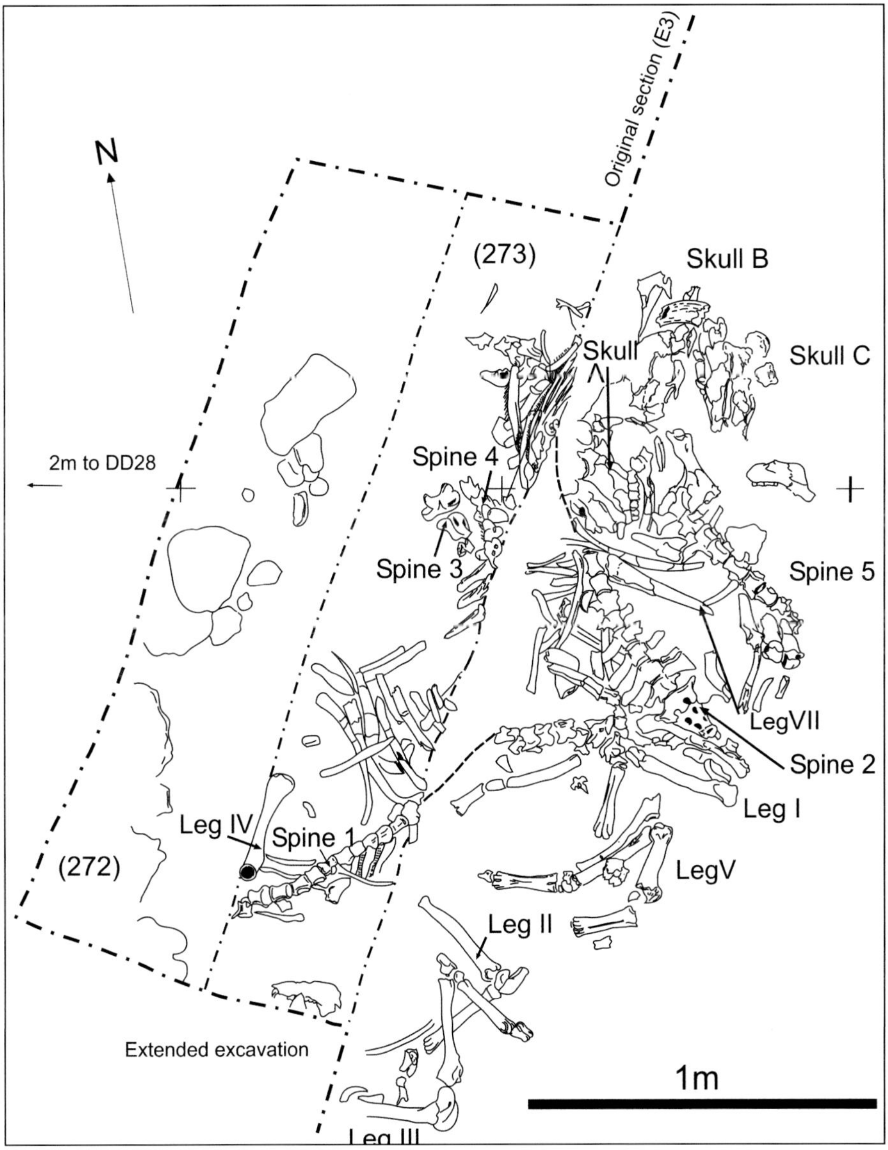

Fig. 12. Plan of cattle skeletons in Quarry pit.

Fig. 13. Cattle skeletons after excavation.

probably later first century AD. Added to the Ditches examples, these may suggest a less prosaic interpretation. In all these examples the deposits appear to be final acts in the infilling of liminal enclosure or ditch features. Whilst these may represent 'rubbish' disposal, in the light of suggestions of the structured deposition of animal remains in the Iron Age (e.g. Hill 1995b), a phenomenon increasingly thought to have also taken place in the early Roman period (e.g. Fulford 2001), we might suggest this deposit represents a deliberate symbolic act of deposition. The evidence from other sites may even imply this was part of a wider practice in the region.

Ditch E(254), Section E6 (Fig. 10) may have been backfilled at roughly the same time as the Quarry pit fills accumulated. The small quantity of ceramic material in its fill dates to the mid first century AD.

Finds

Ceramic group B
Iron Age coin: s.f.162
Brooches: s.f. 154, 156 a and b, 158, 167, 168, 169, 189
Copper alloy: s.f. 159, 161
Iron: s.f. 510, 150
Baked clay: s.f. 191, 193, 197
Touchstone: s.f. 186

Dating evidence

The latest brooch dates to AD 65–70, with features including pre-Flavian finewares and Tiberian-Claudian, Claudian and Neronian samian. Together these suggest the quarry was dug and backfilled by *c.* AD 70 and is therefore potentially contemporary with the building of the villa.

Phase 7: cobbled surface laid over pit (Fig. 7)

Subsequent to the accumulation of layer E(262), a cobbled surface E(252) was laid over the eastern and southern areas of the Quarry pit. The eastern extent of the cobbling closely matched that of the humic layers in the Quarry pit backfill adding support to the likelihood that the truncation of these layers has taken place.

The cobbled horizon probably relates to a similar undated cobbled surface D(93) sealing the eastern terminal of track ditch F and D(82) sealing the outer ditch in Trench D.

Finds and dating evidence

A sherd of Flavian samian.

Phase 8: north–south ditch dug (Fig. 10)

Both the cobbled layer in Trench E and the fill of track ditch F in Trench H are cut by a slight north–south ditch E/H[255] (Fig. 10, Section E4). Finds from the fills of the ditch E(256)/(257)/(258)/(264) appear to be derived from the 'humic' upper fills of the Quarry pit.

Finds

Ceramic Group F
Baked clay: s.f. 391

Dating evidence
Post dates (?)Flavian cobbled surface. Coarsewares suggest a second century AD date.

Trenches F and G: the villa (Structure 1) and vicinity (Figs 14, 16–18)

In its final form Trench F, which exposed the eastern part of the villa (Structure 1) and adjacent features including pathways and the imperfectly-understood Structure 2, comprised a rectangular area of some 380 square metres with its longer axis oriented NNE–SSW. Trench G to the west, which revealed the north-western corner of the building, was 4m square. The features recorded in Trenches F and G can be assigned to ten phases of activity and are described below in chronological order.

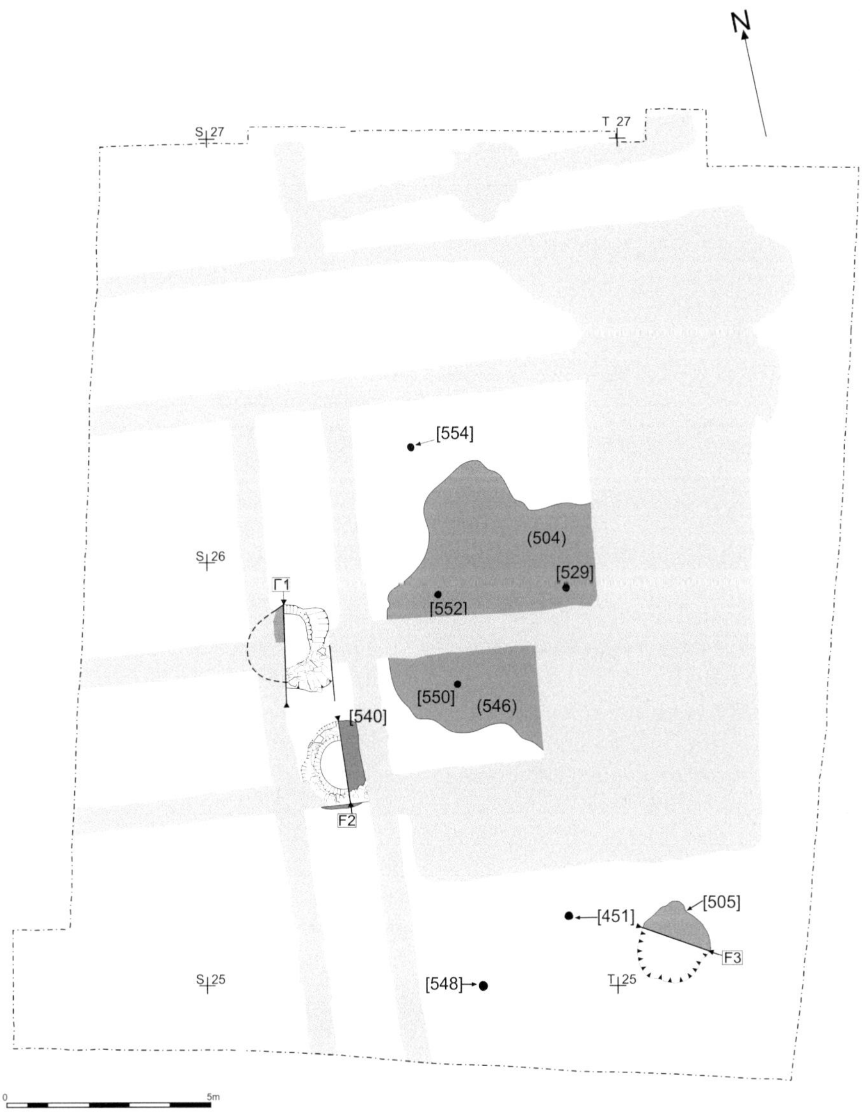

Fig. 14. Plan of pre-villa (late Iron Age) features in Trench F.

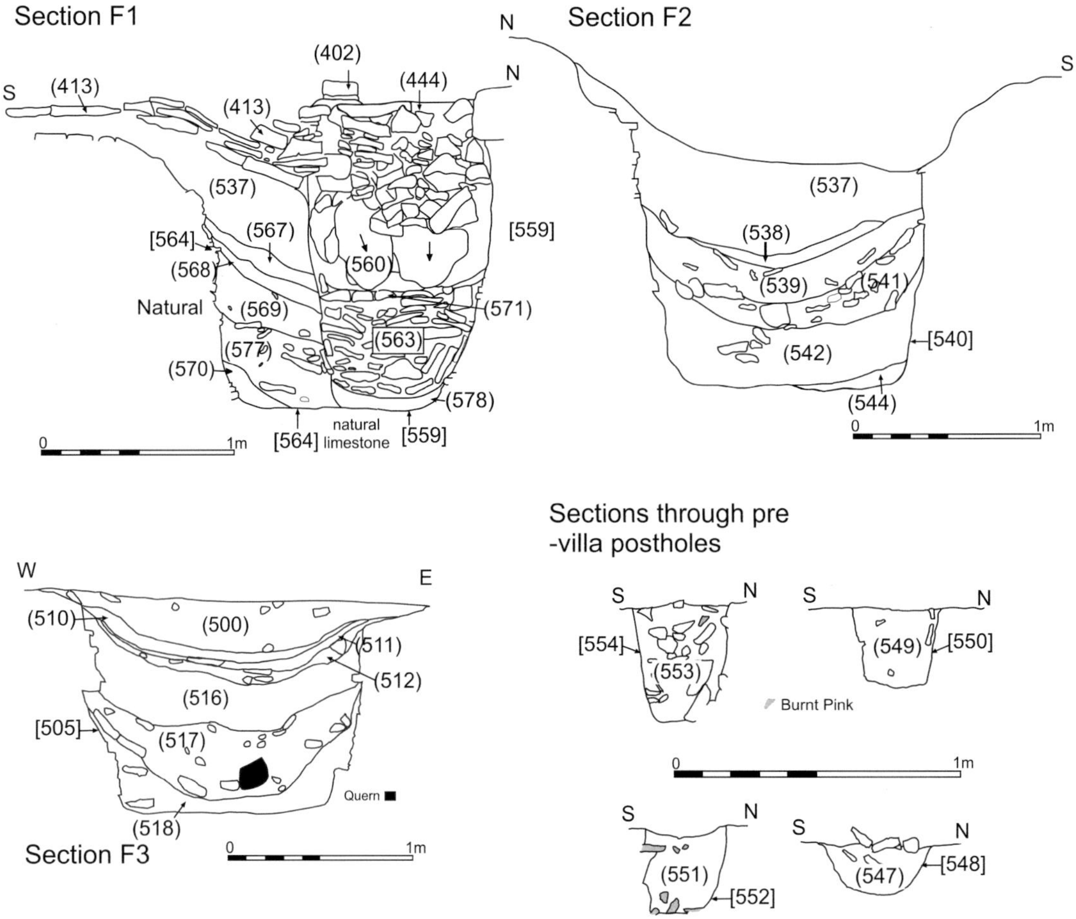

Fig. 15. Sections of Iron Age pits and Iron Age postholes.

Phase 1a: post alignment constructed (Figs 14 & 15)

The earliest features in Trench F appear to be a series of postholes traversing the site from north to south. Three were recognised within the area later defined by room R6 of Structure 1. They were separated by a distance of *c.* 2m and a fourth was recognised some 6m further south. If the stakeholes were arranged at regular intervals, a fifth feature must have been destroyed by walls F(403) and F(402). Further north, additional stakeholes would have been concealed by unexcavated yard surfaces.

The three postholes within the area of room R6, F[554], F[552], and F[550] and the southernmost posthole F[548], had diameters of 0.3–0.35m. Their depths declined with distance south from 0.4m for F[554] to 0.15m for F[548].

The postholes appear to represent the remains of a flimsy post-built structure, probably no more than a fenceline. Although they are considered to predate the accumulation of layer F(504)/(546), the stratigraphic relationship between post-pits and the layer was by no means clear.

Finds
None

Dating evidence
Probably pre-dates layer F(504)/(546) but see below.

Phase 1b: pits dug and used and cobbled surface laid (Figs 14 & 15)
Three Iron Age storage pits were recognised within the excavated area. Additional pits may exist within Trench F sealed by the unexcavated villa deposits.

Two of the pits F[564] and F[540] were situated immediately west of the phase 1a fenceline about 1m apart. The third F[505] was situated 3m east of the fenceline, near the southern edge of the trench. All three pits were cylindrical, narrowing slightly towards the base. The three pits exhibit a considerable degree of uniformity in their dimensions with F[505], F[540], and F[564] having a depth, upper diameter and basal diameter of 1.8m, 1.7m, and 1.10m; 1.25m, 1.72m and 1.14m; 1.2m, 1.7m (estimated), and 1.15m respectively.

Evidence of the last episode of use of pits in the form of F(570), a deposit of carbonised grain up to 0.10m thick, on the base of the south-eastern quadrant of pit F[564]; and F(544), a carbonised deposit on the base of pit F[540], was recognised. No comparable deposit was located in pit F[505].

Between pits F[564] and F[540] a layer of irregularly-laid angular limestone slabs sealed the natural clay. The layer was not detected sealing or slumped into the fills of the pits and is therefore contemporary with or earlier than their use. This layer of slabs is best interpreted as the remains of an area of hard standing associated with the period of use of the pits.

Finds
A number of grain samples were taken from pit deposits (see Huntley below).

Dating evidence
Terminus ante quem provided by phase 2 deposits

Phase 1c: occupation layer accumulates (Fig. 14)
Subsequent to or during the lifetime of the post alignment, an extensive occupation layer F(504)/(546) accumulated in a slight hollow east of pits F[540] and F[564]. The northern, western and southern extent of the layer could be determined but to the east the layer was truncated by the cellar and to the south-east it ran under unexcavated deposits in the eastern wing of Structure 1. The layer occupied much of the area of the later room R6, F(504), and the corridor immediately to the south, F(546), and was truncated by the construction cut of wall F[402].

The layer was up to 0.07m in thickness with the greatest depth towards the south-west. It comprised a dark-grey to black deposit of clay-silt with a high humic content and a considerable quantity of charcoal and carbonised grain. Amongst finds from F(504) were a small quantity of late Iron Age pottery and a small quantity of bronze waste which may imply bronze working in the area, concurring with metalworking waste seen in earlier excavations (Trow 1988a, 53).

A precise relationship between layer F(504)/(546) and the pits could not be established as the layer did not extend as far west as the pits. The presence of considerable quantities of carbonised grain in the layer may suggest that its accumulation took place within the lifetime of the pits. As noted above, the layer appears to postdate the erection of the fenceline, although it is not impossible that the layer accumulated around the base of the posts.

Finds
Ceramic group G1
Copper alloy: s.f. 415, 410, 411, 417, 422
Glass: s.f.404a,b
Iron: s.f. 405

Dating evidence
Ceramic Group G1 contains a small amount of possibly intrusive wheel-turned pottery trampled in from overlying layers but is dominated by L3, a limestone tempered ware found in later Iron Age forms, suggesting the occupation layer accumulated probably in the early first century AD or even first century BC (see discussion in Moore below). The two sherds of glass from layer F(504) cannot be dated more closely than 'Roman' (Shepherd below).

Phase 2: pits backfilled (Fig. 15)
Around the early or mid first century AD, all three pits within Trench F were backfilled. The fill of pit F[505] comprises a series of largely sterile clay-silt lenses and limestone cobbles, with a small quantity of pottery and animal bone in the original (prior to consolidation) upper fill F(516). Fill F(517) contained a virtually entire lower rotary quern stone s.f. 419 and human skull fragments (see Lorentz and Moore below). The nature of this deposit might even be suggested as a structured 'closing' deposit to the pit, common elsewhere in Iron Age Britain (cf. Hill 1995b).

The basal fill of pit F[540] is sealed by a series of slumped sterile layers of natural clay and limestone rubble, one of which F(541) contained a fragment of quernstone. The basal fill of pit F(564) is sealed by a comparable succession of sterile slumped natural clay and silty-clay lenses.

Finds
Ceramic Group G2.
Human bone (Lorentz and Moore below).
Worked stone: s.f.419, 420.
Iron: s.f. 423
Worked bone: s.f. 388, 427, 429

Dating evidence
Ceramic Group G2 and Gallo-Belgic finewares in the backfills of pit F[505] and pit F[540] suggest a date possibly in the early or mid-first century AD for the backfilling of these pits.

Phase 3: occupation debris accumulates (Fig. 14)
Around the middle of the first century AD activity within or in the immediate vicinity of Trench F resulted in a small amount of rubbish being distributed across the site. No new features can be directly attributed to this phase of activity although F(538), the uppermost fill wholly contained within pit F[540] and F[564], appears to have accumulated around this time; subsequent compaction of the original (phase 2) fills of the pits. These fills appear to be dumps of organic debris and both are typified by charcoal flecking. A similar sequence can be detected within pit F(505) where, following the partial compaction of layer F(516) and its underlying contexts, two thin lenses, F(511), and F(512) accumulated in the depression caused by the partly filled pit. The upper of these, F(511) exhibited comparable flecking to F(538) and F(567). Both F(511) and F(567) contained a small amount of pottery. Also attributable to this phase is a small amount of pottery trampled into the upper surface of layer F(504).

Finds
Ceramic Group E2
Copper Alloy: sf.415, 400, 410, 417, 422.

Dating evidence
Ceramic group E2 dates to around the

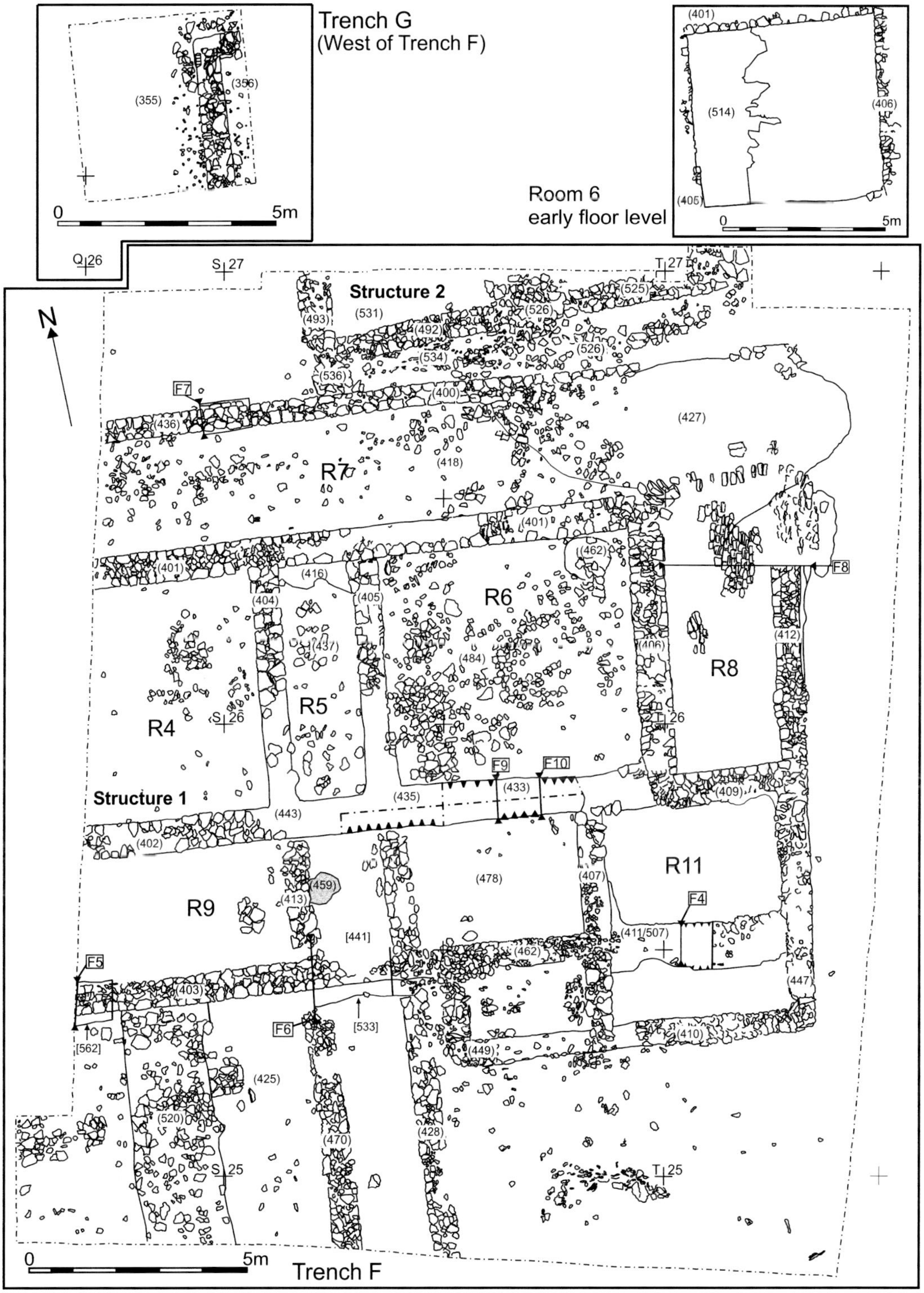

Fig. 16. Plan of Roman features in Trenches F and G.

mid-first century AD. The presence of only Savernake wares (SAV1) and limestone tempered wares (MALV) suggest an early date but the small quantity of material makes it impossible to refine this further.

Phase 4: main villa block constructed (Figs 16–18, 28)

During the third quarter of the first century AD the main block of villa house (Structure 1) was constructed. The block comprises a simple strip building of six rooms – a large west, east and central room (rooms R1, R4 and R6 respectively), a narrow corridor or stairwell between R4 and R6 (room R5), and a pair of small rooms (R2 and R3) between rooms R1 and R4. The block is 30m long east-west and 13m wide north-south. Precise dimensions are available for rooms R5 and R6 only. Room R5 is 1.5m × 5m wide and room R6, 5.5m × 5m. Measurements from aerial photography and based on the position of Trench G suggest that room R6 is the largest of the three large rooms – their size decreasing from east to west.

The outer walls of the building are 0.75m wide and comprise a double facing of dressed local oolite with a rubble core bonded with buff coloured mortar. Where revealed by excavation or by later robbing of footings, the construction trenches for the walls of the building are quite shallow with a maximum depth of 0.4m.

The southern approach to Structure 1 communicated directly with Room 5 and took the form of a path flanked by two dry-stone walls F(428) and F(470) and, in the area immediately adjacent to Structure 1, surfaced with a thick layer of opus signinum F(459). The walls have no footings and survive to a height of only one or two courses, except where F(413) has slumped into the subsidence over pit F(564) caused by the compaction of

Fig. 17. View of Trench F, looking north, after excavation.

layer F(537), where some five courses survive. Interestingly, the path was not aligned perpendicularly to Structure 1 but approaches it at a slight angle, apparently reflecting the alignment of the phase 1 fenceline.

Additional evidence for phase 4 building activity is provided by the upper layers of pit F(505) where, subsequent to the accumulation of F(511), additional slumping of the underlying layers allowed the accumulation of F(510), a layer containing a very high proportion of mortar. The mortar layer, which was presumably trampled into the surface of the pit during the construction of Structure 1, also contained a quantity of pottery. The cobbled floor layer F(484) also dates to this phase and appears to be the primary floor layer in the villa.

Finds

Ceramic groups E1 and E2
Brooch s.f. 426
Iron Age coin: s.f. 385
Copper alloy: s.f. 402
Pellet moulds in F(478): s.f. 254, 421, 255
Worked bone: s.f. 429
Baked clay: s.f. 254, 421, 255

Dating evidence

Ceramic group E2 provides a date of around AD50–70 for the mortar-rich "slumping" layers in pit[505]. Brooch s.f. 426 embedded in wall F(404) can be dated little after AD 70–80 (see Mackreth

Fig. 18. Plan of villa based on aerial photographic and excavated evidence from Trenches F and G.

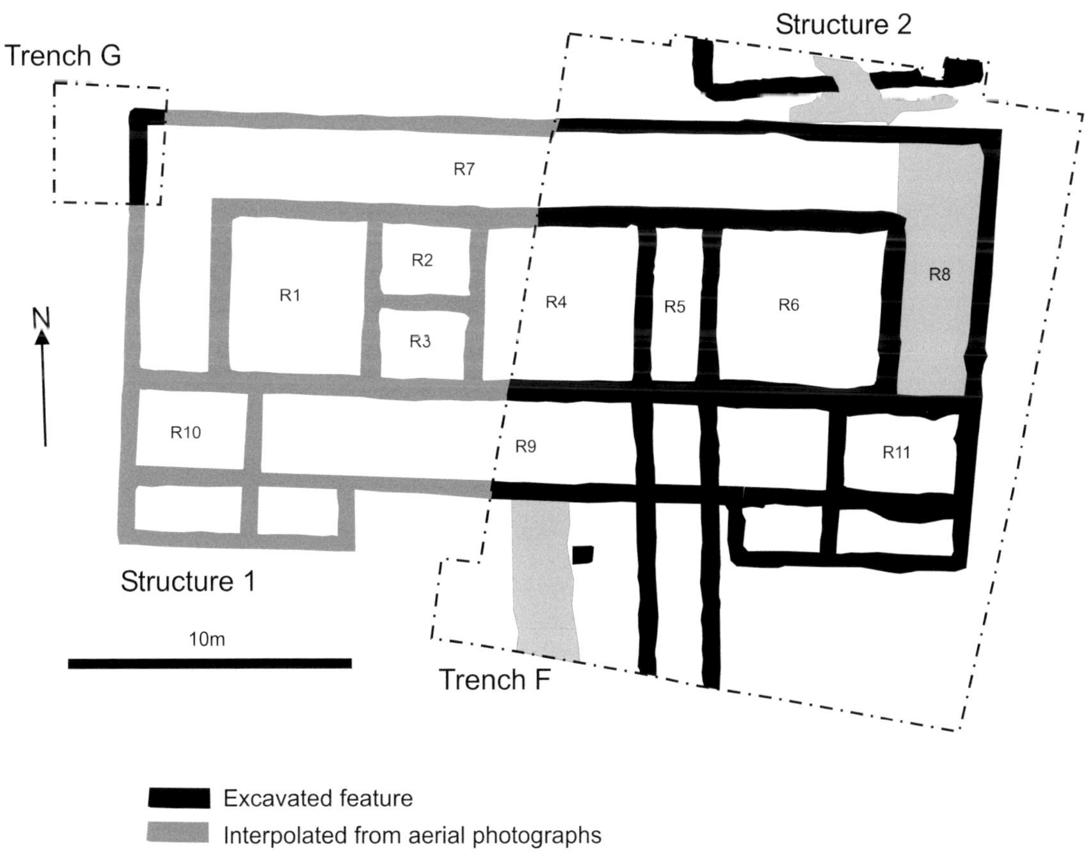

below). Haselgrove (below) dates the Iron Age coin to *c.* 20 BC–AD 10. On this basis it seems safest to date the construction of the main villa building to around the third quarter of the first century AD.

Phase 5: timber corridor (Fig. 16, 25)

Subsequent to the erection of the main block of Structure 1, a timber-framed corridor or veranda was added to the southern side of the block. This corridor may in fact have run on all sides of the block but was only recognised on the southern side. Evidence for the corridor comprised a slot F[533]/[557]/[562] (Fig. 25; Sections F4, F5 and F6) on the same alignment as the later masonry corridor wall F(403), but slightly further south. The slot was excavated at three points, at the western edge of Trench F, where it overlies pit F[540] and at the eastern end of Structure 1. To the west, slot F[562] had probably been enlarged to provide the construction trench for wall F(403) but the vestiges of a deeper slot 1.1m wide were visible below, and were partly overlain by, F(507/411), the footings for wall F(403). Similarly, over pit F[540], F[533] a slot *c.* 1m wide and deeper than the construction trench for F(403) was located. Further east, the same pattern is repeated although F[557], a slot 1m wide, can scarcely be differentiated from the construction trench for wall F(403), F[545].

The slot detected in these sections would have housed a substantial timber sill-beam upon which the outer wall of the veranda was founded. The stratigraphic relationship between the timber veranda and walls F(470) and F(428) has been destroyed by the construction of wall F(403), but it seems probable that both walls were slighted north of the beam slot in order to allow the construction of a raised timber floor for the veranda. No sections of the western, northern or eastern phase 6 corridor walls were carried out and, as a result it is not possible to affirm the existence of a timber corridor on other sides of the main block of Structure 1.

Finds

No finds relating to phase 5 were recovered.

Dating evidence

The construction of the veranda has a terminus post quem provided by the dates of phase 4, and a terminus ante quem provided by phase 7. Therefore, it is likely to date to the early second century AD.

Phase 6: construction of cellar and stone corridor (Figs 19 to 24, 28)

The timber-built veranda was replaced by a stone-built corridor running around the main block. The northern corridor wall, F(400), consisted of two facing courses of flat angular slabs with a rubble infill bonded with yellow-buff coloured mortar and a width of 0.5m (Fig. 25, section F7). The southern corridor wall, F(403), was of similar construction but 0.65m in width. The internal width of the northern corridor was 2.1m and that of the southern 2.6m. As in the case of wall F(402), wall F(403) traversed F[540] one of the backfilled Iron Age storage pits. Unlike wall F(402) (see phase 4 above), construction of F(403) did not involve the building of footings from the base of the pit and later compaction of the pit fills led to its subsidence (Fig. 15, Section F1).

Replacement in stone of the timber veranda coincided with the construction of a cellar at the east end of the block and was part of a major refurbishment of the villa. After surface cleaning, prior to excavation, the area of the cellar appeared as an extensive layer of silt F(427) filling an "L-shaped" zone of subsidence running along the eastern end of the northern

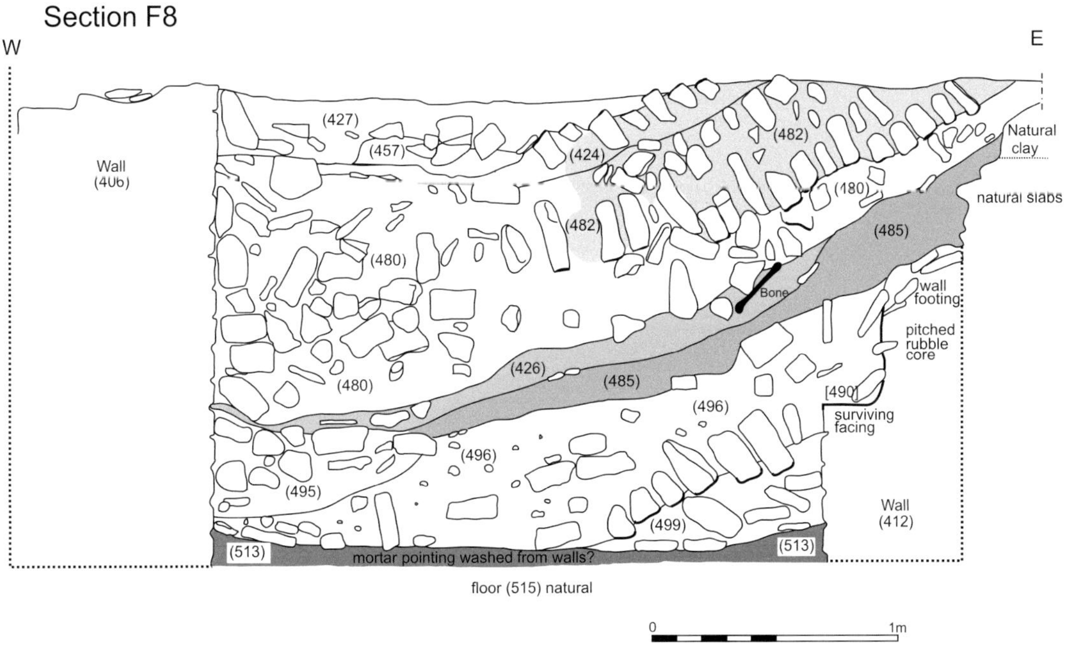

Fig. 19. Section of cellar (F8).

corridor of the main block (see phase 10a below). Once the area of subsidence was recognised as the fill of a cellar, it was decided to preserve a proportion of the feature for future investigation. The evidence of subsidence at the east end of the northern corridor suggests the existence of a ramp or a flight of stairs linking the corridor with the cellar. On this basis, the southernmost 4.2m of the fill of the cellar was chosen for excavation in order to avoid destroying the corridor ramp/stairway-cellar relationship.

Construction of the cellar involved the dismantling of the eastern end wall of the main block and the construction, on the same alignment, of a new wall F(406/475), cutting the footings of wall F(403), and carried up from its western side. The main chamber of the cellar spanned the north–south width of the main block and the northern corridor, although part of this length may have been occupied by a ramp or stairway. The cellar extended as far south as the line of the southern wall of the main block F(403), although the cellar wall F(409) was constructed on a slightly different alignment, confirming it was not contemporary. The east–west width of the cellar chamber was 2.4m. Where wall F(406/475) survived above footing level, it was of double facing course/rubble infill construction 0.8m in width. Below this level F(475), F(409), and F(412) – the western, southern and eastern walls of the cellar – were faced with dressing masonry on the inside edges alone. Behind this facing, the rubble core was carried back to the edge of the Trench F(572). Walls F(409) and F(412) had widths of 0.75m and 0.6–0.7m respectively.

All the walls of the cellar were faced in finely-executed ashlar masonry standing, in the case of wall F(406/475), to a maximum height of 1.90m. The western wall was interrupted by four put-log holes at a height of 1m above the base of the

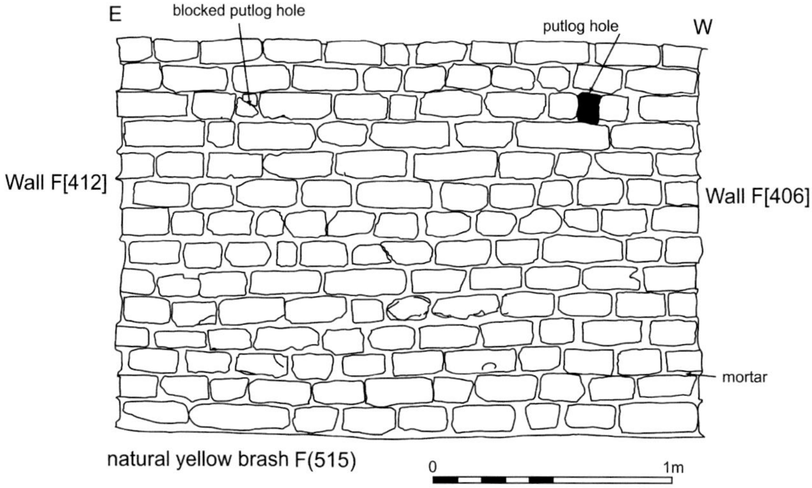

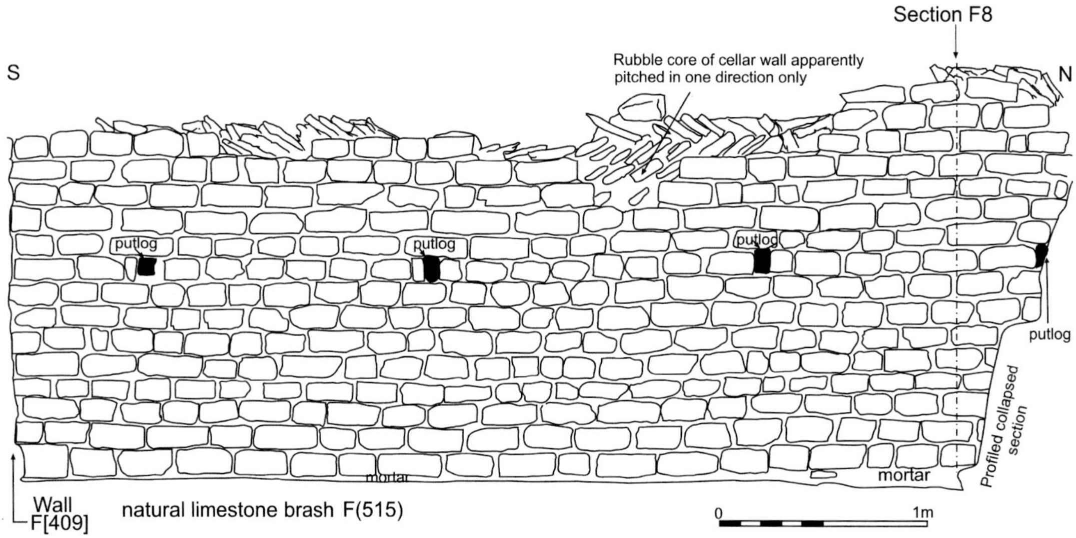

Fig. 20 (top). North facing cellar wall F(409).

Fig. 21 (bottom). East facing cellar wall F(406).

cellar and two further holes at a height of 1.3m (Figs 20, 21, 22 & 24). The eastern wall of the cellar F(412) was in a poorer state of preservation than the western and southern walls, having suffered a partial collapse in antiquity (see phase 8 below). Possibly as a result of this, no put-log holes were recorded. The eastern wall was, however, interrupted by at least one and probably three shallow, splay-sided niches. A series of angled quoins, comprising the southern side of the southernmost niche, survived at a distance of 1.6m north of the junction of walls F(412) and F(409). No evidence for the form of the head of the niche survived in situ although a dressed lintel 0.66m in length was located with a small group of angled quoins amongst F(499) rubble derived from the collapse of F(412). In addition, the same

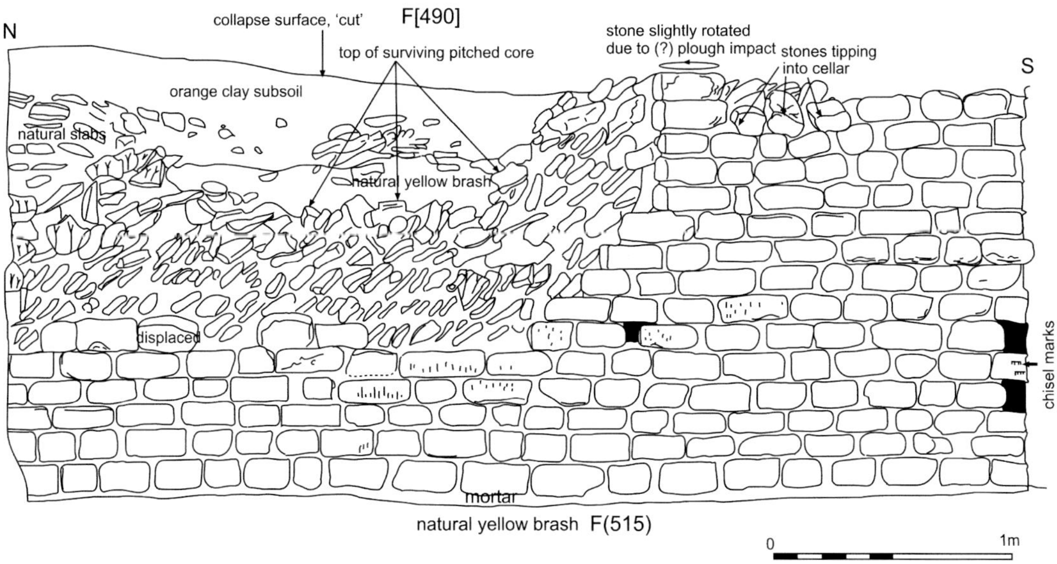

Fig. 22. West facing cellar wall F(412).

rubble layer contained a second group of angled quoins at a distance of some 4m from wall F(409) (i.e. immediately south of section F8, Fig. 19) indicating the approximate position of a second niche and, if the spacing between niches is regular, suggesting the existence of a third.

The base of the cellar was clean natural clay and limestone brash, upon which walls F(175), F(409), and F(412) were directly founded. Any flooring material such as flagstones or tiles had been removed in antiquity or, alternatively, the floor may have been of timber construction. Given the nature of the base of the cellar construction cut, some form of flooring material would have been required.

Aerial photographs of Structure 1 (Fig. 3) confirm that wall F(412) and the eastern end of wall F(400) are not visible as cropmarks due to the subsidence caused by the cellar collapse. The lack of subsidence at the western end of Structure 1 is confirmed both by aerial photographs and by the observations from Trench G (excavation involved the removal of topsoil and surface cleaning only). This suggests that only the eastern end of the structure was provided with a cellar, a proposal which is supported by comparison of other villa buildings with cellars (see below).

A number of floor levels in Room R6 may be datable to phase 6 although their dating is not entirely clear. These include floor F(417), which is located above the phase 4 cobbled surface F(484)

Finds

No finds can be directly associated with the construction of the masonry corridor walls and the cellar. Finds from floor level F(417) may be attributable to this phase.
Wall plaster
Copper alloy: s.f. 263, 262, 273, 242
Glass: s.f. 261a,b, 270, 271a,b, 272, 260

Dating evidence

Dating of this phase cannot be refined beyond the terminus post quem of late first century AD provided by phase 4

Fig. 23. View of the cellar after excavation, looking south.

deposits and the terminus ante quem provided by phase 7 suggesting a date probably in the early second century AD.

Phase 7: construction of wings and metalled path (Figs 16 and 28)

Some time after the construction of the masonry-built corridors, the southern arm of the corridor was modified in order to provide a shallow "wing" at each end of the main block. At the eastern end of the southern corridor 8.5m of wall F(403) was demolished to the level of its footings F(411) in order to facilitate the building of the wing. This involved the construction of wall F(410) to create a 2m deep extension south of the line of the corridor. The extra space created by this extension was subdivided by a north–south partition wall F(407). At its northern end F(407) was built into F(402), the southern wall of the main block and, further south, it sealed F(460)/(461), a layer of demolition debris trampled into the upper surface of F(411). The constructional technique of wall F(410) is not apparent as the wall no longer survives above footing level. The footings comprise a 0.5–0.65m wide cut filled with angular limestone rubble sealed with patches of mortar. In contrast, wall F(407) comprises a similar rubble footing, 300mm in width, above which the surviving wall comprises a double facing of dressed limestone blocks with a core of vertically-pitched rubble and a wash of mortar. The net result of these alterations was to provide a room (R11) some 4m east–west and 5m north–south at the eastern end of the block with the corridor immediately to the west making an "L-shaped" turn southwards.

Very indistinct cropmark evidence at the western end of the block suggests the existence of a similar "wing" (Fig. 3). This suggestion is supported by the faintness of the crop mark of wall F(403) at both its eastern and western extremities, suggesting its demolition in advance of wing construction at both ends. On the basis of this assumption it can be suggested that the axially located pathway F(520), exhibiting as it does an apparent concern for the overall symmetry of Structure 1, best belongs in phase 7. Path F(520) comprises a "linear" zone of limestone cobbling running northwards from the southern limit of Trench F as far north as, and limited by, wall F(403). It is slightly cambered and has an approximate width of 2.5m with its margins, particularly on its eastern edge, rather poorly defined. The path is composed of limestone slabs up to 0.4m in size, occasionally rounded by wear, and with smaller cobbles tamped in to the interstices between larger slabs. The pathway was surface cleaned but not sampled by excavation.

Located on the eastern margin of F(520) and abutted by the metalling of the path is F(425), a rectangular plinth of mortared limestone some 0.62 × 0.78m in size. The purpose of the plinth and its relationship to the pathway is not apparent. It is possible could there have been others that are removed/robbed with other building material and it may represent a colonnade although this seems unlikely.

Floor surface F(437) in the central axial room F may also date to this phase and is overlain by the destruction deposits of phase 9, F(416). However, it is hard to place this surface in any certain phase.

Finds
None

Dating evidence
The construction of the wings must have taken place prior to the collapse of the cellar in Phase 8, suggested as taking place in the third quarter of the second century AD, and after the construction of the stone corridor. It cannot, therefore, be more closely dated than sometime in the early–mid second century AD.

Phase 8: collapse and backfilling of cellar (Fig. 19, section F8)
Around AD 150–175, part of the eastern wall of the cellar F(412) appears to have collapsed into the cellar chamber. The resultant rubble layer (F(499) derived from the collapsed face of F(412) and F(495/496) derived from its core) was piled against the base of F(412) and included the mostly *ex situ* remains of two niche structures (see above). The rubble sealed a very thin layer of mortar F(513) directly sealing the natural base of the cellar. This layer may represent a thin mortar skim for the bedding of a flag or tiled floor although it is equally probable that it merely represents outwashed mortar from the rubble collapse.

It is not clear whether the collapse was the result of controlled demolition or structural failure. The absence of the remains of a flag or tiled floor sealed by F(499) suggests the removal of any such materials prior to the collapse of F(412). In addition, the quantity of rubble involved suggests it derived from the below-ground part of F(412) alone. If F(412) did exist as a masonry wall above ground, the results of demolition were not deposited in the cellar.

Fig. 24. Putlog holes in east facing cellar wall.

It is notable that architectural fragments including window glass and part of a half-length limestone column were recovered from a backfilled ditch some 110m to the south-east during the 1982 excavation (Trow 1988a, 55–58 and fig. 28, no. 9). The backfilling of the ditch was dated to AD 140–160.

Subsequent to the collapse of F(412), the cellar chamber was backfilled with quantities of rubble and domestic refuse. Immediately sealing rubble F(495)/(496)/(499) is F(488), a layer of mortar washed into the cellar from the ruinous core of F(412). In turn, this is sealed by F(489) a deliberately placed dump of rubble in the south-western corner of the cellar and F(491) a charcoal-rich rubbish layer in the south-eastern corner. These fills are below F(485), an extensive and heterogeneous layer of rubbish and demolition debris apparently derived from the eastern edge of the cellar, and F(426) a thick charcoal-rich rubbish dump which seals all the earlier cellar fills and, in places, the surviving courses of wall F(412).

Finds

Ceramic Groups C1 and C2
Copper alloy finds: s.f.279, 284, 306. 308, 326, 335, 338, 348, 368, 380, 401
Lead alloy terminal: s.f. 365
Brooches: s.f.398, 305
Glass: s.f. 297, 321, 316, 319, 293, 304, 344, 359, 286
Pipeclay figurines: s.f 340, 377
Iron objects: s.f. 266, 267, 268
Worked bone: s.f. 269, 275, 283, 296, 300, 303, 309, 311, 312, 320, 321, 323, 324, 325, 329, 330, 332, 333, 336, 339, 341, 347, 349, 357, 369, 371, 375

Note

During excavation, all finds from the interface of contexts F(480) and F(426) were attributed to layer F(480) in order to avoid the possible contamination of the earlier layer by finds from the later. Other than at the interface, layer F(480) contained virtually no finds and, on the basis of a consideration of the characteristics of both layers and the nature of the finds themselves (e.g. joining pottery sherds) it appeared to the excavators that the F(426)/(480) interface finds in fact derive from the upper surface of layer F(426).

Dating evidence

It is probable that there was no appreciable time-lapse between the collapse of wall F(412) and the accumulation of some of the rubbish deposits which seal the derived rubble layer, although the rubbish layers may have taken some time to build up. The rubbish deposits can be dated to AD 150–200 on the basis of the samian, which Willis (see below) describes as a remarkably strong element of samian from AD 120–150. In addition, the glass finds from these contexts suggest a mid-late second century AD date (Shepherd below) and a second century date has been suggested for the pipeclay figurine (Johns below). Similarly, the coarsewares indicate a later second century AD date, with Dorset Black Burnish forms, for example, falling generally between AD 120–200/AD 170–200. The presence of a handful of sherds of later Oxfordshire Colour Coated in F(426) and F(485), and South Midlands Shell Tempered ware, dating to the third–fourth century AD, may indicate the rubbish layers took some time to accumulate before the collapse of the villa wall. However, the secure nature of these contexts is not clear and comments by Trow suggest that some of this material may be intrusive from a later dump of material F(480) which probably accumulated over some time (as late as the third century AD) after the initial dumps took place in the mid–late second century AD. The general impression from the nature of these contexts and overall dating impression suggests that these consisted of short episodes of dumping material and the later sherds may be intrusive from later accumulations of material on the surface.

Phase 9a: destruction of the villa building by fire and collapse of its eastern wall (Figs 16 and 19)

Around the early third century AD, F(406), the eastern end wall of the main block collapsed or was deliberately toppled eastwards, and a substantial chunk of the fallen masonry was thereafter preserved in the upper of the already-demolished cellar. The collapse or demolition may have been the result of a serious fire, traces of which were observed at several points in the building. Evidence for the fire takes the form of the heavily truncated remains of an extensive layer of burnt destruction debris. The latest surviving floor surfaces in rooms R4, R5, and R6 all show traces of what appeared to be burnt daub and limestone fragments and in rooms R4 and R5 thin charcoal-rich lenses survive in locations protected from cultivation damage. F(416), the most substantial of these lenses, is located at the northern end of room R5 protected from ploughing by its proximity to wall F(401). It comprises a silty layer rich in charcoal, burnt daub, friable plaster or mortar, and containing many carpentry nails.

Within the cellar, the demolition debris from the collapse of the end wall F(406) comprised two distinct components. The lowest fill F(480) was composed of a large quantity of faced limestone blocks, frequently burnt, limestone rubble, and large quantities of mortar together with a clay-silt component probably washed into the cellar subsequent to the accumulation of F(480). The number of burnt facing stones in F(490) supports the contention that a major fire was responsible for the destruction of the building.

Partially sealing this layer on its eastern side was F(424) a major section of intact masonry derived from the main-block end wall F(406). The fallen wall comprised a double facing of dressed limestone blocks with a mortared rubble core. On its upper side ten coherent courses survive, on the lower side up to eighteen were recorded, giving a standing height of approximately 2m. On the western side of the cellar, closer to wall F(406), the fallen wall loses its coherence and is replaced by a jumble of rubble, mortar and facing stones.

That the collapse of the end wall took place in the early–mid third century AD is confirmed by careful consideration of the disposition of fills in the cellar and the dating applied to finds above and below the collapsed wall. The finds sealed by the wall are of generally late second century AD date; those overlying the wall belong to the third–fourth century AD.

Two alternative sequences for the filling of the cellar can be proposed. Firstly, that prior to the main-block wall collapse the volume of cellar fills later sealed below the fallen wall was much the same as when excavated (i.e. filling something over 50% of the volume of the cellar and sloping from east to west). Alternatively, the layers sealed by the fallen wall may have completely filled the cellar at the time of its collapse. If the wall collapsed later in the latter part of the third century it is likely that more third century AD material would have accumulated in the depression into which the wall fell. However, there is very little third century material in the cellar and it seems more probable that during the mid–late second century AD the cellar was completely backfilled, level or nearly level with the contemporary ground surface. Subsequent compaction of the organic rubbish layer(s), particularly on the western side of the cellar where they did not overlie the collapsed cellar wall, led to the disposition of the layers recorded during excavation. Similar combinations of rubble and organic-based fills in the Inner Enclosure Ditch appear to have undergone a comparable process of "slumping" (Trow 1988a, 37). Over time, compression of the layers beneath the wall took place, the compaction first accommodating the thickness of the wall itself and then create a depression in which rubbish would accumulate.

The most likely scenario appears to be that the cellar was almost entirely backfilled in the later second century AD prior to the collapse of the end wall in the early third century AD, explaining the presence of some third century material below the wall (see Moore below). The wall then collapsed in the early third century. How this sequence relates to the development of the villa is hard to determine. One scenario is that the abandonment of the villa coincided roughly with the collapse of the cellar in the later second century AD. This is supported by the presence of architectural fragments of contemporary date found in the backfilling of a ditch in Trench A (Trow 1988a, 58). As the building was subsequently demolished the villa was burnt, deliberately or accidentally. The villa's eastern end wall, perhaps a towering gable, may have stood for some time after this demolition before collapsing in to the partially backfilled cellar, probably in the early third century AD. It may seem that the simplest explanation is that the villa was destroyed in an accidental fire and the end wall collapsed sometime later. However, the apparent absence of roofing material recovered in excavation suggests perhaps that the roof was stripped as part of deliberate process of abandonment. A subsequent fire (accidental or deliberate) then destroyed the remaining wooden roof structure. The end wall may not have collapsed until some decades later, in the third century AD.

The material which accumulated above the collapsed wall includes pottery dating to the third–fourth century AD and may relate to an apparent later Roman occupation area located in the south west of the enclosure (RCHME 1976, 85).

Dating evidence

Ceramic Group C2 and D. The terminus post quem of AD 150–170/200 provided by the rapidly accumulating rubbish fills of the cellar and the terminus ante quem of around the early third century AD. Oxfordshire Colour Coated wares dating from between AD 240–400 and Black Burnish ware of similar date in Ceramic Group D in layer F(427) sealing the collapsed wall (see below) suggest this fill of material formed in the third–fourth century AD. It seems likely that F(427) formed over a considerable time after the abandonment of the villa. Material dating to the third century AD in Ceramic Group C2 also indicates there was a period of potentially up to 100 years between the collapse of the cellar wall and the collapse of the end wall. It is harder to determine whether the villa was still occupied over this time and if this collapse marks the abandonment of the villa.

Phase 9b: robbing of walls (Fig. 25)

Several of the wall footings were robbed for stone subsequent to the demolition of the upstanding structure. The most comprehensive robbing was of the footings of wall F(402) south of room G where F[430], a shallow trench of varying depth followed the course of the wall. F(421)/(433)/(434), the fill of the robber trench, comprised a mixture of silty clay and bands of mortar and contained considerable quantities of charcoal and fragments of wall plaster (Fig. 25, section F9 and F10).

Dating evidence

The finds from phase 9b do not allow the digging of the robber trenches to be closely dated. A terminus post quem is provided by the collapse of the end wall (phase 9a) although robbing may have taken place at a considerably later date.

Phase 10: rubbish layer accumulates over cellar

The collapse of the main-block end wall and its slumping deep into the cellar resulted in a shallow depression. Additional collapsed masonry F(457), derived from the collapse of walls F(400) and F(482), accumulated in the north-east corner of the cellar, partially sealing the fallen end wall. The remainder of the void was filled by F(427) and F(477), an accumulation of humic silt and domestic rubbish including a coin, a quantity of broken pottery and butchered animal bones. Material from these deposits dates from the mid third–fourth century AD and appears to be rubbish material accumulating from occupation in the

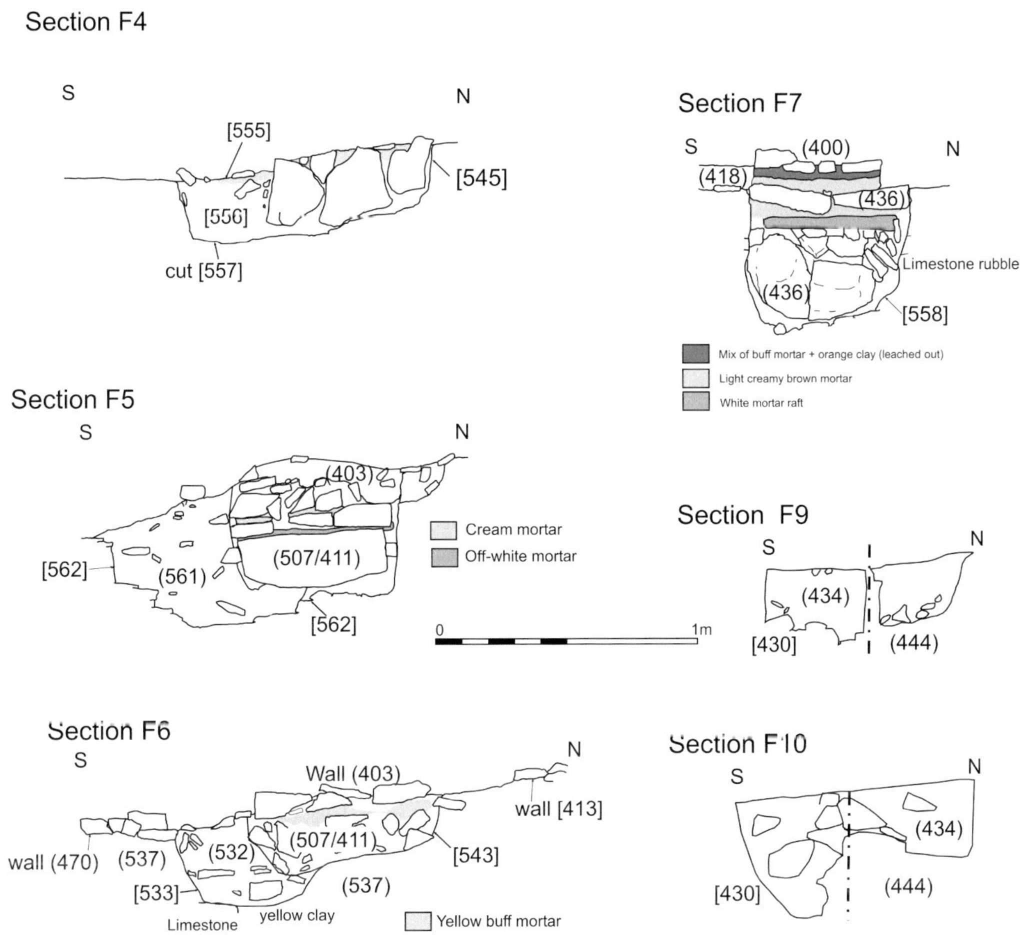

Fig. 25. Sections through villa walls.

vicinity. The discovery of large amounts of third–fourth century pottery in the south west of the enclosure (Fig. 5; RCHME 1976, 86) may indicate occupation moved to this area, representing a move away from the villa building after its collapse or demolition.

Finds

Ceramic Group D
Roman Coin: s.f. 232
Worked bone s.f. 231, 235
Worked stone: s.f. 253
Iron: s.f. 226, 228, 252
Glass: s.f. 236

Dating evidence

The coarse pottery in Ceramic Group D, F(427), can be dated to the third–fourth century AD. The coin of Valerian, which exhibits very little wear, provides terminus post quem of AD 253–260.

Unphased: structure 2 (Fig. 16)

Immediately to the north of the villa part of a rectangular structure was partially uncovered. This consisted of two drystone wall footings, F(493/492) and F(525), separated by a paved entrance way, F(526), facing south-east. Structure 2 is aligned at a slight angle to the main villa block and faces directly onto the north corridor of the villa. The phasing of this structure is uncertain. The rubble layer F(536)/F(531) overlies F(436), the footings of wall F(400), and therefore appears to be later. This layer of rubble also appears to overly the wall footings of F(493/492) and must therefore be later, possible representing its demolition. This may suggest that Structure 2 was constructed prior to the north corridor of the villa (in Phase 6) and this would certainly explain its angled alignment. Finds within the small excavated area of layer F(531), within the structure, date to the first century AD, similar to those in Trench E, further supporting the suggestion of an early date for the structure. The lack of later material, similar to that seen in the cellar contexts for example, may suggest that the second possibility, that it represents post-villa activity, is less likely although this cannot be completely ruled out.

The role of Structure 2 is harder to define. Because only a small section of the structure was revealed it is difficult to determine whether this was a domestic or ancillary building or yard area, although the former seems more likely and it may have been contemporary with the early villa.

Finds
Ceramic Group H
Copper alloy: s.f. 414

PRESERVATION OF THE VILLA

Stephen Trow

Examination of the Ditches site during the late 1970s as part of a rapid evaluation of cultivation damage to archaeological sites in the Gloucestershire Cotswolds indicated that damage to the site was severe. On the basis of this observation the site was not considered suitable for statutory protection and large-scale excavation was suggested as a more suitable response (Saville 1980, 30). One of the aims of the 1982–5 work was to reassess the degree and rate of erosion through limited excavation.

Consideration of the results of excavation between 1982 and 1985 and further study of aerial photographs indicated that preservation of the monument varied considerably across the site. In the southern half of the enclosure it is probable that all horizontal stratigraphy has been removed by ploughing and that those features surviving by virtue of being cut into the underlying bedrock are truncated. In contrast, excavations in the northeast corner of the enclosure have indicated the survival of archaeologically coherent layers outside cut features (Trow 1988a) and excavation on the site of the Romano-British buildings revealed a sequence of similar layers.

Within Trench F, detailed consideration of the survival of the walls of the main villa building (Structure 1) indicates that plough damage increases in severity to the south and east. Sections F5, F6 and F4 (Figs 16 & 25) illustrate the decreasing survival of wall F(403) from west to east. The increased damage southwards is graphically illustrated by the frequency of missing facing blocks from the southern end of wall F(404) and a missing course of blocks at the southern end of F(407) (Fig. 16). Despite this damage, it would appear that the presence of the walls of Structure 1 have lessened the rate of destruction and ensured the survival of underlying Iron Age deposits such as layer F(504). This is illustrated by section F5 (Fig. 25) which shows a rapidly increasing depth of plough-disturbed soil immediately south of the corridor wall F(403) where the plough has bitten deeper after crossing Structure 1. Any interpretation of features associated with the building must, therefore, recognise that up to an extra 0.25m of deposits may have been destroyed south of the building. It is also apparent that the degree of survival of Iron Age layers evidenced within Trench F may be restricted to the immediate environs of the masonry buildings.

On the basis of the enhanced appreciation of survival within the site as well as the importance of the surviving deposits, the site was protected by designation as a scheduled monument in 1988 (Gloucestershire scheduled monument 481). Additionally, the site was removed from cultivation in 2005 and returned to grassland through the Cotswold Environmentally Sensitive Area scheme.

GEOPHYSICAL SURVEY

Tom Moore

Introduction

A new geophysical survey of the enclosure was undertaken in 2006 with the aim of answering some of the questions raised by the recent analysis of the 1984–5 excavations. An earlier survey of the site, undertaken in the 1980s (Trow 1988a, 23–25), whilst revealing some archaeological features, only covered a small area of the enclosure interior and, due to the early nature of geophysical equipment used, the results are not as clear as those obtainable today. It was of particular interest to determine the nature of activity within areas of the enclosure that had not been subject to excavation in order to learn more about the functional nature of the enclosure, the nature and density of Iron Age occupation and the presence of any other Roman buildings.

The Gradiometry survey area (Fig. 26) covered all of the interior and as much of the area outside the enclosure as was possible within the time available. Some areas were not accessible. In particular, the area to the south of the enclosure was partially obscured by maize crop which prevented access to the southernmost part of Barley Slad field. The survey was undertaken with FM256 Gradiometers, with readings every 0.25m and traverses of 0.5m

Interpretation of survey (Fig. 27)

External features

The antenna ditch of the enclosure (A) has long been recognised in aerial photographs (see Fig. 4) and represents a distinctive element to the enclosure suggesting it has greater affinities with late Iron Age non-hillfort enclosures than other Cotswold 'hillforts' (see above). This survey has revealed a second antenna ditch to the south of the one already recognised (B). This also splays out from the south-west entrance, creating an elaborate funnel into the enclosure, reinforcing the similarities between Ditches and banjo-type enclosures and sites such as Gussage-All-Saints. In addition, a second linear runs parallel to the northern antenna ditch (C), apparently representing the formation of a trackway. This appears to run for only a short length, ending in a terminal feature, which may be tentatively interpreted as a large posthole or pit. The area to the south of this trackway contains a number anomalies (E), indicative of pits/postholes but which cannot be reconstructed in to clear archaeological features. Additional faint linear features (F), running apparently parallel to linear feature B, may suggest this also represents a trackway. Alternatively,

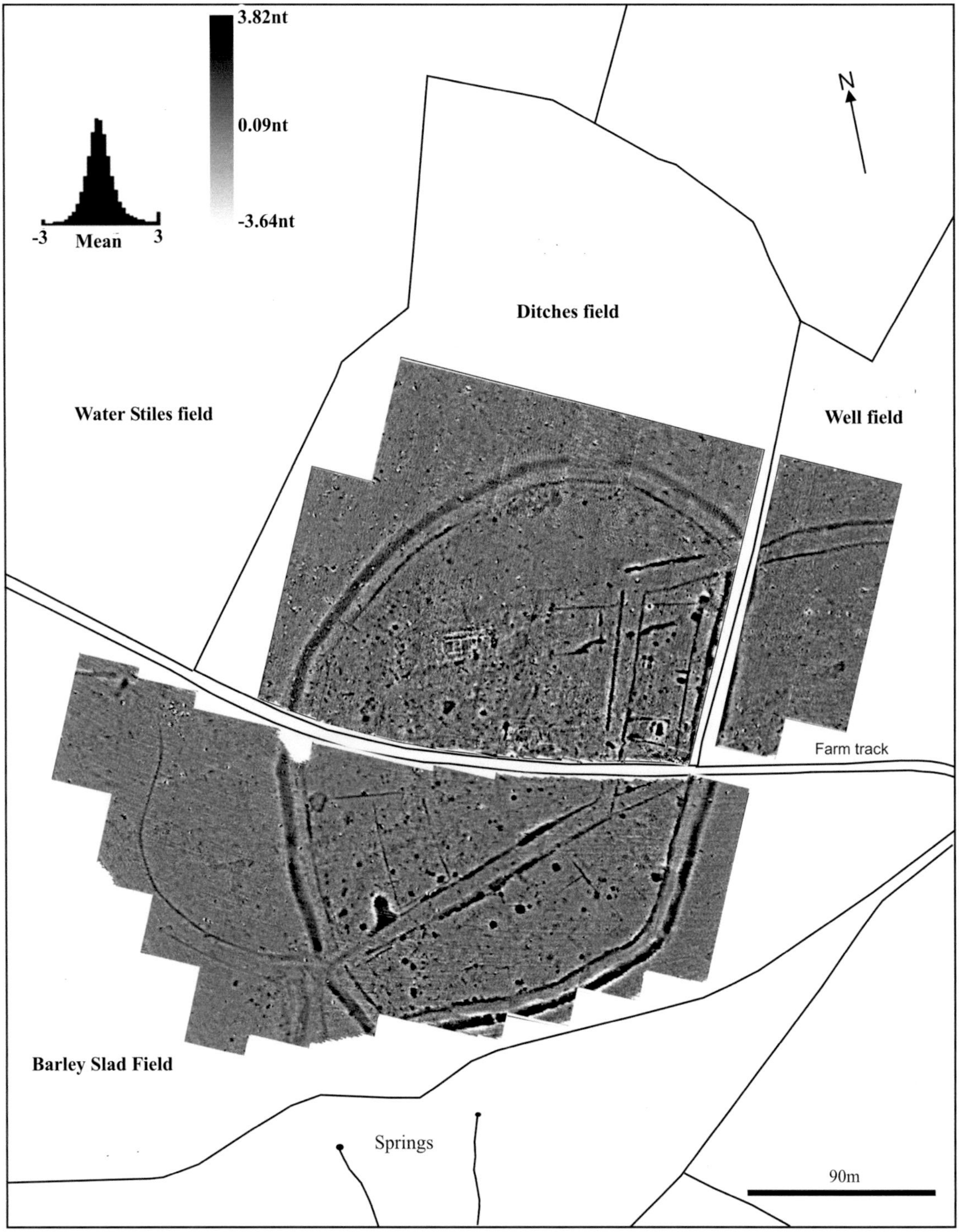

Fig. 26. Gradiometry survey of Ditches enclosure.

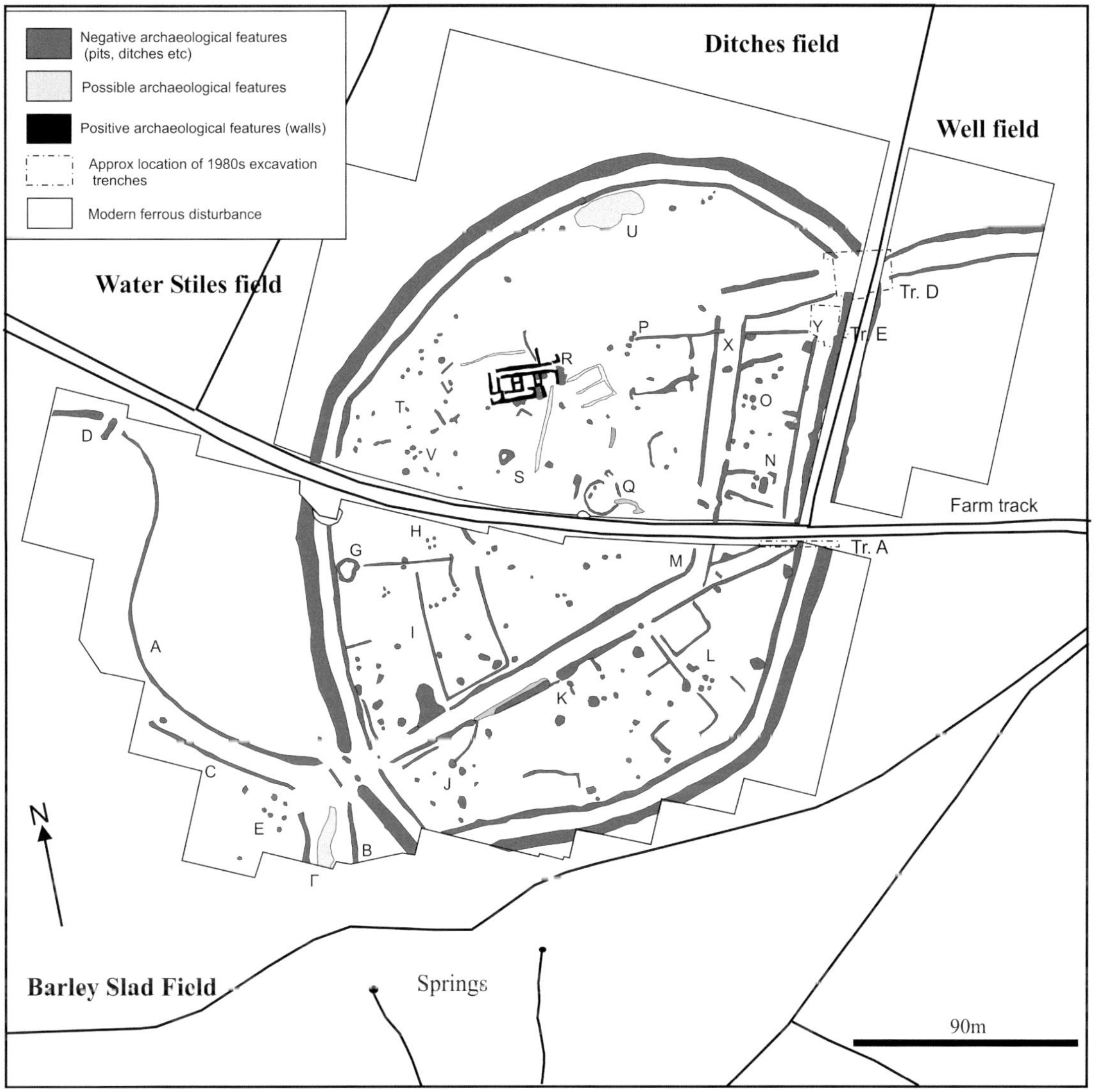

Fig. 27. Interpretative plot of geophysical survey.

these may represent prolonged wear from traffic through the south-west entrance resulting potentially in large amorphous hollowed areas. This is particularly likely if this entrance and trackway were used predominantly for stock.

At the northern end of antenna ditch A, whilst earlier aerial photographs suggest the ditch terminated where an earlier (now demolished) barn stood (D), this survey suggests the ditch curves back to the west. At this point there is an apparent entrance-gap to the south of Water-stiles field, and the linear continues west beyond the survey area.

Internal features

The irregular curvilinear feature G was noted on an earlier aerial photograph (Fig. 4; Trow 1988). This may be a small enclosure for a roundhouse but is too large to be foundation trench. Similar examples of large drainage ditches or small enclosures for later Iron Age roundhouses have been noted elsewhere in the region, for example at Claydon Pike (Allen *et al.* 1984) and Salmonsbury (Dunning 1976). A cluster of postholes or small pits to the east of G may represent the remains of a four-poster structure, usually argued as granaries (H). Further examples might tentatively be postulated in Ditches field at O.

A number of inner enclosures can be noted to the north of the southwest entrance (I). The form of these enclosures may suggest some role for stock corralling. The presence of a number of anomalies that look like storage pits within these enclosures could alternatively suggest other activities took place in this area, although if the enclosures are contemporary with the main trackway, these pits may instead pre-date the enclosures. These enclosures respect the boundary of the inner trackway suggesting they are at least partially contemporaneous, although they do not use the track ditch as their southern boundary. The southern side of one of the enclosures includes a large amorphous feature which could be interpreted as a stone quarry similar to that excavated in Trench E.

The main inner trackway previously noted on a number of aerial photographs (see Fig. 4; Trow 1998a, 2) and recognised as being reverse 'Z' in shape, runs from the southwest entrance to the northeast entrance. The 2006 survey has now revealed that a second trackway, apparently of a different phase, continues to the east beyond the kink in Barley field (M), then turns to the north terminating adjacent to the northeast gate. There is a possibility that this secondary trackway led to another entrance to the enclosure, situated roughly where the modern farm track utilises a causeway to bisect the enclosure. The modern gap created by the farm track might even represents re-use of an earlier causeway through an earlier entrance. However, it is notable that the trackway does not appear to continue on its alignment into Well field, unlike its counterpart to the north, although the presence of hill-wash and overburden related to the modern trackway may obscure any ancient features. It seems somewhat more likely, however, that the ephemeral anomalies visible in this area of Well field relate to prolonged use of the modern entrance to the field at this point. Alternatively, no third entrance existed and the trackway always turned left, running parallel to the Inner Enclosure Ditch. Dating of the trackway ditches at this point seems to indicate that the Inner Enclosure Ditch had already been filled in when the track was in use, although it may have remained as visible boundary (suggested perhaps by its recognition by the later field boundary). The continuation of the east ditch of the main trackway across this junction (M) suggests that this track is of a different phase. It is further noticeable that the linear which appears to join the trackway at Y in Ditches field (P) may also be cut by the later trackway (X) (although see below).

Excavation of the trackway ditches in 1982–3 (Trow 1988a, 38) and 1984 (see above) suggests that the east–west section of the main track leading in to the enclosure from the north-east entrance was constructed in the late Iron Age. The trackway through the north-east gate appears to run to rear of the villa and may be seen to continue, represented by more ephemeral anomalies to the north of the villa building.

Excavation of Trench A across the track ditches, to the south of the modern track, suggested these were "going out of use" by the mid–late second century

AD (ibid., 38) perhaps implying that the orientation of the track running alongside the Inner Enclosure Ditch was first or second century AD in date. Further to the north, the trackway/enclosure ditch at Y appears to have cut through the possibly Flavian cobbled surface laid over the Quarry pit in Trench E and therefore dates perhaps to the second century AD. The linear (P), which appears to run at right angles to this feature and may be related, produced dating evidence suggesting it was backfilled in the later first century AD. In addition, the excavations in Trench E do not suggest that linear P and Y were in anyway related to each other or contemporary, despite this appearing to be the case in the survey plan (see above, Trench E). Therefore, the realignment of the main trackway at X and M appears later than linear P, and possibly trackway Y, suggesting it may date to the second or even third century AD. It may even mark a reorganisation of the trackways within the enclosure related to the later Roman occupation noted within the south east of the enclosure (see below). This would make it post-date the villa structure itself. Despite this dating, it remains possible that the trackway(s) echoed existing routeways through the enclosure, dating back to the first century AD or earlier. It is notable for instance that both appear to respect the central and northern area of the enclosure where the villa structure is situated as well as the central area of the enclosure.

The small enclosures in Ditches field which appear to relate to the main trackway, one possibly having an entrance on to the trackway, contain a number of archaeological features. These include a smaller enclosure at N, inside which is a highly magnetic anomaly. The nature of this features is unclear but there is nothing to suggest it is not archaeological; it may represent a pit containing large amounts of ferrous metalwork, for example. A further possible enclosure can be seen to the south of linear P as well as a more amorphous linear feature running roughly east–west to the south of X. This may represent an earlier linear division of the enclosure interior, although its amorphous nature could imply a geological origin, such as a fissure in the underlying rock strata.

There is at least one entrance on to the main trackway in the southern field (K). This appears to have been elaborated with deep ditch terminals at either terminus. In addition, there is some evidence for a small linear crossing it, possibly representing its closure at some point or representing a narrowing of the ditch to allow for a bridge or features related to some form of gate. Two very large pits, or possibly wells, are also visible within this area and appear to respect this entrance feature. The field name of near by 'Well field' perhaps hints that other wells have been detected in this area in antiquity. A number of similar, large pit like features can be discerned in this area. Whilst some of these are almost certainly wells, the existence of large, limestone lined storage or silo pits has been noted at a number of later Iron Age sites in the region and have been shown to produce relatively similar magnetic anomalies (cf. Marshall 1999; 2001).

To the east, a number of more ephemeral enclosures (L) can be discerned and a narrow trackway may relate to a second entrance on to the main inner trackway. The ephemeral nature of these enclosures is likely to be the result of greater plough damage in this area. These may be related to the occupation noted in this area from fieldwalking evidence collected in the 1970s (RCHME 1976) suggesting later Roman occupation in this area. However, no evidence of stone-built structures was identified in this area, despite the clear recognition of stone structures in Ditches field. This may be the result of greater plough damage (Stephen Trow pers. comm.) or suggest any buildings were more ephemeral, post-built structures.

Villa and central area

The remains of the villa (R) were clearly revealed in the survey and match the plans based on excavated evidence and aerial photographs (see Fig. 18). The cellar excavated in 1985, and the pits revealed beneath the villa, are also visible on the geophysical survey. In addition, there is some indication that the partially excavated structure 2, to the north of the villa, is just visible along with a number of other more ephemeral anomalies. The clarity of the unexcavated walls of the villa suggests that if any other large, masonry structures existed within the enclosure these are likely to have been detected by the survey, although it remains possible that any such features have suffered severe plough damage.

One key question raised by the 1984–5 excavations was how the main villa building related to any other structures in the interior of the enclosure. It is particularly notable that the villa is situated slightly to the north of centre of the enclosure. In addition, the path leading to the villa recognised in 1985, runs in a south-easterly direction rather than running at right angles to the villa structure (see above), although this path was not detected by the geophysics. The geophysical survey may provide some answers to these questions. There is tentative evidence of a curvilinear feature, possibly an eaves drip-gully, located roughly in the centre of the enclosure (Q). This is associated with a number of other anomalies suggestive of possible structures. It is possible that the villa respected the central location of this structure. This survey also indicates that the enclosures visible elsewhere in interior respect this central area, with little evidence for the pits and linears seen to the south.

The location of this curvilinear feature, and the apparent absence of such structures elsewhere in the enclosure, is significant. Is this a late Iron Age roundhouse situated central to the enclosure? If so, the location of the early Roman villa discreet from this building, and the apparent positioning of the path aligned upon the curvilinear structure, may suggest it was still standing and perhaps even in use when the villa was constructed. Examples of roundhouses contemporary with early Roman villas within enclosures are known elsewhere in Britain, for example at Holme House, North Yorkshire (Harding 1984) and possibly contemporary with the earliest rectangular structures at Gorhambury (Smith 1997, 231). At Holme House the circular building is also central to the enclosure and was apparently in use at the same time as the villa building (Fig. 32). Recognition of this structure is highly significant therefore in indicating the role and development of the site.

To the west of this structure and south west of the villa are a number of other potential archaeological features (T), most of which do not form a coherent pattern or structures but are suggestive of pits and postholes probably of Iron Age date, one possibly another four-poster (V). To the north of the villa there is some suggestion that linear P runs further west, possibly marking a boundary contemporary with the earliest phase of the villa (see above). North of this boundary the enclosure appears to be largely absent of features, save for a faint amorphous anomaly at U which may represent quarrying. The apparent lack of features in this area may imply this was reserved for stock or was an open area.

DISCUSSION OF THE IRON AGE AND ROMAN REMAINS

Stephen Trow, Simon James and Tom Moore

Sequence and chronology of the site

For the purpose of discussing the nature and development of the site the phases in Trench E and F above can be combined with the evidence from the 1982–3 excavations and divided in to a number of broader periods of activity at the site (Fig. 28):

Period 1

First century BC–early first century AD: Pre-conquest activity on the site took the form of storage pits and construction of the outer enclosure ditch with the later addition of the Inner Enclosure Ditch. Closer dating of these activities is not possible and the stratigraphic relationships in Trench F and E suggest at least some time depth of activity. (Trench E: phase 1, 2, 3; Trench F: phase 1, 2). The enclosure could have been occupied much earlier than the first century BC but there is currently little evidence for this and, on current finds and the form of the enclosure, a late Iron Age inception is perhaps most likely.

Period 2

Mid first century AD: Between *c.* AD45 and AD50s the site saw considerable activity with the infilling of the Inner Enclosure Ditch and causeway created across the ditch. (Trench E: phase 4, 5; Trench F: phase 3).

Period 3

Later first century AD (AD70s): Building of the main villa block. North–south ditch in Trench E dug. The digging and backfilling of the Quarry pit may date to this period or slightly earlier; the quarry perhaps providing stone for the building of the villa main block. (Trench E: phase 6, ?7; Trench F: phase 4)

Period 4 (Early)

Early–mid second century AD. Addition of timber corridors to villa, later replaced in stone, and construction of the cellar. (Trench F: phase 5, 6)

Period 4 (Late)

Mid second century AD. Addition of wings to the villa. Second episode ('topping-up') of the Inner Enclosure Ditch. (Trench E: phase ?8; Trench F: phase 7)

Period 5

Mid–late second century AD. Collapse of the cellar wall and infilling of cellar. Fire in the villa building? These events may have marked the abandonment or dismantling of the villa and shift to occupation nearby. (Trench F: phase 8)

Period 6

Early third century AD. Collapse of end

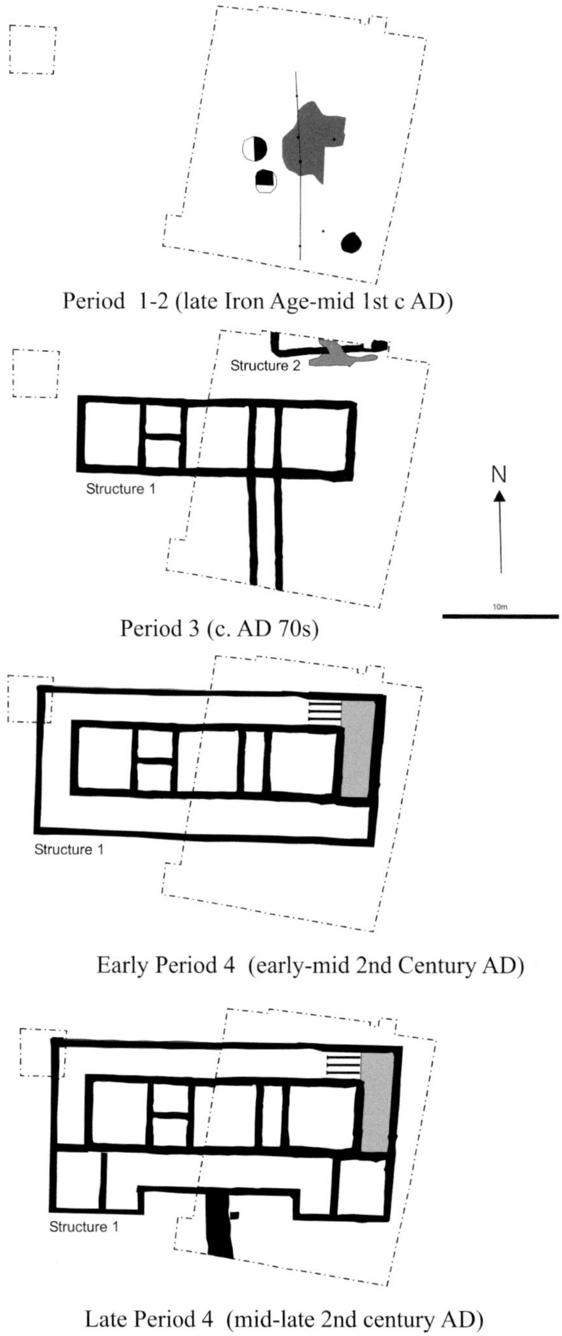

Fig. 28. Phases of activity in Trench F.

wall of main block – probably after villa abandonment. (Trench F: phase 9a, ?9b)

Period 7
Third–fourth century AD. Build up of rubbish in the top of the cellar relating to domestic activity in the vicinity, possibly relating to the pottery scatter in the south of the enclosure. (Trench F: phase ?9b, 10)

The Iron Age enclosure

Several aspects of the character of the Period 1 Iron Age enclosure have already been explored in the report of the 1982–3 excavations (Trow 1988a). The 1984–5 excavations have provided additional evidence for the nature of one of the perimeter ditches of the enclosure and, for the first time, information on features in its interior. Taken as a whole, the 1982–1985 excavations sampled only *c.* 2.5% of the site. Consequently assertions made in the following section must be treated with caution reflecting the limited nature of the evidence. The wider context of the site at Ditches in the later Iron Age and Early Roman period and its relationship to Bagendon will be discussed in more detail in a forthcoming article (Moore *et al.* in prep.).

The enclosure probably originated in the first century BC as univallate with a wide rock-cut ditch and an internal drystone or dump rampart. The size and elevated situation of the enclosure have widely been used to describe the site as a 'hillfort', although the weakly defended entrance and lack of elaboration of the perimeter ditches suggests that military strength was not the primary concern of its builders. The exceptionally late date and form of the site also suggest it fulfilled very different roles to other 'hillforts' in the region, most of which appear to have been abandoned by the first century BC (Moore 2006a).

It is difficult to find plentiful parallels for the enclosure, but in terms of morphology it is best compared with the larger Iron Age curvilinear enclosures of Wessex rather than the developed later Iron Age hillforts of the Cotswolds such as Uley Bury (Saville 1983) and Bredon Hill (Hencken 1938) or the so-called enclosed *oppidum* at Salmonsbury (Dunning 1976). The later phase at Bury Hill, Hampshire, although probably earlier than Ditches, has some parallels in form and contains potential evidence for occupation possibly by a new elite focused on horse rearing. This dates to an apparently short phase of occupation in the second or first century BC (Creighton 2000, 16; Cunliffe and Poole 2000a) with other similar late Iron Age large enclosures at Suddern Farm (Cunliffe and Poole 2000c) and Boscombe Down West (Richardson 1951).

Other possible parallels include Gussage-All-Saints which also has associated antenna ditches (Wainwright 1979). Ditches also resembles some of the late Iron Age banjo enclosures found in Dorset and Hampshire which appear to have been occupied in the late Iron Age (Barrett *et al.* 1991, 235). Similar sites exist in the eastern Cotswolds but are generally undated (Moore 2006b, 143–147). These are characterised by antenna ditches and droveways, similar to those at Ditches, implying a focus on the movement and control of stock. Late in the Iron Age, the non-defensive aspect of the Ditches enclosure was further confirmed by the digging of a second ditch running around the inside edge of the rampart bank, effectively divorcing the rampart from the interior of the enclosure. In this respect Ditches also resembles a number of banjo enclosures where the bank is outside the ditch, a characteristic that has been argued as reflecting the symbolic role of the enclosure boundary rather than any defensive function (Bowden and McOmish 1987; Collis 1996).

Excavated evidence and aerial photographs indicate that the interior of the enclosure contained a considerable number of storage pits. No evidence of buildings was recovered, although subdivision of the enclosure is indicated by the fenceline excavated in Trench F. Most contemporary sites in the Upper Thames valley and the Cotswolds indicate the local indigenous building tradition was for roundhouses with eaves-drip gulleys (Allen *et al.* 1984; Mudd *et al.* 1999, 45), although a number of drystone-built roundhouses of Iron Age date have been noted in the region at Conderton (Thomas 2005) and possibly Bagendon (Clifford 1961). Alternatively, late Iron Age roundhouses in the Upper Thames Valley may have mainly been cob walled structures (Richard Hingley pers. comm.) and this may have also been the case further west, on the Cotswolds. The degree of erosion within the southern half of the enclosure may have rendered any buildings of this type unrecognisable to aerial reconnaissance although the apparent lack of roundhouses may be significant, particularly when compared with the density of structures visible at hillforts such as Uley Bury (Hampton and Palmer 1977). Only one potential candidate for a structure of this type is visible on existing aerial photographic coverage, immediately adjacent to the Inner Enclosure Ditch on the western perimeter of the site, with a second possible example now visible on the 2006 geophysics. It is of course possible that buildings inside Ditches were post-built without gulleys for example, or that the principal structures within the enclosure were limited to its northern half.

Initial construction of the enclosure probably took place in the first century BC (Trow 1988a, 37–38). This date is based primarily on the deliberate deposition of a hoard of currency bars, possibly with ritual significance (Hingley 1990), in a primary position in the outer ditch. However, the later date suggested for some currency bar deposits (Hingley 2005) means it can now be argued that such deposition need not date prior to the first century AD. Recent excavation of two nearby sites at Duntisbourne (Mudd *et al.* 1999) suggests some late Iron Age sites were only occupied for a relatively short space of time in the early–mid first century AD. Ditches may have had a slightly different history with occupation beginning somewhat earlier in the first century BC. It is not possible to closely date the digging or use of the storage pits within the interior of the enclosure, but Ceramic Groups G1 and G2 suggest a later Iron Age date which does not conflict with that indicated by the currency bar hoard. Based on the Gallo-Belgic finewares incorporated in to the fills of pits F[505] and F[540] it appears the pits were backfilled around the early–mid first century AD.

Continued occupation into the period immediately prior to the Roman conquest is attested by a series of Augustan and Augusto-Tiberian fineware sherds and by the Augustan gemstone located during fieldwalking (Trow 1982), although no features indisputably belonging to this period have been excavated. No direct evidence can be adduced for the construction of the Inner Enclosure Ditch. The lack of finds datable before the mid first century AD and the small amount of silting below fills datable to this period suggest that cutting of the inner ditch may not long have preceded its backfilling. That this episode of backfilling dates to *c.* AD 45–55, as suggested in the previous report (Trow 1988a), receives corroboration in the form of a Claudian dupondius copy from layer E(310), derived from inner ditch fill E(320). This provides a terminus post quem of during or soon after the reign of Claudius for the deposition of E(320) and is augmented by a decorated samian bowl from layer E(336) datable to AD 40–55 (see Willis below).

The economy of the enclosure

Evidence for the economy of the Iron Age enclosure derives mainly from the storage pits and associated layer in Trench F and from the contents of the Inner Enclosure Ditch. Whereas the assemblage from the pits relates to the occupation of the enclosure during the second or first centuries BC, the material derived from the ditch provides evidence for the economy of the site on the eve of the Roman conquest and immediately afterwards. This time lapse is apparent in the changes apparent in the faunal assemblage of the two features (see Rielly below).

Crop processing and storage

Analysis of the crops being exploited at Ditches (Huntley below), although based on a small sample of material, suggests the site was consuming rather than producing grain. This is indicated by the high proportion of grain to weeds and the suggestion by Huntley that this material was grown on slightly damp ground rather than the limestone soils in the immediate vicinity. Such evidence supports a wider recent study in the region which has suggested that a number of enclosures, such as Rollright, Oxfordshire, were consuming grain produced on soils other than those in the immediate locality (Stevens 1996). This might suggest some enclosures, possibly including Ditches, participated only in the final stages of crop processing. To some extent this also reflects the pattern from faunal assemblages which indicates that in the mid first century AD a greater proportion of cattle, likely to have come from further down the Bagendon or Churn valleys, was consumed (see Rielly below). This pattern requires further detailed analysis but has important implications for understanding the nature of food production and exchange in the late Iron Age. Other evidence for crop processing survives in the form of the lower stone of a rotary quern deposited in the fill of pit F(517). An upper stone from a similar rotary quern was recovered during the 1983 excavation (Trow 1988a, 57–58). The stone formed part of the roadway leading to the north-eastern entrance and may belong to an equally early phase.

Three storage pits were recognised during the partial excavation of Trench F. It is possible that other examples remained unlocated in the northern half of the trench, although no obvious subsidence of unexcavated villa contexts indicated their presence. Consideration of aerial photographs of the enclosure and the new geophysical survey (Figs 4 and 26; Trow 1988a) suggests that it probably contains more than 100 comparable pits. The pits are cylindrical in shape with an average diameter of 1.4m and depth of 1.2m. The survival of undamaged structures sealing two of the pits suggests no truncation due to cultivation damage. These dimensions are well within the normal range for similar storage pits in Wessex, although the average volume they provide, 1.85 cubic metres, is rather lower than the average volume of pits at Danebury (Whittle 1984). Little comparative data exists for similar pits in the region dug into limestone, but the Ditches examples compare well with an example from Wood House, Guiting Power, with a diameter of approximately 1.5m and a depth of 1.1m (Gascoigne 1973), and the diameters of a group of truncated pits at Guiting Power (Saville 1979, 132). It can be estimated that each of the excavated pits in Trench F could have held approximately 1300kg of grain.

Animal husbandry

The cattle-rich assemblage already known from Ditches has been a focus for debate in studies of the 'Romanization' of diets in the first century AD (Rielly 1988 and below, Hambleton 1998; Albarella 2007). This assemblage has been supported by material from the 1984–5 excavations which suggests a focus on cattle consumption in the mid first century AD yet an apparent shift back to an apparently 'un-Romanized' diet predominating in sheep after the mid first century AD. The emphasis on cattle in the mid first century AD and the possibility of a local source may suggest an emphasis on cattle rearing at the Bagendon-Ditches complex. We may be seeing a transition to a more 'Romanized' (or Gallo-Belgic) diet in this period, possibly alongside other changes in drinking and eating habits, perhaps related to the high status nature of the occupants as they attempted to emulate the lifeways of the kingdoms in south east England and their contemporaries in Gaul. To what extent cattle consumption was restricted to those of high status or marked a general shift in foodways is less clear, however. Such an emphasis on high status food consumption may have continued in the second century with the high proportion of pig consumed and evidence for chicken (see Rielly below). The form of the enclosure discerned from the geophysics survey (Figs 5 and 27), with an emphasis on trackways, enclosures and antenna ditches also suggests an emphasis on animal husbandry and management in the early Roman period, and possibly in the late Iron Age.

Crafts and industrial activity

Sheep made up a significant component of a generally cattle-dominated animal bone assemblage in the first century AD. Although their age distribution suggests they were not kept specifically for their wool (Trow 1988a; Rielly below), the artefactual evidence indicates that textile processing was carried out on the site. Finds include limestone and ceramic spindle whorls, triangular loomweights, and bone pins and bobbins. No classic weaving combs have been recovered from these conquest period contexts although small find s.f.366 may have performed a similar function. A similar range of textile processing tools were recovered by Clifford at Bagendon (1961, 151 and pls LII, LVII) suggesting that non-intensive textile production was an element of the economy of both sites. That the production of textiles took place earlier in the lifetime of the enclosure is demonstrated by the fragment of a worked bone bobbin from pit F[564].

The evidence of metalworking from the first century deposits is all indirect and *ex-situ*. That iron and copper working was taking place at Ditches is established by examination of various slags and crucible fragments (Trow 1988a, fiche 1/A6). The presence of currency bars on the site may also indicate that ironworking activity was established at an early date. More concrete evidence for smelting and smithing activities was recorded at Bagendon (Clifford 1961, 186–196) and provides an indication of the level of technology to be expected at Ditches. Of particular interest is the evidence for coin manufacture which occurs on both sites. At Ditches this takes the form of fragments of baked clay pellet-moulds, used in the manufacture of coin blanks, recovered from the Inner Enclosure Ditch, from Trench F and from fieldwalking. The moulds occur in two types apparently corresponding to the production of large gold and smaller silver denominations. This evidence for goldworking is complemented by the recovery from the inner ditch of a fragment of gold foil and a touchstone with traces of gold on its surfaces. The evidence for bronze working recovered in previous excavations (Trow 1988a, 53) further indicates the apparent role of Ditches as a producer of a variety of types of metalwork. This appears to have included the production of coin blanks; possibly the site acted as a mint although the metalworking evidence suggests these were not the only items being produced. All the coin moulds were found within layer F(478) which may date to phase 4, the period of the villa construction. It seems most likely that these were redeposited from earlier coin production in the immediate vicinity, although the possibility that coin production was taking place immediately before or at the time the villa was constructed cannot be ruled out. At Bagendon, a concentration of pellet moulds and associated coins was taken by Clifford to imply the location of a native 'mint' (Clifford 1961, 16, 98) although, as at Ditches, it can only be established with certainty that it was a location for the production of coin blanks. The dating of the 'mint' area at Bagendon remains open to question but is likely to date to around the mid–first century AD. On the basis of present evidence, the striking of the coins may have occurred at Ditches or Bagendon, at both sites or a third location. Discovery of part of another possible coin mould from the late Iron Age site at Wycomb (Timby 1998, 321) implies further complexity in where, and by whom, late Iron Age coins were produced. In addition, limited evidence from the Inner Enclosure Ditch in the form of clay kiln furniture may suggest limited pottery manufacture on site as well.

'Structured deposition' at Ditches?

A number of elements in the treatment of remains at the site suggest some intentional structuring in the deposition of animal and human remains. The deposition of cattle remains in the final phase of the Quarry pit appears to be structured, possibly symbolically (although see Rielly below), and can be paralleled at a number of other sites in the region including The Bowsings (Marshall 1991) and Abbeymead (Atkin 1987) where similar treatment of animal remains appears to have taken place. At these sites as at Ditches, cattle were deposited in boundary features in the later half of the first century AD, both apparently as closure deposits in the final use of these features. Elsewhere, both in the region and beyond, the placement of animal remains in boundary features as part of 'structured deposits' is a common occurrence on Iron Age sites (Bowden and McOmish 1987; Hill 1995a) and with such symbolic activities and structuring of space increasingly recognised in the Roman period (e.g. Fulford 2001). Rielly also notes a variation in the deposition patterns of animal remains. To this can be added the deposition of fragments of human skull alongside a quern stone in pit F[505] which echoes the apparent symbolic deposition of quern stones elsewhere in the region (see Roe below, Moore 2006b).

A hoard of currency bars was deposited within the outer enclosure ditch, excavated in 1982–3 (Trow 1988a, 40), also reflecting the widespread symbolic deposition of these artefacts in boundary features (Hingley 1990; 2005). The continuation of such practices in to the mid–late first century AD, particularly on sites such as Ditches, which in traditional terminology were highly 'Romanized', indicates the complexity of practices taking place in the first century AD and the potentially complex sets of identities and belief systems which even communities exhibiting relatively 'Romanised' lifestyles could engage.

Another unusual element to the deposition patterns noted at the site is the high proportion of brooches (30), dating to the mid first century AD, recovered from sections of the Inner Enclosure Ditch, both in the 1982–3 and 1984–5 excavations. The two areas excavated were approximately 100m apart and, if the deposits found in these sections are typical, might suggest around 250 brooches were deposited in this area of the feature. The presence of rich deposits of metalwork and other material in enclosure features has been widely acknowledged elsewhere (Hingley 2006) and is seen at the site itself with the currency bar hoard found in the outer enclosure ditch (Hingley 1990; Trow 1988a, 40). In addition, the presence of material deposited on the eastern or south-eastern edge of enclosures has been widely recognised on Iron Age sites as part of symbolic patterns of deposition (e.g. Hill 1995b; Parker-Pearson 1996). The possibility, therefore, that brooches were deliberately deposited in this area, potentially as an act of conspicuous consumption and/or as some other kind of symbolic act must be considered. In addition, the number of brooches from these ditch sections, if representative of a larger deposition pattern perhaps indicates the wealth of material culture potentially present on the site at this time.

The Romano-British villa (Structure 1)

The main villa block appears to have been built during the third quarter of the first century AD. More precise dating is difficult, but a terminus ante quem of *c.* AD80 provided by brooch s.f. 426 and the ceramic evidence from pit F[505] (and material sealing the primary floor of room R6) suggest construction in the early Flavian period. The need to accommodate the construction of the main block, addition of the timber veranda, its replacement in stone and the associated construction of the cellar, insertion of wings and the use and demolition of the cellar, all before the backfilling of the cellar in the mid–late second century AD, further supports the proposed early foundation. Even allowing for a very rapid succession of constructional phases, it is unlikely that the villa could have been constructed later than the end of the first century AD. Such a later foundation date, would require a 40 year hiatus in the occupation sequence of Trench F, which receives no support from the ceramic record (Willis below). The early villa structure appears to have been complemented by at least one ancillary building, Structure 2, which was partially revealed. The role of this structure in not entirely clear but may have provided additional accommodation or storage facilities. Further buildings should perhaps be expected in the wider enclosure, as seen at Gorhambury (Neal *et al.* 1990).

On the basis of this early construction date, the Ditches building does not conform to the common pattern for villa development in the region. The majority of excavated Cotswold villas were constructed in the third or fourth centuries AD with only a few sites originating as early as the second century (Holbrook 2006, 106–108; RCHME 1976, xxxviii). A similar late development for villa establishments is suggested elsewhere in the south-west (Branigan 1977, 34–6). Other early villas may be postulated in the Cotswolds, on the basis of claimed arretine pottery from Rodmarton (Clifford 1961, 211; RCHME 1976, 98), a probable late Iron Age ditch and Terra Nigra from Waltham (Hirst n.d.) and early material from Great Witcombe (RCHME 1976, xxxviii) but in all cases the evidence is ambiguous. In addition, at Frocester rectangular buildings were constructed within the later Iron Age enclosure in the second century AD, although such structures can hardly be termed a 'villa' and the site only developed large masonry buildings somewhat later, in the third century AD (Price 2000, 87).

Nationally, the incidence of villa buildings constructed and occupied in the first century AD is difficult to determine. Leech and Leach (1982, 66), for example, have noted that a substantial proportion of villa sites in southern Somerset and northern Dorset have produced evidence of first or second century activity, but it is unclear whether these sites boasted villa buildings so early. Unfortunately, the positive identification of first century villa buildings is complicated by the likelihood of early occupation on the site of many later villa establishments and the early date of the majority of excavations of known early villa sites. In many cases, as at Frocester, whilst these sites were continuously occupied from the first century AD (or earlier), villa buildings were often only built later, in the third century AD, as appears to have been the case at Marshfield, Southern Gloucestershire (Blockley 1985).

The majority of villa buildings which can confidently be attributed to the first century AD are clustered in the south-east of England (Fig. 33; Black 1987), including sites such as Gorhambury (Neal *et al.* 1990) and Lockleys (Ward-Perkins 1938) in Hertfordshire. The Ditches building is one of a limited number of early villas peripheral to this group. Additional examples include the early Flavian examples in Oxfordshire, including Shakenoak (Brodribb *et al.*

1971a), and those in Northamptonshire, including Mileoak, dated to AD 65–75 (Green and Draper 1978) with further possible examples including the building situated within Ham Hill hillfort, Somerset (Branigan 1977, 39–40), although the evidence from the last is questionable. A number of other first century AD villas have been postulated (see Black 1987) most in South East England. Further afield, Holme House, North Yorkshire, whose situation is somewhat similar to Ditches, may also have originated in the late first century AD, although the dating of the site remains uncertain (Richard Hingley pers. comm.). Ditches represents the westernmost known example and is at present exceptional. The development of the villa at Ditches, therefore, casts light on the nature of the transition from pre-Roman societies and landownership to the post-conquest landscape; enabling wider questions over settlement form, house design and identity in early Roman Britain to be explored below.

Ditches and other villa buildings compared

The first villa

Early Roman villas in Britain can be divided in to a number of distinct layouts, including strip buildings or 'row houses', 'cottage houses', courtyard villas and winged corridor houses, although definitions of these groups differ (see Black 1994; Hingley 1989; Smith 1997) and indeed defining early villa buildings is problematic. Ditches develops through a range of these layouts, exhibiting a sequence of development comparable to a number of other villas in southern Britain and northern Gaul (Fig. 29).

The extent to which villas buildings developed from rectilinear timber buildings of late Iron Age tradition is uncertain (Smith 1997, 219) but, unlike south-eastern England, there is little evidence of such buildings in the region prior to the Roman conquest, or anything similar to the early Roman timber buildings known from Frocester (Price 2000). There is no evidence for any rectilinear timber building at Ditches prior to the stone built villa. It is, however, entirely possible that the remains of a timber precursor were entirely obliterated by the foundations of the villa (as appears to have been the fate of most traces of an early timber phase at Gorhambury: Neal *et al.* 1990, 27, 39), or perhaps one was located elsewhere in the enclosure, as at Piddington (Friendship-Taylor 2002; 2006).

The form of the first phase of Ditches villa belongs to Smith's 'row type house' (1997, 51). It has also been referred to as a 'strip building' and can also be placed within the broader group of 'cottage houses' discussed by Hingley (1989, 38). Especially early parallels are seen at Park Street and Lockleys (Black 1994, 101). Ditches' early form can also be paralleled at Boxmoor, Hertfordshire and Brixworth, Northamptonshire (Black 1994). The first phase of some villas in northern Gaul consists of a similar arrangement, as at Herouville-Lebisey, Calvados; Boos Le Bois Flahault, Seine-Maritime (Smith 1997, 53); a range of examples in the Somme (Ferdiere 1988, 173) and examples in Picardie, such as Behen (Bayard 1996).

The similarity in form between these Gaulish and British examples of similar date may indicate a continental influence in this design. Black (1994, 100), however, questions the Gaulish origin of this type of villa suggesting a common, possibly military-inspired, source for this type rather than representing an import from Gaul. However, the apparent similarities between early Roman villas in Gaul and Britain and lack of obvious military prototypes, suggest a military source

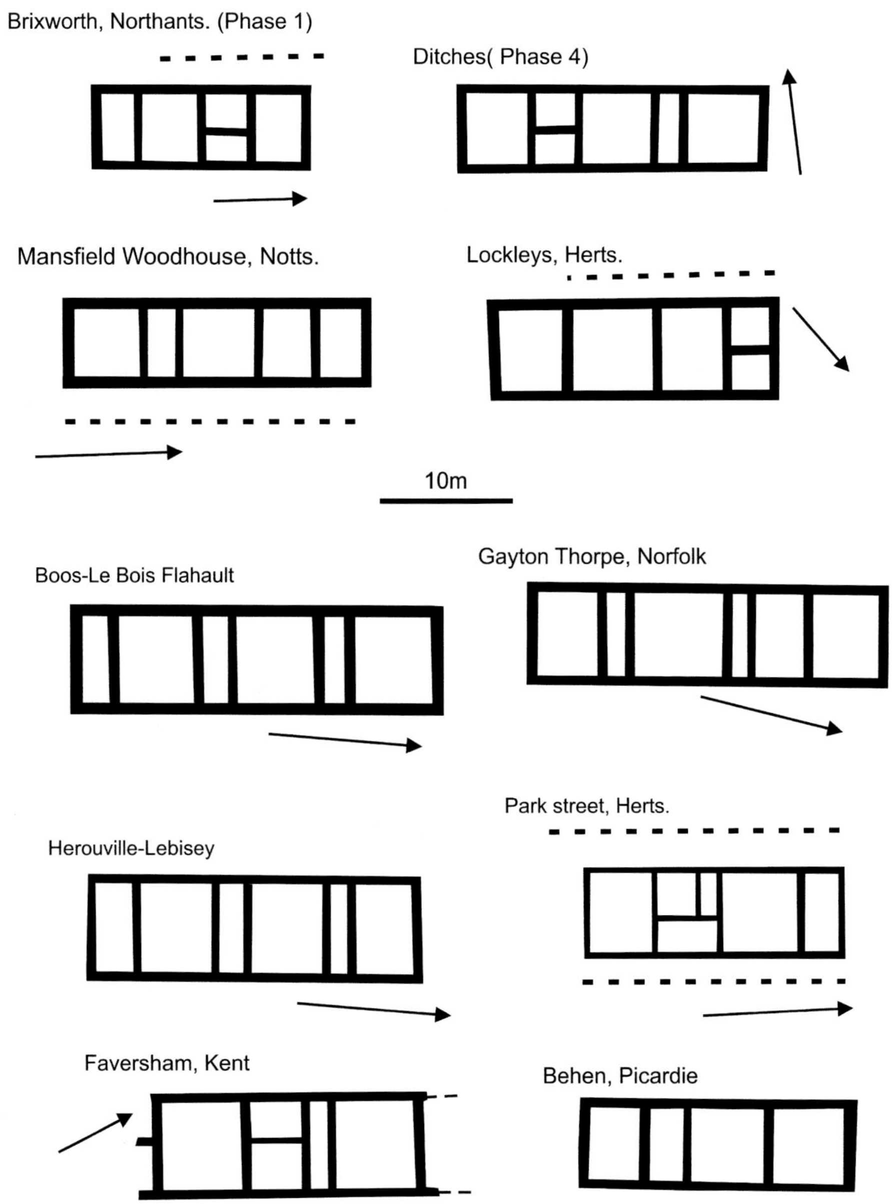

Fig. 29. Comparison of Ditches villa phase 4 and other early villas.

for these layouts is unlikely. It has also been suggested that the courtyard and winged-corridor villas were derived from continental prototypes in Italy and Gaul respectively, but that the strip-building (or row house) may have had its roots in indigenous building traditions in south-eastern Britain (Rodwell and Rodwell 1985, 41).

It is also notable that the development

of Ditches has similarities with Gorhambury and a number of other Hertfordshire villas. Considering the possible close links between the Bagendon complex and the Hertfordshire region, particularly *Verlamion* (Verulamium), in the late Iron Age, suggested by the pottery, coin and textual evidence (Moore *et al.* forthcoming), inspiration for the Ditches villa may have derived from this area and perhaps indirectly from Gaul. However, it seems that the masonry phase of the Gorhambury villa developed somewhat later than that at Ditches (probably around AD 100) although the overall layout and design have a number of similarities (Neal *et al.* 1990, 38–45). The question of origins for this form remains open to debate but current evidence suggests the row house type design was a common characteristic of early villas in southern Britain and northern Gaul, reflecting perhaps the close links between these regions prior to, and after, the Roman conquest.

Other contemporary or near-contemporary row houses vary from the compactness of the buildings at Park Street and Lockleys, Hertfordshire and Brixworth, Northamptonshire to the extended form of the Eccles villa in Kent (Black 1994, 101). Exact parallels for the Ditches building in terms of date, as well as plan and size, are difficult to provide. The (presumed) first phase of the building at Little Milton, Oxfordshire, as plotted from aerial photographs, is identical to the Ditches villa in size and plan, but remains undated (Drury 1982, 297). The main range at Ditchley, Oxfordshire consists of a similar row house arrangement to that at Ditches and was constructed probably in the early Flavian period although the excavator believed the wings to have been part of the initial design (Raleigh-Radford 1936; cf. Booth 1999). North Leigh, Oxfordshire also has a somewhat similar arrangement, although the wings here too appear to have been part of the original design whilst its primary phase dates later than Ditches, in the early second century AD (Ellis 1999, 204).

The early use of masonry in the construction of the Ditches villa building is of considerable significance. Despite the lack of surviving details of the interior decoration of the building, the full-height stone walls of the main range (see above) and the quality of the ashlar employed in the phase 6 cellar confirm its considerable status. Walthew (1975, 195) has noted not only the apparent backwardness of town-house planning with respect to villa-house development, but also the comparatively precocious use of masonry for villa building. Although the Cotswolds are an area in which the early use of masonry might be expected, due to the suitability of local stone for building such structures, the technology involved had to be imported and was probably not readily available in the first century AD. Certainly, in neighbouring Cirencester, current evidence suggests masonry was not employed on a large scale for private accommodation until the latter part of the second century (Holbrook 1994, 63), bearing out Walthew's assertion and further emphasising the uniqueness, in a local context, of the Ditches building. It has been suggested that the expertise for early Romano-British masonry structures came from the Roman army. However, the army engaged in a limited amount of masonry construction work in first century Britain and civilian Gallic masons are a more probable source of skilled labour (Blagg 1984).

The developed villa

In the later first or early second century AD, in phase 5, a timber corridor or veranda was added at least to the southern side of the main block. This was then

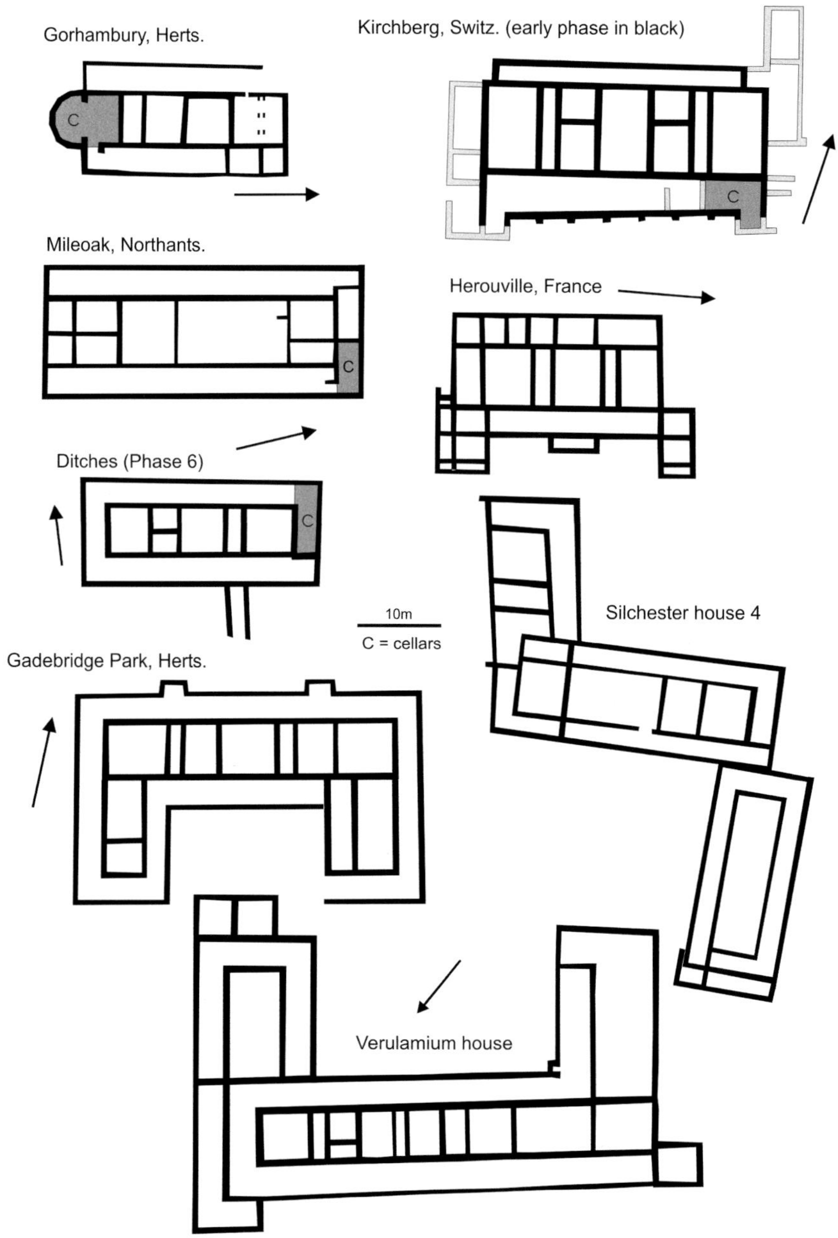

Fig. 30. Comparison of Ditches villa phase 6 and other corridor villas.

replaced in phase 6 by a stone built corridor, which certainly encompassed the whole building. Within Trench F there was no evidence for sub-division of the corridor other than by the southern wall of the cellar. Aerial photography suggests a similar absence of partitions in the western half of the building except a wall separating the southern from the western corridor on the line of the front of the main range. The overall effect of these additions was, therefore, to provide an 'ambulatory' around the main block.

The addition of corridors to simple row houses can be paralleled elsewhere and appears to have been a widespread development (Fig. 30). Normally this involved the addition of a single corridor as seen at Little Milton, Oxfordshire, and Piddington, Northants. (Friendship-Taylor 2006, phase 3) or two corridors, as at Boxmoor, Hertfordshire (Drury 1982, 297), to the front or back of the main range. The construction of a timber veranda on the southern side of the main block, can also be paralleled elsewhere, for example at Lockleys and Mansfield Woodhouse, Nottinghamshire where a corridor was apparently preceded by a timber construction. The addition of corridors on both sides of the main block can also be noted further afield at Herouville-Lebisey, Boos-Le Bois Flahaut (Smith 1997, 51–53) and Behen (Bayard 1996, 176) in northern France. The addition of corridors is conventionally interpreted as providing sheltered communication between rooms, not least for service purposes, the latter interpretation is supported by the presence of cellars in or below a number of examples, including Ditches. In some instances, therefore, they may also have fulfilled storage roles. Walthew (1975) has remarked on the repetition of this pattern in villas and town-houses interpreting it as indicative of a central dining room flanked by service corridors and storerooms. In contrast, Smith (1978, 120) has suggested that the addition of corridors, at Ditches at least, changed the roles of the rooms behind and shifted the entrance to a central position.

Few parallels are known for the Ditches phase 6 plan, with corridors on all four sides of the main block. At Kuttingen Kirchberg, Switzerland a row house similar to Ditches was supplied with both front and rear corridors, one of which contained a cellar at one end, similar to Ditches (Smith 1997, 66). Ovillers, Somme exhibits a large porticus (covered walkway or corridor, potentially open and supported by columns) that ran around the entire building (Smith 1997, 142). Gorhambury, Park Street and Shakenoak also boasted corridors at both front and back in certain phases. Park Street appears to have had a corridor around the entire block in period VI; this also incorporated a cellar (Black 1987, fig. 39). However, at most other sites, including Shakenoak and a number of continental examples, the construction of corridors appear to be contemporary with construction of wings, features which were separate, later additions at Ditches.

The corridor at Ditches, in its later phases, can alternatively be regarded as comprising two discrete components, a frontal porticus and an uninterrupted three-armed gallery, rather than a unified four-sided ambulatory. If this interpretation is accepted, several additional parallels can be provided for the gallery. The villa at Flocques, Somme, for example, has a similar three-armed corridor although it lacks the frontal porticus (Smith 1997, 142) and the Park Street corridor may have been three sided (Black 1987, 94 and fig. 39). The second-century building at Walton Heath, Surrey, as reinterpreted by Black (1987, fig. 53), the second-century villa at Ashtead, Surrey, and the late second or third-century villa at Keston, Kent (Philp *et al.* 1991, 80), may also exhibit this feature. The parallels mentioned above lend weight to Black's suggestion (1987, 139) that this arrangement may belong to a north Gallic architectural tradition. Also linked architecturally to this group of

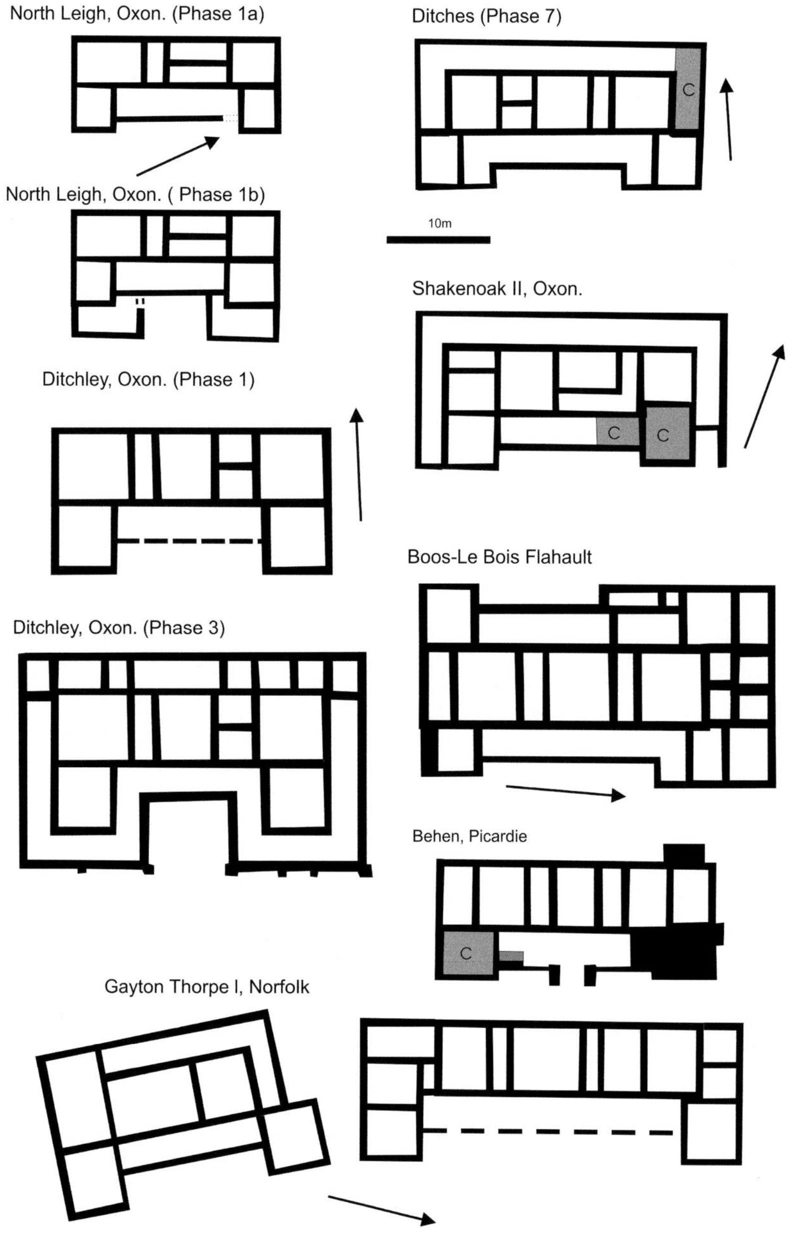

Fig. 31. Comparison of Ditches villa phase 7 and other winged second century AD villas.

buildings are a series of winged buildings with wholly encompassing corridors such as Gadebridge, Box and Ditchley (Figs 30 and 31).

Amongst other early villa houses, comparisons can be made with the Mileoak and Shakenoak B buildings. The first century AD structure at Mileoak,

Northamptonshire appears to be built on a similar plan with a corridor, incorporating a cellar, surrounding the main range (Green and Draper 1978, fig. 5). Here, however, the corridors at the ends of the range are subdivided. Widespread stone-robbing, and a general lack of phasing evidence, obscure whether these partitions are original or later insertions. It has been suggested that the Mileoak plan is a hybrid form between the strip-building and the winged villa (Rodwell and Rodwell 1985, 41). Similar considerations certainly apply to the phase 6 Ditches building, which represents a transition between the types both in plan and in actual sequence. The mid-second century remodelling of building B at Shakenoak provides an additional link between the forms. Prior to alterations the building comprised a main range almost wholly surrounded by a continuous corridor with two slight wing rooms (Smith 1997, 71).

Interestingly, some of the best parallels for the corridor on all four sides of the main block occur in urban rather than rural contexts, although Perring (2002, 36) has suggested that corridor and porticos were a later adoption in towns than in the countryside. In their earliest designs buildings 4 and 5 in insula XXXIII at Silchester both appear to comprise a central range with a surrounding corridor. Building 4, which is believed to be early in the town's constructional sequence, was of timber-framed construction on a foundation of flint rubble, brick and tile. Building 5, which post-dated building 4, was of masonry construction but of similar plan (Boon 1974, 190). A survey of Romano-British building types by Berry (1951, 30) drew attention to the apparently unique plan of these buildings which he regarded as "outside the typological development of the accepted standard forms" while Boon (1974, 189) sought a possible precursor of the plan in the Claudian timber building excavated at *Camulodunum*. Further parallels also exist at town houses in Verulamium (Fig. 30). Considering the potential links in the conquest period between the two late Iron Age *oppida* at Silchester and Bagendon, the cross fertilisation of such arrangements should also perhaps be considered, as should the influence of early urban dwellings upon rural architecture and vice versa. We might also question whether the distinction between urban and rural architecture is as pronounced at high status locations such as in the vicinity of an '*oppidum*'.

The entrances to Ditches also highlight a number of interesting aspects of the design and layout of early villas. The 'passageway' (room R5) in the Ditches building did, as has often been suggested, act as an entrance and may lend weight to Drury's (1982, 295) interpretation of the rooms as a set rather than Smith's suggestion that such arrangements might have been arranged for more than one household. Smith (1997, 53), in contrast, has suggested Ditches was a row house with two entrances, although there is little evidence for this. The axial entrance, which potentially marked the unified nature of the building, was probably not established until the addition of wings in phase 7. In the light of the evidence for the phase 5 entrance at Ditches, it seems likely that those elements imposing frontal symmetry on essentially asymmetric ranges (e.g. the wings at Ditchley and Boxmoor) should be considered as possible later additions.

Another aspect of Ditches' layout, shared with other early Roman villas but rarely commented on, is the tendency for their entrances to face south or south-east. The entrance at Ditches, revealed by the excavated access paths, faced due south and can be placed within this broader pattern. Whilst it is possible to explain this patterning in terms of a functional choice of a south-facing aspect (Ditches looks out over a valley), studies on the orientation of Iron Age roundhouses have stressed the importance of south/south-easterly orientations, possibly relating to cosmological references as well as any functional requirements (e.g. Oswald 1997), and this is a pattern matched by Iron Age houses in the region (Moore 2006b). Considering the early nature of Ditches villa and its location within an Iron Age enclosure we should perhaps consider to what extent 'Iron Age' concepts of structuring space may have informed the layout of early Roman structures rather than regarding these forms as entirely based on external, continental influences and concepts of social space. The suggestion that the orientations of early Roman villas in Picardie also exhibit at least some tendency towards an easterly facing direction (Haselgrove 1995), and considering the apparent similarities in form between Ditches and early villas in Gaul discussed above, may suggest early villas in southern Britain also continued to emphasise the traditional importance of such orientations, whether cosmological, functional or both.

As we have seen, in its original form, the Ditches building belonged to the 'strip-building' or 'row-house' tradition and, in an evolutionary sequence paralleled by a number of other villa buildings, was remodelled as a 'half-H' winged-corridor house in the early second century AD. It involved the addition of (presumably) two wing rooms, the alteration of the corridor fronting the main range so that it turns to flank these new rooms, and the establishment of an axial approach path. The resultant design places the building amongst a group of winged corridor villas with 'half-H' plans which elsewhere have been dated to the late first or second centuries AD and are considered to be of Gallo-Roman inspiration (Rodwell and Rodwell 1985, 41; Walthew 1975, 197). Parallels include Darenth, Kent and Gayton Thorpe, Norfolk and continental examples such as Herouville-Lebisey and Boos-Le Bois Flahaut (Fig. 31). The winged form of Ditches also has parallels with the first phase of the villa at North Leigh, Oxfordshire, constructed in the early second century AD (Ellis 1999). The early phase at Ditchley, too, appears similar in form with two wings on a simple strip unit. In some ways, therefore, Ditches follows a sequence which is paralleled in the region and follows some villas which also start relatively early and continued to develop in to the second or third century AD. Unlike some of those examples, however, Ditches did not continue into in the third century AD, but instead appears to have been destroyed and abandoned.

Early Roman rural cellars

During phase 6, the Ditches villa was augmented by the construction of a cellar and the remodelling, in stone of corridors on three, possibly four sides of the original range (Figs 23 & 24). Entrance to the cellar was by means of stairs or a ramp in the northern corridor. Cellars are known or inferred from twenty-one British villa buildings (Brodribb *et al.* 1971b, 21; Perring 1989, table 2). Cellars are also present at a number of contemporary Gallic villas such Behen, Picardie (Bayard 1996, 176) and one recently excavated at Moulon, Ile-de-France (Archeoaaccea 2005), which has led many to suggest these acted as the inspiration for both urban and rural cellars in Britain (Perring 1989, 289; Rodwell and Rodwell 1985, 45).

With exceptions, such as Barton Court Farm, Oxfordshire (Miles 1986), and in contrast to cellars in an urban context, rural cellars generally belong to first- and second-century AD buildings (Perring 1989, 279), a fact which is reflected in their largely south-easterly distribution. The Ditches example is the westernmost recorded, a distinction previously held by Shakenoak. The addition or insertion of a later cellar into a pre-existing building can be paralleled at a number of sites including Barton Court Farm; Faversham, Kent; and, probably, Park Street. In the latter two cases, the cellars appear to have been constructed within an existing corridor (Neal 1974, 90), something also known from continental examples such as Mudlesheim, Germany (Smith 1997, 81). These provide parallels for Ditches where the cellar was probably laid out on the lines of the timber-built corridor of phase 5.

Several possibilities have been advanced for the uses of villa cellars (Brodribb *et al.* 1971b; Miles 1986, 31; Perring 1989). Arguably the most convincing function, particularly when communication with the cellar is from inside the building rather than outside, is the cool storage of perishable foodstuffs such as smoked and salted meat, fish and dairy products. The cellar's location, on the north-east side of the building protecting it from the summer sun may support such a suggestion. As at Ditches, wall niches are frequent occurrences in cellars and can be seen in contemporary examples at Gorhambury (Neal *et al.* 1990, 47) and Shakenoak (Brodribb *et al.* 1971b, 22), either singly or in groups (Perring 1989, 285). This has led to suggestions of a ritual role or even funerary function (Rodwell and Rodwell 1985, 47). Although the unelaborate decor of most cellars makes this uncertain, it appears to have been the case with at least some examples, such as Lullingstone, Kent (Meates 1979). Perring (1989, 288–291) has also argued that the presence of 'votive deposits' in many cellars points to their ritual function, noting in particular the presence of glass jugs and Venus figurines in a number of cellars. To Perring's list can now be added the finds from the cellar at Ditches, but to what extent the assorted material had any 'votive' element remains unclear. Cellars, of course, may have had a range of functions, including both ritual observances and mundane roles; religious and functional considerations were certainly not mutually exclusive in antiquity. The occurrence of cellars predominantly in first and second century AD contexts may also indicate that they marked some form of continuation or Iron Age preference for subsurface storage. This is potentially also related to a continued symbolic significance of such places for offerings and observances to chthonic deities or fertility rites. The evidence for such roles for Iron Age storage pits comes from the common presence of structured deposits within many examples, the example from Ditches being no exception (see above).

Examples such as Ditches may indicate the persistence of multiple roles for underground storage facilities from the Iron Age into early Roman times. The multiple functional and ritual roles for other subterranean storage chambers (also suggested for the souterrains and fogous of northern and south-western Britain which frequently date to the first and second centuries AD: Harding 2004, 197) may imply that cellars in early Roman Britain held similar multiples roles. Alternatively, as Perring (1989, 292) suggests, any ritual role for these structures may have been inspired by Roman fertility cults. However, the lack of evidence for the use of the cellar at Ditches (which appears to have been stripped before the wall collapse) makes determining its use difficult. Whatever the roles of villa cellars the reason for the apparent link between cellars and early Roman villas needs to be explained.

Ditches villa: conformation and appearance

From the information provided by its foundations, the intact cellar, fallen end wall of the main block and other architectural remains found on the site, it is possible to draw reasonably detailed conclusions regarding the orientation, layout, form of the superstructure and general appearance of Ditches villa during its various phases. From the first laying out of the original strip building (phase 4), it seems the house had clear front and rear sides: it faced south, across the Bagendon valley. Initially the main entrance was probably into room R5 from the south, as the walled approach suggests. Since the demarcated approach led to the space between them, this implies that the central (R4) and/or eastern (R6) rooms were especially important, at least in terms of (semi-)public space, and may imply that the western rooms (R1 to R3) were more private. Such an internal arrangement may well have persisted, behind the later symmetrical façade with axial approach path (below). The functions of the later wing rooms are unknown.

Apart from the implications of the two successive approach paths, we have no indication of the location of doorways and routes of access into and around the building, with the exception of the Phase 6 cellar for which there are surface indications of an access ramp or (more likely) stairs from the north corridor (a rear, service corridor?).

It was suggested above that the narrow room R5 was probably simply an access lobby, providing sheltered, indirect entry to the flanking rooms; there is no reason to suppose it was also a stairwell to any upper level. The building was in all probability single storey. The only area where there is a real likelihood of two superimposed levels, from phase 6, the cellar, which may have been floored over to carry the east corridor over it to the back of (and into?) the eastern wing room. This would create a subterranean room with limited headroom. While this is perfectly practicable, there is also the possibility that it was not floored over. The space between corridor roof and cellar floor perhaps constituted a deep, open space, with plenty of headroom for hanging things. Here, sheltered from summer heat by the end wall, and perhaps lofty gable, at the end of the main block, was a cool corner, especially if the corridor on the rear and sides of the house had few and small windows.

At least once the stone corridor system was added in phase 6, the slope of the roof will have required the rooms of the main block to have been lofty, even if there was no clerestory for direct illumination of the interior. However, a clerestory, like that seen on the villa model from Fontoy, Moselle (Massy 1989), seems likely, at least on the sunny southern side, although perhaps not on the north-facing rear. The house appears to have boasted glazed windows: window glass was in use on the site before the mid-second century AD (Trow 1988a, 55–58, fig. 28, no. 9). If there was a clerestory, then the main rooms will have been about as high as they were wide, making; rooms R1, R4 and R6 roughly cubic.

The collapsed end wall in the cellar represents mortared masonry standing at least 3m above the surviving intact foundation, although its upper part is lost. The fallen wall suggests that the outer walls of the main block were stone-built to full height. The well-preserved masonry of the cellar give us a good impression of the high-quality, regular masonry employed at least during this late phase, while the put-log holes preserved in the cellar walls reveal something of the construction techniques employed. However, the late villa may not have been entirely of stone construction. Deposits of what seemed to be daub in the late fire debris inside the building might suggest that the upper parts of some walls were of wattle-filled timber framing. If, when the corridors were built, the main block was elevated (e.g. to provide a clerestory), perhaps the addition was timber framed. There were certainly timber elements in the earlier stages of its development (e.g. phase 5 timber veranda), and it is possible that the later corridors were also timber-framed on a stone footing.

Recovery of part of a half-height column from a mid-second century deposit (Trow 1988a, 55–58 and Fig. 28, no. 9) suggests that the southern, frontal corridor at least (and probably alone) boasted a colonnade on a low wall. In its most developed state (Phase 7), the building was quite pretentious, with its symmetrical, winged façade, at this stage if not earlier incorporating a colonnade.

With regard to the conformation of the roof, the fallen wall was not preserved to a great enough extent to tell us whether it supported a tall gable as opposed to a hipped roof. Neither is there any indication of roof pitch. Evidence of roofing materials is noticeably thin. Was this because of careful salvaging after the final fire? Or because the roofing material was actually organic: wooden shingles or even thatch, as has been suggested for a number of other early Roman villas (Friendship-Taylor 2006, 3)? The latter seems implausible, at least for the last, relatively pretentious phase of the building. Could the lack of remains of roofing materials suggest that the building had been stripped of these before it burned?

The villa produced no evidence of several features often thought to typify Romano-British villas in the Cotswolds and elsewhere: it lacked mosaics, hypocaust systems, or a bath. However, this is probably primarily, even solely, because of its unusually early chronology; it would have been very surprising to find these at such an early date in a country residence in Britain, outside the context of exceptional sites such as the Italianate 'palace' of Fishbourne (Cunliffe 1971a; b; Cunliffe 1998; Manley and Rudkin 2003) and other rare early examples such as that at Gadebridge (Neal 1974, 6). In Britain such features are only common from the third century onwards. Nevertheless, even without these luxurious extras, the Ditches house was pretentious for its time, comprising what would have been a startling combination of alien features. It is also possible that a bath complex may await discovery elsewhere in the enclosure, although the recent geophysical survey suggests this is unlikely.

In the later first century AD, for local people first seeing the building from a distance, there was the novel prospect of a precisely orthogonal structure, which on approach would reveal itself to result from the foreign technologies of mortared stone construction, plastered and painted walls, window glazing and (perhaps) equally novel roofing materials. If permitted to enter, the visitor encountered a complex of rooms accessed and half-hidden by lobbies and, later, corridors, which offered an unprecedented controlled gradation of semi-public and more private spaces. And within a couple of generations, further visually striking architectural novelties were incorporated, including a colonnade, and an imposing symmetrical façade with axial approach. While a modest villa by later Cotswold standards, in its day Ditches will have been a startling expression of alien taste and of wealth, arising in the midst of a familiar but transformed place of local power, prominent in the landscape and highly visible from Ermin Street, the Cirencester-Gloucester road, across the valley.

Continuity and ownership

Who controlled Ditches in the late Iron Age? Who transfigured the site in the early decades of Roman rule, and why? Why was it not simply abandoned (as nearby Bagendon soon was)? Its archaeology, contemporary context and comparison with other sites helping explain the continuity of site status from late Iron Age to early Roman times, and hint at the kind of individual or group in control (Creighton 1992).

Firstly, there is the very early construction of the Roman-style building, erected in masonry in the third quarter of the first century AD, probably without a timber precursor. Few villas were built so early in Britain, and most were in south east England, making Ditches doubly unusual. It was also built in an exceptionally elevated situation. Most Cotswold villas occupy sheltered valley-side situations, straddling or below the spring line for gravity-fed water supply. The high exposed position of the Ditches building appears poorly suited to 'Roman' tastes.

Martins' (2005, 75) point that location may often have been about "being seen" as much as Roman concepts of aesthetics, is highly relevant here; specifically, being seen to relate to an existing sense of place. The new building, like the surrounding enclosure, was widely visible in the landscape, not least from Ermin Street, the new Roman road across the valley to the west linking nascent *Corinium* (Cirencester) with *Glevum* (a legionary base soon to become a *colonia*). Most significantly, it will also have been starkly apparent to those familiar with the landscape that the building was situated within the important pre-existing Iron Age enclosure dominating the upper Bagendon valley and forming part of the greater late Iron Age '*oppidum*' (see below). Relating the building to this pre-existing complex was perhaps *the* overriding factor in choosing its location. However, its erection was also contemporaneous with reduction of the Ditches enclosure earthworks.

It is especially hard to judge who controlled Ditches in the late Iron Age, whether a wealthy individual or family, or some more communal arrangement. Unfortunately, Rivet's comment that we have little clear understanding of the nature of wealth or social structure in the late Iron Age (1969, 182) remains largely true. Geophysical survey suggests there may have been a major central roundhouse at the site, but its existence, let alone its chronology or function as residence rather than meeting place, remain hypothetical. It is therefore better to reserve judgement, and for the late Iron Age to refer to 'decision-makers' at Ditches, which could have been a place where power was negotiated between multiple interests in the region rather than the base and residence of one. However, construction of a single Roman-style house, evolving through several phases thereafter, suggests that, from very early under Roman rule if not before, Ditches was dominated by a single family (or perhaps succession of families). Who, then, were they, and why did they so radically alter the aspect of the site?

One conceivable interpretation is that Ditches was taken over by alien incomers soon after AD 43. Appropriating an existing place of political importance, demolishing the earthworks which symbolised native power and imposing a foreign-style residence in their midst could be seen as the marks of conquerors expressing domination of the landscape in the most obtrusive manner. Roman military equipment at the site might seem to support such an hypothesis. However more detailed consideration of the Ditches evidence is inconsistent with such an explanation.

For all its alien, intrusive aspect, the villa was not imposed on the topography of Ditches in the way that, in other provinces, centuriated Roman landscapes obliterated what went before. Rather, it respected and related to the place in which it was built. Certainly, the Iron Age enclosure earthworks were substantially reduced, and outshone by the startlingly novel orthogonal architecture and constructional techniques of the new house. Yet, if diminished, the earthworks were not erased, their lines and entrances continuing to define the place: they were likely used to evoke continuity from the pre-Roman past, to legitimise the transformed present represented by the villa they encompassed. Similar phenomena are attested elsewhere.

Other early villas were situated in late Iron Age enclosures, most famously Gorhambury where, like Ditches, the Roman-style house appears to represent high-status continuity from pre-conquest times (Fig. 32; Neal *et al.* 1990). An early 'villa' lies within an early Iron Age hillfort at Alfred's Camp, Berkshire (Gosden and Lock 2003), although here direct continuity is uncertain. Air photography reveals a villa inside an Iron Age banjo enclosure at Micheldever (Fasham 1987, 63; Wilson 1974) and another within a larger pre-Roman earthwork at Tidbury (Wilson 1974). Ditchley villa is also surrounded by a 'banjo-like' enclosure (Richard Hingley pers. comm.), although the extent of pre-Roman occupation is disputed (Booth 1999, 44). Other villas in the region also appear to relate to banjo enclosures, e.g. Rodmarton (Moore 2007). Villa are also known from other Iron Age enclosures, at Frocester, Gloucestershire (Price 2000), Holme House, North Yorkshire (Harding 1984) and Dalton Parlours, West Yorkshire (Wrathmell and Nicholson 1990), but somewhat later than Ditches, these do not indicate radical change immediately following Roman annexation. Other Roman buildings located in late Iron Age enclosures are known from Hampshire and Berkshire (Gosden and Lock 2003, 78), e.g. an aisled building at Houghton Down, Hampshire (Cunliffe and Poole 2000b) and one possibly within the hillfort at Ham Hill, Somerset (see above). However, in many cases, these cannot be termed 'villas', a first century AD date cannot be established, nor is continuity with late Iron Age occupation certain.

Forest Hill, near Mildenhall, Wiltshire, may constitute a closer parallel to Ditches (Fig. 32). Here a villa lies within an Iron Age enclosure which finds from the vicinity suggest might be part of a late Iron Age '*oppidum*' (Corney 1997). Like Ditches, this may represent placement of a villa within an existing pre-Roman 'elite' centre. Similar relationships between early villas and an *oppidum* complex may be seen closer to Ditches at Grim's Ditch, Oxfordshire (Copeland 1988), where several stood within the late Iron Age earthworks. These include Shakenoak and Ditchley, both established in the first century AD (Trow and James 1988). At Blacklands, Somerset, another possibly early villa is associated with a late Iron Age enclosure similar to that at Ditches (Lawes 2006).

Within the old Ditches enclosure, the new building was located to face onto what perhaps in the Iron Age was already a defined central open area. Across this, it also looked towards the putative site of a major central roundhouse which, if correctly identified, like some comparators at other villas may still have

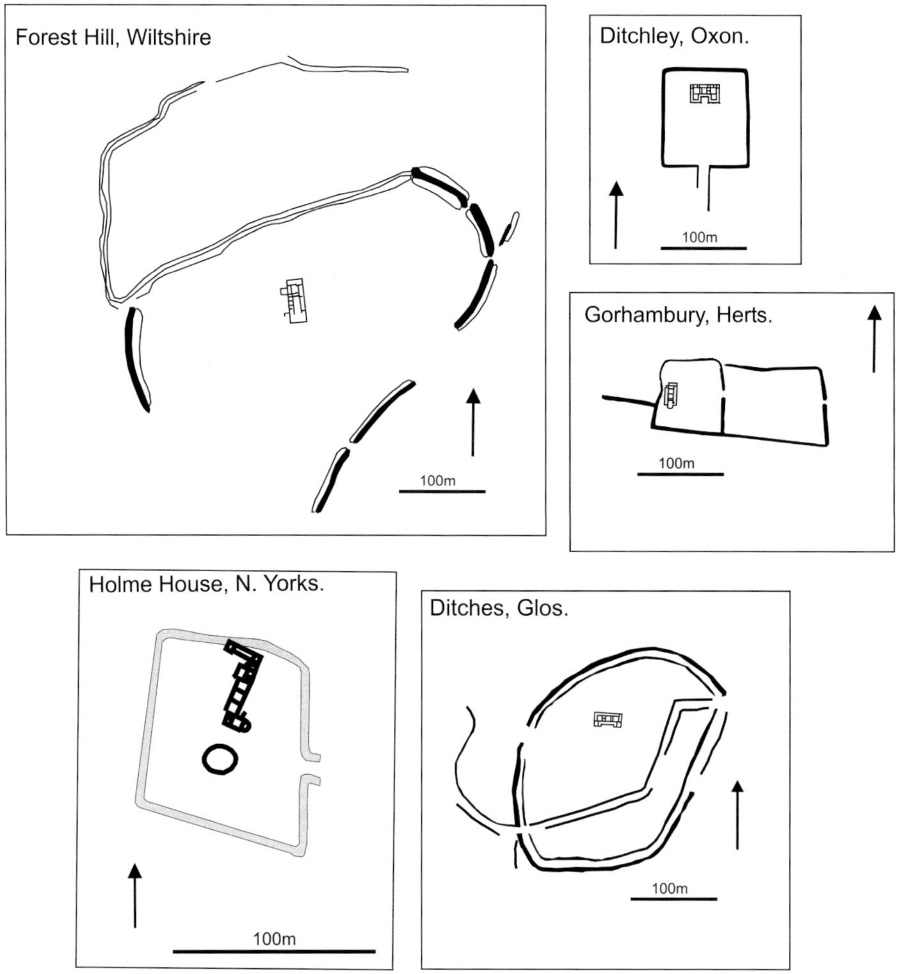

Fig. 32. Early Roman villas in late Iron Age enclosures.

been standing at least during the early phases of the Roman house. Circular buildings contemporary with villas are known at Holme House, North Yorkshire (Harding 1984), Ringstead, Northants., Bancroft, Bedfordshire (Smith 1997, 254–5), Stanwick, Northants. (Mudd 1999, 244) and Shakenoak, Oxon. (Brodribb *et al.* 2005, 423–425). Reinterpretation as circular buildings of second-century 'threshing floors' at nearby Barnsley Park (Webster 1982; Smith 1997, 238), and possibly at Ditchley (Raleigh-Radford 1936, 26), also suggests roundhouses continued as important elements of villa complexes. Circular structures of Roman date are also known elsewhere in the region and are contemporary with rectangular buildings, e.g. at Birdlip Quarry in the third century (Mudd *et al.* 1999, 243). Such structures have frequently been interpreted as representing servant or slave quarters (Webster 2005, 172–6), or 'backward' or poorer communities (e.g. Brodribb *et al.* 2005, 424), although such simplistic social models have been challenged (Hingley 1989, 34). Central location of roundhouses at some villa sites clearly indicates their social importance to these communities (Smith 1997, 254), perhaps representing continued reference to earlier *high* status structures. The magnetic anomaly suggesting a major roundhouse in the middle of the Ditches enclosure is a key target for future investigation.

Romano-British villas in general have long been seen as mostly built by indigenes adopting imperial lifestyles rather than by colonial incomers, and this seems the more likely explanation even of the exceptional sequence at Ditches. The hypothetical powerful family controlling it in early Roman times was evidently concerned to emphasise its connections to the indigenous British past, and in practice seem also to have 'stayed British' in other fundamental aspects of life, such as basic dietary preferences (see Reilly). This, then, looks like a story of local continuity through the upheavals of the mid-first century AD. Yet at the same time, the owners of Ditches did reduce the earthworks, and did erect a foreign-style residence in its midst. If Britons, what were their motivations for all this, and how did they resource the project?

The new Ditches building represents considerable investment of wealth (Martins 2005), involving technical expertise in architecture and construction techniques from elsewhere. (Slighting the earthworks also demanded extensive resources, of labour if not money, around the same period). Rivet (1969) related development of villas to increasing profitability of Romano-British agriculture from the second century onwards. If so, those built earlier were funded in other ways: expenditure by the Roman state, investment by foreign merchants (Todd 1978, 201–2), realisation of pre-existing wealth by a native aristocracy, or perhaps borrowed money. Roman senators are known from literary sources to have provided loans to British provincial elites (Creighton 2006, 45).

Wherever the source of the means, through the twentieth century the motivation for building villas was traditionally understood in terms of simple acculturative 'Romanization': native British aristocrats aping as best they could understand or afford the 'self-evidently superior' culture of their imperial masters. Black, for example, has argued that in building villas, native elites were following the governor Agricola's call to construct "something a Roman would call home" (1994, 107). Many current understandings, influenced by post-colonial perspectives, allow for more active engagement by these groups, not as passive recipients but as knowing agents pursuing their own interests, within the constraints of the asymmetries of power in a newly-conquered province (classically, Millett 1990). Southern British native elites did not simply copy, but selected and reinterpreted Roman culture to fit their circumstances, producing a new provincial version of it. They did this because it was necessary and useful to them. Necessary, because adherence to Roman values and lifestyle was required for participation in the ruling strata of the empire, and useful because this gave them a secure place within the new order, and some access to the broader horizons of imperial life. In return for rapprochement with Rome and controlling their social subordinates, emperor and soldiers would back their authority at the local level. They were 'becoming Roman' (Woolf 1998), but partly on their own terms.

Initially, their participation in the imperial enterprise may have been largely military. Ditches and some other early

Fig. 33. Selected probable and possible first century AD villas in Britain.

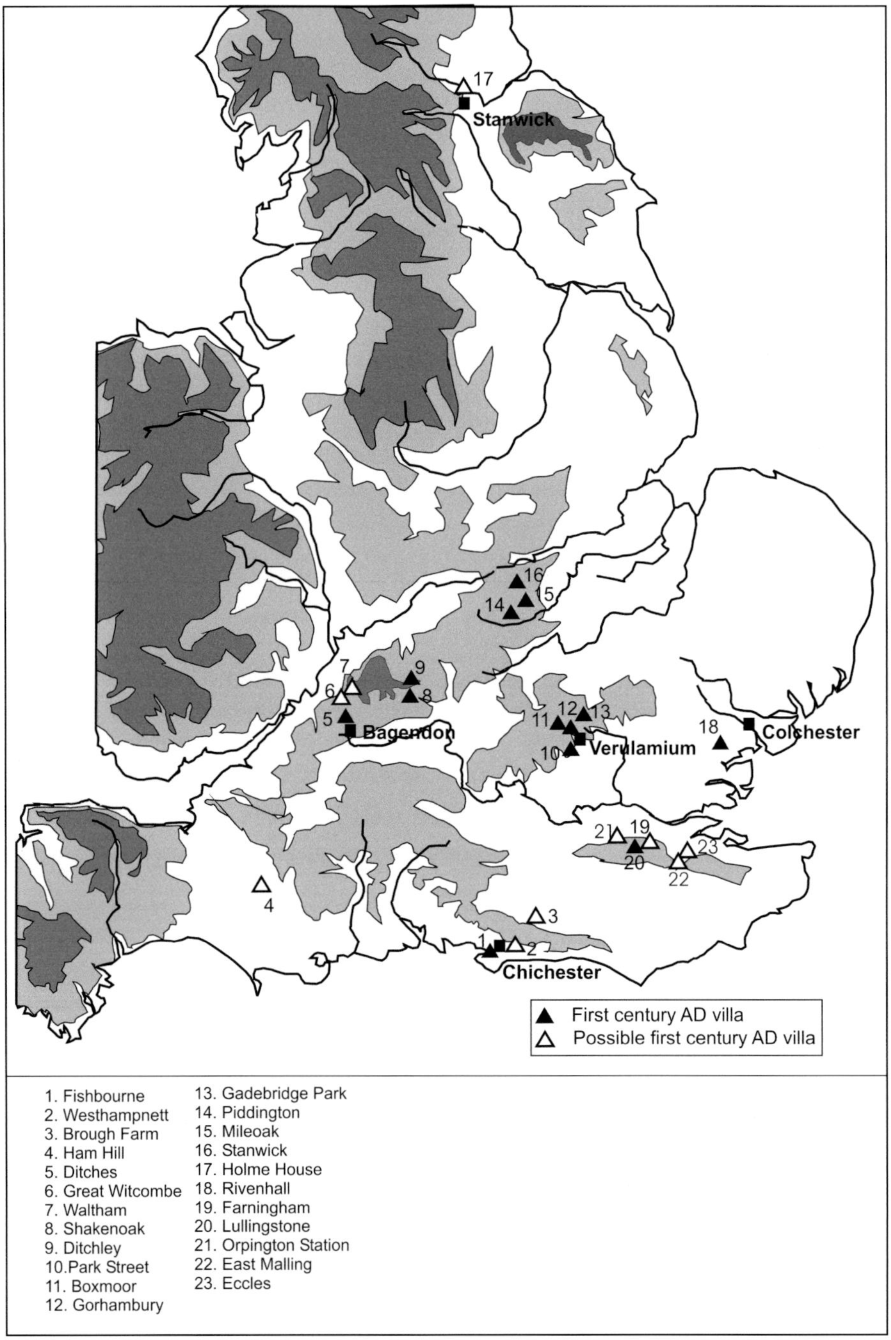

villas and settlements have produced Roman military equipment (James 1988), including Gorhambury, Claydon Pike and Whitton (Black 1994, 108). Rather than attesting the presence of Roman soldiers, this more likely reflects the adoption of Roman military equipment by prominent Britons (Black 1994). It is likely that British male aristocrats served as allies with, if not directly in, the Roman military during the conquest period (Creighton 2006, 47–50). However, their role soon become primarily civil. As Ditches villa was in its early phases, local self-government, run by indigenous elites, was nascent and would soon be based on new 'native' towns like *Corinium*.

For native elites, adopting the trappings of the new dominant power, military and especially civil, signalled not only their membership of an emergent provincial ruling class which would come to have closer symbiotic ties with the emperors than with the majority of their own fellow provincials. It also offered striking new ways of expressing ascendancy over, and increased separation from social subordinates. At Ditches, construction of a villa within the Iron Age enclosure represents continuity of power, but this was now expressed in radically different terms, overtly expressing cultural, and by implication political integration into the new imperial order. It must have been especially striking in the southwest, as exceptional in the region at that time. Ditches can be compared to other Claudio-Neronian residences in Britain, particularly Fishbourne. Whilst Ditches villa looks very modest beside the Fishbourne, many of the motives behind the construction of such unusual buildings in early Roman contexts may have been similar. Fishbourne has been suggested as the palace of a client king ruling alongside the early province. Possibly succeeding a pre-conquest high status site (Creighton 2001; 2006), Fishbourne emphasises both the adoption of Roman tastes and imperial links similar in kind, if not scale, to the transformation at Ditches. This process may well have been early at both sites because it was already underway prior to the conquest, indicated at Ditches by imports like the Augustan intaglio.

However, in detail, the picture is more complex and interesting. For their own developing version of 'Romanness', the decision-makers at Ditches were not drawing solely, or even primarily, on the Italianate culture of emperors and senators as the 'palace' at Fishbourne clearly did: in plan at least it would not have looked out of place on the Bay of Naples. Neither was it derived from that of the large nearby community of lesser Roman citizens, at the legionary base of *Glevum*, just 19 km west-northwest over the Cotswold scarp. This was partly because they aspired not just to Roman lifestyle, but to *elite* lifestyle. Into the AD 70s, *Glevum* certainly accommodated several equestrian officers and a couple of senators (the legionary legate and a youthful military tribune) but, though doubtless comforted by fine tableware and furnishings, these gentlemen were slumming for brief periods of military service in semi-permanent timber accommodation. *Glevum* offered no useful architectonic model for a country residence. For their notions of 'Romanness' the Ditches villa builders looked less to Italy, or to Italians in Britain, than to Gaul.

The idea of the villa as a masonry country house is certainly to be traced to Italy, but the forms seen in the successive phases at Ditches are not – at least, not directly. The 'row house' and its elaborations with corridors and wings are temperate-zone interpretations of such residences, designed to catch, rather than protect from the sun. Parallels to the Ditches villa are to be found in northern France, some with similar structural sequences, and developing within existing late Iron Age enclosures as at Behen, Picardie (Bayard 1996; Collart 1996). Perhaps reflecting similar continuity of ownership from Iron Age to Roman times, these sequences have led to suggestions that layout and form of such villas may have their antecedents in late Iron Age Gaulish timber buildings rather than in Italy, although the constructional techniques are a Mediterranean innovation (Haselgrove 1995, 71). Ditches clearly drew on such versions of the villa evolving in Gallic provinces flourishing from the time of Augustus, and developing their own provincial interpretations of Roman lifestyle and material culture.

It is not necessary to invoke immigrant owners to explain the Gaulish aspect of villas like Ditches (Black 1987, 25; 1994). British elites were seeking models of Roman civilian elite lifestyle to copy and adapt, and the most accessible were offered by the provincial aristocracies of Gaul. By the mid-first century AD many Gallic aristocrats possessed Roman citizenship, and some were equestrians. But British emulation of Gallo-Roman rather than Italian culture was no simple matter of proximity. Like contacts with the imperial house, southern British links with Gaul antedated Claudius. Insular societies were under strong Gallic influence before either region fell under the cultural dominion of Rome (Hill 2002). Indeed we can speak of 'Gallicization' of pre-conquest southern British elites, reflected in coinage, imported pottery and changing burial rites, and involving limited movement of Gauls across the Channel (Creighton 2000; 2006; James 2001; Woolf 1998). Through this process, as they were taken up in Gaul Greco-Roman ideas, tastes and styles were transmitted to the island and to centres like Ditches, before Caesar (coinage) and after (wine, wheel-thrown pottery). With both areas within the empire from the 40s, Gaul naturally continued its role as cultural conduit, and one of its next key exports was villa design.

Were the occupants of late Iron Age Ditches, then, already in direct contact themselves with Gaul and with the imperial regime? Possibly, but perhaps most connections were indirect. Cross-Channel cultural and political links were primarily articulated through networking between elite families and individuals in Britain with their equivalents in Gaul, and with the imperial house. The main focus of British participation in these interactions lay in the south-east and Thames basin; regions north and west of this were less integrated. The Ditches-Bagendon complex emerged at the upper end of the Thames basin, on the periphery of this sociopolitical network which increasingly included petty dynasts and Roman-sponsored kings (Creighton 2001; 2006). Consequently, engagement of Ditches' occupants with wider cross-Channel networks was mediated through the social, economic and political links they had developed with elite groups to the east, which reflected in the archaeology of Ditches and Bagendon, e.g. in ceramics and in 'native' coin types (Moore 2007). The form of the early villa, similar to examples in the Verulamium region, suggests that after the Claudian annexation, Ditches' connections to Gallo-Roman society were likely to have remained via these connections to a region which, at *Camulodunum* and soon London, also accommodated the main foci of Roman rule – and access to imperial patronage.

It is possible that the builder of Ditches villa was one of the smaller dynasts within these networks at the time of the Claudian annexation, perhaps even one of those named on local 'Dobunnic' coinage, and he or his family had long controlled the site. Or perhaps the builder had recently secured it for himself, as victor among a group of Cotswold communities scrambling for position during the upheaval of establishing Roman power. Someone building such a regionally-exceptional residence surely aspired to, and likely achieved Roman citizenship. By the later first century, with the developing villa remaining an eye-catching novelty to travellers on Ermin Street, for his descendant or successor even equestrian status is conceivable. Perhaps when the villa burned down in the second century, the owners were direct descendants of those who controlled Ditches long before Claudius. Or maybe it had passed into new hands by bequest or purchase, to others who saw themselves as Dobunni, or to relatives whose main connections were down the Thames Valley. Either way, the new Romans of Ditches likely had some Gaulish blood, for like the insular aristocracies of the following millennia, the groups with which they were affiliated intermarried beyond the island.

The story of Ditches is complex but fascinating. Far into the Roman period those controlling this place simultaneously prized continuity of fundamental Late Iron Age British traditions, alongside a strong desire to be elite Romans – but their 'Romanness' was not Italianate. Rather it was based on Gallic interpretations of Roman aristocratic lifestyle, reflecting also the established prestige of Gaulish culture in southern Britain. As the people of Ditches 'became Roman', then, they were also being Gallic, and at the same time hanging onto their British roots.

Ditches enclosure and the Bagendon '*oppidum*'

In order to understand the significance of the Ditches enclosure and villa it is also necessary to explore its relationship with the Bagendon dyke complex. Further detailed discussion of the nature of the roles of the Bagendon complex within the context of the later Iron Age and Roman landscape are the subject of a number of articles (Moore 2007; Moore *et al.* forthcoming) but some initial observations can be made here.

Despite the limited excavations at both sites, representing only small samples of the overall areas of the two sites, some analysis of their roles and relationship can be offered. The most obvious points in the relationship of the two sites is their proximity and contemporaneity. The excavated areas of the two sites are some 3.5km apart, although the Ditches enclosure is only some 2km from the northernmost of the Bagendon linear earthworks. Central to the relationship between sites is also their shared association with the Bagendon Brook; the Bagendon dyke complex straddles the mouth of the valley and controls its junction with the River Churn whilst the Ditches enclosure overlooks the head of the valley and controls its source.

The recent excavations at Duntisbourne Grove, Middle Duntisbourne (Mudd *et al.* 1999) and Stratton (Wymark 2003) have revealed that late Iron Age occupation was not limited to these two sites but spread over a far wider area and may be comparable to similar complexes at Verulamium and Colchester (Fig. 2). In the case of the former sites it appears these were possibly only occupied for a short time in the first century AD, as appears to have been the case at Bagendon.

Both the Ditches enclosure and Bagendon were occupied during the first century AD. Reinterpretation of the material from the Clifford excavations at Bagendon (Swan 1975), has been argued as indicating a floruit of activity in the excavated area in the early years of the Roman conquest, in contrast to Clifford's chronology which emphasised occupation from as early as the AD 20s (Clifford 1961, xix). The extent to which

Bagendon had significance prior to the conquest remains open to debate, and the problematic dating of some pottery types provides further uncertainty (Timby 1990; Willis 2000a). Haselgrove (below) also suggests the coin evidence may indicate earlier occupation or activity at Bagendon than that suggested by Trow (1988a, 76) and Swan (1975). The nature and extent of pre-conquest activity at Bagendon, therefore, remains uncertain, with even the date of the dykes themselves unclear; further discussion of these points will be provided with the report on the 1980s Bagendon excavations (Moore *et al.* forthcoming). However, it appears that the intense period of activity at the site, revealed through the excavations by Clifford (1961) and those by Trow and Reece (Moore *et al.* forthcoming), may have been relatively short lived and may have ceased by around the AD 60s. In contrast, Ditches has a much more extended chronology with evidence for continuous occupation from as early as the second or first century BC well into the Romano-British period.

This proximity and partial contemporaneity of the two sites is reflected in the similarity or common origin of much of the artefactual evidence derived from conquest-period contexts. Most apparent for the first century coarse pottery, with the ceramic repertoire of both sites comparable in the range of both forms and fabric, it is also evident in the similar ranges of worked bone tools, iron artefacts, and objects associated with textile processing. The similarities in material culture significantly also include a variety of prestigious items, often imported, which attest to the high status of the two sites. Both ceramic assemblages include a selection of fine tablewares of Gaulish, British, and to a lesser extents Italian origin. Both sites have yielded imported glassware and, considering the relatively small areas excavated, both have produced large quantities of British coins and brooches. In addition, fieldwalking in the Ditches enclosure has produced an unstratified Augustan intaglio of Mediterranean origin which is likely to have been a pre-conquest import (Trow 1982).

One particularly significant feature which both sites share is the presence of clay pellet-moulds generally considered to be involved in the production of British coinage. Large quantities of these mould fragments were recovered at Bagendon and led to its identification as the mint and 'capital' of the Dobunni (Clifford 1961). Both sites have produced such slab-moulds and analysis has indicated that the larger moulds retain gold traces and the smaller silver traces mirroring the mainly large gold and small silver denominations of the local Dobunnic coinage. Although only a small number of mould fragments have been recovered from the Ditches enclosure, the utilization of gold on the site is confirmed by the recovery, from the Inner Enclosure Ditch, of a fragment of gold foil (Trow 1988a, 51) and a touchstone with traces of gold alloy on its surfaces (Trow *et al.* below). It seems certain that, even if the actual striking of native issues was not taking place on either site, the production of coin flans in both silver and gold took place at both, concurrently or successively.

The establishment of a villa within the Ditches enclosure provides a contrast with the absence of known 'Roman-style' settlement at Bagendon. This may relate to the different roles of the sites prior to the conquest; the presence of the Augustan period intaglio and material perhaps suggest high status occupancy at the Ditches enclosure with an emphasis on production at Bagendon. For example, several early Roman coins were recorded from the Ditches enclosure, including a Claudian dupondius copy, whilst no early Roman coins are known from Bagendon. Similarly, the two items of Roman military metalwork from Ditches can also be argued as possible indication of conquest period high status occupants (see above). Trow (1988a, 82) has also stressed the apparently more 'Romanized' nature of the mid first-century animal bone assemblage at Ditches, contrasting with that at Bagendon, and this has subsequently been confirmed by the faunal remains from the 1984–5 excavations (see Reilly below). However, the presence of large quantities of coins and finewares at Bagendon suggests the difference in status activity may be a matter of detectable but limited degree.

The range of prestigious items recovered from both Ditches and Bagendon cannot be paralleled at any other site in the region except (and here on a far more limited scale) Salmonsbury. Although only limited sampling has taken place at a number of other late Iron Age sites, such as those at Duntisbourne and Wycomb, there is no present evidence to indicate any of these held the status of Ditches. That two sites of such status should occur in close proximity suggest they were intimately connected and, alongside the recent discoveries at Duntisbourne, and possibly the Tar Barrows near Cirencester (Reece 2003), should perhaps best be regarded as elements of a single, even wider complex sprawling over kilometres of landscape, comparable in extent, if perhaps not in intensity, with sites like *Camulodunum*. On the basis of current evidence it appears that the Ditches enclosure represents the location of the earliest activity within the complex and was also the focus of the highest status occupation. The importance of the Ditches enclosure within the wider Bagendon complex appears to have been perpetuated into the Roman period with the construction of a precociously Romanised residence in the same location.

As discussed above, the construction of the villa must have represented the realisation of considerable wealth and also acted as a bold statement of political affiliations, new ways of living and using domestic space. The villa's location and date suggest it was most likely built by the descendants or successors of the occupiers of the enclosure who, perhaps whilst emphasising their social and political affiliations and membership of the new Roman provincial order, also wished to maintain a link to the location and role which had maintained their pre-conquest authority. The nature of that authority and its complexity are the subject of further examination (Moore 2007; Moore *et al.* in prep.) but the evidence of coin minting and imported ceramics points in the direction of a community or individual with considerable power in the late Iron Age.

The Bagendon complex may have represented a location for such individuals to maintain control over exchange between the early Roman military province in southern England and the non-Romanised midlands, west and south-west. It has been suggested elsewhere (Trow 1990) that the Bagendon earthworks represent a gesture towards the control of a valley already dominated by the Ditches enclosure, and that the sudden expansion in material wealth apparent at both Ditches and Bagendon is the result of this control of exchange networks. Whilst this model remains valid we should also consider that the community within the Bagendon complex saw an opportunity to advance their status and position by forging links with the client kingdoms to the south and east and indirectly with Gaul and the Roman empire. It seems that in many ways the

Bagendon complex was on the periphery of existing social and economic networks, such as the exchange of Malvern ware pottery, and its emergence corresponds with the development of new power relationships with communities to the east and abroad (Moore 2007). As such, the development of the villa at Ditches represents a continued association by this community with the power, political influence and tastes of elites of south-eastern England, Gaul and the Roman empire as a whole.

This view provides an alternative approach to the interpretation of the Bagendon complex as a proto-urban *oppidum* superseded by the Roman town of Cirencester advanced by Clifford (1961). Instead the development of both Ditches and Bagendon follow the political and economic fortunes of presumed regional elites as political influence and links were developed, maintained and expressed. As Ditches developed into a Roman villa, with occupation in the vicinity potentially as late as the fourth century AD, Bagendon apparently declined in the Flavian period contemporary with the development of the Roman town of *Corinium* (Cirencester) 4km to the south. It is probably simplistic to see the decline of the activity at Bagendon as purely the movement of the population to the new town although it must have no longer had a role as a possible production centre for coins or other material. There may not have been a smooth transition or continuity at all late Iron Age settlements; occupation at the Duntisbourne sites appear to have ended by the Flavian period, certainly by the time Ermin Street was constructed over the ditches and possibly earlier (Mudd *et al.* 1999, 96). Therefore, whilst Ditches appears to provide evidence of the continued high status of a pre-Roman elite family which had occupied the earlier enclosure, this may not have been a widespread phenomenon or even one in which all members of the pre-existing Ditches community participated. Whilst some elements of continuity in status may have taken place, others in the wider Bagendon complex may have been dispossessed of their position as a changing set of markers for wealth and power emerged in the post-conquest era. We should be careful, therefore, not to see Ditches as representing a smooth evolutionary transition from Iron Age state to Roman *civitas*; within a wider context Ditches can be placed in a far more complex and fluid picture of social change in the late Iron Age and early Roman period with varying groups vying for status and power in the new Roman province (Moore 2007; Moore *et al.* in prep.).

The decline of the Ditches villa is somewhat harder to discuss, based as it is on a rather limited set of evidence. It seems most likely that the villa was either deliberately dismantled or was dismantled after an accidental fire had destroyed the building in the mid–late second century AD. The evidence of third and fourth century material from the latest layers on the site and apparent dense scatter to the south of the villa (RCHME 1976, 85) may indicate that the community moved to other, as yet un-investigated, buildings to the south. The absence of stone structures on the geophysical survey suggests that if they did, these were timber built structures rather than a villa-style building. Alternatively, the household may have moved to another location. As discussed above, the hilltop location of the Ditches villa is unusual compared to other villas in the Cotswolds and it possible the occupiers moved to a new villa in a more typical Cotswold location; on a sheltered valley side with nearby water supply.

It is perhaps simplistic to see the end

of occupation of the villa at Ditches in the later second century as a subsequent decline in the status or fortunes of the villa's occupants; the villa appears to have been abandoned in a short space of time rather than declined. However, that a once powerful family had finally lost their social pre-eminence remains a tantalising possibility.

We have stressed above that the development of the villa at Ditches was directly involved in emphasising to a wider community the memory of previous locations of power, including the earlier enclosure at Ditches and its place in the wider *oppidum* complex of Bagendon (cf. Creighton 2006), as well as expressing new social, political and financial links. It is, therefore, of interest to note that by the late second or third century AD, this symbolic geography was no longer as important as it had been in late first and early second century AD. Unlike the Gorhambury enclosure, or other significant early Roman features at towns like Verulamium and Colchester (Creighton 2006, 130), and perhaps the Tar barrows at *Corinium* (Cirencester) (Reece 2003; Creighton 2006), the Ditches enclosure and villa were out of sight of the town at *Corinium*. Does the decline of the villa at Ditches perhaps imply that associations with earlier symbols of power were no longer essential or significant to the inhabitants or to communities nearby as expressions of power? Had the memory of the late Iron Age dynasts faded, leaving power and authority to be expressed through somewhat different means, as perhaps expressed by the development of the much larger Cotswold villas at sites like Chedworth?

GALLO-BELGIC AND LOCAL FINEWARES

Val Rigby

Catalogue

Trench E

Quarry pit

E(252), GABTN, platter, Cam 13
E(253), GABTN, platter, Cam 14, AD 50–75
E(253), GABTN, platter, Cam 8
E(253), GABTN, beaker, Cam 120
E(253), GABTN, cup, Cam 56
E(261), GABTN, platter, Cam 14, AD 50–75 (Fig. 34, 5)
E(261), GABTR3, beaker, Claudian
E(261), GABTR2, pedestal beaker
E(261), NOGWH, butt beaker, Cam 113, Pre-Flavian
E(261), NOGWH, flagon, Cam 163, Pre-Flavian
E(263), GABTR3, beaker
E(273), GABTR3, beaker Cam 112/Cam 84
E(281), GABTR3, beaker
E(281), NOGWH, flagon
E(281), WW, flagon
E(281), WW, flagon
E(284), GABTN, platter, Cam 8
E(285), GABTR3, beaker
E(285), NOGWH, flagon
E(286), GABTN, platter, Cam 13

Inner Enclosure Ditch

E(318), same vessel as E(319)
E(319), FWB, ribbed collar type flagon, Cirencester TF11, Pre-Flavian
E(320), beaker, Cam 94, Central Gaulish?, Pre-Flavian
E(320), FWB, butt beaker, Cam 113, Claudian-Neronian
E(320), ABING, butt beaker, Cam 113, Pre-Flavian
E(320), ABING, butt beaker
E(337), butt beaker, Cam 113, unusual fabric, Pre-Flavian (same vessel as in E(320))

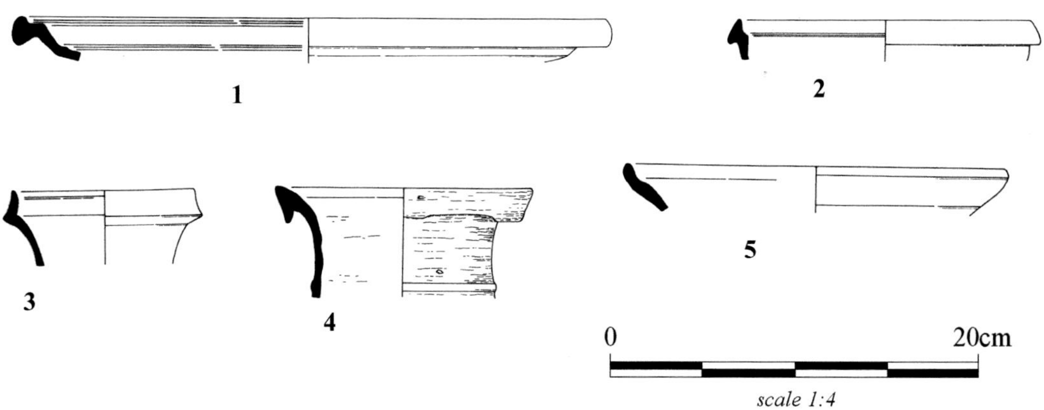

Fig. 34. Gallo-Belgic pottery.

E(337), ABING, beaker, Cam 91, Cirencester fabric 11?
E(338), FWB, beaker, Cam 91, same vessel as in E(337)

Ditch E[255]
E(264), GABTN, platter with central stamp A]CVT[II], AD 20–50. Probably Acutus III, P32, Die 03BCI, reorded also at Colchester, Chichester and Verulamium.
E(264), WW, beaker.

Trench F
Iron Age pits
Pit F[505]
F(500), GABTN, platter. Cam 3/5 variant, late Augustan (?) (Fig. 34, 1)
F(500), GABTR3, beaker sherd
F(511), GABTR1, (c) platter Cam 7 or 8, late Augustan to Claudian
F(511), GABTN, cup Cam 56c, Tiberian-Neronian (Fig. 34, 3)
F(511), NOGWH, flagon Cam 161/163, Tiberian-Neronian (Fig. 34, 4)

Pit F[540]
F(538), GABTR3, girth beaker Cam 84, late Augustan-Claudian
F(538), GABTN, platter Cam 12, late Augustan-Tiberian

Phase 1c. Occupation layer
F(504), WW, Cam 113, Tiberian-Claudian

Phase 4. Primary floor level of Structure 1
F(478), GABTR1c, platter Cam 8
F(478), NOGWH, butt beaker Cam 113
F(484), GABTN, flagon Cam 161/163
F(484), GABTN, platter
F(484), GABTN, beaker
F(484), GABTR3, girth/butt beaker
F(484), GABWH, beaker, Cam 114
F(484), WW, beaker Cam 113
F(484), WW, beaker Cam 114
F(514), NOGWH, flagon base Cam 161/163, Tiberian-Claudian
F(514), GABTN cup

Phase 6. Later floor level
F(417), WW, beaker Cam 113

Fill of cellar
F(426), GABTN, small platter, Tiberian-Neronian
F(426), NOGWH, flagon
F(427), GABTR2, Cam 7c, 15BC–AD20

Phase 9b. Fill of robber trench
F(434), GABTN platter sherd

Subsoil and unstratified
F(440), GABTR1c, Cam 8 variant with marked offset and sharp moulding, Tiberian (Fig. 34, 2)
F(u/s), GABTR3, Cam 84 (same vessel as F(538)
F(u/s), GABTN, platter Cam 7/8, Tiberian – pre-conquest
F(u/s), GABTN, cup rim Cam 58, AD 50–75
F(u/s), Burnt WW, butt beaker Cam 114, Tiberian-Claudian
F(u/s), GABTN platter Cam 12

Discussion

The Gallo-Belgic finewares from the 1984–5 excavations at Ditches comprise an assemblage of relatively small and abraded sherds with few joining fragments. The assemblage adds to the material already known from Bagendon excavations (Clifford 1961), the earlier Ditches excavations (Rigby 1988) and more recent finds from Middle Duntisbourne and Duntisbourne Grove (Timby 1999a, 329–332) which might also be regarded as part of the 'Bagendon complex'. Overall, the assemblage provides evidence of occupation by people interested in acquiring 'Romanized' pottery in the pre-conquest period, possibly as early as AD 10. Only the vessel forms commonly represented in southern Britain have been identified at Ditches and Bagendon. A platter, *Camulodunum* form 7 is definitely a late Augustan or early Tiberian product. The latest piece is a Terra Nigra platter *Camulodunum* form 14, a type current *c.* AD 50–70, the remaining pieces fall in the date range between AD 10–60, most clustered around AD 30–60. The absence of platter form Cam 16, conventionally dated to AD 50–85 because of its occurrence on Agricolan forts in Scotland, is worth noting despite the small size of the sample. The identification of local copies of imported pottery, made in the Upper Thames Valley, in the assemblage provides further potential evidence of potters well versed in Roman potting techniques in the region. At least in the first instance these may have been non-local to the area or even immigrants from Gaul. The kiln fired quartz-sand tempered fabrics of these copies are in marked contrast to the products of indigenous potters and required a different set of skills. Tiberio-Claudian forms were copied demonstrating a growing demand for thin-walled colourful specialised vessels in the immediately post-conquest period.

Amphorae catalogue

Quarry pit

E(251)

BATAM Dr. 20, handle, 31g

Inner Enclosure Ditch

E(320)

BATAM Dr. 20, body sherd, 115g

Cellar fill

F(495)

BATAM Dr. 20, body sherd, 135g

F(480)

BATAM Dr. 20, 7 body sherds, 429g

THE SAMIAN

Steven Willis

Introduction

The samian (*terra sigillata*) from the 1984–5 excavations amounts to 256 sherds weighing 3542g. An aggregate of *c.* 164 vessels are represented with a rim equivalence (EVE) of 9.765. This is a sizable sample, especially from a rural site, and together with the material from the earlier seasons sheds valuable light on the chronology and nature of the site. The sherds are generally quite fragmentary, with the exception of a proportion of the material from the cellar fills; degree of fragmentation notwithstanding, the sherds are in a good state of preservation. They do not show adverse weathering, suggesting benign soil environments. The gloss surfaces have accordingly survived, though they tend to be dull. All but a handful of sherds could be attributed to form, while in all cases the source was discernable. A total of 31 contexts contained samian; the unstratified samian was not examined. In essence the works in 1984 investigating the Inner Enclosure Ditch and the Quarry yielded samian dating to the mid first century AD, while the area examined in detail in 1985 (Trench F) produced a later group of second century date. The majority of the assemblage (182 sherds) came from contexts associated with the filling of the cellar. Several stamps are present.

Format of samian catalogue

The catalogue lists all samian sherds from the excavations submitted for identification and dating. The catalogue adheres to a consistent format. Each entry per context relates to an individual vessel represented in that context. Sherds are ordered by trench, phase and context, then the following data are given: the number of sherds and their type (i.e. whether a sherd is from a rim, base (footring), or body of a vessel, or, indeed, if it consists of a full profile), the source of the item, (South Gaulish is abbreviated to SG, Central Gaulish to CG and East Gaulish to EG; in the case of Southern Gaul the La Graufesenque industry is abbreviated to LG, and for Central Gaul, Lz represents Lezoux and LMV, Les Martres-de-Veyre), the vessel form (where identifiable), the weight of the sherds in grams, the percentage of any extant rim (i.e. the RE figure, where 1.00 would represent a complete circumference) or base (i.e. the BE figure) and the rim and base diameters, and an estimate of the date of the sherd in terms of calendar years (this being the date range of deposits with which like pieces are normally associated). Any decoration is then described. Oswald's figure types (Oswald 1936–7) are referred to following the standard convention, for example O.1926a would be his type

1926a. Similarly, the decorative details catalogued by Rogers (Rogers 1974) are simply referred to as, for instance, Rogers B105, without quoting the bibliographic reference. The presence of other features such as burning, trimming and repair is also noted.

Geoff Dannell, who had catalogued the samian from the 1982–3 seasons, kindly examined a number of sherds from the early deposits excavated in 1984 and his observations and notes are incorporated in the catalogue below.

Catalogue of the samian

Trench E

by Steven Willis with Geoff Dannell

Phase 4. Inner enclosure ditch

E(319)

- Body, SG LG, Drag. 29, 4g, probably *c.* AD 40–55.
- Two body sherds, SG LG, Drag. 15/17, 4g, *c.* AD 40–70.

E(320)

- Rim, SG LG, Drag. 15/17, 4g, RE: 0.07, Diam. 180mm, *c.* AD 40–55.
- Two conjoining rim sherds, SG LG, Drag. 15/17, 8g, RE: 0.08, Diam. 180mm, *c.* AD 40–60.
- Rim, SG LG, Drag. 15/17, 5g, RE: 0.03, Diam. 170mm, *c.* AD 40–60. From a different vessel from the item above.
- Body, SG LG, small Drag. 27, 1g, *c.* AD 40–70.
- Body, SG LG, small Drag. 30, 2g, *c.* AD 40–70. No decoration is represented.
- Body, SG LG, small hemispherical cup, 2g, *c.* AD 40–70. Burnt. Different vessel from the small Drag. 27 of like date.
- Body, SG LG, Drag. 15/17, 3g, *c.* AD 40–100.
- Body, SG LG, Drag. 18, 1g, *c.* AD 40–100.
- Base, SG LG, cup, probably Drag. 27g, 3g, BE: 0.12, Diam. 60mm, *c.* AD 40–100.
- Body, SG LG, small hemispherical cup, 2g, *c.* AD 40–100.
- Body, SG LG, probably from a platter, 1g, *c.* AD 40–100.
- Body, SG LG, Drag. 29, 6g, *c.* AD 45–60. A small area of decoration is represented at the carination which is defined by bead bordering; in the upper zone is a tendril arrangement, while in the lower zone is a leafy motif.

E(336)

- Rim, SG LG, Drag. 29, 55g, RE: 0.10, Diam. 220mm, *c.* AD 40–55. This vessel is probably the product of one of the workshops associated with SENICIO. A number of the details appear on work with his internal stamp. The large leaves from the lower zone are on a bowl from Mainz (Knorr 1919, Taf. 76F), together with a similar striated rod. The small astragalus binding looks like that from Neuss (Knorr 1919, Taf. 77L), and the hollow rosette is on a bowl from Valkenburg (info. from the late Prof. Jan-Kees Haalebos), which is itself very close to a published form 29 there (cf. van Giffen 1940–4, Afb. 583) in the style of MARINVS (a stamped one from the same mould is in the Museum of London). The bud motif from the upper zone is also known at Valkenburg on a 30 (van Giffen 1940–4, Afb. 59.2), signed in the mould by MASCLVS; his lozenge-shaped leaf is similar to that which appears in the work of SENICIO. (Fig. 35, no. 2)

Phase 6. Top of quarry fill

E(253)

- Body, SG LG, Ritt. 5, 1g, *c.* AD 30–55.

E(261)

- Rim, SG LG, Drag. 27 with rouletted rim, 1g, RE: 0.025, Diam. 120mm, *c.* AD 30–55.
- Body, SG LG (pale paste), Drag. 27, 2g, *c.* AD 30–55.

E(262)

- Two body sherds, SG LG, Ritt. 12, 3g, *c.* AD 40–55.
- Three body sherds, SG LG, probably Drag. 27, 7g, *c.* AD 40–55.

E(273)

- Two body sherds, SG LG, Drag. 15/17, 7g, *c.* AD 40–55.

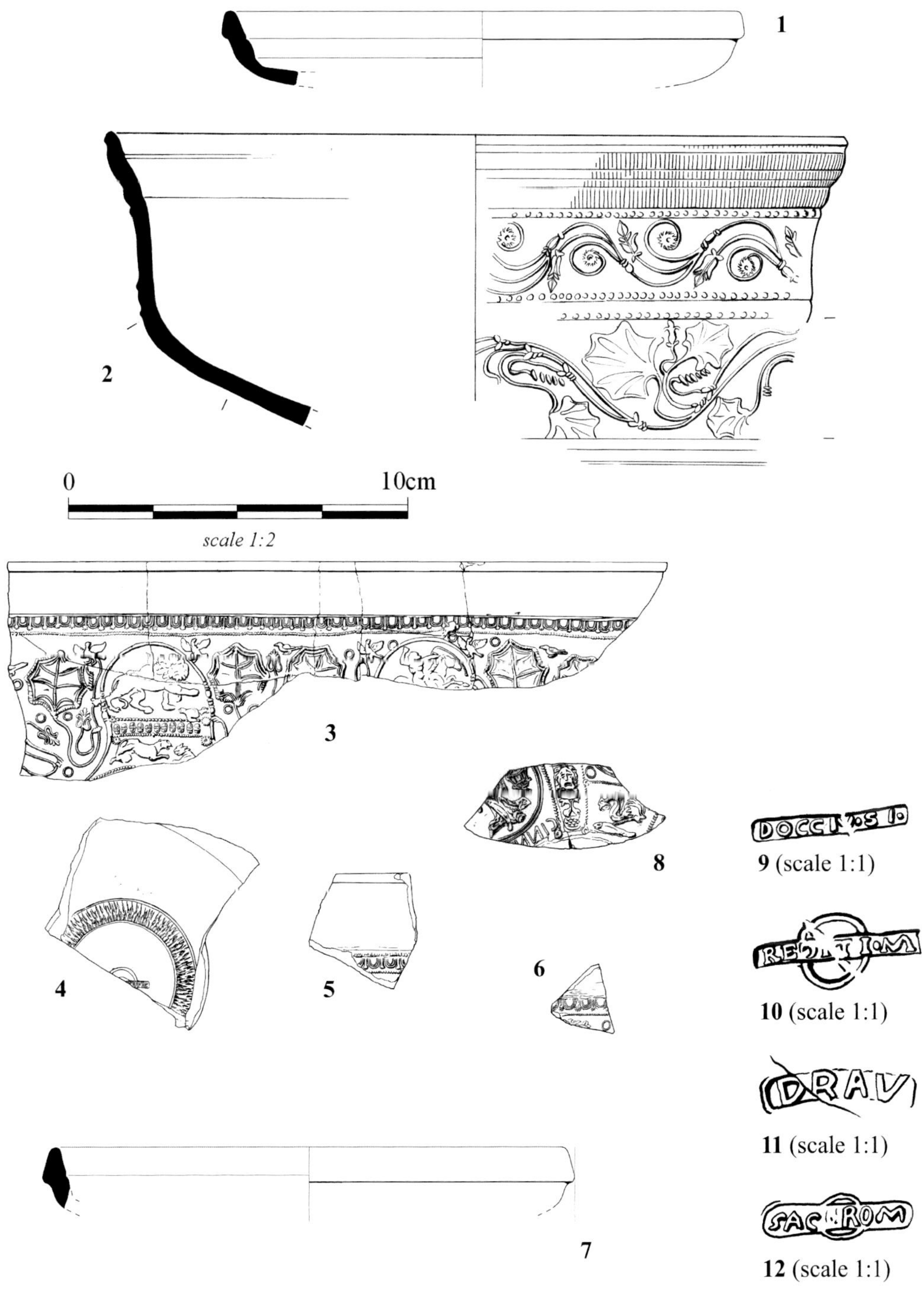

Fig. 35. Samian pottery.

E(281)
- Base, SG LG, small Drag. 27g, 2g, BE: 0.12, Diam. 40mm, *c.* AD 40–70. A tiny fragment from a stamp is represented but is not identifiable.
- Body, SG LG, probably Drag. 29 or 30, 1g, *c.* AD 40–100.
- Base, SG LG, probably from a platter, 2g, BE: 0.06, Diam. *c.* 90mm, *c.* AD 40–100.
- Body, SG LG, from a cup or platter, 1g, *c.* AD 40–100.
- Two conjoining body sherds, SG LG, from a bowl or dish, 3g, *c.* AD 40–100.
- Body, SG LG, Drag. 29, 3g, *c.* AD 55–70. An area showing fine straight gadroons from the lower zone of decoration is represented.
- Body, SG LG, probably Drag. 18, 3g, *c.* AD 70–100. A tiny fragment from the stamp is represented. From the same vessel as represented in context 252.

E(283)
- Body, SG LG, Drag. 29, 1g, *c.* AD 40–55.

E(286)
- Flake, SG LG, form not identifiable, 1g, probably *c.* AD 40–55.

E(299)
- Body, SG LG, platter, being a Drag. 15/17 variant, 1g, *c.* AD 30–55.
- Body, SG LG, from a hemispherical cup, or small bowl or dish, 1g, *c.* AD 40–80.

E(303)
- Two body sherds, SG LG, Drag. 18, 3g, *c.* AD 40–100.

Phase 7. Cobbling sealing Quarry pits
E(252)
- Body, SG LG, cup, 1g, probably *c.* AD 40–55.
- Body, SG LG, Drag. 18, 12g, *c.* AD 70–100. Evidently stamped 'CALVS['. Not illustrated. Another sherd from this vessel occurs in context 281.

Phase 8. North–south boundary ditch
E(264)
- Body, SG LG, Drag. 27, 1g, *c.* AD 30–55.
- Body, SG LG, Drag. 18, 3g, probably *c.* AD 40–55.

Trench F
by Steven Willis

Phase 3. Iron Age pit [540]
F(538)
- Rim, Arezzo, Loes. 1a, 8g, RE: 0.09, Diam. 150mm, *c.* AD 1–40. After Loeschcke 1a (cf. *Camulodunum* 2a (Hawkes and Hull 1947)). Geoff Dannell examined this item and confirms an Arezzo source; he has dated the item as Augustan-Tiberian. Abraded. (Fig. 35, no. 1)

Phase 4. Building of the villa
F(484)
- One rim sherd and a conjoining body sherd, SG LG, Ritt. 5, 1g, RE: 0.05, Diam. 100mm, *c.* AD 30–50. This vessel has an extremely thin wall with a good quality slip. Geoff Dannell has examined this item which he identifies as Tiberian-Claudian.

Phase 6? Floor layer
F(417)
- Body, CG Lz, Drag. 18/31, 52g, *c.* AD 120–150. Burnt.
- Body, CG Lz, Drag. 33, 10g, *c.* AD. 120–200. Burnt. Two drilled holes occur, evidently for repair via riveting.

Phase 8. Cellar fills
F(488)
- Rim sherd and body sherd, from same vessel, SG LG, Drag. 18 or 18/31, 1g, RE: *c.* 0.03, Diam. *c.* 190mm, *c.* AD 50–110.
- Rim, CG Lz, Drag. 18/31, 5g, RE: *c.* 0.02, Diam. not identifiable, *c.* AD 120–150.
- Body, CG Lz, Drag. 27, 4g, *c.* AD 120–160.
- Rim, CG Lz, Drag. 33, 6g, RE: 0.07, Diam. 130mm, *c.* AD 120–160.
- Two conjoining body sherds, CG Lz, large Drag. 33, 19g, *c.* AD 120–200. The item appears to have been trimmed around at the junction of the vessel wall and floor and the footring also seems to have been removed creating a disc About half of the floor of this vessel is represented

and it is possible that this 'disc' has been chopped in half. A fragment of a stamp is represented reading ']MA' ligatured, but is not possible to identify given that this is a common die ending and in this case is not characterized by distinguishing features.

- Four body sherds, all same vessel, CG Lz, Déch. 72, 16g, *c.* AD 150–200. The decoration is of incised cut glass style, similar to Oswald and Price 1920, Pl. 77, no 4. Other sherds from this vessel occur in contexts 426 and 485.

F(489)

- Body, CG Lz, Drag. 33, 4g, *c.* AD 120–170.
- Body, CG Lz, Drag. 37, 8g, *c.* AD 120–200. An area of decoration occurs arranged in panels defined by bead rows with rosette terminals; a vertical panel is represented here with a composite motif forming continuous loops; also represented in a separate panel is a leaping animal.
- Rim, EG Trier, Drag. 31, 2g, RE: 0.03, Diam. 180mm, *c.* AD 160–220. Another sherd from this vessel occurs in context 491.

F(491)

- Body, CG Lz, Drag. 37, 7g, *c.* AD 120–150. An area of decoration occurs; part of the ovolo band is represented; this is finely executed with a double border, no central projection and with a tongue defined by twisted cord ending in a rosette terminal; below is a fine bead border with a small ring depicted in the field of decoration; this ovolo type is similar to Rogers's types B28 and B59. (Fig. 35, no. 6)
- Rim, CG Lz, Drag. 33, 7g, RE: 0.14, Diam. 110mm, *c.* AD 120–170.
- Rim, CG Lz, Drag. 33, 3g, RE: 0.05, Diam. 100mm, *c.* AD 120–170. Different vessel from the above item.
- Body, CG Lz, Drag. 33, 8g, *c.* AD 120–170. Apparently from a separate vessel to the other examples of Drag. 33 from this context.
- Rim, CG Lz, Drag. 33, 4g, RE: 0.06, Diam. 130mm, *c.* AD 120–200. Different vessel from the above items.
- Three body sherds, all same vessel, CG Lz, Drag. 33, 12g, *c.* AD 120–200. Possibly from same vessel as above but uncertain.
- Body, CG, Drag. 38, 9g, *c.* AD 130–200. The fabric is pale brown with a coarse slip.
- Rim, CG Lz, Drag. 31, 12g, RE: 0.06, Diam. 190mm, *c.* AD 150–200 (probably *c.* AD 150–170).
- Body, CG Lz, probably Drag. 31, 1g, *c.* AD 150–200.
- Body, CG Lz, probably Drag. 31, 2g, *c.* AD 150–200. From different vessel from the above item.
- Rim, EG Trier, Drag. 31, 8g, RE: 0.05, Diam. 180mm, *c.* AD 160–220. Another sherd from this vessel occurs in context 489.

F(495)

- Rim, CG Lz, Drag. 18/31, 4g, RE: 0.06, Diam. 190mm, *c.* AD 120–140.
- Body, CG Lz, Drag. 18/31, 5g, *c.* AD 120–140. From different vessel from rim above.

Phase 8. Upper fills of cellar

F(426)

- Body, CG LMV, Drag. 37, 8g, *c.* AD 100–125. In the style of Donnaucus; a further sherd from this vessel occurs in context 480.
- One rim sherd and two body sherds, CG LMV, Drag. 37, 48g, RE: 0.08, Diam. 210mm, *c.* AD 100–125. From the same vessel as the bowl represented in 485.
- Body, CG LMV, Drag. 37, 9g, *c.* AD 100–130. An area of decoration occurs; part of the ovolo border is represented, the ovolo being defined by a single border and with no central projection; the tongue is represented by a twisted cord stem ending in a very fine rosette; below is a bead border; decoration is arranged in panels; only part of the decorative field is represented but includes the spiral Rogers S63 and a small petalled roundel.
- Rim, CG Lz, Drag. 42 cup with handle and barbotine trailing, 23g, RE: 0.17, Diam. 110mm, *c.* AD 120–140.
- Rim, CG Lz, Curle 11, 31g, RE: 0.12, Diam. 180mm, *c.* AD 120–145.

- Body, CG Lz, Drag. 18/31, 10g, *c.* AD 120–145.
- Body, CG Lz, Drag. 18/31, 5g, *c.* AD 120–145.
- Rim, CG Lz, Drag. 18/31, 25g, RE: 0.13, Diam. 180mm, *c.* AD 120–145.
- Rim, CG Lz, Drag. 18/31, 2g, RE: 0.05, Diam. 170mm, *c.* AD 120–150.
- Rim, CG Lz, Drag. 18/31, 5g, RE: 0.05, Diam. 170mm, *c.* AD 120–150.
- Rim, CG Lz, Drag. 18/31, 9g, RE: 0.01, Diam. uncertain, *c.* AD 120–150.
- Rim, CG Lz, Drag. 18/31, 2g, RE: 0.04, Diam. *c.* 170mm, *c.* AD 120–150.
- Rim, CG Lz, Drag. 18/31, 21g, RE: 0.09, Diam, 190mm, *c.* AD 120–150.
- Two rim sherds, CG Lz, Drag. 18/31, 11g, RE: 0.09, Diam. 190mm, *c.* AD 120–150.
- Body, CG Lz, Drag. 18/31, 13g, *c.* AD 120–150.
- Body, CG Lz, Drag. 18/31, 7g, *c.* AD 120–150.
- Profile sherd, CG Lz, Drag. 18/31, 91g, RE: 0.07, Diam. 180mm, BE: 0.35, Diam. 80mm, *c.* AD 120–150.
- Rim, CG Lz, Drag. 18/31, 47g, RE: 0.19, Diam. 190mm, *c.* AD 120–150.
- Profile sherd, CG Lz, Drag. 18/31, 77g, RE: 0.17, Diam. 170mm, BE: 0.10, Diam. *c.* 80mm, *c.* AD 120–150.
- Base, CG Lz, Drag. 18/31, 60g, BE: 0.35, Diam. 90mm, *c.* AD 120–150. The vessel has been trimmed around crudely at the junction of the wall and vessel floor.
- Body, CG Lz, Drag. 36, 6g, *c.* AD 120–150.
- Rim, CG Lz, from bead rimmed vessel, 1g, RE: *c.* 0.04, Diam. uncertain, *c.* AD 120–150.
- Body, CG Lz, form not identifiable, 3g, *c.* AD 120–150.
- Six rim sherds, four body sherds and one base sherd, all same vessel, CG Lz, Drag. 18/31R, 359g, RE: 0.41, Diam. 250mm, BE: 0.46, Diam. *c.* 96mm, *c.* AD 120–160. Part of a short stamp is represented, ending ')M'; this stamp is unidentified.
- Three rim sherds conjoining, CG Lz, Drag. 18/31R, 49g, RE: 0.17, Diam. *c.* 260mm, *c.* AD 120–160.
- Base, CG Lz, hemispherical cup, probably Drag. 27, 17g, BE: 0.35, Diam. 60mm, *c.* AD 120–160.
- Rim, CG Lz, Drag. 27, 1g, RE: 0.06, Diam. 130mm, *c.* AD 120–160. Burnt.
- Body, CG Lz, Drag. 27, 5g, *c.* AD 120–160.
- Rim, CG Lz, from bead rimmed vessel, 1g, RE: *c.* 0.03, Diam. uncertain, *c.* AD 120–160.
- Body, CG Lz, Drag. 33, 3g, *c.* AD 120–175.
- Rim, CG Lz, Drag. 18/31 or 31, 2g, RE: 0.05, Diam. 170mm, *c.* AD 120–200. Abraded.
- Rim, CG Lz. Drag. 18/31 or 31, 7g, RE: 0.07, Diam. 190mm, *c.* AD 120–200.
- Rim. CG Lz. Drag. 18/31 or 31, 3g, RE: 0.06, Diam. 170mm, *c.* AD 120–200.
- Body, CG Lz, Drag. 18/31 or 31, 3g, *c.* AD 120–200.
- Rim, CG Lz, Drag. 18/31 or 31, 3g, RE: 0.03, Diam. uncertain, *c.* AD 120–200.
- Base, CG Lz, Drag. 30, 131g, BE: 0.34, Diam. 100mm, *c.* AD 120–200. The only decoration represented is a poorly impressed astragalus terminal and the terminal of a twisted rope motif.
- Rim, CG Lz, Drag. 30 or 37, 4g, RE: *c.* 0.02, Diam. uncertain, *c.* AD 120–200. Burnt. An 'x' mark has been inscribed on the interior surface.
- Base, CG Lz, Drag. 33, 10g, BE: 0.50, Diam. *c.* 38mm, *c.* AD 120–200. Not stamped. The vessel appears to have been crudely trimmed around at the junction of the vessel floor and the footring. Approx. half of the footring and floor are represented and the fracture across the floor is smooth, evidently through some deliberate abrasion; this item may have been used as a rubber or polisher.
- Rim, CG Lz, Drag. 33, 17g, RE: 0.23, Diam. 100mm, *c.* AD 120–200.
- Two conjoining rim sherds, CG Lz, Drag. 33, 26g, RE: 0.14, Diam. 130mm, *c.* AD 120–200.
- Body, CG Lz, Drag. 33, 1g, *c.* AD 120–200.
- Body, CG Lz, Drag. 33, 3g, *c.* AD 120–

200. Different vessel from above item.

- Body, CG Lz, small Drag. 33, 2g, *c.* AD 120–200.
- Body, CG Lz, Drag. 33, 3g, *c.* AD 120–200.
- Rim, CG Lz, Drag. 33, 1g, RE: 0.05, Diam. 110mm, *c.* AD 120–200.
- Rim, CG Lz, Drag. 33, 1g, RE: 0.05, Diam. 110mm, *c.* AD 120–200. From a different vessel to the above item.
- Body, CG Lz, Drag. 33, 1g, *c.* AD 120–200.
- Body, CG Lz, bowl or dish, 3g, *c.* AD 120–200.
- Body, CG Lz, bowl or dish, 3g, *c.* AD120–200.
- Body, CG Lz, bowl or dish, 8g, *c.* AD 120–200.
- Body, CG Lz, bowl or dish, 6g, *c.* AD 120–200.
- Body, CG Lz, bowl, 12g, *c.* AD 120–200.
- Base, CG Lz, hemispherical cup, 22g, BE: 1.00, Diam. *c.* 44mm, *c.* AD 120–200. Not stamped.
- Body, CG Lz, form not identifiable, 1g, *c.* AD 120–200.
- Body, CG Lz, form not identifiable, 1g, *c.* AD 120–200.
- Body, CG Lz, form not identifiable, 3g, *c.* AD 120–200.
- Two base sherds, same vessel, CG Lz, Drag. 44, 63g, BE: 0.39, Diam. 70mm, *c.* AD 130–200. There is some evidence for burning on both sherds. The interior floor of the vessel shows signs of wear.
- Four rim sherds and one body sherd, all same vessel, CG Lz, Drag. 18/31-31 (transitional), 61g, RE: 0.38, Diam. 190mm, *c.* AD 135–165.
- Two conjoining body sherds, CG Lz, Drag. 37, 29g, *c.* AD 135–175. A section of decoration occurs; this is arranged in panels and medallions; the panels are divided by bead borders with small ring terminals; in one vertical panel occurs the composite motif Rogers Q1; to the right is a panel with two fish types represented, these being Oswald O.2386 and O.2418; a further panel contains a medallion with plain double border below are the letters 'CINN' before the sherd breaks; the characters are retrograde, being a stamp of Cinnamus ii; the medallion includes the urn motif (Stanfield and Simpson 1958, fig. 47, no. 6) and the figure of Victory O.809. (Fig. 35, no. 8)
- Eight rim sherds and two base sherds, all same vessel, CG Lz, Drag. 18/31, 331g, RE: 0.92, Diam. 180mm, Base Diam. *c.* 90mm, *c.* AD 140–160. Stamped 'DOCCIV.SF', this being a vessel of the workshop of Doccius ii of Lezoux; products of this workshop are often ascribed a mid rather than early Antonine date. This vessel is nearly complete. (Fig. 35, no. 9)
- Two rim sherds and two full profile sherds conjoining, CG Lz, Drag. 33, 100g, RE: 0.60, Diam. 110mm, BE: 1.00, Diam. 42mm, *c.* AD 140–175. Stamped 'REDITI.M', this being a stamp of Reditus of Lezoux, die 3c; the earliest work of this source is dated from *c.* AD 135, but this particular die occurs on form 31 so a date after *c.* AD 140 is likely in this case (cf. Hartley in Rodwell 1988; Dickinson 1999, 86). (Fig. 35, no. 10)
- Seven rims, three body sherds and one base sherd, all same vessel, CG Lz, Drag. 18/31R, 369g, RE: 0.63, Diam. 270mm, BE: 0.30, Diam. *c.* 90mm, *c.* AD 145–160. Part of a stamp is represented reading ']OFFIC'; this is probably the work of Ruttus of Lezoux, die 1a, and the stamp represented here then may have originally read 'RVT+OFFIC'; this stamp occurs in an early to mid Antonine pit at Alcester (Dickinson 1996, 593). (Fig. 35, no. 4)
- Rim, CG Lz, Drag. 31, 6g, RE: 0.07, Diam. 170mm, *c.* AD 150–170. Burnt.
- Base, CG Lz, Drag. 31, 23g, BE: 0.24, Diam. 80mm, *c.* AD 150–175. Worn interior.
- Two conjoining base sherds, CG Lz, Drag. 31, 91g, BE: 0.52, Diam. *c.* 90mm, *c.* AD 150–185. Stamped 'DRAV[CIM', this being a stamp of Draucus ii of Lezoux; vessels of this workshop occur on the Antonine Wall; the form range includes forms 27, 79/80 and Lud. Tg/Tx; a date for this item after *c.* AD

160 is quite probable. (Fig. 35, no. 11)

- Eight rim sherds and three body sherds, all same vessel, CG Lz, Drag. 31, 131g, RE: 0.55, Diam. 180mm, *c.* AD 150–200.
- Rim, CG Lz, Drag. 31, 7g, RE: 0.08, Diam. 180mm, *c.* AD 150–200. Burnt.
- Body, CG Lz, Drag. 31, 3g, *c.* AD 150–200.
- Body, CG Lz, Drag. 31, 6g, *c.* AD 150–200.
- Body, CG Lz, Drag. 31, 4g, *c.* AD 150–200.
- 2 conjoining body sherds, CG Lz, Drag. 31, 15g, *c.* AD 150–200.
- Body, CG Lz, Drag. 31, 8g, *c.* AD 150–200.
- Body, CG Lz Déch. 72, 1g, *c.* AD 150–200. Cut glass style decoration. Sherds from the same vessel occur in contexts 485 and 488.
- Rim, EG Trier, Drag. 31R, 24g, RE: 0.06, Diam. 270mm, *c.* AD 160–260.

F(480)

- Body, SG LG, Drag. 33, 6g, *c.* AD 40–100. Burnt.
- Rim, CG LMV, Drag. 37, 13g, RE: 0.07, Diam. 200mm, *c.* AD 100–125. Decoration: a part of the ovolo band is represented with the type appearing similar to Rogers B28 and B59; this may well be a vessel in the style of Donnaucus (see above). This rim is from the same vessel as represented in 426, but is from a different vessel to that by the same potter present in context 485. (Fig. 35, no. 5)
- A complete profile sherd and two rim sherds, conjoining, CG Lz, Drag. 18/31, 103g, RE: 0.37, Diam. 170mm, BE not recorded, Base Diam. *c.* 70mm, *c.* AD 120–150.
- Rim, CG Lz, Drag. 18/31 or 31, 2g, RE: 0.01, Diam. uncertain, *c.* AD 120–200.
- Rim, CG Lz, Drag. 33, 2g, RE: 0.05, Diam. *c.* 130mm *c.* AD 120–200.
- Body, CG Lz, bowl or dish, 7g, *c.* AD 120–200.

F(485)

- Five rim sherds and two body sherds, all from same vessel, CG LMV, Drag. 37, 335g, RE: 0.65, Diam. 210mm, *c.* AD 100–125. Decoration: part of the ovolo band is represented, the type being similar to Rogers' B59 (Stanfield and Simpson 1958, Fig.11); this is defined by a double cordon with no central projection; the tongue is somewhat indistinct but ends in a fine rosette terminal; below is a bead border. The decoration is arranged in an open scroll; within one lobe is the horseman, O. 251 (Oswald 1936–7) within a semi-circular band; in another is a large lion, not in Oswald; in upper lobes appears the large leaf, Rogers J1; the distinctive double D motif occurs in a band below the lion (Stanfield and Simpson 1958, Fig. 11. no. 8); occurring as a filler is the bird, O. 2315a; some rings also appear as space fillers; all of these features indicate this vessel to be in the style of Donnaucus. Further sherds from this vessel occur in context 426. (Fig. 35, no. 3)
- Rim, CG Lz, from a beaker, probably Déch. 67, 1g, RE: 0.07, Diam. *c.* 64mm, *c.* AD 120–150.
- Rim/wall sherd and a conjoining profile sherd (*c.* 95% of vessel), CG Lz, Drag. 33, 86g, RE: 0.78, Diam. 110mm, BE: 1.00, Diam. 40mm, *c.* AD 120–200. The item is stamped 'SACIROM' being the work of Saciro of Lezoux; this is an infrequently represented workshop and its dating is not refined; this stamp is documented by Hofmann (1985, 30, Pl. XIII, 167.1). (Fig. 35, no. 12)
- Body, CG Lz, Drag. 33, 1g, *c.* AD 120–200.
- Rim, CG Lz, bead rimmed bowl, 3g, RE: *c.* 0.03, Diam. not recorded, *c.* AD 120–200.
- Body, CG Lz, bowl, 5g, *c.* AD 120–200.
- Rim, CG Lz, Drag. 31, 6g, RE: 0.07, Diam. 190mm, *c.* AD 150–175.
- Body, CG Lz, Déch. 72, 1g, *c.* AD 150–200. Other sherds from this vessel occur in contexts 426 and 488.

Phase 8–10. An upper fill of the cellar
F(456)
- Body (essentially a flake), CG Lz, form not identifiable, 1g, *c.* AD 120–200.

Phase 9/10. Patch of burning in south corridor
F(469)
- Rim, CG Lz, Drag. 31, 1g, RE: *c.* 0.02, Diam. *c.* 190mm, *c.* AD 120–150.
- Rim, CG Lz, Drag. 46, 14g, RE: 0.25, Diam. 88mm, *c.* AD 120–150.
- Base, CG Lz, probably Drag. 38 or Walters 81, 4g, BE: 0.06, Diam. *c.* 70mm, *c.* AD 130–160.
- Rim, SG Montans, Drag. 36, 9g, RE: 0.14, Diam. *c.* 160mm, *c.* AD 135–155.

Phase 9/10. Soil over path
F(497)
- Rim, probably Arezzo, Loes. 1a, 2g, RE: 0.07, Diam. 150mm, *c.* AD 1–40. Geoff Dannell confirms a Augustan-Tiberian date for this vessel. This item is possibly slightly burnt. Abraded. This is a different vessel from the one represented in context (538). (Fig. 35, no. 7)
- Body, CG Lz, Drag. 37, 1g, *c.* AD 120–200. A tiny area of decoration is represented with no details discernable.
- Body, CG Lz, Drag. 31, 2g, *c.* AD 150–190. A fragment of stamp occurs reading 'ALBV[', being, apparently, the work of Albucius of Lezoux; this stamp resembles that recorded by Hofmann (1985, 28, Pl. XI, 10.7).

F(498)
- Base, CG Lz, from a small hemispherical cup, perhaps Drag. 27, 1g, BE: 0.13, Diam. 40mm, *c.* AD 120–150.
- Body, CG Lz, Drag. 37, 5g, *c.* AD 120–200. An area of decoration is represented arranged in a scroll.
- Body, CG Lz, hemispherical cup, 4g, *c.* AD 120–200. The footring appears to have been deliberately removed. The floor of the vessel is not stamped.

Phase 9/10. Pit fill
F(442)
- Two rim sherds and 1 body sherd, all same vessel, CG Lz, Drag. 27, 12g. RE: 0.21, Diam. 110mm., *c.* AD 120–140.
- Body, CG Lz, cup/small bowl, 2g, *c.* AD 120–140. An unusual form. Burnt.

Phase 9a. Robber trench fill
F(467)
- Base, CG Lz, Drag. 31R, 14g, BE: 0.08, Diam. *c.* 100mm, *c.* AD 160–200. Burnt.

Phase 10. Deposit in hollow above cellar backfill
F(427)
- Base, CG Lz, bowl or dish, 2g, BE: *c.* 0.04, Diam. *c.* 90mm, *c.* AD 120–150.
- Body, CG Lz, bowl or dish, 2g, *c.* AD 120–170.
- Base, CG Lz, probably Drag. 18/31 or 31R, 2g, BE: 0.07, Diam. 80mm, *c.* AD 120–200.
- Two base sherds and a conjoining body sherd, CG Lz, Drag. 33, 13g, BE: 0.01, Diam. *c.* 60mm, *c.* AD 120–200. This base has been trimmed at the junction of the vessel wall and the floor and crudely finished. A fragment of a stamp is present which may read 'GE' or 'CF' but is poorly impressed.
- Body, CG Lz, Drag. 33, 2g, *c.* AD 120–200. Very glossy slip. Different vessel to that represented by the base sherds.
- Body, CG Lz, bowl or dish, 1g, *c.* AD 120–200. Essentially a flake.

The samian from Trench E

The samian ware recovered from the Inner Enclosure Ditch in 1982–3 comprised a moderately sized ensemble of mainly Claudian material with two items from Arezzo. Nothing was necessarily later than *c.* AD 45/50 (Dannell 1988). Sherds from 15 samian vessels were recovered in 1984 from this feature, again with a similar chronological character. The deposits investigated in 1984 yielded no

Arretine; all of the samian is from La Graufesenque. Whilst attention to this samian (by itself) suggests that it might have been deposited at any time in the pre-Flavian period, tellingly none of it is necessarily post-Claudian (cf. Table 1) and so a strong consistency exists in terms of the dates of the samples from this feature.

The samian from the top Quarry Fills (see Catalogue) is again all from La Graufesenque. It includes some potentially earlier samian than the Inner Enclosure Ditch (cf. Table 1), but also has a later emphasis too, and two post-Claudian items occur (a Drag. 29 and a sherd from a stamped platter (see below)). Significantly, the date of this samian group is in accord with the observation (cf. above) that these layers may derive from the disturbance and re-deposition of the Inner Enclosure Ditch filling. Whether from the Inner Ditch or the Quarry these samian sherds display little evidence that they had been in long use prior to breakage/deposition.

Of the 15 samian vessels represented amongst the pottery from the Inner Enclosure Ditch all are identifiable to generic form. These comprise decorated bowls, cups and platters (Table 2), all of types typical of the mid first century AD. The same number of samian vessels was represented amongst the sample from this feature investigated in 1982–3 (Dannell 1988). These comprised 2 decorated bowls, 4 cups and 9 platters. Hence from this feature the two samples (totalling 30 vessels) give the following composition: decorated bowls 6 (20%), cups 8 (26.7%), and platters 16 (53.3%). The proportion formed by decorated vessels is quite modest at a fifth, this figure being significant since often the percentage of samian present comprising decorated types is an indicator of site status. The Ditches complex was obviously of some standing at this time, as reflected in the absolute quantity and range of samian present at this comparatively early date, as well as via other indexes. The comparatively low proportion of decorated forms present is probably a function of the date of the group since generally it seems that proportionately less decorated vessels were produced in samian ware around the mid first century AD than subsequently (Willis 2005); cups and platters are especially prominent generally amongst samian assemblages at this time.

As Table 2 shows, a similar number of samian vessels was recovered from the Top Quarry Fill during the works reported here. The sixteen vessels identifiable to type are of similar form to those from the Inner Enclosure Ditch, with no surprises (cf. Table 2); decorated

Table 1. Summary of the dates of the samian vessels from the Inner Enclosure Ditch and the Top Quarry Fills, Trench E.

Date Range	Period	Inner Enclosure Ditch	Quarry Fills	Totals
c. AD 30–55	Late-Tiberian/Claudian		4	4
c. AD 40–55	Claudian	3	5	8
c. AD 40–60	Claudian/early Neronian	2		2
c. AD 40–70	Claudian/Neronian	4	1	5
c. AD 40–80	Claudian/early Flavian		1	1
c. AD 40–100	Claudian/Flavian	5	5	10
c. AD 45–60	Claudian/early Neronian	1		1
c. AD 55–70	Neronian		1	1
c. AD 70–100	Flavian		1	1
Totals:		**15**	**18**	**33**

	Inner Enclosure Ditch	Quarry Fills	Totals
Decorated Bowls:			
Drag. 29	3	2	5
Drag. 29 or 30		1	1
Drag. 30	1		1
Plain Bowls:			
Ritt. 12		1	1
Bowls or Dishes:			
Indeterminate		1	1
Cups:			
Ritt. 5		1	1
Drag. 27	2	4	6
Indeterminate	2		2
Cup or Platter:			
Indeterminate		1	1
Platters:			
Drag. 15/17	5	2	7
Drag. 18	1	2	3
Indeterminate	1	1	2
Totals:	**15**	**16**	**31**
(Form not identifiable)		2	2
Aggregate Totals:	15	18	33

Table 2. The composition of the samian from the Inner Enclosure Ditch and the Top Quarry Fills by form. Numbers record the instances of each category. All vessels represented here are in South Gaulish La Graufesenque fabric.

vessels (bowls) account for 18.7% of the group, reflecting the pattern seen with the Inner Ditch.

The average sherd weight of the samian from the Inner Enclosure Ditch is 5.9g, which is comparatively low (see below) indicating that this samian had undergone a process or processes leading to considerable fragmentation. However, the average sherd weight for the 24 sherds of samian in the case of the Quarry Fills is a mere 1.8g, a remarkably low figure. This advanced state of fragmentation is consistent with the interpretation of this material as redeposited (see above). It is possible perhaps that the material was intentionally broken prior to deposition since these pieces seem beyond the optimum breakage point for samian. It is interesting to note in this connection that the Quarry Pit is associated with what appear to be structured deposits of animal remains (see elsewhere, this report). Could it be that the samian in this feature was ritually broken (cf. Chapman 2000)?

Only four other sherds of samian were recovered from this area in 1984. Two were from the cobbling sealing the Quarry pits and the other two came from the north–south boundary ditch (contexts 252 and 264 respectively; see Catalogue). All were from La Graufesenque, with three dating to the late Tiberian-Claudian bracket. The fourth item (from the cobbling) was Flavian and indeed, notably from the same vessel as the latest samian sherd from the top of the filling of the Quarry, so perhaps the tiny fragment from the Quarry filling (context 281) might be intrusive.

The samian from Trench F

The samian from this trench is dominated by second century Lezoux products. The majority of the samian from this trench comes from the layers filling the cellar, which reflect this pattern. Two sherds from Arretine vessels occur, comprising a Loeschcke 1a platter from pit F[540], where it is associated with other mid

Date Range	Period	Totals
c. AD 40–100	Claudian/Flavian	1
c. AD 50–110	Claudian/early Trajanic	1
c. AD 100–125	Trajanic/early Hadrianic	2
c. AD 100–130	Trajanic/early Hadrianic	1
c. AD 120–140	Hadrianic	3
c. AD 120–145	Hadrianic/early Antonine	4
c. AD 120–150	Hadrianic/early Antonine	19
c. AD 120–160	Hadrianic/early Antonine	8
c. AD 120–170	Hadrianic/Antonine	4
c. AD 120–175	Hadrianic/Antonine	1
c. AD 120–200	Hadrianic/Antonine	37
c. AD 130–200	Hadrianic/Antonine	2
c. AD 135–165	Late Hadrianic/Antonine	1
c. AD 135–175	Late Hadrianic/Antonine	1
c. AD 140–160	Early Antonine	1
c. AD 140–175	Antonine	1
c. AD 145–160	Early Antonine	1
c. AD 150–170	Antonine	1
c. AD 150–175	Antonine	2
c. AD 150–185	Antonine	1
c. AD 150–200	Antonine	11
c. AD 160–220	Mid Antonine/early 3rd century	1
c. AD 160–260	Mid Antonine/mid 3rd century	1
Total:		**105**

Table 3. Summary of the dates of the samian vessels from the fills of the Cellar (contexts 426, 480, 485, 488, 489, 491, 495).

first century AD pottery, and a rim probably from a platter of Loeschcke form 1a, from context F(497). There are also sherds from three vessels from La Graufesenque including a cup of Ritterling form 5 dating to the late Tiberian–early Claudian period. These items indicate activity during the era *c.* AD 30–55 in the area of the subsequent villa. Arretine *terra sigillata* is known from other locations in the region of the Ditches complex, in association with indigenous settlements. This is testimony to the importance of these sites and the connectivity of the region with wider distribution networks in the Late Iron Age and conquest era.

The rarity of South Gaulish samian amongst the sample from Trench F is noteworthy given the sequence of occupation at the Ditches complex. This is particularly germane with regard to the Flavian period when samian was imported into Britain in large quantities, being, socially, widely available (Willis 1998a; 2005). The implication is that this area was not being used in a manner leading to deposit formation in the later first century, or if it had been, any such deposits have been lost.

Whilst the bulk of the samian from these trenches is from Lezoux, dating to between *c.* AD 120–200 there is a strong showing of samian dating to the period *c.* AD 120–150. This holds for the assemblage generally and for the samian recovered from the cellar fills. Table 3 shows the composition of the samian from the cellar by date. Amongst the 105 vessels represented there are just two items of Claudian–early Trajanic date (*c.* AD 40–110) testifying to the comparative lack of residuality amongst this group (the items being a burnt Drag. 33 and a platter that is potentially late first century/Trajanic and which may have been extant in the second century). Table 3 indicates that there are 40 vessels dating to the period *c.* AD 100–165, nearly 40% of the sample. Contrastingly there are only 17 vessels dating to after *c.* AD 150, which is less than 20%. Normally in Britain sites of all types occupied through the second century will show samian assemblages that are dominated by material post-dating *c.* AD 150 (Willis 2005), but not so here.

Significantly in terms of the chronology of the layers filling the cellar, samian from contexts attributed to Ceramic Group C1 includes items that are potentially the latest samian represented in the cellar fill deposits, including the Trier vessel from F(489) and F(491) (see below). Contexts F(488), F(489), F(491) and F(495) attributed to Ceramic Group C1 are, in terms of the dates of the samian present, not distinguishable from contexts F(426),

F(480) and F(485) belonging to the later Ceramic Group C2. It would seem that the samian from the cellar represents a continual supply and consumption of samian at Ditches through the second century until the mid-Antonine period (*c.* AD 165/170 perhaps) when the list stops. The ratio of 18/31s to 31s (normally dated *c.* AD 120–150 and *c.* AD 150 to 200 respectively) can be taken as an index of dating (noting the bias in favour of 31's since they belong to an era of greater supply of samian to Britain), this ratio being 20:15 (cf. Table 4). The samian from elsewhere in this trench displays a similar end date to that from the cellar.

A few more chronological details can be noted regarding the samian from the cellar. Three vessels from Les Martres-de-Veyre occur, all decorated bowls of Drag. 37 form. Production at this

Source: **Form Type:**	South Gaulish La Grauf.	Central Gaulish Les Martres	Central Gaulish Lezoux	East Gaulish Trier
Decorated Beakers / Jars:				
Déch. 67			1	
Déch. 72			1	
Decorated Bowls:				
Drag. 30			1	
Drag. 30 or 37			1	
Drag. 37		3	3	
Bowls:				
Indeterminate			3	
Plain Bowls:				
Drag. 31R				1
Drag. 38			1	
Drag. 44			1	
Curle 11			1	
Bowls or Dishes:				
Indeterminate			5	
Cups:				
Drag. 27			4	
Drag. 33	1		23	
Indeterminate			1	
Dishes:				
Drag. 18/31			20	
Drag. 18/31 - 31			1	
Drag. 18/31 or 31			6	
Drag. 18/31R			3	
Drag. 31			14	1
Drag. 36			1	
Drag. 42			1	
Dish or Platter:				
Drag. 18 or 18/31	1			
Totals:	**2**	**3**	**92**	**2**
(Form not identifiable)			6	
Aggregate Totals:	**2**	**3**	**98**	**2**

Table 4. The composition of the samian from the Cellar by source and form. Numbers record the number of instances of each category.

source experienced its main floruit *c.* AD 100–125 when it was the main supplier of samian to the North-West provinces; however, the exported quantities were much lower than that coming from La Graufesenque in the later first century or Lezoux from *c.* AD 120. Hence, that only three vessels from this source occur amongst this sample cannot be taken as a straight-forward indicator of a lack of activity at the Ditches complex at this time. Les Martres imports in Britain are dominated by two forms: the Drag. 37 and the 18/31 platter and it is evident that 37s from this source were typically in use well into the second century (Willis 2005). Hence these Les Martres bowls in the cellar deposits may have formed part of a contemporary 'in use' assemblage at the site, alongside the Lezoux plain and decorated forms which are normally given a later date.

A second point of detail to make with regard to the samian from the cellar is that there is a useful ensemble of five samian stamps from layer F(426). The date brackets for these items (see Catalogue) cluster coherently around the earlier Antonine period and closely support a prospective date of deposition for this layer of *c.* AD 165/170 (that is on the grounds of the samian evidence alone).

Finally, considering the date of the cellar fills, attention to what is present and absent is telling. Only two East Gaulish vessels are present, both from Trier and potentially constituting the two latest samian vessels in the group, dating to after *c.* AD 160. East Gaulish samian is generally infrequent in Britain but any group of Antonine date of any size is likely to contain some examples. This small presence amongst the cellar group is consonant with the suggested date of the deposit. More broadly, no forms diagnostically late second century occur, such as samian mortaria nor some of the Ludowici forms, while there are no late second century decorated bowls. The Drag. 31R bowl is another indicator of later second century date and there is only one example present, this being one of the Trier vessels (cf. Table 4).

Only 10 vessels from the cellar deposits come from decorated forms, forming *c.* 10% of the sample identifiable to form (cf. Table 4). Decorated samian vessels likewise form a small percentage amongst the samian from this trench generally (Tables 5 and 6). This is a low showing by any comparison (cf. Willis 2005, where the average for villas and other rural sites in Britain is established at *c.* 20%), and is especially remarkable given that the proportion of decorated samian in a group might be considered an index of wealth and status. However, recent work has shown that rural sites that might by other indicators be considered high status (e.g. via building type, materials and architectural details), including villas, often have low proportions of decorated samian, with the proportion not higher than that at farmsteads (Willis 2005, Tables 35 and 42). One explanation is that at villas and other higher status sites in the countryside alternatives were in use such as glass vessels and silver or other metal table ware (Evans 1993, 110). This may well, for instance, have been the case at Fishbourne, where a similarly low proportion of decorated samian occurs (Willis 1998a; 2005). The sheer quantity of samian from the Ditches complex is testimony to the level of supply of samian and both consumers' interest in it and their ability to afford it. Decorated forms, being essentially beakers and bowls, will have been associated with drinking and perhaps presenting food at meals; possibly other non-samian pottery forms took these roles in the second century – Severn Valley Ware tankards for instance.

Source: **Form Type:**	Italy Arezzo	South Gaulish La Grauf.	South Gaulish Montans	Central Gaulish Les Martres	Central Gaulish Lezoux	East Gaulish Trier
Decorated Beakers / Jars:						
Déch. 67					1	
Déch. 72					1	
Decorated Bowls:						
Drag. 30					1	
Drag. 30 or 37					1	
Drag. 37				3	5	
Bowls:						
Indeterminate					3	
Plain Bowls:						
Drag. 31R					1	1
Drag. 38					1	
Drag. 38 or Walters 81					1	
Drag. 44					1	
Curle 11					1	
Bowls or Dishes:						
Drag. 18/31 or 31R					1	
Indeterminate					8	
Cup or Bowl:						
Indeterminate					1	
Cups:						
Ritt. 5		1				
Drag. 27					6	
Drag. 33		1			25	
Drag. 46					1	
Indeterminate					2	
Dishes:						
Drag. 18/31					21	
Drag. 18/31 - 31					1	
Drag. 18/31 or 31					6	
Drag. 18/31R					3	
Drag. 31					16	1
Drag. 36			1		1	
Drag. 42					1	
Dish or Platter:						
Drag. 18 or 18/31		1				
Platters:						
Loeschcke 1a	2					
Totals:	**2**	**3**	**1**	**3**	**110**	**2**
(Form not identifiable)					7	
Aggregate Totals:	**2**	**3**	**1**	**3**	**117**	**2**

Table 5. The composition of the samian from 1985 by source and form. Numbers record the number of instances of each category.

Source: / Form Type:	Italy Arezzo	South Gaulish La Grauf.	South Gaulish Montans	Central Gaulish Les Martres	Central Gaulish Lezoux	East Gaulish Trier
Decorated Beakers / Jars: 0.7 % of Group						
Déch. 67					0.07	
Déch. 72					P	
Decorated Bowls: 8.7 % of Group						
Drag. 30					P	
Drag. 30 or 37					0.02	
Drag. 37				0.72	0.08	
Bowls: 0.3 % of Group						
Indeterminate					0.03	
Plain Bowls: 1.9 % of Group						
Drag. 31R					P	0.06
Drag. 38					P	
Drag. 38 or Walters 81					P	
Drag. 44					P	
Curle 11					0.12	
Bowls or Dishes:						
Drag. 18/31 or 31R					P	
Indeterminate					P	
Cup or Bowl:						
Indeterminate					P	
Cups: 29.5 % of Group						
Ritt. 5		0.05				
Drag. 27					0.27	
Drag. 33		P			2.22	
Drag. 46					0.25	
Indeterminate					P	
Dishes: 56.1 % of Group						
Drag. 18/31					2.26	
Drag. 18/31 - 31					0.38	
Drag. 18/31 or 31					0.22	
Drag. 18/31R					1.21	
Drag. 31					0.85	0.08
Drag. 36			0.14		P	
Drag. 42					0.17	
Dish or Platter: 0.3 % of Group						
Drag. 18 or 18/31		0.03				
Platters: 1.7 % of Group						
Loeschcke 1a	0.16					
Totals:	**0.16**	**0.08**	**0.14**	**0.72**	**8.15**	**0.14**
(Form not identifiable)					0.07	
Aggregate Totals:	**0.16**	**0.08**	**0.14**	**0.72**	**8.22**	**0.14**

Table 6. The composition of the samian from 1985 by source and form. Numbers record the Rim Equivalence (EVE) for categories. Total RE 9.46.

Considering the samian from Trench F more generally the presence of a vessel in Montans fabric may be noted, this being a Drag. 36 from F(469) dating to the mid second century. Samian from this source is occasionally present in assemblages from British sites but typically as singletons or in small numbers (Willis 2005). A second uncommon form is the Drag. 42 dish from F(426) with handle and barbotine trailing. Part of a small bowl/cup form, of Hadrianic date, was present in F(442).

The average sherd weight of the samian from the cellar fills is 17.7g (182 sherds/3216g). This is a comparatively high figure indicating that the deposit includes comparatively unfragmented items that have not been subject to attritional processes. A comparison with the average sherd weight of the samian from the Inner Enclosure Ditch is signal in this respect (cf. above). The 339 samian sherds from the excavations at Orton's Pasture, Rochester, dating to *c.* AD 70–110, have an average sherd weight of 13.1g (Willis 2000b), the 173 sherds of samian from St Nicholas Street Leicester, 1965–6, Phases 1–4, dated *c.* AD 30–110 have an average weight of 13.2g (Willis in press) and the 380 sherds from Meole Brace 1988–90 dating to *c.* AD 155–240 have an average of 15.2g (Ellis *et al.* 1994). Context and variability in site formation activities are key in this respect, but attention to such details as average sherd weight data can be a pointer to the nature of these processes in specific cases. Ditch fills are generally associated with pottery of particularly low average weight (cf. Martin 2007) so it is not necessarily surprising to see that this is the case with the sample from the Inner Enclosure Ditch.

Four vessels show signs of alteration. A cup from F(498) seems to have had its footring deliberately removed and a Drag. 18/31 dish from F(426) has been trimmed round at the junction of the vessel wall and floor; cases of the latter seem to sometimes relate to the inversion of the vessel to use the footring as a small shallow dish and sometimes a lamp (Willis 2005), whilst other uses are conceivable. A third vessel, from F(426), had been trimmed at the junction of the vessel floor and the footring, but it has been broken across the base with the fracture showing abrasion, so the item may have been being used as an improvised rubber or polisher, potentially of metal surfaces as has been noted elsewhere (Willis 1998b). Finally, a Drag. 33 cup from F(488) had been refashioned to produce a disc. One vessel has been drilled for repair, this being a Drag. 33 from F(417).

THE COARSEWARE POTTERY

Tom Moore

Methodology

Around 4,000 sherds (55kg) of coarse pottery were recovered from the 1984 and 1985 excavations. These have been quantified using rim equivalents (RE), weight and sherd numbers (see graphs). Only the stratified assemblages have been fully quantified by fabric and form.

A new fabric series was established which has been closely correlated to the fabric series established by Stephen Trow (1988b). This was done to enable close comparison between the 1982–3 assemblage and the 1984–5 material and has also been used to quantify the material from Bagendon (1979–1981), which displays a number of similarities in fabrics and forms with the first century AD deposits from Ditches. This allows for quantitative comparison between the two sites in form and fabric, discussion of which can be found in the analysis of material from Bagendon.

The assemblage was divided on the basis of fabric assessed from a fresh break using a binocular microscope. In some areas fabrics represent variants of the same pottery groups and have been combined under the general groups/names below. Where possible, parallels with Trow's earlier fabric types are provided and with major assemblages elsewhere, including Frocester (Timby 2000), Duntisbourne Grove, Middle Duntisbourne, Birdlip Quarry (Timby 1999a), Conderton Camp (Morris 2005), Uley West Hill (Leach 1993) and Cirencester (Rigby 1982). In order to facilitate easy comparison with Trow's report on the 1982–3 excavations the same form types were used with additions added for the 1984–85 assemblage where form parallels could not be discerned in the existing form groups. Form and fabrics were paralleled with large published assemblages from the region in order to provide specific parallels and dates, these included Weston-under-Penyard-Ariconium (Willis 2000a), Bagendon (Clifford 1961), Uley West Hill (Leach 1993), Frocester (Timby 2000), Kingsholm (Darling 1985), early and late Roman Cirencester (Cooper 1998; Rigby 1982), Thornill (Timby 2004) and the Ermin Street sites at Duntisbourne and Birdlip Quarry (Timby 1999a). Comparisons in form and fabric were also made with the National Fabric series (Tomber and Dore 1998) and with Tyers (1996).

Fabrics

Fabrics for the earlier contexts were divided in to the same groups as in Trow (1988b) for comparison between the 1982–3 and 1984–5 excavations. Trow divided the fabrics in to broader groups as follows. The corresponding 1984–5 fabrics have been grouped as close as possible in to these groups:

Group A: handmade, limestone tempered Iron Age tradition pottery (84–5 fabrics: MALV, L1, L2, L3).
Group B: handmade/wheel turned grog tempered wares (84–5 fabrics: GROG1, GROG2, GROG3).
Group C: (84–5 fabric GROGBAG).
Group D: early Severn Valley Wares (84–5 fabrics: SVWO/R).
Group E: Savernake wares (84–5 fabrics: SAV1–6).
Group F: finewares (GROGFW, WW, FWB, including samian, Gaulish imports and amphorae.

Groups A–F match Trow's fabric groups (1988b, 64). Further groups G–M have been added to include fabrics not grouped by Trow and those only present in the later contexts (see below). Because of the predominantly later date of most of these wares, these have not been used to compare with the 1982–3 assemblage. The fabric descriptions below have been grouped together under the major wares.

Forms

In order to compare with the coarse pottery from the 1982–3 report the form types have been grouped in to the same groups outlined by Trow (1988b) with additions to include forms not present in 1982–3 assemblage. These groups are divided as such (see Trow 1988b, 64):

Group 1: Jars in Iron Age tradition forms (JA and JB).
Group 2: bead rimmed vessels (JC).
Group 3: storage jars (JG).
Group 4: wide mouthed and necked bowls (BC and BD) (includes JK; straight necked jars).
Group 5: carinated bowls (BE).
Group 6: platters (DA).
Group 7: beakers (K).

The following additional groups have been added to Trow's groups:

Group 8: Flanged bowls (FB) (found in SVWs, OXCC and BB wares).
Group 9: Tankards (TK).
Group 10: Flagons (FL).
Group 11: Tripod vessel (DC).
Group 12: Samian derived forms (found solely in SVWs) (SD).
Other: includes other forms including bases which do not fit the existing categories above.

Fabric descriptions

Group A: Limestone tempered wares

MALV1: Black-grey with inclusions rarely exceeding 2mm, with burnished surfaces, occasionally decorated with vertical burnished hatching.
Forms: everted rims jars and storage vessels.
Parallels: Trow fabric 1; Timby 1999, MALVL1; Peacock B1; GL TF 33.
Date: Iron Age–first century AD.

MALV2: Dark-grey black (occasionally varying with firing to oxidised reddy light brown areas on interior surfaces, e.g. Fig. 43, no. 156). Inclusions include abundant limestone and occasional organic voids.
Forms: jars with everted rims and storage vessels.
Parallels: Trow fabric 1.
Date: Iron Age–first century AD.

L1: Coarse fabric with frequent inclusions. Inclusions of abundant limestone. A dark-black grey core with orange-brown to black-brown exterior surfaces. Possibly local origin.
Forms: Iron Age form jars and storage vessels.
Parallels: Trow fabric 2?
Date: first century BC–first century AD.

L2: Limestone tempered ware rarely found in both the 1982–3 and 1984–5 excavations, may be of local manufacture.
Forms: uncertain.
Parallel: Trow fabric 3.
Date: Iron Age.

L3: Black fabric with few inclusions, friable and void ridden. The limestone inclusions are generally small and whiter than those in fabrics L1 and 2. Dark grey black but some vessel have yellow/orange brown area and black areas of varying firing. Inclusions of frequent voids (up to 2mm) from organic temper and limestone inclusions (0.1–2mm diameter).
Forms: Iron Age handmade forms, small usually upright jars (see Ashville form B; DeRoche 1978).
Parallels: Trow 3?
Date: Occurrence in association with Savernake wares suggests possibly early first century AD (see below).

Group B: Grog tempered wares

The grog-tempered wares include the finer ware (Trow 1988b: Group C), GROGBAG, and the coarser grog tempered wares (Trow 1988b Group B), fabrics GROG1, GROG2 and GROG3. The finer fabric is dominated by platters, many imitating imported forms and local imitations of Terra Nigra (see above). Fabric GROG2 and GROG3 includes rare examples of flagon, similar to examples from Bagendon (see Fig. 42, no.124).

GROG1: (a) A highly mixed, dark blue-grey fabric with a range of inclusions, usually orange interior and black burnished exterior (except in (b) cases). Exterior surfaces are varied between orangey-brown and patches of black-brown reduction indicating varied firing.
Forms: appears in jar/beaker and platter forms. A platter from F(510) can be paralleled at Middle Duntisbourne (Timby 1999a, no. 91) . One straight sided vessel is decorated with lattice decoration and horizontal ribs (Fig. 42, no. 129).
Parallels: Trow fabric 7; Uley fabric 2.
Date: early–mid first century AD.

GROG2: slight soapy textured fabric with frequent grog inclusions and occasional organic voids. Surfaces are usually smoothed. Most have a grey-brown core with reddish brown margins (a) some oxidised to a red-brown (b).
Forms: found in Hofheim flagons, bowls and carinated jars.
Parallels: Trow fabric 6, Cirencester fabric 3 and 24.
Date: first century AD.

GROG3: (a): Dark grey-black fabric. Gritty, hard sandy fabric with common white mica. Exterior brown-grey burnished/ cc exterior, (b): grey core fabric with orange-brown exterior. Inclusions include abundant grog with occasional quartz. Brown-red coated exterior, patchy.
Forms: platters.
Parallels: Trow fabric 9.
Date: Forms can be paralleled at Bagendon, mid first century AD.

GROG4: Occurs in Iron Age forms but reflect the broader pattern of this group.
Forms: Forms occur in the Iron Age forms similar to MALV.
Parallels: Trow fabric 6.
Date: first century AD.

GROG5: Rare, brown fabric with frequent grog inclusions.
Forms: everted rim jar (Fig. 36, no.21).
Parallels: Trow fabric 21.
Date: first century AD.

Group C: 'Bagendon Black' grog tempered ware

GROGBAG: A fine grained moderately hard black-grey fabric with rare grog inclusions. Exterior surfaces on reduced versions (a) are dark grey-black to brown in places with orange-brown margins. Some (rarer) examples are oxidised to an orange-red (b). Known as Bagendon Black it occurs in relatively large quantities at Bagendon (Clifford 1961) and was noted at Cirencester. Locally made.
Forms: found in platters and bowls which can be paralleled at Bagendon.
Parallels: Trow fabric 8; Cirencester fabric 8.
Date: early–mid first century AD.

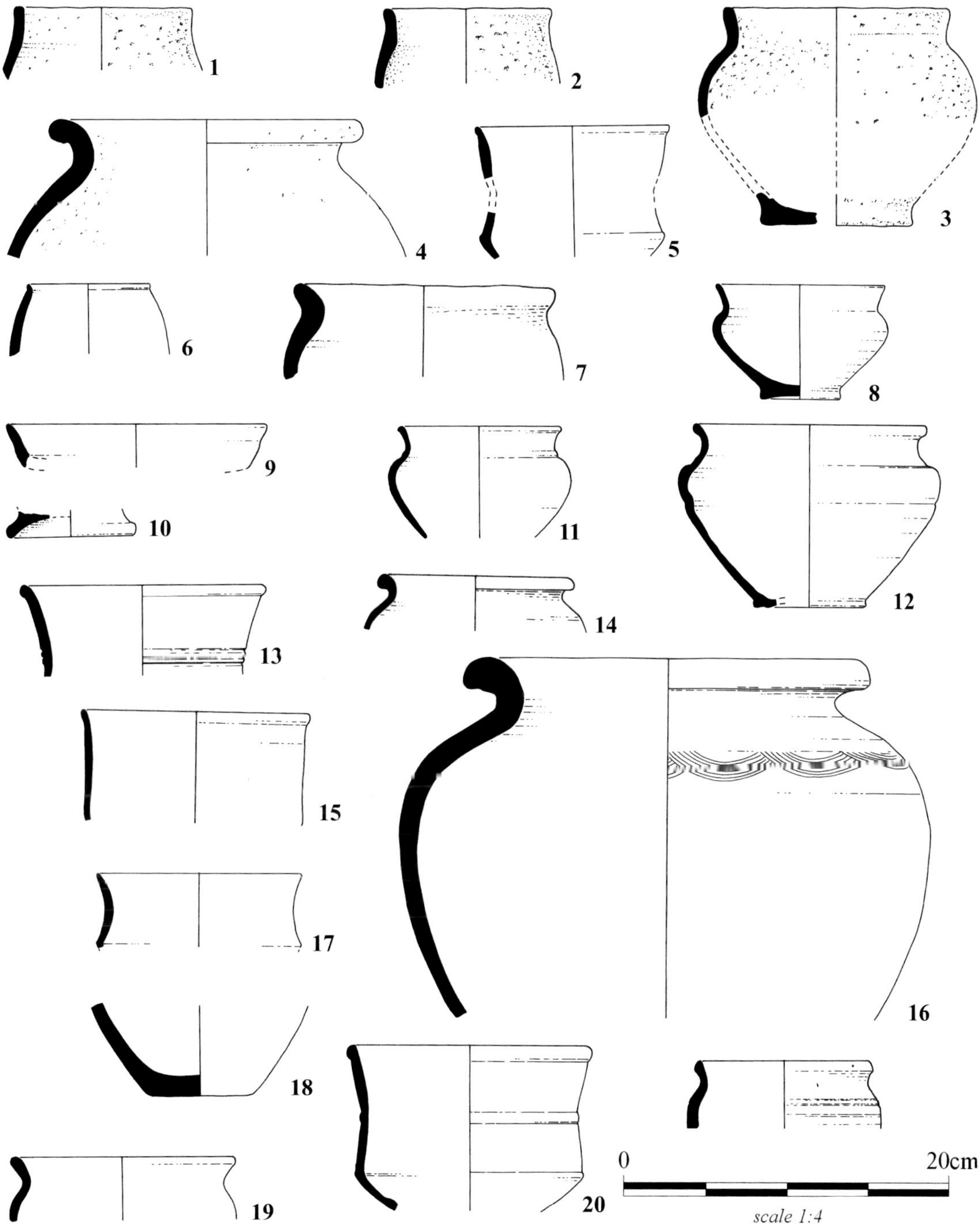

Fig. 36. Coarse pottery.

Group D: Severn Valley wares

Oxidized Severn Valley Wares

SVWO(E)1: Red-orange fabric, occasionally with grey core (see Webster 1976, Timby 1990 for more detailed discussion).

SVWO(E)2: Variant of SVWO(E) with smoothed red-brown burnishing on exterior surfaces.

SVWO(L)1: Finer variant of SVWO fabric with fewer inclusions. The exterior of vessels are usually burnished to a smooth orange-cream finish.

Unoxidized Severn Valley Ware

SVWR(E)1: Unoxidized fabrics in SVW forms.

SVWR(E)2: Variant of SVWR, light blue grey core with reduced dark grey margins.

SVWR(L)1: Blue grey core with frequent inclusions of dark grey grog and charcoal. Occasional small fleck of limestone and occasional organic voids.

Parallels: Trow fabric 13, 14, 45; Cirencester 1–4 (early Severn Valley wares) 106–9 (late Severn Valley Wares) Frocester (Timby 2000) TF24; Uley (Leach 1993) fabric 7, 10, 11. Willis (2000a) O10-O24; SVWO (Timby 1999a).

Forms: Severn valley wares are found in a range of forms. As discussed by Willis (2000a), there is some variation between the form types in different fabric groups within Severn Valley Ware. The early Severn Valley ware fabrics are dominated by the carinated bowls (Group 5) and wide mouthed/necked bowls (Group 4) with limited amounts also found in flagons, tankards and storage jars. The dominance of flange bowls, samian derivatives and tankards, which can all be broadly dated to the second–third century AD (Webster 1976), in fabric SVWO(L), emphasises the apparently generally later date of this fabric. Some storage jar forms and bowl forms can be found in both early and late contexts. Whilst Willis (2000a) gives a date range of between AD100–300 for these forms it may be possible to date these slightly earlier on the basis of some finds from Ditches.

Date: The date of Severn Valley wares has been the topic of considerable debate (Timby 1990; 1999a, b; Webster 1976; Willis 2000a) with some suggestion they emerge prior to the conquest. The dating of Ditches does not allow this possibility to be refined although it is clear they occur in contexts which date to around AD 45–50 and occur in association with later Iron Age forms and fabrics. The earlier date for SVWO(E) fabrics is emphasised by the forms they occur including carinated cups (BE4), a first century AD form which was replaced by the later tankards of the second century AD (see Webster 1976). These fabrics still occur in later contexts, although in most cases are likely to be residual. Both the forms and contexts in which fabric SVWO(L) occurs suggests a broad chronological distinction between these fabrics.

Group E: Savernake wares

SAV1: Light yellow-grey illsorted fabric with abundant inclusions of quartz, grog and rare charcoal. Exterior surfaces vary but are often dark blue-grey with interior surfaces light grey. The variation in this fabric may reflect the varied sources known. SAV2: Blue grey fabric with frequent (black and red) grog inclusions (less than 1mm), occasional quartz and limestone inclusions, frequent voids. Exterior surfaces are blue-grey. SAV3: Possibly a Savernake type (quartz inclusions). SAV4: A dark grey variant with higher inclusions of grog temper. SAV5: Grey core. Abundant grog (red and black) inclusions and frequent limestone inclusions. Black coated exterior.

Parallels: Trow fabric 11, Cirencester fabric 6; Gloucester fabric 6.

Forms: Found in bead rim and storage jar forms (see Swan 1975).

Date: There has been considerable debate over the date of the Oare and Savernake wares, some seeing a purely post-conquest date (Swan 1975), others an inception prior to the conquest. The Ditches material does not lend any conclusion to the debate but further emphasises the high proportion of this material in assemblages of mid–late first century AD date. Judging by the lack of material in later contexts (apart from residual sherds) these wares appear to have been largely replaced by the North Wiltshire Greywares (see below) in the second century AD (cf. Cooper 1998, 332; Tyers 1996, 195).

Group G: North Wiltshire wares

Whitehill Farm wares

NWWH: Light grey, sandy hard textured fabric with few inclusions, occasional grey grog. Interior and exterior surfaces are sometimes blue-grey with blue grey margins.

Forms: Found in forms from Whitehill Farm, North Wiltshire (see Anderson 1979). Many of the forms, particularly the dishes and bowls imitate Black Burnish forms whilst some of the wide mouthed bowls have affinity with some Severn Valley forms.

Parallels: Trow fabric 34; Anderson (1979); Timby (2001, R13&R11?); Cirencester fabric 98.

Date: Whitehill Farm wares appear to replace the Savernake wares in the early second century AD continuing to be produced in to the third century AD (Anderson 1979). Cirencester sees a peak in the consumption of these wares from *c.* AD 150 onwards (Cooper 1998, 341).

North Wiltshire greywares

NWG1: Coarse, sandy grey-brown fabric, rare inclusions. Exterior margins are darker-grey with brown-grey surfaces. Interior surfaces have frequent white colour coat (?) surfaces. Possibly an imitation of Dorset Black Burnish from N. Wiltshire.

Forms: Bowls in imitations of Dorset Black Burnish forms, similar to those indicated by Anderson (1979) for the Whitehill Farm wares.

Parallels: Trow fabric 12?

Date: Anderson (1979) gives dates in the second century AD for most of the similar forms to those found at Ditches although dates in to the third century AD are possible.

NWG2: Hard, gritty, even textured sandy grey ware with light blue-grey core and light grey exterior and interior. Inclusions of occasional charcoal and uncommon dark grey and orange grog. Rare examples are oxidised to an orange buff on interior and exterior. This grey ware may have a North Wiltshire origin.

Forms: see above.

Parallels: Trow fabric 16.

Date: first–third century AD.

NWG3: hard fired, light grey-beige fabric with grey colour-coat exterior? Found in forms similar to North Wiltshire (Anderson 1979).

Forms: see above.

Parallels: Trow fabric 75.

Date: second–third century AD.

Group H: Dorset Black Burnished wares

DORBB1: Dorset Black Burnished ware 1 (see Tyers 1996 for description). Dorset Black Burnish ware makes up 13% of the overall assemblage from the site, greater when only later contexts are included, which corresponds well with nearby sites such as Frocester (Timby 2000).

Forms: flange bowls and dishes typical of second–third century AD (Holbrook and Bidwell 1991; Tyers 1996).

Parallels: Trow fabric 32, Cirencester fabric 74, Gloucester TF4.

Date: late first–fourth century AD.

Group I: Oxfordshire Colour Coat wares

OXCC: Oxford red colour coat. A fine buff-orange fabric with occasional remnants of red colour coat on exterior and interior.

Forms: third–fourth century AD forms.

Parallels: Young (1977).

Date: Young (1977) indicates second–fourth century AD.

OXWC: Oxford white colour coat ware. A coarse, orange-brown fabric with white-cream colour coat exterior and interior. Found in a thin walled vessel. Only three sherds of this fabric were recovered,

representing sherds from one vessel in F(426).
Parallels: Young (1977, 93); Ariconium (Willis 2000a) fabric 30–31?; Trow fabric 40.
Date: Young (1977), third century AD; Willis (2000a), second–fourth century AD.

South West White Slipped ware

SWS: Cream-white slip with grey core and orange margins.
Forms: Flagons (Fig. 39, no.74).
Parallels: Cirencester fabric 95; Gloucester TF15; Frocester TF34; SOWWS (Timby 1999a).
Date: late second–third century AD.

Group J: Fine Oxidised Fabrics

OXS1: Orange-cream fabric, hard sandy texture with few inclusions. Occasional red grog inclusions and flecks of charcoal. In some examples has a grey core with oxidised surfaces.
Forms: Found in Tankard forms similar to those seen in SVWs (Webster 1976), also some flagon examples.
Parallels: Trow fabric 42.
Date: second century AD?

OXS2/ABING: Orange-buff fabric with frequent sand inclusions, gritty texture. Occasional grog inclusion, dark grey and red grog inclusions. Usually reduced with light grey exterior and interior surfaces. Considered to have a source in Abingdon area.
Forms: Beakers.
Parallels: Trow fabric 23.
Date: first century AD.

OXS3: Mid buff-grey core with orange-buff-brown interior and exterior surfaces. Hard, gritty texture with occasional inclusions of ?quartz and very occasional charcoal flecks. Surface has faint traces of barbotine decoration around middle of vessel 58.
Forms: beakers.
Parallels: Trow fabric 35.
Date: second century AD.

OXS4: Rare, hard, flaky, gritty fabric well fired grey core with orange margins. Slightly micaeous with inclusions of grey and orange grog (up to 0.2mm) and uncommon grey pellets. The exterior surface has a dark brown slip.
Parallel: Trow fabric 21.
Date: first century AD.

Central Gaulish Colour Coat

CGCC: Orange-red fabric with red-brown colour exterior (in some cases grey interior). Sand hard texture. The exterior surface has barbotine decoration. Rough-cast beakers in Central Gaulish forms, may be copies from North Wiltshire (Wanborough) see Anderson (1979, 1981), Greene (1973) and Cooper (1998).
Forms: found in roughcast beakers.
Parallels: Cirencester Fabric 141; Trow fabric 36/37.
Date: early–mid second century AD.

North Wiltshire Colour Coat

NWCC: Orange-red fabric with grey core. Sandy hard texture. An imitation of Gaulish vessels made in North Wiltshire (Wanborough) see Anderson (1979, 1981), Greene (1973) and Cooper (1998). Fabric hard to distinguish from the Gaulish originals.
Forms: found in roughcast beakers.
Parallels: Cirencester Fabric 85.
Date: parallels in Cirencester date to AD150–170.

Group L: Local Black Burnished wares

Sandy black burnished wares

MICBB: A hard fired sandy abrasive fabric. Usually dark grey black exterior surface and black-brown core. Burnished with often sandy-abrasive texture on interior surfaces. Timby (2000) suggests a north Wiltshire origin.
Forms: jars in early forms, later in Black Burnish imitations
Parallels: Trow fabric 10; Frocester Fabric 32; Uley fabric 4; Cirencester fabric 5.
Date: At Frocester dated to between mid first century AD–second century AD (Timby 2000, 135) and elsewhere

regarded as predominantly later first century AD (Leech 1993, 224). Imitation of Dorset Black Burnish forms suggests it continues in to the second century AD.

Black burnish reduced sandy ware

MICSW1: Orange-yellow sandy fabric with occasional white inclusions and very occasional red grog inclusions (up to 1mm diam). Exterior surfaces are burnished black with a light-grey mottled interior surface.
Forms: Whitehill and Black Burnish imitations.
Parallels: uncertain.
Date: second–third century AD.

MICSW2: Orange-yellow hard, smooth fabric with few inclusions, including frequent mica. Exterior surfaces are hard burnished grey-black surfaces with mica visible.
Forms: Whitehill and Black Burnish imitations.
Parallels: Trow fabric 27 and 29?
Date: later first–second century AD.

MICSW3: Coarse orange sandy fabric with grey exterior.
Forms: Whitehill and Black Burnish imitations.
Parallels: Trow fabric 17; 30.
Date: first–second century AD.

Group K: Local Greywares

GW1: Coarse black-grey grey fabric. The interior surface is a lighter-beige grey with an interior varying between mid-blue grey and lighter areas. Sandy inclusions are abundant together with grog, flecks of charcoal. A source in North Wiltshire is possible although the fabric has close parallels to Black Burnish ware and the form of vessel (Fig. 43, no.151) is close to Savernake forms.
Forms: bead rimmed jars (found in Savernake wares) and in later contexts Black Burnish style forms (Fig. 37, no. 40).
Parallels: Trow fabric 12.
Date: first–third century AD.

GW2: Coarse, ill sorted grey fabric, dark grey core with light grey margins and surfaces. Occasional dark grey grog and rare orange grog (less 0.2mm). Some examples have wiped dark grey slip.
Forms: found in imitations of Dorset Black Burnish wares and bowls.
Parallels: Trow fabric 38.
Date: second–third century AD?

GW3: Beige-grey fabric with grey (colour coat) exterior and interior. Inclusions include quartz, grey grog (<1mm) and small red grog. The fabric has some similarities with Savernake wares but is finer. This fabric is rare; probable source in North Wiltshire.
Forms: Storage jars and bead rimmed (Savernake) forms.
Parallels: Trow fabric 12.
Date: first–second century AD.

GW4: Mid-grey micaeous greyware.
Forms: storage jars and imitations of Black Burnish North Wiltshire forms.
Parallels: uncertain.
Date: second–fourth century AD.

GW5: Soft, sandy beige-yellow fabric with light-grey micaeous exterior.
Forms: imitations of Dorset Black Burnish vessels; possible North Wilts origin?
Parallels: Trow fabric 74.
Date: second–fourth century AD.

GW6: Dark grey fabric, with mica inclusions. Very rare, similar forms to Sandy Black Burnish wares.
Forms: storage jars and imitations of Black Burnish.
Parallels: Trow fabric 73.
Date: second–fourth century AD.

Group M: Miscellaneous

Mancetter Hartshill white ware (Mortaria)

MAHWH: Fine cream-white hard fabric with inclusions of quartz (see Tomber and Dore 1998); very rare.
Forms: Mortaria.
Parallels: Tyers (1996, 123); Tomber and Dore (1998, MAHWH).
Date: second–third century AD.

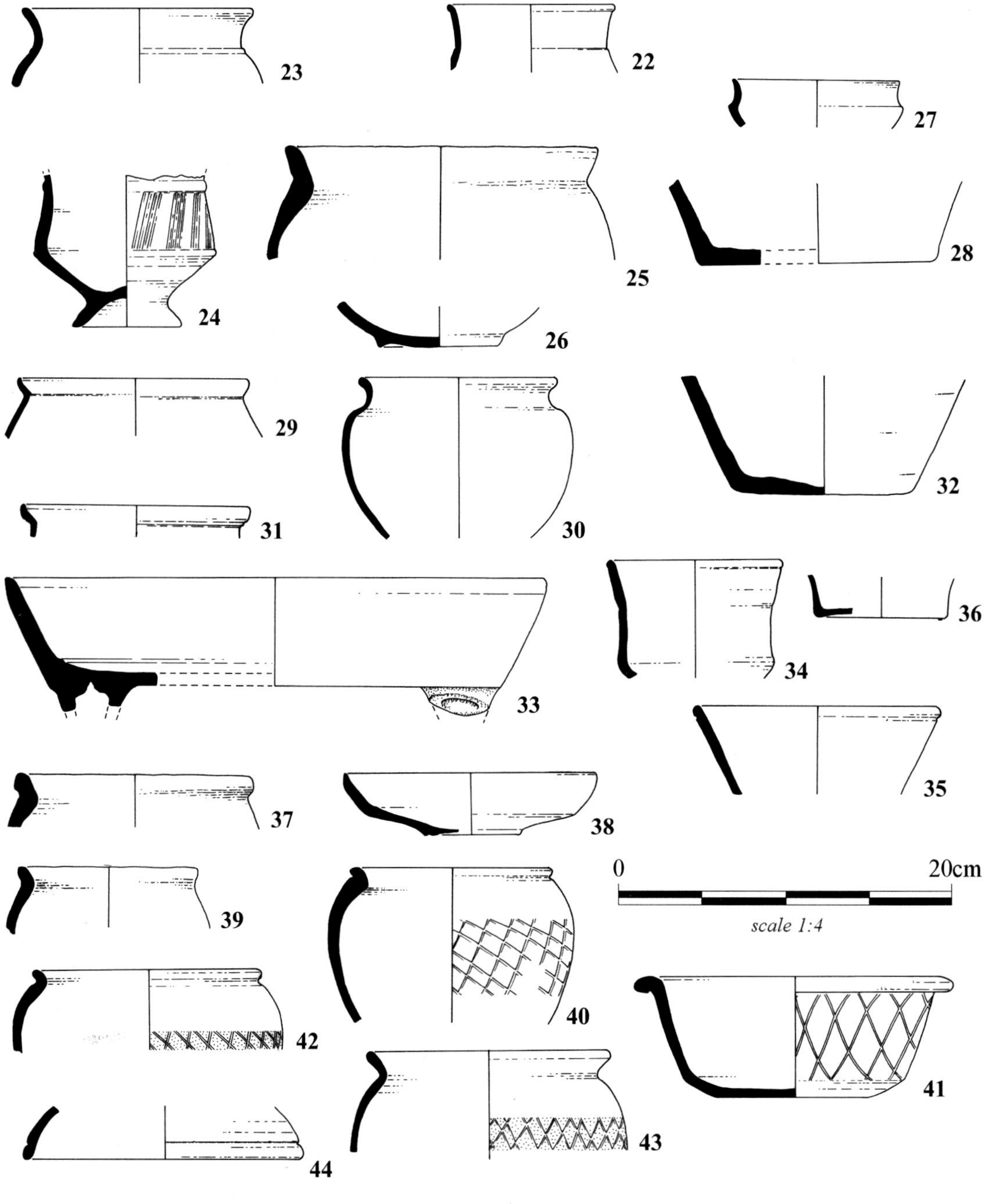

Fig. 37. Coarse pottery.

South Midlands Shell tempered ware

SH1: A hard black-brown fabric with abundant large shell inclusions (see Tomber and Dore 1998). This fabric is found in only a handful of vessels in later contexts.
Forms: The form of the single definable vessel (Fig. 39, no. 80) can be paralleled elsewhere (Tyers 1996, 192).
Parallels: Tyers (1996, 192), Tomber and Dore (1998, ROBSH).
Date: Dated from third–fourth century AD (Tyers 1996, 193); found occasionally in Cirencester in fourth century AD contexts (Cooper 1998). Its presence in F(426) and F(480) appears to confirm the late date of the latter deposit. Chronology of this fabric beyond its core area is usually defined at AD 300–400 although a somewhat earlier date is possible.

Local Shell Tempered ware

SH2: Hard, coarse shell tempered fabric distinct from SH1. Possibly comparable to local shelly fabrics, noted in Oxfordshire and Worcestershire.
Forms: unknown.
Parallels: ?ROMSH (McSloy 2006).
Date: first–third century AD, possibly with origins in the late Iron Age.

Group F: Finewares

North Gaulish White ware

NOGWH: blue-grey core with white oxidised exterior, imported from Northern Gaul (Tomber and Dore 1998, 22).
Forms: Found in flagons and beakers.
Parallels: Trow fabric 48; NOG WH (Tomber and Dore 1998, 22).
Date: first century AD.

GROGFW: (a) Dark grey core with oxidised red-orange exterior and grey-beige reduced interior. Tempered with occasional fossil limestone. (b) with cream exterior and interior surfaces. Found in fineware forms, similarities with GROG5. Local fabric?
Forms: present in beakers.
Parallels: Trow fabric 24.
Date: mid-first century AD.

FWS: Creamy-white sandy fine fabric
Forms: Flagons and beakers.
Parallel: Trow fabric 28.
Date: mid-first century AD.

FWB: pale-buff fineware fabric, poss imported.
Forms: found in beaker and flagon forms.
Parallels: FWBUFF (Timby 1999a, 324).
Date: first century AD.

FWW: White fineware; uncertain type source.
Forms: parallels in Cirencester (Rigby 1982).
Parallels: uncertain.
Date: first century AD.

FWBG: pale grey-buff fabric, rare. Local origin?
Forms: Hofheim flagon forms.
Parallels: uncertain.
Date: first century AD.

FWOXID: hard fired, fine sandy oxidised orange fabric
Forms: beakers.
Parallels: FWOX (Timby 1999a, 324).
Date: first century AD.

WW: white-grey hard fired fabric with occasional red inclusions, found in fineware forms, including Cam. Forms 113 and 114 and flagons.
Forms: Butt beakers and flagons (see Fig 43, 154).
Parallels: ?Frocester TF22 (Timby 2000, 132).
Date: early/mid-first century AD.

WSOXID: blue-grey hard fine fabric oxidised to buff.
Forms: Flagons.
Parallels: uncertain.
Date: second century AD?

GABTN: Gallo-Belgic Terra Nigra (see Tomber and Dore 1998, 15–16)

GABTR: Gallo-Belgic Terra Rubra (see Tomber and Dore 1998, 17–19)

GABWH: Gallo-Belgic White ware (see Tomber and Dore 1998, 22–24)

Fabric	No. of Sherds	RE	Weight (g)
ABING/OXS2	13	0.225	45
AMPH	1		115
DORBB1	4		40
FWB	16		56
FWS	33	0.15	100
GROG1	12	0.47	288
GROG2	24	0.51	305
GROG3	8	0.76	126
GROG4	4		143
GROG5	5	0.05	41
GROGBAG?	53	1.815	505
GW1	3	0.65	149
GW2	1	0.07	72
GW4	3		39
L1	46	1.07	603
L2	9		44
MALV1	9	0.66	355
MALV2	83	0.63	892
MICBB	28	0.42	311
MICGW	15	0.22	74
MICSW1	1		5
MICSW3	2		3
NWG1	18		805
NWG2	2		18
OXS2	1		18
SAV1	27	0.3	1266
SAV2	39	1.57	4567
SAV4	1	0.05	17
SAV5	2	0.1	39
SAV6	1		12
SH2	5	0.05	45
SVWO(E)1	55	2.24	983
SVWO(E)2	89	2.34	973
SVWR(E)1	15	0.26	160
SVWR(L)1	4		53

Table 7. Fabrics in ceramic group A.

Discussion of key groups and catalogue of illustrated sherds

Ceramic group A

Backfilling of the Inner Enclosure ditch (Trench E, Phase 4)

Contexts E(338), E(320), E(319), E(340), E(336/337) (Table 7)

This material derives from the infilling of the enclosure ditch. This overlays the initial silting of the ditch which, despite the relative size of the contexts, were sterile of pottery. This fact may point to the earlier date of these contexts resulting in the lack of 'Romanized' mid-first century AD material.

Finewares in group A include Dr. 20 amphorae, Camulodunum forms in Abingdon and local fabrics (Rigby above) and samian (Willis above), all of which imply a Claudian-Neronian date. The continuity of many Malvern ware 'Iron Age' forms after the Roman conquest has now been widely recognised, at Frocester (Timby 2000) and the Duntisbourne sites (Timby 1999a), with Willis (2000a) suggesting some forms such as JB4 (Fig. 37, no. 39) date from the first century BC to as late as AD 75. Similar examples at Middle Duntisbourne derive from early–mid first century AD contexts. The prevalence of forms such as JB4[.2] at Ditches and Bagendon, but apparent lack of similar forms at Conderton (Morris 2005), which has been suggested as abandoned in the second century BC, reinforces the impression that such types may date no earlier than the first century BC–first century AD. The bead rimmed vessels in Limestone fabrics (Fig. 41, no. 121), apparently a local product, can be paralleled at Frocester and Preston (Timby 1999a; 2000) deriving from middle–late Iron Age contexts, although again they may have continued in use in to the later first century AD (Timby 2000, 127). These contexts also have a large component of Savernake wares, particularly the large storage vessel which were found in abundance at Bagendon (Clifford 1961, 266–7). Swan's (1975) dating of similar material had suggested a date between the conquest and AD 70s although, in similar fashion to the Severn Valley wares, the evidence from some sites could suggest a pre-conquest origin. The large number of necked bowls (Fig. 36, no. 11) and carinated beakers (Fig. 36, no. 13, 19, 26) in early Severn Valley ware fabrics, are likely to date no later than the first century AD (Timby 1990), although they could date to before the conquest. Bowls in the grog fabrics (Fig. 41, no. 122) can be paralleled at Bagendon and Cirencester dating earlier than the AD 60s. Finewares, mostly in local fabrics, occur in pre-Flavian Camulodunum forms (see Rigby above). The overall impression from the 1984 excavations supports the earlier suggestion that the Inner Enclosure Ditch was infilled in the mid–first century AD, between *c.* AD 45–55 (Trow 1988a, 37), the lack of early second century AD material in the upper fills implying that the ditch was completely backfilled by the end of the first century AD.

Fig. 36, 11 [15] BD3[.2], SVWO(E)2, E(338), parallels (Timby 1990, no. 57); Date: mid–late first century AD.

Fig. 36, 12 [16] BD2[.3], MICBB, E(338), parallels Frocester (Timby 2000, no. 142, 135 in same fabric), Cirencester (Rigby 1982, no. 209), Thornhill (Timby 2004, no. 51), Date: late first–early second century AD.

Fig. 36, 13 [17] BE4[.3], SVWO(E)1, E(338), parallels Ditches 1982–3 (Trow 1988, no. 119, 70), (Timby 1990, no. 43); Date: mid first century AD.

Fig. 36, 14 [18] JC N1, GROG1, E(319), parallels early Cirencester (Rigby 1982, no. 361, 242); Date: first century AD

Fig. 36, 15 [19] BE, SVWO(E)1, E(319), parallels (Timby 1990, no. 42); Date: mid–late first century AD.

Fig. 36, 16 [20] JG2 N1, SAV1, E(320), parallels Ditches 1982–3 (Trow 1988b, no. 126), Bagendon Form 173; Date: mid–late first century AD.

Fig. 36, 17 [21] BE5, MICBB, E(320), parallels Ditches 82–3 (Trow 1988b, no. 121), Bagendon Form 99; Date: mid first century AD?

Fig. 36, 18 [22] base form A, MALV1, E(320); Date: late Iron Age–first century AD

Fig. 36, 19 [25] BC3, GROG1, E(320); Date: first century AD

Fig. 36, 20 [26] BE4[.3], SVWO(E)2, E(320), parallels Kingsholm (Timby 1990, no. 43); Date: first century AD.

Fig. 36, 21 [27] JB7[.2], GROG5, E(320); Date: first century AD

Fig. 37, 22 [28] BE4[.5], GROG2, E(320), parallels Timby (1990, no. 47); Date: mid–late first century AD

Fig. 37, 23 [29] BC3[.3], SVWO(E)1, E(320), parallels Frocester (Timby 2000, no. 114); Date: first century AD.

Fig. 37, 24 [30] BE4[.3], SVWO(E)1, E(320), parallels Frocester (Timby 2000, no. 167, 166); Date: first century AD.

Fig. 37, 25 [31] JB5[.2], MALV2, E(320), parallels Frocester (Timby 2000, no. 39); Date: late Iron Age–mid first century AD

Fig. 37, 26 [32] base form P, SVWO(E)2, E(320), parallels Duntisbourne Grove (Timby 1999a, no. 111); Date: mid first century AD

Fig. 37, 27 [33] BE2[.2], GROGBAG, E(320), parallels Bagendon form 100; Date: mid first century AD.

Fig. 37, 28 [34] base form N12, GROG4, E(320); Date: late Iron Age–mid first century AD.

Fig. 37, 29 [35] KB3[.3], FWW, E(320), parallels Early Cirencester (Rigby 1982, no. 188 in same fabric), Bagendon Form 62 (Clifford 1961, fig. 50, no. 12, 16), Oare (Swan 1975, no. 55); Date: early–mid first century AD

Fig. 37, 30 [36] BC2, GROG3, E(320); Date: mid–late first century AD.

Fig. 37, 31 [37] KB2[.1], FWW, E(320), parallels Bagendon Form 62a; Ariconium (Willis 2000a, fig. 19, no. 5); Date: early–mid first century AD.

Fig. 37, 32 [38] base N11, NWG1, E(320); mid–late first century AD.

Fig. 43, 154 [39] rim, FL, WW, E(320)

Fig. 37, 33 [40] DC1[.5], SVWO(E)2, E(320); Date: late first century AD.

Fig. 37, 34 [41] BE4[.5], SVWO(E)1, E(320), parallels Frocester (Timby 2000, no. 165), Timby (1990, no. 43); Date: mid first century AD.

Fig. 37, 35 [42] BE4, SVWR(E)1, E(320), parallels Frocester (Timby 2000, no. 167); Date: first–early second century AD.

Fig. 37, 36 [43] base tankard, SVWO(E)1, E(320); Date: first–second century AD?

Fig. 37, 37 [44] JB6[.1], MALV1, E(320), parallels Duntisbourne Grove (Timby 1999a, no. 110?); Date: first century AD.

Fig. 37, 38 [45] DA1[.3], GROGBAG, E(320), parallels Bagendon Form 12; Date: mid first century AD?

Fig. 37, 39 [46] JB4 N1, MALV2, E(320), parallels Duntisbourne Grove (Timby 1999a, 109), Frocester (Timby 2000; no. 95), Ariconium (Willis 2000a, fig. 13, no. 7); Date: late Iron Age–mid first century AD.

Fig. 41, 109 [139] base form R, GROG1, E(340), parallels Ditches 82–3 (Trow 1988b, no. 76); Date: mid first century AD.

Fig. 41, 110 [140] BDN2, MICBB, E(340), parallels Cirencester (Rigby 1982, 378), Thornhill (Timby 2004, no. 51); Date: late first century AD.

Fig. 41, 112 [142] BC3[.2], SVWO(E)1, E(340), parallels Webster (1976, no. 20), Ariconium (Willis 2000a, fig. 19, no. 11); Date: first–second century AD.

Fig. 41, 114 [145] JG N8.1, SAV1, E(340), parallels Bagendon Form 175, Oare (Swan 1975, no. 52), middle Duntisbourne (Timby 1999, no. 87); Date: mid first century AD.

Fig. 41, 115 [146] DA3 N1, GROGBAG, E(318), Ditches 1982–3 (Trow 1988b, no.108), Bagendon Form 17. Cirencester (Rigby 1982, no. 89) Date: mid first century AD.

Fig. 41, 118 [149] BC4 N, GROGBAG, E(340), parallels Ditches 1982–3 (Trow 1988b, no. 29), Bagendon Form 117; Date: first century AD.

Fig. 41, 119 [152] D, GROG1, E(337); Date: first century AD

Fig. 41, 120 [153] JC3[.6], GW1, E(336), parallels Cirencester (Rigby 1982, no. 132), Frocester (Timby 2000, no. 125), Bagendon Form 151 (Fig. 54, 11), Oare (Swan 1975, no. 33); Date: first century AD

Fig. 41, 121 [156] JB3 N1, MALV2, E(336); parallels Frocester (Timby 2000, no. 90); Date: late Iron Age–first century AD.

Fig. 42, 122 [157] BC3 N2, GROGBAG, E(339), parallels Bagendon Form 116d, Cirencester (Rigby 1982, 430); Date: mid first century AD–pre AD60s.

Fig. 41, 123 [158] JB3 N3, L1, E(340); Frocester (Timby 2000, no. 54), Duntisbourne Grove (Timby 1999a, no. 110); Date: first century BC–first century AD.

Fig. 42, 142 [151] JC3[.5], GW1, E(336), parallels Uley West-Hill (Leach 1993, no. 57), Bagendon Form 146–147, Thornhill (Timby 2004, no.80); Date: mid–late first century AD.

Fig. 43, 143 [143] BE2[.2], GROGBAG, E(340), parallels Bagendon Form 100a; Date: first century AD.

Fig. 43, 147 [47] KB1[.2], OXS, E(320).

Ceramic group B

Quarry pit backfilling (Trench E, phase 6)

Contexts: B1 E(310); B2 E(273), E(261), E(281), E(285), E(286), E(287), E(299), E(253/284/262); B3 Cobbled surface E(252) (Table 8)

Silt layer E(310) lies directly on the eastern side of the Quarry pit, apparently deriving from E(320), the Inner Enclosure Ditch, and includes small numbers of similar wares. The other contexts represent the infilling of the Quarry pit, apparently marking a series of dumps of material and have been treated here as a coherent group, as they were by the excavators. This group includes a range of similar fabrics and forms to those in the Inner Enclosure Ditch (ceramic group A). These contexts include similar, necked bowls in early Severn Valley wares (Fig. 40, no. 94), whilst grog tempered vessels

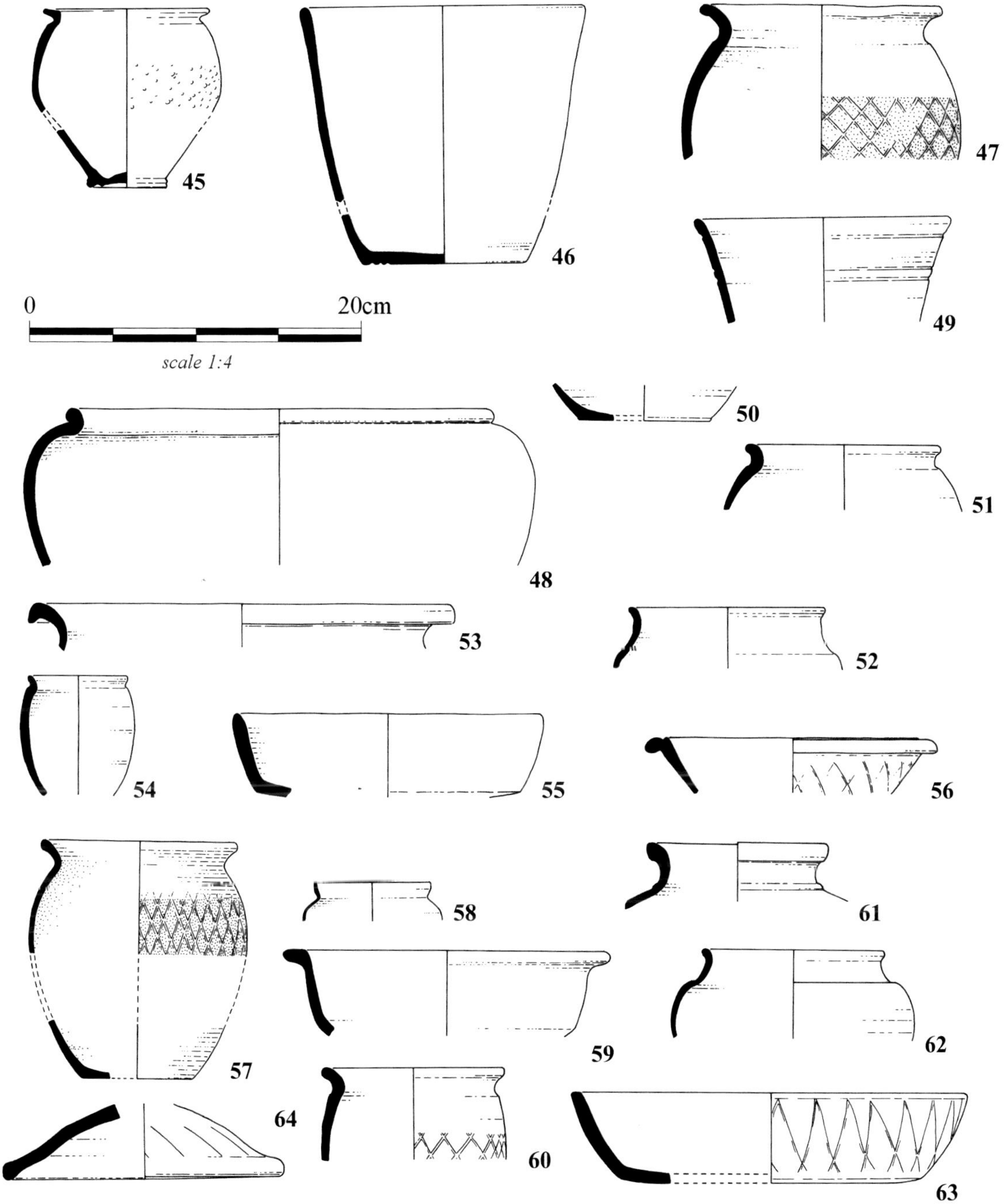

Fig. 38. Coarse pottery.

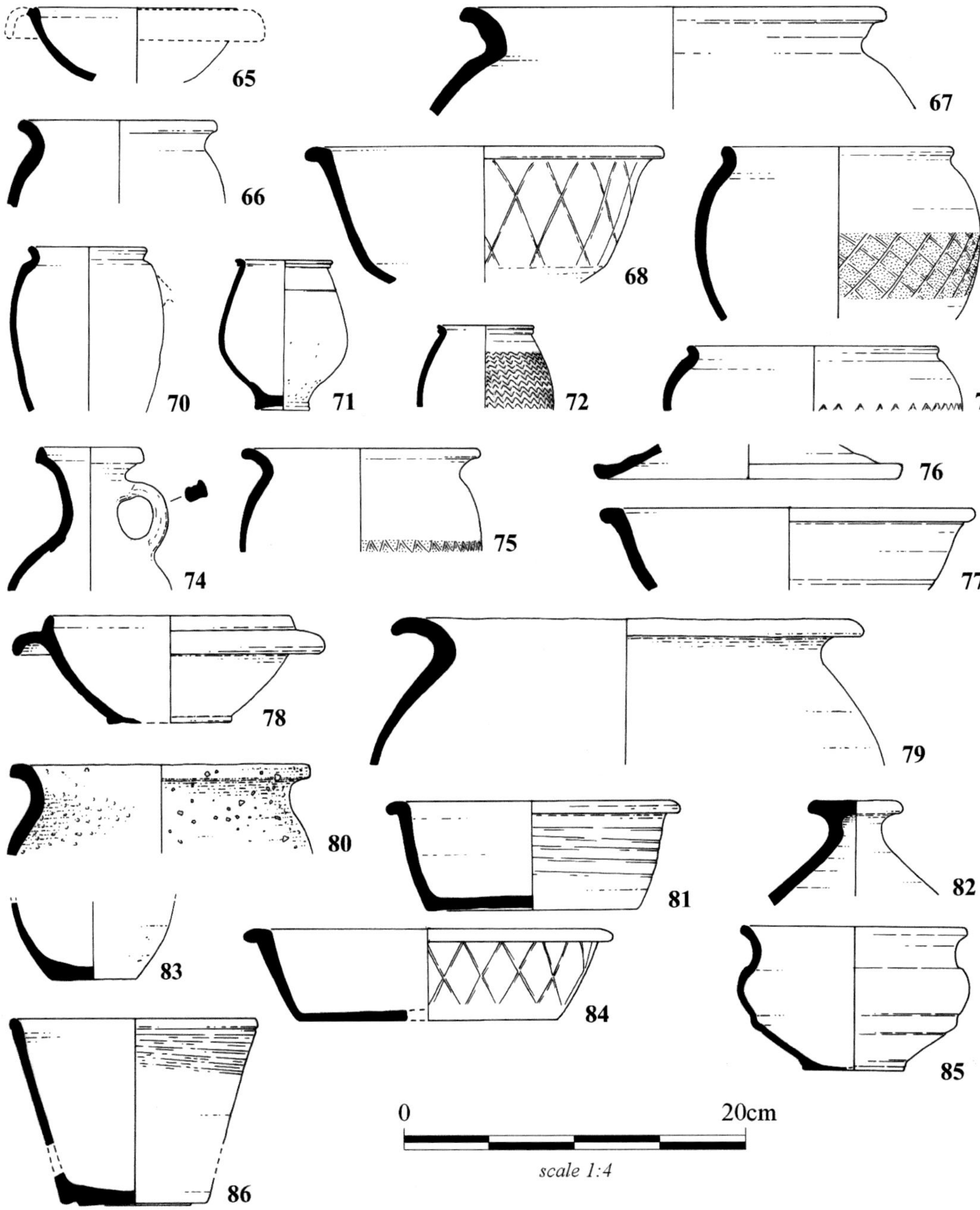

Fig. 39. Coarse pottery.

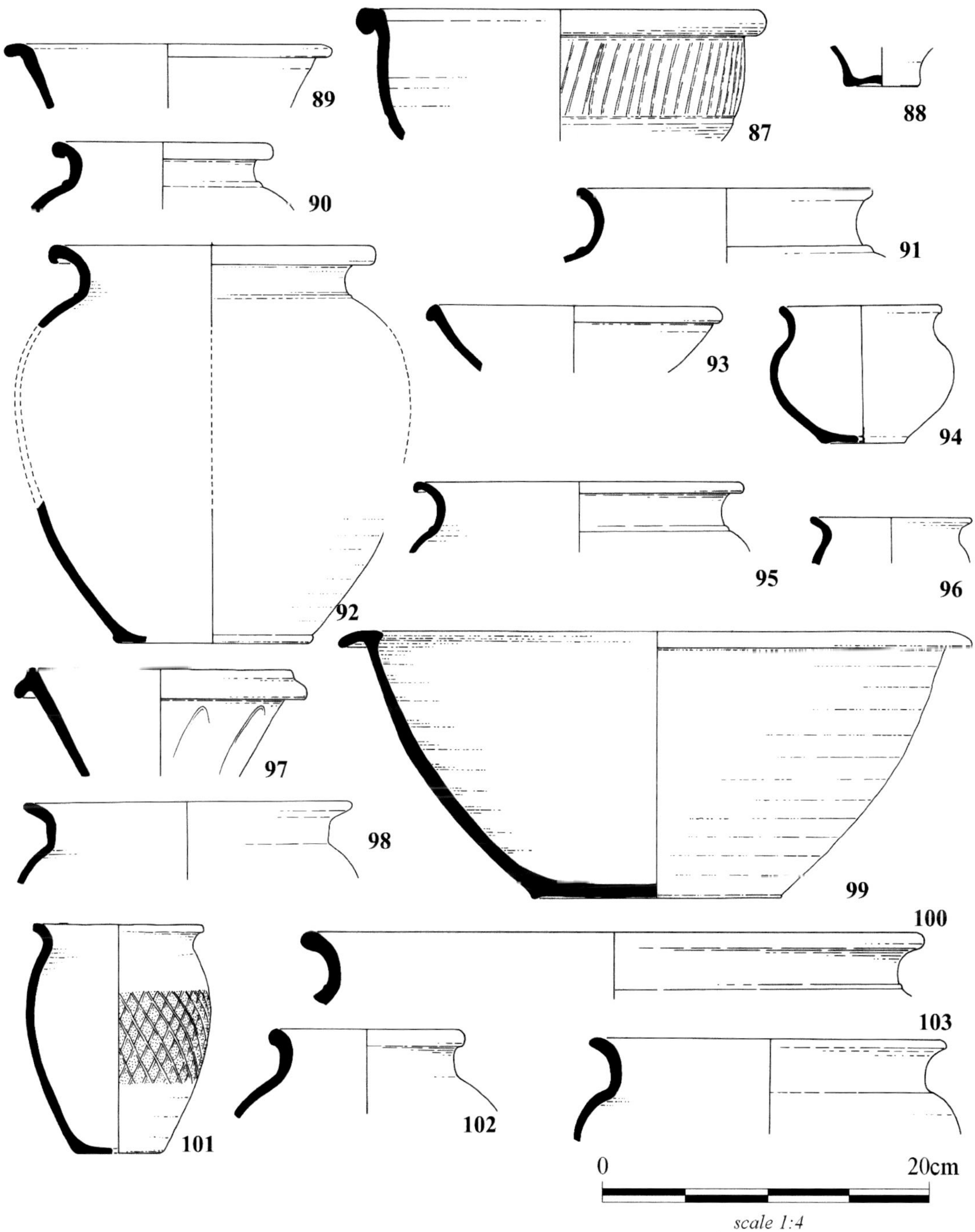

Fig. 40. Coarse pottery.

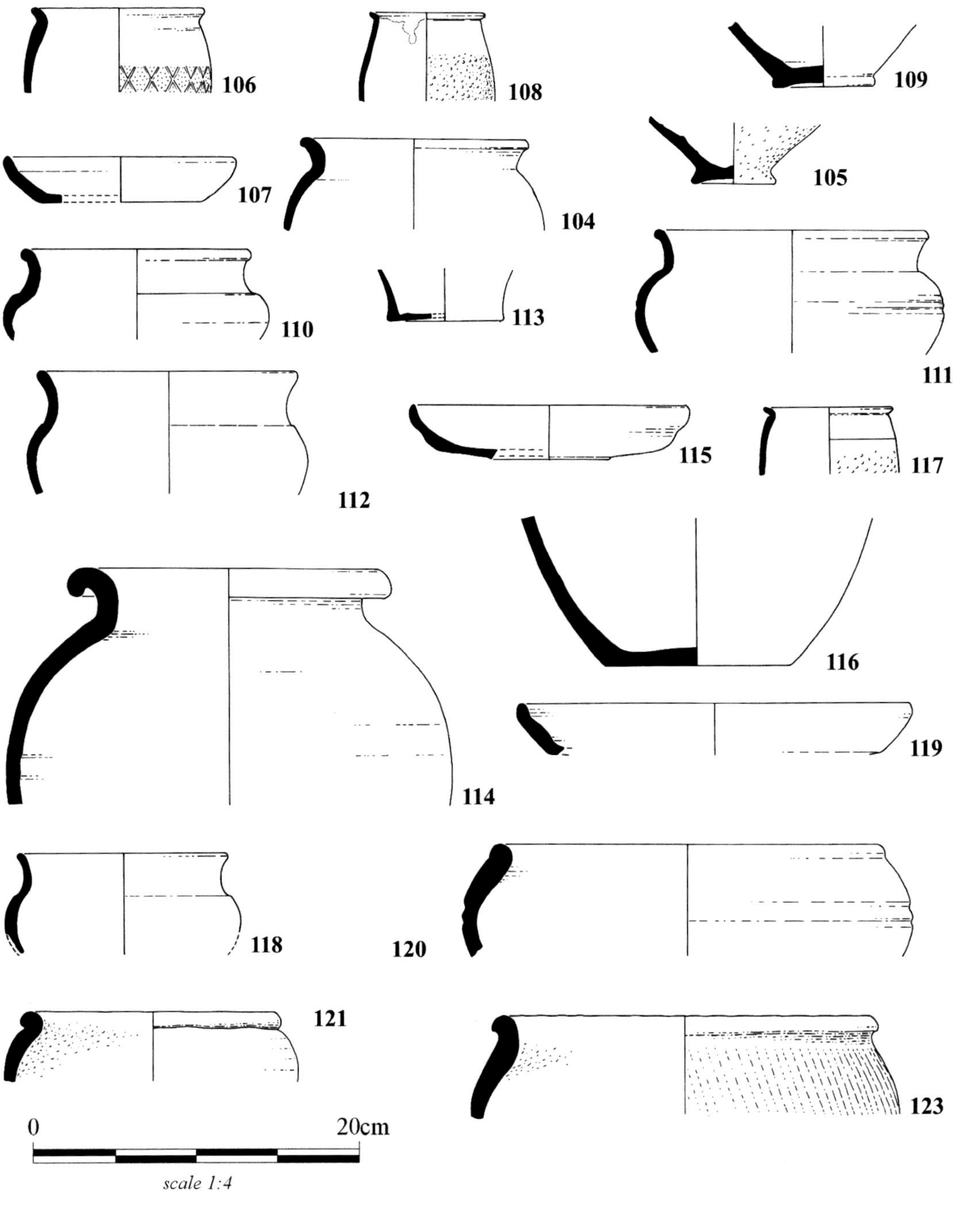

Fig. 41. Coarse pottery.

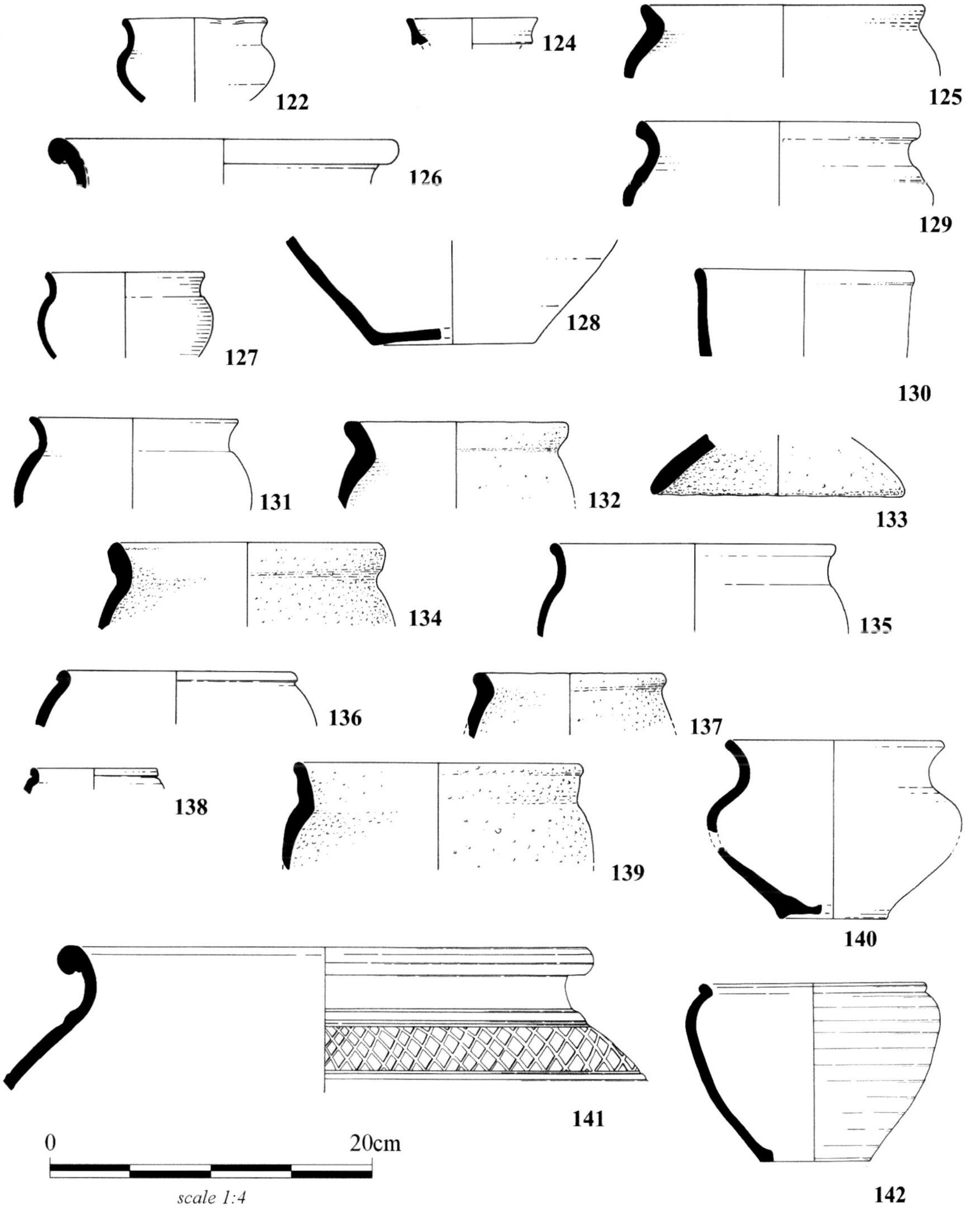

Fig. 42. Coarse pottery.

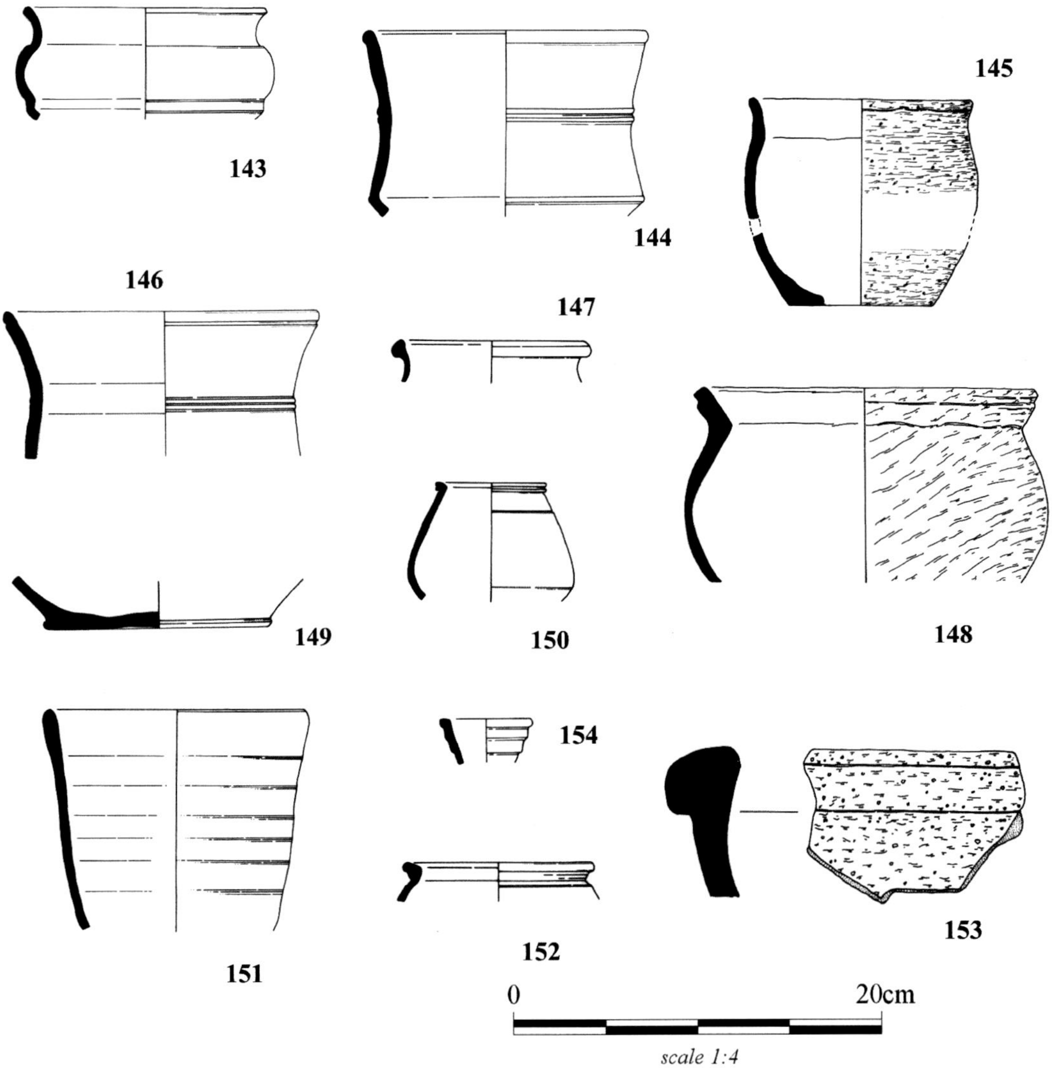

Fig. 43. Coarse pottery.

such as (Fig. 42, no. 131) are unlikely to date later than the third quarter of the first century AD. These contexts also include a large quantity of Iron Age tradition vessels in a range of forms (Fig. 42, no. 132, 133, 134) which are unlikely to date any later than the AD 70s (Timby 1999a; Willis 2000a) as well as a large quantity of Savernake storage vessels (Fig. 42, no. 136) and a flagon rim which is likely to be no later than the AD 70s on the basis of parallels from Cirencester. Together, the lack of late first century or second century AD material from these contexts indicates the Quarry pit was completely backfilled in the third quarter of the first century AD. The cobbled surface laid over the Quarry pit E(252) contains a very small amount of early Severn Valley wares and grog wares of mid–late first century AD date, associated with Flavian samian (see Willis above), suggesting the quarry was backfilled in the late first century AD, possibly contemporary with construction of the villa.

Fig. 40, 94 [118] BC N7, SVWO(E)1, E(281), parallels Ariconium (Willis 2000a, fig. 29. no. 11); Date: first century AD.

Fig. 42, 124 [159] Flagon, FL2, GROG2, E(281), Ditches 1982–3 (Trow 1988b, no. 74), Cirencester (Rigby 1982, no. 299); Date: later first century AD (pre-Flavian?).

Fig. 42, 125 [160] Handmade jar, JB7 N1, GROG1, E(281), parallels Ditches 1982–3 (Trow 1988b, no. 118), Bagendon Form 161 (fig. 53, no. 3), Frocester (Timby 2000, no. 94); Date: late Iron Age– first century AD.

Fig. 42, 126 [161] JG N6, SAV1, E(261), parallels Bagendon Form 173, Uley West-Hill (Leach 1993, no. 72), Swan (1975, no. 52); Date: mid–late first century AD.

Fig. 42, 129 [162] BC3[.2], SVWO(E)2, E(281), parallels Ditches 1982–3 (Trow 1988b, no. 112), Bagendon Form 116?; Date: mid–late first century AD

Fig. 42, 128 [163] storage jar, JG Base2, SAV1, E(281); Date: first century AD?

Fig. 42, 129 [164] BC N4, GROG1, E(299), Bagendon (Fig. 52, 11); Date: first century AD.

Fig. 42, 130 [165] BE3[.1], SVWR(L)1, E(299), parallels (Timby 1990, no. 42); Date: mid first century AD.

Fig. 42, 131 [166] BC N3, MICSW2, E(299), parallels Bagendon Form 120 (fig. 52, no. 11); Date: mid–late first century AD.

Fig. 42, 132 [167] JB5, L1, E(299), parallels Bagendon Form 161 (Fig.55, no. 9); Date: late Iron Age–first century AD.

Fig. 42, 133 [168] LID4, L1, E(299); Date: late Iron Age–mid first century AD

Fig. 42, 134 [169] JB9, MALV2, E(273), parallels Middle Duntisbourne (Timby 1999a, no. 93); Date: mid first century AD (before AD65?).

Fig. 42, 135 [171] BC3[.2], SVWO(E)1, E(273), parallels Webster (1976, Fig. 4, no. 20), Ariconium (Willis 2000a, fig. 19, no. 11); Date: mid–late first century AD.

Fig. 42, 136 [172] bead rimmed jar, JC3[.5], SAV1, E(261), parallels Ditches 1982–3 (Trow 1988b, no. 123), Uley West-Hill (Leach 1993, no. 57), Bagendon Form 146; Date: early–mid first century AD.

Fabric	No. of sherds	RE	Weight (g)
DORBB1	5		22
FWOXID	15		26
FWS	10		24
GABTN	9	0.1	69
GABTR2	1		2
GABTR3	8	0.05	14
GROG1	105	1.21	933
GROG2	37	0.29	362
GROG5	4		130
GROGBAG	15	0.19	98
GROGFW	1		9
GW1	1		3
L1	91	0.75	678
L2	51		539
L3	2		15
MALV1	57	0.67	417
MALV2	55	2.42	446.5
MICBB	17	0.05	78
MICSW2	15	0.51	111
MICSW3	15	0.2	139
NOG WH	4		76
NWG1	5		51
NWG2	3	0.24	12
OXS1	1		5
OXS3	1	0.05	3
SAV1	68	0.91	985
SAV2	9		389
SAV3	5	0.05	57
SAV4	2		29
SAV5	6		86
SVWO(E)1	87	1.52	797
SVWO(E)2	48	1.62	441
SVWR(E)1	18	1.65	201
SVWR(L)1	43	0.89	424
UNC	17	0.23	26
WW	14		71

Table 8. Fabrics in ceramic group B2.

Fabric	No. of Sherds	RE	Weight (g)
AMPH	1		135
CGCC	1	1	3
DORBB1	76	2.36	1163
GROG3	1		15
GW1	4		73
GW2	25	1.07	426
GW4	2		11
GW5	4	0.17	51
MICBB	6	0.13	33
MICGW	1		14
MICSW3	4		14
NWCC	2	0.2	8
NWG1	7	0.52	168
NWG2	5	0.48	191
NWG3	8		36
NWWH	13	0.36	351
OXS1	5		11
OXS3	12	0.25	119
SWS	1		5
SH2	1		6
SVWO(E)1	3		242
SVWO(E)2	3		96
SVWO(L)1	23	0.81	2030
SVWR(E)1	1		5

Table 9. Fabrics in ceramic group C1.

Fig. 42, 137 [174] handmade jar, JB6[.2], MALV2, E(261), parallels Frocester (Timby 2000, no. 88); Date: late Iron Age–mid first century AD.

Fig. 42, 138 [175] JC3 N1, UNC, E(261), Bagendon Form 154; Date: first century AD.

Fig. 42, 139 [176] JB7, MALV, E(287), parallels Middle Duntisbourne (Timby 1999a, no. 88); Date: late Iron Age–first century AD.

Fig. 42, 140 [177/8] BC N5, GROG1, E(253/287), parallels Ditches (Trow 1988b, no. 76), parallels Bagendon Form 102; Date: mid first century AD.

Fig. 43, 144 [150] BE4[.3], SVWO(E)1, E(253), parallels Webster (1976 fig. 9, no. 59), Timby (1990, no. 43), Ariconium (Willis 2000a, Fig. 22, 12). Date: first century AD.

Fig. 43, 146 [170] BE4[.3], SVWO(E)1, E(273), parallels Webster (1976, no. 59), Timby (1990, no. 43); Date: first century AD.

Fig. 43, 148 [6] JB5 N1, MALV, E(281), parallel at Middle Duntisbourne (Timby 1999, no. 88); Date: late Iron Age–late first century AD.

Ceramic group C1

Collapse of cellar wall (Trench F, phase 8)

CONTEXTS: F(488), F(489), F(491), F(495) (TABLE 9)

These contexts include the material contemporary with the collapse of the cellar wall, or immediately after F(495), F(488), F(491) and those immediately overlying the cellar wall. They have been distinguished from the larger dumps of material which overlie them, although some contamination from above layers is possible. Unfortunately, no ceramics were recovered from the contexts underlying the cellar wall F(499) and F(490) making dating the collapse of the cellar wall difficult. This group is dominated by Dorset Black Burnish wares, North Wiltshire grey wares, Severn Valley wares and other local grey wares. The Dorset Black Burnish forms tend to suggest a mid–late second century AD date with little that can be placed later (Fig. 37, nos 41, 42, 43). This is supported by the North Wiltshire-Whitehill Farm grey wares which are in forms dating predominantly to the second century AD (Fig. 40 no. 103), whilst the Severn Valley ware flanged bowl (Fig. 40, no. 99) is likely to date to the second–third centuries AD. Roughcast beakers, possibly North Wiltshire copies of North Gaulish types (Anderson 1979; 1981), can also be dated to the middle decades of the second century AD (Fig. 39, no. 72; Fig. 41, no. 108). The lack of third century AD material supports the impression from the samian that the cellar wall probably collapsed in the middle of the second century AD.

Fig. 37, 40 [49] JC BBtype1, GW1, F(491), parallels (Holbrook and Bidwell 1991, form 9.1?); Date: late first century AD.

Fig. 37, 41 [50] DA BB2, DORBB1, F(491), parallels Ariconium (Willis 2000a, Fig. 22 no. 22); Date: late second century AD.

Fig. 37, 42 [52] JC BBtype1, DORBB1, F(491); Date: late first–early second century AD (Holbrook and Bidwell 1991).

Fig. 37, 43 [54] J BBtype3.1, DORBB1, F(491), parallels Frocester (Timby 1999a, 187), (Holbrook and Bidwell 1991, form 19.1a; Woodward et al 1993, 229); Date: late first to early third century AD.

Fig. 37, 44 [56] Lid, MICBB, F(491), parallels Uley West Hill (Leach 1993, no. 65); Date: late first–early second century AD.

Fig. 38, 45 [58/48] KF1[.1], OXS3, F(491); Date: late first–early second century AD (Greene 1973, 66).

Fig. 38, 57 [73] J BBtype3, DORBB1, F(489), parallels Frocester (Timby 2000, 186), Uley West-Hill (Leach 1993, 169) (Holbrook and Bidwell 1991; Woodward *et al.* 1993); Date: late first–early second century AD.

Fig. 39, 72 [88] K N7.1, NWCC, F(488), parallels (Anderson 1979, fig. 7. 2; cf. Greene 1973; Webster 1993, 300), possible local product; Date: mid second century AD.

Fig. 40, 99 [124] FB1, SVWO(L)1, F(488), Webster (1976, no. 50: second–third century AD), Tewkesbury (MacRobert 1993, no. 24). Date: late second century AD.

Fig. 40, 100 [128] JG N1, SVWO(L)1, F(488), parallels Ariconium (Willis 2000a, fig. 21, no. 4). Date: late first century AD.

Fig.40, 101 [129] J BBtype4, DORBB1, F(488), parallels Frocester (Timby 2000, no. 187). Date: late first–early second century AD (Woodward et al 1993, type 1; Holbrook and Bidwell 1991, 19.1: late first century AD).

Fig. 40, 102 [130] J GW, GW2, F(488), Date: second–third century AD.

Fig. 40, 103 [131] J GWtype3, NWWH, F(488), parallels Uley West-Hill (Leach 1993, no.171), Thornhill (Timby 2004, no.52); Date: second century AD.

Fig. 41, 104 [132] J BBtype2, GW2, F(488), parallels Ariconium (Willis 2000a, fig. 11 no.5), Frocester (Timby 2000, no. 187), (Holbrook and Bidwell 1991, late first–early second; Woodward *et al.* 1993, AD100–250); Date: mid–late second century AD.

Fig. 41, 106 [135] C BBtype2.1, DORBB1, F(488), parallels Frocester (Timby 2000, no. 190), Uley West-Hill (Leach 1993, no. 165, 167), Ariconium (Willis 2000a, fig. 12, no. 10), (Holbrook and Bidwell 1991, form 18.1); Date: late first century AD.

Fig. 41, 107 [136] DA N1, SVWO(L)1, F(488), parallels Ariconium (Willis 2000a, fig. 20. no. 23), (Webster 1976, no. 73). Date: mid–late first century AD.

Fig. 41, 108 [137] K N7, NWCC, F(488), (Anderson 1981); Date: mid–late second century AD.

Fig. 41, 116 [147] base N2, SVWO(E)1, F(488), parallels (Webster 1976, no. 8?); Date: first–third century AD?

Fig. 43, 149 [55] base form N10, NWWH, F(491), parallels Anderson 1979, no. 3; Date: second–third century AD.

Fig. 43, 152 [57] C BB GW1, NWG2, F(491), parallels Uley West-Hill (Leach 1993, no. 107); Date: late first century AD.

Ceramic group C2

Dumps of material in cellar prior to collapse of the end wall F(406) (Trench F, phase 8)

Contexts: F(426), F(485), F(480) (Table 10)

The majority of material from the large dumps of material in the cellar below the collapsed end wall are of mid–late second century AD, some possibly of early third century AD date, including Dorset Black Burnish wares (Fig. 38, nos 47, 51, 54, 55, 56; Fig. 39, nos 69, 70, 73), Severn Valley ware (Fig. 39, no. 86), North Wiltshire grey wares (Fig. 32, no. 49, 77) and North Gallic beakers of mid second century AD date (Fig. 39, no. 71).

Fabric	No. of sherds	RE	Weight (g)
AMPH	7		429
CGCC	8	0.55	51
DORBB1	325	6.2	5265
GABTN	1		9
GROG2	1		10
GROG3	1		5
GW1	41	0.39	860
GW2	41	0.88	323
GW4	19	0.21	198
GW5	17		329
GW6	3		87
MAHWH	2		107
MICBB	21	0.72	226
MICGW	12	0.04	94
MICSW2	1		5
MICSW3	9		41
NOG WH	1		17
NWCC	6	0.5	65
NWG2	42	0.87	418
NWG3	13		158
NWWH	94	2.695	2159
OXCC	6		62
OXS1	74	1.5	1001
OXS3	2		5
OXWC	3		39
SAV1	3		41
SAV2	1		25
SAV3	1	0.02	2
SH1	8	0.3	133
SVWO(E)1	33	0.28	286
SVWO(E)2	41	0.06	1220
SVWO(L)1	49	0.97	983
SVWOXID	7		84
SVWR(E)1	3		85
SVWR(E)2	3	1.02	309
SWS	25	0.16	167
WSOXID	9		54

Table 10 Fabrics in ceramic group C2.

However, the presence of Oxfordshire Colour Coat wares in F(426) and F(485), (see Fig. 39, no. 65), dating to the late third–early fourth century and a handful of sherds of South Midlands shell tempered ware (Fig. 39, no. 80), dating to the third–fourth century, is problematic. It is notable that these sherds make up a very small proportion of the assemblage representing only a handful of sherds from all contexts and are in contrast to the majority of materials, coherent date in the second century AD. The presence of these later sherds is in contrast to the otherwise coherent nature of the assemblage and may indicate this material was deposited as late as the third century AD. However, it is possible that these sherds represent contamination from later layers, and certainly Trow suggests in his excavation notes that the differences between some layers, particular F(426) and F(480) were not altogether clear, and these may represent intrusion from later contexts. It should also be noted that, at least in one case, adjoining sherds were found between F(491) and F(426). Alternatively, these layers could be dated to the third century AD, pushing back the collapse of the villa end wall to the third century AD.

Fig. 38, 46 [59] TK3, OXS1, F(480), parallels Webster (1976, form 42), Frocester (Timby 2000, 164, 163); Date: second–third century AD.

Fig. 38, 47 [62] J BBtype2, NWG1, F(480), parallels Frocester (Timby 2000, 187); Date: mid–late second century AD (Holbrook and Bidwell 1991).

Fig. 38, 48 [63] JC N2, SAV5, E(326), parallels Swan (1975, no. 29), Bagendon Form 147, Early Cirencester (Rigby 1982, no. 358), Watchfield (Biddulph 2004, no. 7); Date: mid first century AD–early second century AD.

Fig. 38, 49 [64] TK4, NWWH, F(426), parallels Anderson (1979), tankard in similar fabric Thornhill (Timby 2004, no. 85); Date: second century AD?

Fig. 38, 50 [65] base form N8, GW5, F(426); Date: uncertain.

Fig. 38, 51 [66] JC BB1type2, DORBB1, F(426), parallels Frocester (Timby 1999a, no. 206); Date: late second century AD (Holbrook and Bidwell 1991, form 35.2).

Fig. 38, 52 [67] BC N10, MICBB, F(426), parallels Wanborough; Date: late first–early second century AD.

Fig. 38, 54 [70] CBBtype2, DORBB1, F(426), parallels Frocester (Timby 1999a, 190), Uley West-Hill (Leach 1993, no. 166). Date: late second century AD (Holbrook and Bidwell 1991, form 2.1).

Fig. 38, 55 [71] D BB type3, DORBB1, F(426), parallels Uley West-Hill (Leach 1993, 159), (Woodward *et al.* 1993, no. 235 – late second century; Holbrook and Bidwell 1991); Date: mid–late second century AD.

Fig. 38, 56 [72] FB BBtype3, DORBB1, F(426), parallels Uley West-Hill (Leach 1993, 156), (Woodward *et al.* 1993, no. 224; Holbrook and Bidwell 1991, form 43?); Date: mid second–early third century AD.

Fig. 38, 58 [74] K N8, OXS1, F(426), Date: uncertain.

Fig. 38, 59 [75] DA BB6, NWG1, F(426), parallels Ariconium (Willis 2000a, fig. 12, no. 12); Date: late second–early third century AD.

Fig. 38, 60 [76] J BBtype3.2, DORBB1, F(426), parallel Birdlip Quarry (Timby 1999a, no. 153). Date: late first–late second century AD (Woodward *et al.* 1993, type 8; Holbrook and Bidwell 1991, form 9.4?).

Fig. 38, 61 [77] J GW type4, NWG2, F(426), parallels narrow necked jars (see Anderson 1979, fig. 8, no. 2; Timby 2004, no. 42); Date: second century AD.

Fig. 38, 62 [78] BD2[.3], MICBB, F(426), parallels Uley West Hill (Leach 1993, no. 59); Date: late first–early second century AD.

Fig. 38, 63 [79] D BBtype2.1, DORBB1, F(426), parallel Frocester (Timby 2000, no. 192). Usk (Webster 1993, 33.2), (Holbrook and Bidwell 1991, no. 58.1); Date: mid–late second century AD.

Fig. 38, 64 [80] LID4, SVWR(E)2, F(426), parallels Late Cirencester (Cooper 1998, no. 84); Date: second–third century AD.

Fig. 39, 65 [81] FB3, OXCC F(485), parallels Young (1977, C44.2); Date: AD270–350.

Fig. 39, 66 [82] Jar, J BB type 2, GW2, F(426), (Holbrook and Bidwell 1991, form 26.1c); Date: AD 120–200.

Fig. 39, 67 [83] J BBtype6, DORBB1, F(426), parallels Uley West-Hill (Leach 1993, no. 173), Ariconium (Willis 2000a); Date: AD120–200.

Fig. 39, 68 [84] DA BB2, DORBB1, F(426), parallels Ariconium (Willis 2000a, fig 12. no. 22), Frocester (Timby 2000, no. 195), (Holbrook and Bidwell 1991); Date: late second–early third century AD.

Fig. 39, 69 [85] JC BB1type2, DORBB1, F(426), (Woodward *et al.* 1993, type 1); Date: late first–early second century AD.

Fig. 39, 70 [86] C BBtype2, DORBB1, F(426), parallels Frocester (Timby 2000, no. 190), Uley West-Hill (Leach 1993, no. 167), Holbrook and Bidwell 1991, form 8.1); Date: mid–late second century AD.

Fig. 39, 71 [87] K N 7, CGCC, F(426), parallels Late Cirencester (Cooper 1998, no. 30: AD150–170), North Gallic version, date to AD80–140: Anderson 1981, 336); Date: mid second century AD.

Fig. 39, 73 [89] JC BB1type1, DORBB1, F(426), (Holbrook and Bidwell 1991, 15.3); Date: second century AD.

Fig. 39, 74 [91] FL, SWS, F(426), parallels Frocester (Timby 2000, 201); Date: second–third century AD

Fig. 39, 75 [92] J BBtype1, DORBB1, F(426), parallel Frocester (Timby 2000, no. 184), (Woodward *et al.* 1993, type 3); Date: second–early third century AD

Fig. 39, 76 [93] LID1, NWWH, F(426), parallels Anderson (1979, no. 7) Roughground (Green and Booth 1993, fig. 89.12), Thornhill (Timby 2004, no. 77); Date: second–third century AD.

Fig. 39, 77 [94] DA G1, NWWH, F(426, 485, 488), parallels Cirencester (Cooper 1998, no. 57), (Anderson 1979, no. 10); Date: second century AD.

Fig. 39, 78 [95] SD1, SVWO(L)1, F(426, 489), parallels Webster (1976, no. 63). Date: second–fourth century AD.

Fig. 39, 79 [96] J BBtype2, DORBB1, F(426), parallels Frocester (Timby 2000, no. 184, 185); Date: second–third century AD.

Fig. 39, 80 [97] Jar, J GW type6, SH1, F(426), parallels: Tyers (1996, 193, no. 1), Watchfield (Biddulph 2004, no. 19); Date: third–fourth century AD.

Fig. 39, 81 [99] DA G2, NWWH, F(426); Date: second century AD?

Fig. 39, 82 [100] LID1, NWWH, F(426), parallels Anderson (1979, no. 7); Date: second–third century AD

Fig. 39, 83 [101] J BB base, DORBB1, F(480), parallels Frocester (Timby 2000, no. 186), Uley West-Hill (Leach 1993, no. 172); Date: second–third century AD?

Fig. 39, 84 [102] DA BB1, DORBB1, F(485), Usk (Webster 1993), Dorchester (Woodward *et al.* 1993, type 22:); Date: mid–late second century AD.

Fig. 39, 85 [103] BD2 N3, NWG2, F(485), parallels Anderson (1979, no. 3) Thornhill (Timby 2004, no. 51); Date: second century AD.

Table 11. Fabrics in ceramic group D.

Fabric	No. of sherds	RE	Weight (g)
DORBB1	104	0.46	713
GROGBAG	1		14
GW1	4		19
MICSW3	9		40
NWG1	11	0.28	90
NWG2	101	1.66	1576
NWWH	18		69
OXCC	3	0.17	27
OXS1	2	0.15	41
SAV1	3		53
SVWO(E)1	3	0.09	46
SVWO(E)2	1		11
SVWR(E)1	11	0.11	89
GABTR2	1		3

Fig. 39, 86 [106/105] TK1, SVWO(L)1, F(485, 426), parallels Webster (1976, no. 41). Date: second–third century AD.

Fig. 40, 87 [107] BC GW1, NWWH, F(485); Date: second–third century AD.

Fig. 40, 88 [108] C BBtype1, DORBB1, F(485), parallels Uley West-Hill (Leach 1993, no. 165); Date: uncertain.

Fig. 41, 105 [133], base K, NWCC, F(485), base of beaker; parallels North Gaulish beakers Form 1 or copy (Anderson 1981); Date: late first–early second century AD.

Fig. 42, 141 [90], JG G3, NWWH, F(426).

Fig. 43, 150 [51] K N7, CGCC, F(485), parallels Late Cirencester (Cooper 1998, no. 30); Date: late second–early third century AD.

Fig. 43, 151 [61] TK3, OXS1, F(480), parallels Webster (1976, form 42), Uley West-Hill (Leach 1993, no. 131). Date: second–third century AD.

Ceramic group D

Build up of soil after abandonment of villa (Trench F, phase 10)

CONTEXTS: F(427) (TABLE 11)

Pottery in the hollow of material above the collapsed end wall in the cellar indicates it accumulated in the third–fourth century AD. This includes a quantity of Oxford Colour Coated wares (Fig. 40, no. 93) and late forms of Dorset Black Burnish wares (Fig. 40, no. 97) dating to the to the late third–fourth century AD, and also appears to paralleled in some of the grey wares (Fig. 40, nos 89, 96). The range of pottery from F(427) is likely to relate to activity in the vicinity of the villa subsequent to the villa's abandonment, represented by the collapse of the end wall.

Fig. 40, 89 [112] Bowl, GB, OXS3, F(427), parallels Anderson (1979, fig. 8, no. 11); Date: third–fourth century AD.

Fig. 40, 90 [113] J GW type4.1, NWG2, F(427), parallels Anderson (1979, fig 8. no. 2), Thornhill (Timby 2004, no. 42); Date: second century AD?

Fig. 40, 91 [114] JG N1(a), SVWO(E)1,

F(427), parallels Ariconium (Willis 2000a, fig. 25, no. 4), (Webster 1976, no. 2); Date: late first–early second century AD.

Fig. 40, 92 [115] JG G1, NWG2, F(427); Date: second–third century AD.

Fig. 40, 93 [116] FB6, OXCC, F(427), parallels Young (1977, C45.3); Date: AD270–400.

Fig. 40, 95 [120] JG G1.1, NWG2, F(427); Date: second–third century AD.

Fig. 40, 96 [121] J GWtype5, SVWR(E)1, F(427); parallels Ariconium (Willis 2000a, fig. 29, no. 2); Date: second–fourth century AD.

Fig. 40, 97 [122] FB BBtype1, DORBB1, F(427), Frocester (Timby 2000, no. 194), (Holbrook and Bidwell 1991, 45.1c?), (Woodward *et al.* 1993, type 25: AD250–400); Date: AD250–400.

Fig. 40, 98 [123] J GW type5, NWG2, F(427); Date: second–third century AD.

Ceramic group E1

Primary floor level of early villa (Trench F, phase 4)

CONTEXTS: F(484), F(514) (TABLE 12)

The presence of fabric L3 in these contexts indicates the early date for the construction of these floor levels, although it should be remembered that some of this material may have been residual from pits in the vicinity. The presence of early grog wares alongside Savernake wares emphasises a date in the mid–late first century AD. As with the mortar slumping in the top of the Iron Age pits, these early floor levels contain significant numbers of finewares, including imports and Whitewares in beakers dating from the first half of the first century AD (see Rigby above).

Ceramic group E2

Slumping of mortar and material in to Iron Age pit (Trench F, phase 4)

CONTEXTS: F(500), F(510), F(511), F(538) (TABLE 13)

The slumping of material in to the top of the Iron Age pit F[505] and F[540] also provides evidence for the first phase of the construction of the villa. It is more debatable as to what extent this material aids in dating of the Iron Age pits, all of this material coming from the upper backfill layers. It is possible that the storage pits had been partially backfilled at an earlier date (see Ceramic group G2). This material provides dating evidence for the 'topping up' of the pits, activity perhaps immediately prior to, and contemporary with, the construction of the first villa. Within this material a platter in grog ware (GROG1) can be paralleled at Middle Duntisbourne (Timby 1999a, 332) and dated to around the mid-first century AD. Other sherds in these contexts occur in MALV, GROGBAG fabrics, Early Severn Valley and Savernake wares, which include late Iron Age forms and Savernake storage vessels consistent with a mid first century AD

Table 12. Fabrics in ceramic group E1.

Fabric	No. of sherds	RE	Weight (g)
GROG1	7	0.1	53
GROG2	7		41
GROG5	1		28
L1	10		24
L3	4		10
MALV2	12		42
MICBB	1		4
SAV1	9	0.2	243
SAV3	1		6
SAV5	1	0.07	5
SVWO(E)2	4		8
SVWR(L)1	2		12
GABTN	5		27
GABTR3	2		2
GABWH	1	0.1	12
FWOXID	1		1
WSOXID	1		15
WW	8	0.15	40
NOG WH	7		210

date. This is supported by the presence of an Augustan-Tiberian samian sherd in F(538) (see Willis above) and a range of imported Gallo-Belgic finewares and local copies in F[505] and F[540] which can be paralleled in the early–mid first century AD (cf. Rigby above), some material in the upper layers of pit F[505] dating potentially as late as the Neronian period. Overall, the assemblage emphasises the likelihood of construction of the villa in the latter half of the first century AD, potentially representing direct continuity from occupation associated with the Iron Age pits.

Fig. 36, 4 [8] JG2, SAV1, F(538), parallels Bagendon Form 174; Date: mid–late first century AD.

Fig. 43, 153 [7] BH N1, L1, F(538), parallels Frocester (Timby 2000, no. 62); Date: late Iron Age–early first century AD.

Fig. 36, 9 [13] DA N2, GROGBAG, F(500), parallels at Cirencester (Rigby 1982, no. 198 in similar fabric), similar to Bagendon Form 16 (Cam2 copy?); Date: early first century AD.

Fig. 36, 10 [14] K Ped, GROG3, F(500), Bagendon Form 36 (copy of Cam74?); Date: early–mid first century AD?

Ceramic group F

North–South ditch E[255] (Trench E, phase 8)

CONTEXTS: E(268), E(265), E(264) (TABLE 14)

The north–south ditch post-dates the Flavian cobbled surface (see above) and the coarsewares cannot refine the date of this feature further, although the substantial amounts of Iron Age tradition and first century fabrics such as Savernake

Table 13 (left). Fabrics in ceramic group E2.

Fabric	No. of sherds	RE	Weight (g)
GROG1	23	0.125	125.5
GROG2	1		1
GROG5	1		3
GROGBAG	3	0.06	12
GROGFW	5		15
L1	44	0.15	97
L3	76		76
MALV2	19		95
MICBB	8	0.4	33
SAV1	18	0.08	69
SAV2	1		28
SAV4	4		70
SAV5	5		116
SVWO(E)2	6	0.5	24
SVWR(L)1	5		253
FWOXID	1		3
GABTN	5	0.32	71
GABTR1C	4		6
GABTR3	1		1
NOG WH	2	0.2	37

Table 14 (right). Fabrics in ceramic group F.

Fabric	No. of sherds	RE	Weight (g)
GROG1	7		48
GROG2	3		32
GROG5	1		62
GROGBAG	5		25
L1	13	0.17	79
MALV1	6	0.17	39
MICGW	5	0.11	29
SAV1	8	0.05	96
SAV2	1		5
SAV3	1		18
SAV4	1		60
SAV6	1		61
SH2	1		20
SVWO(E)1	23	0.47	136
SVWO(E)2	8		60
SVWR(L)1	5		54
WW	1		4
GABTN	1		1

and early Severn Valley wares alongside the apparent lack of second century AD suggests it is likely to be late first century AD in date. One sherd of Terra Nigra with a stamp is likely to date from AD 20–50, and is presumably residual (see Rigby above).

Ceramic group G1

Late Iron Age occupation layer (Trench F, phase 1c)

CONTEXTS: (504, 546) (TABLE 15)

The material in the occupation layer is heavily dominated by fabric L3. This is a distinctive and early fabric on the site, found in forms (JB8/JB8[.2]; Fig. 36, nos 1, 2, 3) which can be placed in a later Iron Age context with parallels at Conderton and Frocester ranging in date from the second century BC to early first century AD. The presence of a handful of sherds of early Severn Valley and Savernake wheel thrown wares has been argued in the past by Trow to be intrusive; however, the earlier dating suggested for both wares in recent years means they could be of pre-conquest date and need not alter a pre-conquest date for the occupation layer. The presence of a fine, White ware beaker of Tiberian-Claudian date (see Rigby above) also supports an early–mid first century AD date for the layer.

The unusual jar (Fig. 36, no. 3) in fabric L3 is rare, with few parallels noted from other late Iron Age sites, such as Frocester or Conderton. This form echoes the grog tempered bowls of the early–middle first century AD, seen both at Ditches and Bagendon in significant numbers and may be a precursor to such forms or a copy in local ware. This may also imply a relatively late date for the context, possibly in the early–mid first century AD. Depending on the implications of the presence of the wheel thrown ware sherds, the other material suggests the occupation layer dates somewhere between the first century BC and mid first century AD.

Fig. 36, 1 [1] JB8[.2], L3, F(546), parallels at Conderton Camp (Morris 2005, 123: R10), Frocester (Timby 2000, no. 8?); Date: later Iron Age.

Fig. 36, 2 [2] JB8[.2], L3, F(504), parallels at Conderton Camp (Morris 2005, 123: R4), Frocester (Timby 2000, no. 89); Date: later Iron Age.

Fig. 36, 3 [3] JB8, L3, F(504), uncertain parallels; Date: early–mid first century AD?

Fig. 43, 145 [4] JB8, L3, F(504), parallel at Thornhill Farm (Timby 2004, no. 17). Date: late Iron Age–early first century AD.

Ceramic group G2

Backfilling of Iron Age pits (Phase 2?)

CONTEXTS: F(516) (TABLE 16)

Dateable material from all the pits was only available from the upper layers and the mortar slumping in the very uppermost layers (see Ceramic Group E2). In reality, only context F(516) can be equated with the primary backfilling of the pits and produced dateable material, the upper layers (discussed

Table 15 (left). Fabrics in ceramic group G1.

Table 16 (right). Fabrics in ceramic group G2.

Fabric	No. of sherds	RE	Weight (g)
L1	7		51
L3	53	0.88	412
SAV1	2		20
SVWO(E)1	1		1
WW	3	0.07	12

Fabric	No. of sherds	RE	Weight (g)
GROG1	24	1.3	233
GROGFW	15		24
MALV1	6	0.08	87
SAV1	6		81
SAV2	1	0.07	10

below) all potentially representing mortar 'slumping' or topping up at a later date. The relationship between these two events remains somewhat unclear, however, and the length of time between these events may not have been particularly long. The fabric and forms in F(516) stress a mid first century AD date for the backfilling of the pits, with a typical assemblage of grog wares, Savernake wares and limestone tempered wares (Fig. 36, nos 5, 6, 7, 8). The notable lack of fabric L3 may stress the chronological distinction between this material and the other limestone wares, also apparent in the different forms between the groups, the latter including classic Malvern ware forms. The lack of imported finewares is also notable, although the small amount of material from this context makes any assessment problematic.

Fig. 36, 5 [9] BE4, GROG1, F(516), parallels Bagendon Form 107b (cf. Timby 1990, no. 43 but not ESVW), Date: early–mid first century AD.

Fig. 36, 6 [10] JC2[.1], GROG1, F(516), parallels Ditches 82–3 (Trow 1988b, no. 35) and Bagendon (Form 155). Date: mid first century AD.

Fig. 36, 7 [11] JB4[.2], MALV2, F(516); Date: late Iron Age–first century AD.

Fig. 36, 8 [12] BC1[.4], GROGBAG, F(516), Bagendon Form 117; Date: mid first century AD?

Table 17. Fabrics in ceramic group H.

Fabric	No. of sherds	RE	Weight (g)
GROG1	4		15
L1	1		8
L3	1		3
NOGWH	1		1
OXS1	2		22
SAV4	1		8
SVWO(E)1	9	0.25	43
SVWO(E)2	1		5

Ceramic group H

Structure 2 (unphased)

CONTEXT: F(531) (TABLE 17)

Only a small amount of material came from contexts associated with Structure 2 and the uncertain nature of the structure entails that assessing its date from the pottery is problematic. However, combined with the limited structural relationships evident, some inferences can be made. The assemblage bears close resemblance to others from mid–late first century AD contexts. Layer F(531), inside Structure 2, contains early Severn Valley wares in bowl forms, a handful of late Iron Age fabric sherds (L1 and L3), a sherd of North Gaulish white ware and a flagon in OXS1 (Fig. 41, no. 113). The overall impression is of a mid–late first century AD date. Whilst some of this may be residual, it seems likely that the debris accumulated after the abandonment of Structure 2 and thus dates it destruction, probably in the early second century AD when the north corridor of the villa was constructed. Alongside the apparent limited relationship between the wall footings, this may suggest it was constructed prior to the north corridor of the villa although perhaps not prior to the main body of the villa, possibly in the late first century AD.

Fig. 41, 113 [144] K base, OXS1, F(531); Date: mid first century AD?

Discussion

The fabrics from Ditches (Table 18) provide a broad range of material from the early first century to third century AD. Before discussing the overall assemblage it is worth noting that whilst the assemblage is relatively large the majority of material derives from a small number of features which may have formed relatively rapidly. These include the cellar assemblage, which incorporates the vast majority of later ceramics, and the enclosure ditch

	Sherds	RE	Weight	Sherds%	RE%	Weight%
ABING/OXS2	15	0.225	66	0.4	0.2	0.1
AMPH	9		679	0.2	0.0	1.2
CGCC	10	2.55	63	0.2	2.2	0.1
DORBB1	525	15.26	7266	13.1	13.3	13.1
FWB	16		56	0.4	0.0	0.1
FWBG	3	0.25	59	0.1	0.2	0.1
FWOXID	18		33	0.4	0.0	0.1
FWS	46	0.15	130	1.1	0.1	0.2
GABTN	24	0.44	219	0.6	0.4	0.4
GABTR1C	5		12	0.1	0.0	0.0
GABTR2	2		3	0.0	0.0	0.0
GABTR3	17	0.05	35	0.4	0.0	0.1
GABWH	1	0.1	12	0.0	0.1	0.0
GROG1	219	7.645	2086	5.5	6.7	3.8
GROG2	93	3.105	834	2.3	2.7	1.5
GROG3	22	0.76	204	0.5	0.7	0.4
GROG4	5	0.2	151	0.1	0.2	0.3
GROG5	18	0.4	290	0.4	0.3	0.5
GROGBAG	98	4.495	903	2.4	3.9	1.6
GROGFW	38	0.12	123	0.9	0.1	0.2
GW1	53	3.18	1104	1.3	2.8	2.0
GW2	67	2.08	821	1.7	1.8	1.5
GW3	1		13	0.0	0.0	0.0
GW4	41	1.51	385	1.0	1.3	0.7
GW5	23	1.06	390	0.6	0.9	0.7
GW6	3		87	0.1	0.0	0.2
L1	248	2.38	2330	6.2	2.1	4.2
L2	60		583	1.5	0.0	1.0
L3	120	1.83	736	3.0	1.6	1.3
MAHWH	2		107	0.0	0.0	0.2
MALV1	197	5.22	1571	4.9	4.5	2.8
MALV2	79	1.58	913	2.0	1.4	1.6
MICBB	86	2.49	723	2.1	2.2	1.3
MICSW1	8	0.17	26	0.2	0.1	0.0
MICSW2	18	0.67	121	0.4	0.6	0.2
MICSW3	28	0.32	155	0.7	0.3	0.3
NOG WH	17	0.3	370	0.4	0.3	0.7

Table 18. Fabric quantities from all contexts 1984–5.

	Sherds	RE	Weight	Sherds%	RE%	Weight%
NWWH	125	5.445	2579	3.1	4.7	4.6
NWCC	10	0.7	95	0.2	0.6	0.2
NWG1	83	2.67	1733	2.1	2.3	3.1
NWG2	297	6.56	4305	7.4	5.7	7.8
NWG3	21		194	0.5	0.0	0.3
OXCC	11	0.17	95	0.3	0.1	0.2
OXS1	88	2.25	1061	2.2	2.0	1.9
OXS3	26	1.04	164	0.6	0.9	0.3
OXWC	4		44	0.1	0.0	0.1
SAV1	166	2.35	3696	4.1	2.0	6.7
SAV2	57	1.69	5117	1.4	1.5	9.2
SAV3	14	0.13	165	0.3	0.1	0.3
SAV4	20	0.05	356	0.5	0.0	0.6
SAV5	17	0.36	371	0.4	0.3	0.7
SAV6	2		73	0.0	0.0	0.1
SH1	9	0.35	146	0.2	0.3	0.3
SH2	6		58	0.1	0.0	0.1
SVWO(E)1	283	14.66	3126	7.1	12.8	5.7
SVWO(E)2	255	8.83	3147	6.4	7.7	5.7
SVWO(L)1	76	2.66	3045	1.9	2.3	5.5
SVWR(E)1	52	3.26	612	1.3	2.8	1.1
SVWR(E)2	7	1.02	359	0.2	0.9	0.6
SVWR(L)1	76	1.77	951	1.9	1.5	1.7
SWS	25	0.16	167	0.6	0.1	0.3
WSOXID	18		86	0.4	0.0	0.2
WW	27	0.22	132	0.7	0.2	0.2
TOTALS	4010	114.89	55536	100.0	100.0	100.0

Table 18 continued. Fabric quantities from all contexts 1984–5.

and quarry assemblages, which produced the majority of first century AD material. Much smaller assemblages from the occupation layers and early floor levels, whilst modest, provide more explicit dating of first century AD activity on the site.

Overall, the range of fabrics reflects the picture seen at most comparable rural settlements in the region. A dominance of north Wiltshire products, beginning with the Savernake wares in the first century AD and continuing with the Whitehill Farm wares, North Wiltshire Colour Coated and greywares is representative of the pottery at Cirencester (Cooper 1998) and further afield at other rural settlements like Frocester (Timby 2000). The small proportions of later material such as Oxfordshire Colour Coat and South Midlands Shell tempered ware reflects the limited amount of third–fourth century AD pottery on the site as a whole and reinforces the relatively early abandonment date suggested above.

Trow divided his fabrics and forms in

to broader groups to allow for assessment of variation (see above). Despite some differences in fabric definitions, the 1984–5 material can be similarly grouped to allow comparison, although problems in comparing these must be borne in mind. There is only really benefit in comparing the 1984 material (deriving from features such as the Quarry pit and Inner Enclosure Ditch, and the potentially early material from Trench F), with the 1982–3 excavations as the large 1985 assemblages represent a chronologically distinct group, in both the fabrics and forms represented. In some instances residuality may be a factor, with earlier material in later contexts, although the large size of the main assemblages suggests this is unlikely to lead to erroneous dates.

Dividing the fabrics in to the same broad groups as the 1982–3 groups (Trow 1988b) reveals a number of patterns (Table 19, 20). Whilst there are quantitative differences (a smaller number of finds in these fabric groups from 1984), the proportions of quantities in the assemblage compare relatively well, with similar proportions relative to each other of each group (for example in the Savernake wares), although there is less of Group C in the 1984 assemblage. Factors influencing this comparison include variance in identification and somewhat different categorisation between the two assemblages (particularly in defining

	Trench F(1985)*			**1982–3 Excavations****		
	Sherds	**RE**	**Weight (g)**	**Sherds**	**RE**	**Weight (g)**
Group A	51.9	24.4	30.9	29.4	23.7	25.7
Group B	15.1	33.6	17.1	15.6	19.5	13.8
Group C	0.7	1.5	0.4	12.4	12.3	10.6
Group D	6.2	17.8	11.8	23.4	32.6	23.8
Group E	10.9	9.2	22.4	10.1	4.5	22.2
Group F	15.1	13.6	17.4	9.1	7.4	3.9

*only includes probable first century AD, or earlier, contexts
** after figures in Trow 1988b, microfiche

Table 19. Comparison of Trow's fabric groups by % of assemblage from presumed Late Iron Age or first century AD contexts in Trench F compared with 1982–3.

	Trench E (1984)*			**1982–3 Excavations****		
	Sherds	**RE**	**Weight**	**Sherds**	**RE**	**Weight (g)**
Group A	26.8	22.7	19.0	29.4	23.7	25.7
Group B	15.4	14.6	12.9	15.6	19.5	13.8
Group C	5.4	8.9	3.5	12.4	12.3	10.6
Group D	28.7	39.7	24.9	23.4	32.6	23.8
Group E	11.7	11.1	36.2	10.1	4.5	22.2
Group F	12.0	3.0	3.4	9.1	7.4	3.9

*only includes fabrics ascribable to Trow's groups
** after figures in Trow 1988b, microfiche

Table 20. Comparison of Trow's fabric groups by % of assemblage from all contexts in Trench E compared with 1982–3.

finewares) and in the types of areas excavated. Comparing the contexts from Trench F, including the pre-villa pits, occupation layer and early floor levels with 1982–3 proportions (Table 19), the higher representation of group A (handmade Iron Age fabrics) and smaller proportion of Group D (Severn Valley wares) may emphasise the potentially slightly earlier dates for a number of the contexts in Trench F, such as the occupation layer, than those encountered in the 1982–3 excavations. The latter comprised primarily the enclosure ditches, representing assemblages dating from the mid–late first century AD whilst a number of the Trench F contexts may be of early first century AD date. The relatively high proportion of finewares in Trench F is also notable, although this may be explained by the inclusion within the 1985 group of the local fineware copies of Camulodunum forms. To what extent this represents a real difference in 'high-status' activity between the villa area and the edges of the enclosure therefore remains unclear.

By contrast, comparison of the groups from Trench E (Table 20) shows a far greater similarity to Trow's figures from 1982–3. This perhaps reflects the similar nature of the features encountered; the Inner Enclosure Ditch and Quarry pit being similar in date, form and content to the features investigated in 1982–3.

Comparison of the late Iron Age contexts in Trench F and Trench E with comparable assemblages elsewhere is also instructive. The quantity of fineware fabrics, such as the beakers in Whitewares, and grog tempered finewares copying many of the Camulodunum forms, is certainly far greater than contemporary rural sites such as Frocester and Duntisbourne Grove, each of which contain only a very small number of Gallo-Belgic imports (Timby 1999a; 2000). Quantative comparisons with the Duntisbourne sites (Timby 1999a, 334) is more problematic. Whilst these sites have smaller assemblages overall (Timby 1999a, 330, 334), the size of contemporary assemblages (i.e. those likely to be first century AD in date) is more comparable, certainly for those of early first century AD date. Middle Duntisbourne Group 4 (Timby 1999a, 330) has the most comparable assemblage, but even here only four sherds of GABTN derive from an assemblage of 707 sherds compared to ten from 319 sherds in Ceramic Groups E1 and E2, although the number of GABTR3 are more comparable (Middle Duntisbourne, 3 sherds and Ditches E1/E2, just 2). Comparing such relatively small numbers is difficult and should not necessarily be taken as a firm indicator of status but potentially suggests that Ditches contains slightly higher proportions of finewares compared to comparative rural settlements. However, further quantative comparison between sites in the Bagendon-*oppidum* complex is required in order to determine the potentially varied nature of activity. It is particularly important to determine whether the late Iron Age occupation at Ditches was indeed of higher status than that at Bagendon, as perhaps indicated by the construction of the early Roman villa, or whether it was part of a continuum of such sites. In addition, only small areas of relevant contexts have been excavated at the Duntisbourne sites with contexts closer to possible occupation areas, like those at Ditches, potentially likely to include greater numbers of finewares.

Comparing the forms in the 1982–3 assemblage with that from 1984 (Table 21) is restricted by similar problems, with probable variations in form classifications and some areas of methodology. Comparison by form using Trow's original grouping, for example, suffers from the large representation of 'other' (representing base forms not assessed by Trow) which have been excluded from these figures. In particular, these comparisons are made on the published report in Trow 1988b, not on re identification of the 1982 3 material. However, some broad comments can be made about the variation in the prevalence of form groups between the two assemblages. Overall proportions of material are relatively similar with comparably high proportions in the two assemblages of Group 1 (Iron Age form jars), Group 4 (wide mouthed/necked bowls) and similar proportions of Group 5 (Carinated jars) and Group 2 (bead rimmed jars). There is some disparity apparent between the numbers for Group 3 (storage jars), which may also be reflected in fabric differences. There also appears to be a greater prevalence of Group 7, beakers, in the 1982 3 assemblage than in 1984. These two differences combined could represent differences in activities between the two areas with apparently more dining equipment in the areas examined in 1982–3 as opposed to emphasis on storage vessels in the Quarry pit areas. Whether such difference reflects real variation in activities in the vicinity of these areas is unclear but may imply they represent somewhat different depositional processes.

The early Roman material from the 1984 and 1985 assemblage from Ditches matches other early Roman sites from the region and closely resembles the pottery from the 1982–3 excavations. Grog tempered wares in local fabrics can be directly paralleled in form with examples from Middle Duntisbourne and Bagendon (Clifford 1961, Trow 1988b, Timby 1999a), stressing the contemporary and similar nature of these sites and supporting the impression that they represent part of a wider complex (see below). Fabrics such as L3 may date as early as the first century BC but can be refined little more than this. Association of L3 with early Severn Valley wares and Savernake wares may also support arguments by Timby (1990) that Severn Valley wares in particular can be pushed back in to the pre-conquest period, and that late Iron Age forms and fabrics continued in to the mid–late first century AD. Some of the jars (JB8) in Iron Age fabrics can be paralleled at Conderton Camp, which appears to have been abandoned in the second century BC (Morris 2005), indicating the longevity of such forms in the region in to the first century BC and early first century AD. Certainly the Malvern fabrics, and their associated forms, may have been in use as late as the AD70s (Timby 1999a; Willis 2000a).

For the later assemblages, the large quantities of finewares, particularly samian, in Ceramic Group C2 alongside large amounts of Dorset Black Burnish ware, may support the suggestion that the later contexts represent the abandonment of the villa; the fills of these contexts representing the wholesale dumping of large amounts of ceramics. The apparently unusually large sherds of samian noted in this group (see Willis

Table 21. Comparison of Trow's Form groups by % of the assemblage in Trench E compared with 1982–3.

	Trench E (1984)		**1982–3 Excavations**	
	Weight (g)	**RE**	**Weight (g)**	**RE**
Group 1 (JA–JB)	16.69	24.77	29.00	25.27
Group 2 (JC)	3.48	2.78	3.83	4.43
Group 3 (JG)	39.76	11.02	10.53	4.54
Group 4 (BC-BD)	19.45	41.75	32.16	41.90
Group 5 (BE)	14.24	13.05	10.75	9.50
Group 6 (DA)	5.45	4.31	6.76	6.70
Group 7 (K)	0.94	2.31	6.98	7.67
* after figures in Trow 1998b, microfiche				

above), may also suggest that this material was the result of a single 'dumping' episode, rather than the result of long term rubbish accumulation.

The vast majority of the pottery excavated from the villa complex falls within a date range of the second–third century AD and is evident in the coarsewares, particular those from North Wiltshire which dominate other Roman sites such as Cirencester between the mid–late second century AD and also Dorset Black Burnish wares. This is matched by close dating of the samian wares to the middle of the second century AD (see Willis above). The comparability in material with Cirencester is notable, with a similar range of types of material being supplied to the two sites in the mid–late second century AD, seen for example in the cellar assemblage (cf. Cooper 1998, 332). In addition, the similarities in the range of material in early contexts in the cellar to that from Wanborough (Greene 1973; Anderson 1979), dated to the early second century AD (Green 1973, 64) emphasises the chronological focus of activity in that period. Whilst some third century AD, and possibly some fourth century AD, material is present from the site the small number of these items support the structural evidence in suggesting that the villa was abandoned by the third century AD. The Oxford Colour Coated wares and South Midlands shell tempered wares derive predominantly from general activity of an uncertain nature which took place in the vicinity of the villa and may relate to nearby sites which are known about (e.g. RCHME 1976) or have yet to be identified. The small quantities of this material emphasises that Ditches flourished in the first–early third century AD in contrast with other villas elsewhere in the Cotswolds.

Like other sites in the region, early Severn Valley wares, Malvern wares and Savernake wares dominate the early context assemblages. Perhaps most notable in the assemblage, in line with other excavations of sites in the area, is the close connection between fabrics and forms. Storage jars predominate in Savernake forms, carinated jars and necked bowls in Early Severn Valley wares, platters and jars in grog wares, some imitating Gallo-Belgic imports, whilst Iron Age forms for storage and cooking jars continued to be produced in Malvernian, and to some extent, local limestone fabrics. This close relationship between forms and fabric suggests that as early as the mid-first century AD the community at Ditches had a well structured and developed exchange network to obtain specific pottery types from workshops to perform specific functions, either as table wares or for storage and cooking.

The possible evidence of kiln furniture dating to the mid-first century AD, represented by the firebars from the Inner Enclosure Ditch, E(320) (see Baked Clay below; Annette Hancocks pers. comm.), seems to imply that pottery manufacture may have been taking place on the site, at least temporarily. Little can be said about the nature and extent of this activity but similar material was recovered from late Iron Age/early Roman enclosure ditches and pits at Grange Park, Northants. (Hancocks 2006, 162), albeit in far greater quantities, apparently indicative of small-scale pottery manufacture and of a relatively transient nature (ibid., 164). Considering Rigby's observations above that some of the local copies of Gallo-Belgic wares may have been made in the Upper Thames Valley, the possibility that the Ditches community was engaged in pottery manufacture should be kept in mind, particularly considering the other evidence for the 'industrial' activities of coin making and metalworking recognised at the site.

A perhaps overly sharp divide appears between the first century and second century AD pottery from Ditches. In the early second century AD the bead rimmed vessels of Savernake ware were replaced by the North Wiltshire wares (see above; Anderson 1979) and Dorset Black Burnish ware became prominent by the late second and third century AD (Cooper 1998, 332–333). The grog and finewares of the first century AD are replaced predominantly by an abundance of samian which appears to reach its peak supply in the second century AD (Willis above). The later material from Ditches appears to closely reflect developments in Cirencester, in both fabrics and forms, with the similar range of North Wiltshire grey wares, black burnished wares and colour coated wares and imports from Dorset and beyond. The two large assemblages from the site, however, in the cellar and those from the Inner enclosure ditch and Quarry pit may somewhat skew the picture from the site. Both appear to represent 'dumps' of material which may have accumulated relatively rapidly and represent 'snap shots' of pottery consumption in the mid–late first century AD and later second century AD rather than an accurate reflection of consumption patterns over this period. However, the limited amount of later Roman pottery from the assemblage emphasises the impression that the villa was abandoned by the third century AD.

BROCHES

Donald Mackreth

All are of a copper alloy, unless otherwise indicated

Late La Tène

1 E(319), s.f.177 Iron. (Fig. 44, no. 5). The spring probably has eight coils. The hook is long enough to run a short way along the head of the bow which may have a rounded section; corrosion hides this detail. The lower bow is missing. (X-Ray, 70 KV, 30 secs)

2 E(320), s.f.187 Iron. (Fig. 44, no. 7). The wings appear to be plain, the bow roughly oval in section. Of the spring, only the chord is left, still held by a short hook. (X-Ray, 70 KV, 30 secs)

3 E(250), s.f.151 Iron. (Fig. 44, no. 2). The spring is complete and has, apparently, six coils. The hook is very short, barely touching the head of the bow. The wings seem to be plain. The bow has a flat back and a rounded front. The lower part, with the catch-plate, is missing. (X-Ray, 70 KV, 30 secs)

The preceding three are Colchesters, see after Brooch 7 for comment.

4 E(340), s.f. 185 Iron. (Fig. 44, no. 6). Some of the spring is missing, but the left-hand side is complete and shows that there had only been three coils. The full length of the bow is present with the catch-plate along with the return. (X-Ray, 70 KV, 30 secs)

5 E(281), s.f.168 Iron. (Fig. 44, no. 4). Although hard to see, there may only be three coils with an internal chord. The bow is circular in section and tapers to a pointed foot with a small catch-plate behind. (X-Ray, 70 KV, 30 secs)

6 E(281), s.f.167 Iron. (Fig. 44, no. 3). Although complete, the brooch is in pieces. The pin is whole with a loop at the top. The X-ray shows that the head of the bow is rolled-over to house an axis bar for what is in effect a hinged-pin. The bow has a circular section and tapers to a pointed foot with a small catch-plate behind. (X-Ray, 70 KV, 30 secs)

7 F(426), s.f.398 Iron. (Fig. 44, no. 8.). Very accreted (4738), there seems to have been four coils with an internal chord. The bow is circular in section tapering towards the missing foot. (no X-Ray)

The only Late La Tène brooches in this collection are of iron. Although this material was frequently used in the late pre-Roman Iron Age, there are usually several copper alloy brooches as well. Whether the absence of the latter material is significant can only be seen when tested against the only large, dated collection to have been published so far, The King Harry Lane cemetery, St. Albans (Stead and Rigby 1989).

To understand the nature of the overall collection recovered, it is necessary to examine its dating. The authors of the report acknowledge that the cemetery may have begun as early as 15 BC, but preferred to use AD 1 (ibid., 83), and this has had a knock-on effect on the dating of Phases 2 and 3 leading to what

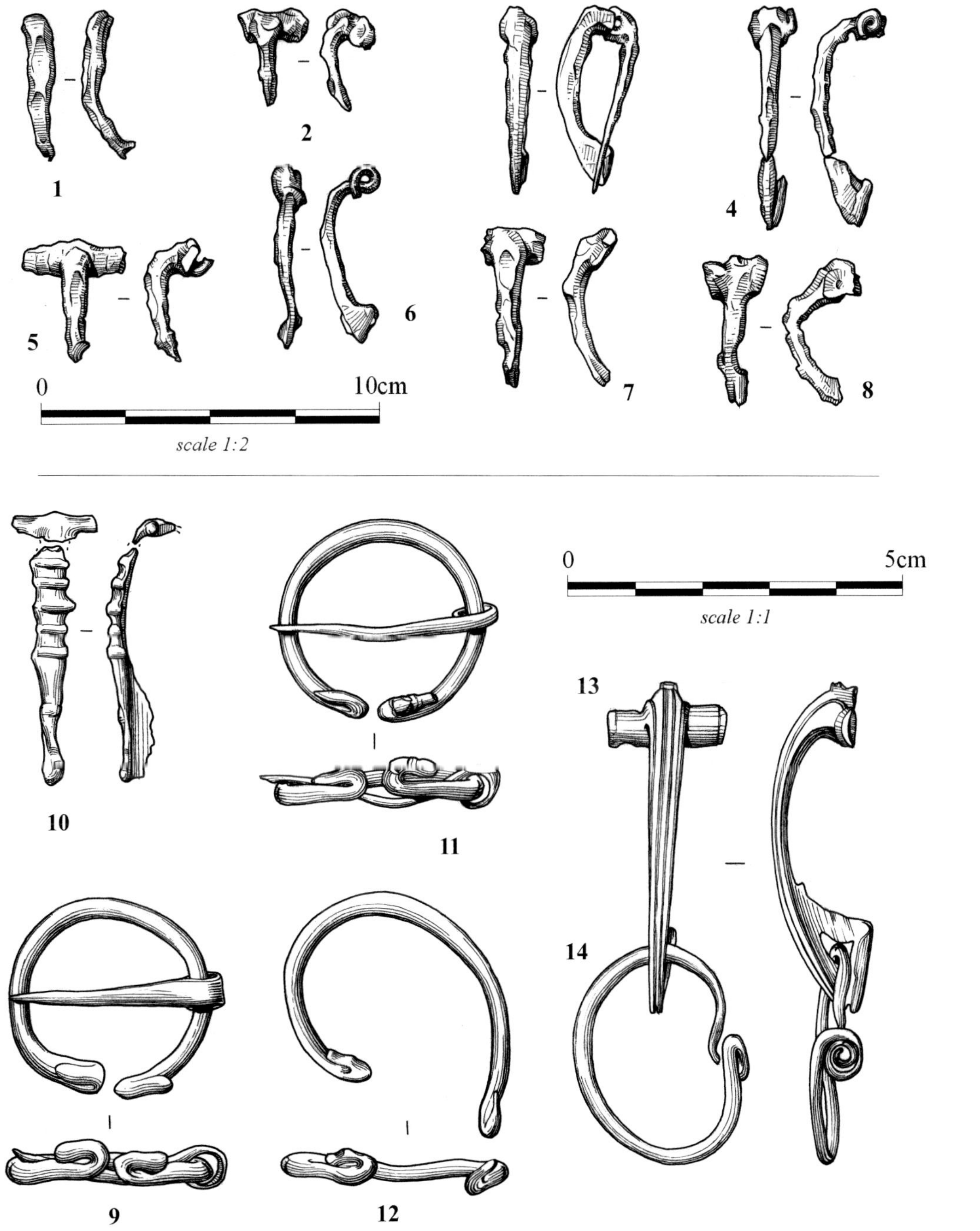

Fig. 44. Brooches.

the writer considers to be an unacceptably late date for the end of Phase 3. There are no Colchester Derivatives, save one (ibid., 354, fig. 154, g.316.4) and there is no real Hod Hill (ibid., 334, fig. 132, g233.3), types which are abundant from AD 40/45 in the former case and AD 43 in the latter, and yet if the following table is examined there can only be one conclusion.

Stead and Rigby dating:
Phase 1 – AD 1–40
Phase 2 – AD 30–55
Phase 3 – AD 40–60
Phase 4 – AD 60+

Mackreth dating:
Phase 1 – 15BC–AD 30
Phase 2 – AD 20–40
Phase 3 – AD 35–55*
Phase 4 – AD 45+

More than half of the brooches in the cemetery according to the published dating must be after the conquest, yet where is the other part of the spectrum of brooches which occur abundantly a few hundred metres away? They are not there. If, however, the dating is moved back to the earliest possible in the report, and the phases adjusted according to the right-hand column in the table, practically all of the problem disappears. There is the matter of the * attached to the terminal date of Phase 3. This is an acknowledgement that a great many of Colchesters and Langton Downs, and some Rosettes continue beyond the conquest and in that sense the AD 55 date should be allowed to stand, save for the cemetery itself: there is still the major absence of types concurrent with survivors in use. The terminal date of the cemetery is emphatically early with the bulk of the burials having been committed to the ground before AD 43/5.

Now let us see what this means in terms of the distribution of iron Colchesters through the phases of iron Colchesters. Phase 1, G *75.4*, G 84.2, *G 123.3*, *G 211.2*, *G 235.2*, *G249.2*, G 256.3, G 268.4, *G 296.4*; Phase 2, G 13.5, *G 73.5*, *G 108.2*, *G 143.4*, G 283.3, G 338.2, *G 420.4*, G 420.3; Phase 3, *G 135.3*, *G 106,3*, G 204.4, G 207.2, G 289.4. In other words, nine from Phase 1, eight from Phase 2 and five from Phase 3, there is none in Phase 4. This presents a classic curve: present in numbers at the beginning, almost as many in Phase 2 and a tailing off in Phase 3. In truth, so few graves are given to Phase 4 that presences and absences in it are neither here nor there. Those brooches which are in italics have catch-plates which belong to the earliest strand of Colchesters: fretting. In terms of the re-dating I have given to the phases, all are pre-conquest and there is no reason to think that the three from Ditches should be dated otherwise. It is a salutary lesson when the writer has only been able to find one brooch from other sites which is similarly firmly pre-conquest: Skeleton Green AD 15–25 (Partridge 1981, 137, fig. 66.5). Of course, a cemetery is a specialised set of deposits and the question of residuality does not arise.

As for Brooches 4–7, they are *Drahtfibel* Derivatives and not particularly close as none has what might be called a rod-like bow. Brooch 4 has a three-coil spring, and Brooch 5 probably does as well. The dating of these is: Dragonby, late first century BC–early first century AD (May 1996, 235, fig. 11.2,16); Bagendon, *c.* 20/25 BCA–D 43/45 (Clifford 1961, 168, fig. 29,5); Bishopstone, Iron Age (Bell 1977, 131, fig. 63,30); Dragonby, Iron Age (May 1996, 235, fig. 11.2,18, fig. 11.3,28, 30); Dragonby, late Iron Age–early Roman (ibid., 233, fig. 11.1,11 & fig. 11.2,13); Dragonby, mid first century (ibid., 235, fig. 11.1,12); Lullingstone, first century (Meates 1987, 102, fig. 47,278); Ditches, AD 40–60 (Trow 1988a, 46, fig. 22,12); Gussage All Saints, before AD 75 (Wainwright 1979, 108, fig. 82,1006); Ditches, Claudian-Neronian (Trow 1988a, 46, fig. 22,14). There are a further twelve which cover the rest of the Roman period into the fifth century. There should be little doubt that these iron brooches are essentially Iron Age in date.

However, Brooch 4 had only three coils. Those in copper alloy are a mark of the extreme south-east, but those in iron are not really found there. The sites producing the dating indicate this: Skeleton Green, *c.* 10 BC–AD 20 (Partridge 1981, 132, fig. 66,1); Silchester, AD 25–15 BC (Fulford and Timby 2000, 325, fig. 150,17); Silchester, AD 40–50/60 (ibid., 325, fig. 149,7, fig. 150,20, 22); Great Oakley, Northants, late first–near the end of the second century (Meadows 1992, 93, not illus). The example from Ditches suits this broader distribution and the dating again points to the Iron Age.

Colchester derivatives

8 E(262), s.f.156 (Fig. 44, no. 13). Found with copper alloy penannular brooch (see below) threaded through its pierced catch plate, its spring is missing. It had been held by a rear-ward facing hook and the corrosion behind the left-hand wing bears the imprint of three coils. It is now certain that the hook merely held the chord, the spring itself being soldered to the left-hand wing. The surviving part of the hook has two concave cuts. Each wing is slightly curved to seat the spring and has a groove at its end. The front of the bow has two V-sectioned ridges down it with a step on each side. The sides and back of the bow are flat, each rear corner has a broad chamfer. The catch-plate has a three-sided opening, two being concave. The top edge of the catch-plate has a small step before joining the bow. The brooch had been tinned or silvered and is very finely finished in all its details.

The type is named after its most consistent feature: Rearhook. The type is overwhelmingly East Anglian and so concentrated in the northern part that it can be called the Icenian brooch. This is emphasised even more by the remarkable circumstance that, of all the brooch types studied by the writer, it is the only one which can be described as having come to an abrupt end. Normally, the curve produced by potting the dates of contexts shows the period when most were being consigned to the ground and then there is a long tail somewhere in which there is the final date when survivors in use were no longer to be seen: see Brooch 9. This does not apply to the Rearhook, there is no tail. Not that all Rearhooks became unwearable either because it was not wise to be seen wearing the badge of a defeated tribe, or because the workshops ceased to exist, many were no doubt taken by Roman soldiers as grisly mementoes. This may well have applied to the example from Ditches, in which case, although the terminal date for the type can be set firmly in the bracket AD 60/65, this specimen may have continued for a few years longer.

9 (+), s.f.224 (Fig. 45, no. 3). The spring is held in the Polden Hill manner; an axis bar through the coil passes through a pierced plate at the end of each wing; the chord is held by a rearward-facing hook. The brooch is only 35mm long, but is highly detailed. Each wing has a bald moulding at its end. The bow is clasped by curved mouldings rising from the wings. The hook rises from an area outlined by a chisel-cut V pointing towards the top pair of divided lenticular bosses on the bow itself. There are six angled pairs of bosses. On the upper and middle part, the four central pairs form saltires lying across the width of the bow. The bottom pair end in ridges bordering a central groove along the whole bow in the upper part of which is a beaded ridge. The foot-knob runs all

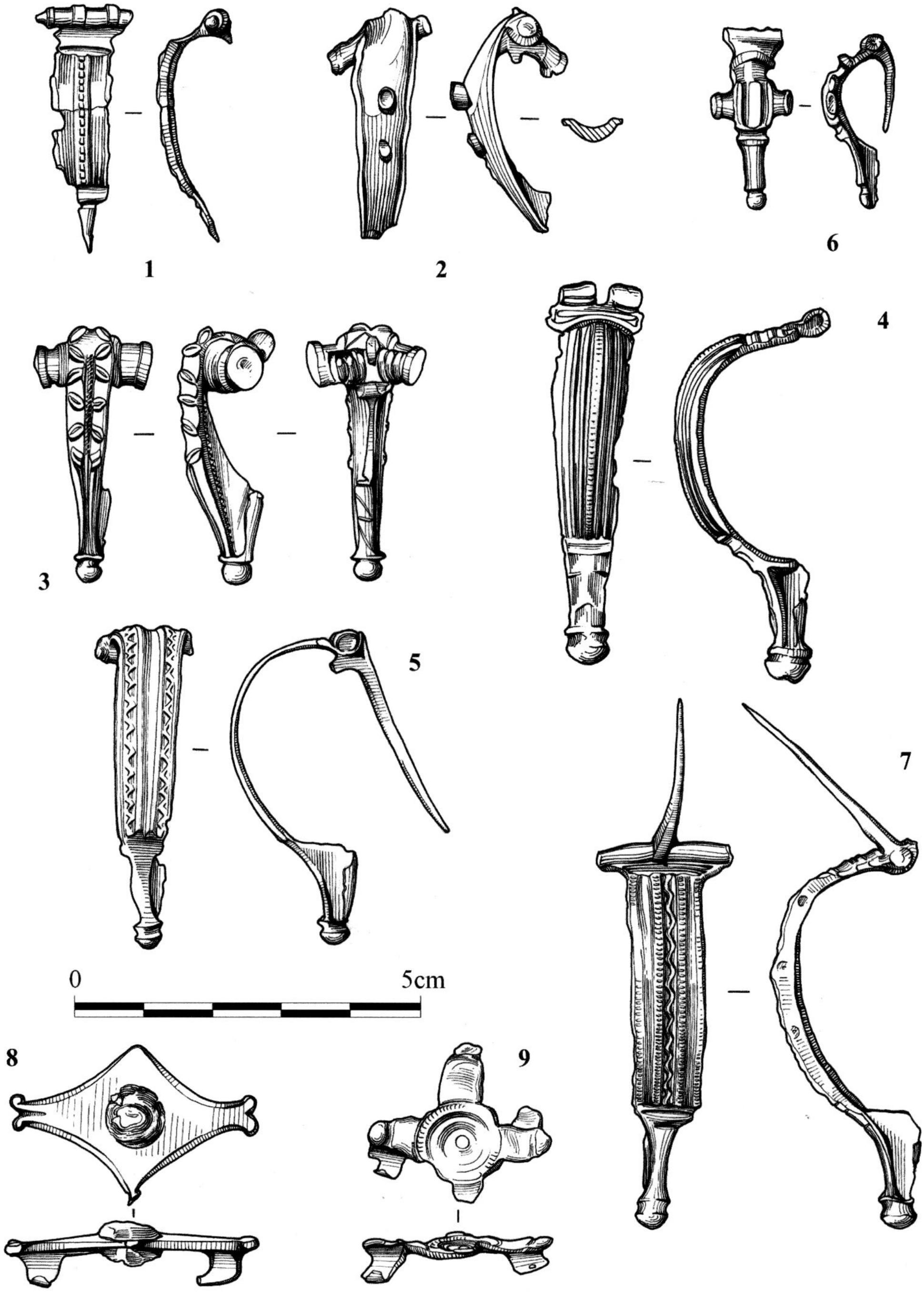

Fig. 45. Brooches.

round and has a small cross-moulding across its top. The catch-plate has a line of rocker-arm ornament down both sides next to the bow and the return has two repeats of a cross-groove with a diagonal one below.

Of all the terms given by Collingwood to brooches to act as an *aide memoire*, the name Dolphin has perhaps stuck more than most. However, it has been indiscriminately applied, and should be reserved for members of the present family where the head of the bow distinctly over-rides the wings. The family is diverse and was very widely traded, but it was made and at home in the West Midlands and the Marches, a major variation with a hinged pin belonging specifically to the southern Pennines. Rather than discuss the dating of this particular design for which the writer has only one context, it is better to review the dating of all varieties.

Arranged in the order of the beginning of each date-range of the full type is: Derby, three examples, late first-early second century (Dool and Wheeler 1985, 283–4, fig. 123,4,5); Croft Ambrey, three examples, *c.* AD 75–160 (Stanford 1974, 144, fig. 67,2,4,5); Wroxeter, AD 80–120 (Bushe-Fox 1916, 23, pl.15,5); Shakenoak Farm, Oxon, early second century (Brodribb *et al.* 1968, 95 fig. 27,7); Verulamium, AD 115–130 (Frere 1972, 114, fig. 29,10); Worcester, before 120 (Darlington and Evans 1992, 73, fig. 37,1); Leicester, early–mid second century (Clay and Pollard 1994, 145, fig. 74,23); Derby, *c.* AD 120–150 (Dool and Wheeler 1985, 283–5, fig. 124,8); Watercrook, 120–190 (Potter 1979, 210, fig. 84,11); Worcester, *c.* AD 130–170 (Darlington and Evans 1992, 73, fig. g32,3); Wall, Staffs, Hadrianic–early Antonine (Gould 1967, 17, fig. 7,7); Caerleon, Hadrianic–Antonine (Zienkiewicz 1986, 170 fig. 54,5); Wilcote, Shakenoak Farm, mid second–mid third century (Brodribb *et al.* 1971, 118–9, fig. 47,70); Derby, AD 150–175 (Dool and Wheeler 1985, fig. 123,6); Baldock, AD 150–180 (Stead and Rigby 1986, 113, fig. 45,83); Whitton, Glam, before 160 (Jarrett and Wrathmell 1981, 169, fig. 69,12); Tewkesbury, AD 160–200 (Hannan 1993, 64–5, fig. 18,4); Exeter, late second–early third century (Holbrook and Bidwell 1991, 235, fig. 101,20); Tewkesbury, 200–250 (Hannan 1993, 64, fig. 18,3); Worcester, three examples, earliest third century (Darlington and Evans 1992, 73, fig. 37,4,5 and not illus.) and *c.* AD 240–300 (ibid. 1992, 73–5, fig. 37,6); Gloucester, late third century (Hurst 1986, 39, fig. 22,1); Prestatyn, late third–early fourth century (Blockley 1989, 92, fig. 10); Derby, late third–fourth century (Dool and Wheeler 1985, 283–5, fig. 125,11); Gadebridge, before mid-fourth century (Neal 1974, 123, fig. 54,14); Gloucester, late fourth century (Hassall and Rhodes 1975, 66, fig. 26,1); Cirencester, two examples, AD 375–410/20 (McWhirr 1986, 104, fig. 77,1,2).

If these date-ranges are arranged as a bar chart, the beginning of the *floruit* is obviously close to 75 and runs strongly through to *c.* AD 150/175. There is a group which persists into the early third century, but the link back to the main run is weak and it should be seen as being residual, and thereafter all are clearly residual. The only example from the Polden Hill Hoard (British Museum, 46, 3–22, 125) should say more about the dating of the hoard than about the brooch.

Headstud relative

10 F(426), s.f.305 (Fig. 45, no. 2). The pin was hinged, the axis bar being housed in thin circular-sectioned wings. Corrosion may hide one or two mouldings at the end of the surviving one. The bow is broad with

a step down each side and once tapered to a foot. The stud is tall for its diameter and contains traces of a bubbly enamel. The lower bow has corrosion accretions hiding any other decoration.

Not a member of the classic Headstud varieties, this belongs to a clutch which belong to the south-west, but the dating is not strong: Camerton, AD 90–200 (Wedlake 1958, 225, fig. 52,26).

Wroxeter

11 Square 012, 1986 barley slad. (Fig. 46, no. 2). The spring is held between two pierced lugs behind the flat head of the bow. The chord is internal. The head-plate is well curved but is straight across the top from which rises a cast-on loop on a pedestal. The head of the bow has straight sides with a central beaded ridge and three divided lenticular bosses down each side. The ridge ends in a small nib and the knob is replaced by a small lenticular boss on each side at the top of the lower bow. This has a median ridge, a step down each side and tapers to a foot with a large projection to either side.

A member of a group rather than a family, there is a fairly close parallel at Cirencester (unpublished CIR 64, CII (24), sf.44, AW (952)) and others also related occur in Gloucestershire, but only one in the overall group is dated: 5668 Derby, AD 115–140 (Dool and Wheeler 1985, 293, fig. 128,133).

Aucissa-Hod Hills

12 1987 field-walking, Ditches Field (Fig. 45, no. 4) The head-plate has a broad central flute and there is a small ridge across the top of the bow. This arrangement is repeated at the bottom of the upper bow which has a beaded ridge down each side and another sunk in the centre of the swelled front. The lower bow is short with an arris down the centre. The separately made foot-knob has a cross-moulding around its top. The brooch was once tinned or silvered.

13 E(261), s.f.154 (Fig. 45, no. 5). The simple broad flute with a small ridge on each side across the head-plate is repeated at the base of the upper bow. This has a deep and wide central hollow. On each side is a broad face with a series of triangular cells which leave a reserved chevron between them. The foot-knob is like that on the previous brooch.

Brooch 12 is a studier casting than any of the main Aucissa group. It also has beading on the edges of the bow and lacks the head-plate of the main series. It stands in the line of development from the Alesia towards the Aucissa itself. However, there is little indication of its date, save that it ought to precede the more famous type, that standing at the very end of the development and immediately before the final development of the Hod Hill.

Brooch 13 is a reminder that, while it was the Aucissa proper which was the ancestor of the Hod Hill in its commonest forms, other types also had a hand in the development. In this case it was the version in the Alesia-Aucissa line which had a central flute. These, being rarer, have a much more restricted number of dated examples: King Harry Lane, unphased (Stead and Rigby 1989, 314, fig. 116, g158.2) and Phase 3 (ibid. 326, fig. 127, g205.3) both before *c.* AD 55, if not AD 45: see Comment after Brooch 7; Colchester, AD 43/44–61 (Hawkes and Hull 1947, 322, pl. 96,125); Colchester, 49–61 (ibid., 322, pl. 96,126); Wroxeter, before *c.* AD 130 (Webster 2002, 102, fig. 4.7,23) Bancroft, late first–late century (Williams and Zeepvat 1994, 299, fig. 136,48). The example from Wroxeter could have arrived as early as AD 55/60 and the one at Bancroft have come from the Iron Age–Roman interface there. On the whole, both Brooch 12 and Brooch 13 would have been survivors in use at AD 45 and may have continued as such to AD 60/65.

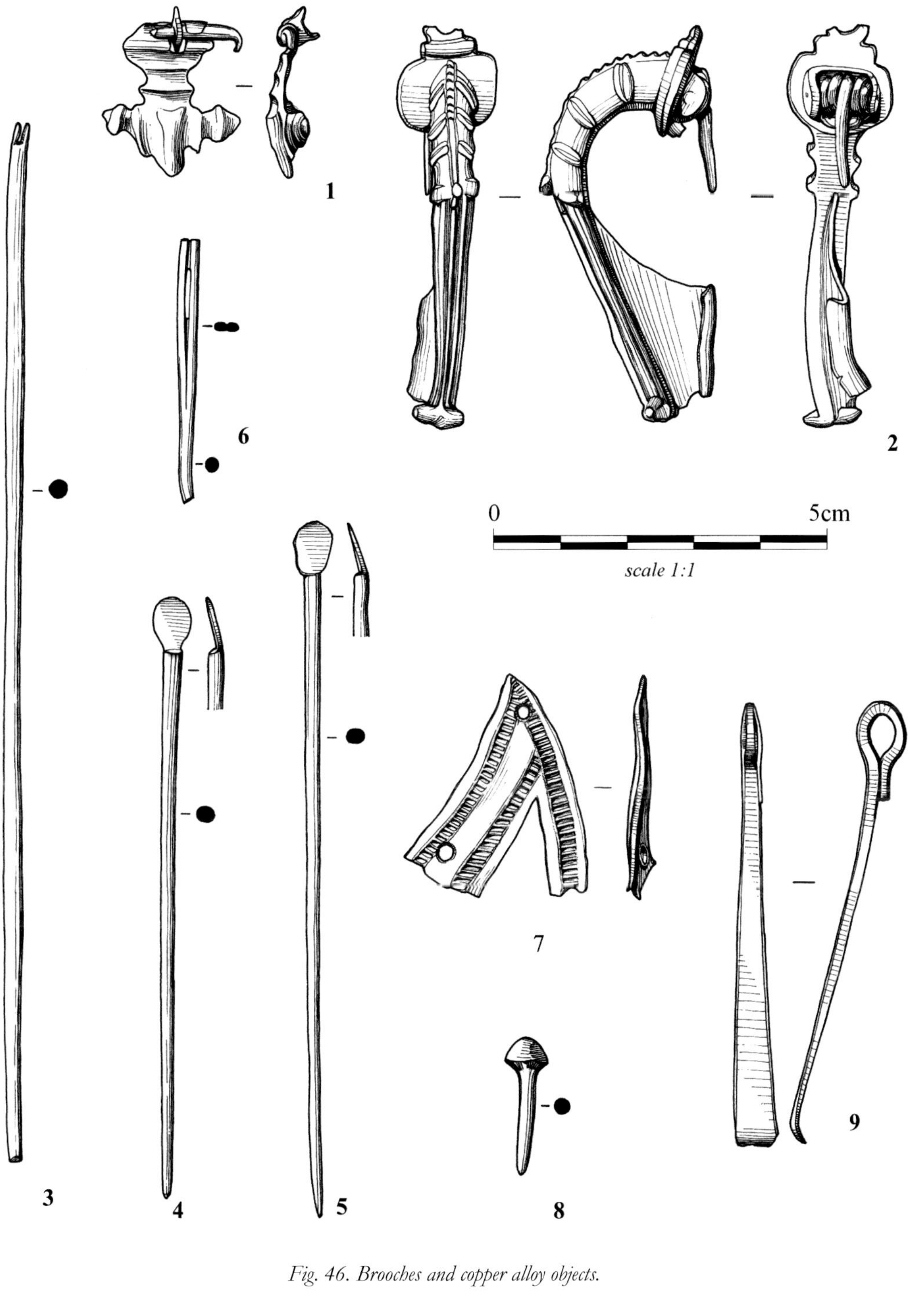

Fig. 46. Brooches and copper alloy objects.

14 E(286), s.f.169. (Fig. 45, no.7). The knobs on the ends of the axis bar survive. The head-plate narrows towards the bow and has a buried ridge between two cross-flutes. The bow is thick with a flute down each side with beaded borders and a sunken wavy line down the centre. The line was formed by punching a cast ridge on alternate sides. There were at least three, and probably four, iron bars through the bow to carry knobs on each side. None of these survives. The upper bow ends in a cross-flute offset by a step on each side. The lower bow is thin and straight-sided. The separately made foot-knob has a very wide cross-flute round its top.

15 (+), s.f.180, Tr.G (Fig. 45, no. 1). In poor condition and in two pieces, the knobs on the axis bar are present. The design on the head-plate has been reduced to a single thin ridge next to the bow. This has a slack profile, a flute down each side and a sunken bead-row down the centre. Like the last, there are iron bars through the upper bow, this time three and, again, the knobs do not survive. The upper bow is stopped by a cross-flute and the lower bow is thin and, apparently, plain. The foot-knob is missing.

Both of these are members of a "type" identified by M. R. Hull (Clifford 1961, 176) who took the chief feature to be iron bars carrying beads and knobs, or knobs alone through parts of the brooch. Thereafter, the use of series of projections simulating these, albeit badly, provided another strand. However, the boundaries are blurred, not only in development, but in what really defines a type. Hull was right to see the distinctive feature appearing firstly on Aucissa-like brooches, but he illustrates (ibid., figs 34–5) the very reason why it is difficult to be sure that it is a genuine type. He included designs standing as separate groups in their own right: the distinctive feature is purely decorative.

Both of these brooches are of the same basic design and based on one of the parallel designs of the Aucissa proper. The available dating is: Bagendon, two examples, 20/25–43/45 (Clifford 1961, 177, fig. 33,2,4); Silchester, AD 40–50/60 (Fulford and Timby 2000, 332, fig.153,62); Colchester, AD 43/4–48 (Hawkes and Hull 1947, 323, pl. 97,139); Bagendon, AD 43/45–AD 47/52 (Clifford 1961, 177, fig. 33,3,5); Old Winteringham, before AD 75 (Stead 1976, 198, fig. 99,90); Harlow temple, before AD 120 (France and Gobel 1985, 77, fig. 39,24); Canterbury, AD 100/110–AD 300/320 (Blockley *et al.* 1995, 975, fig. 408,93). Basically, the date-range ends *c.* AD 50.

Hod Hills

16 E(299), s.f.189 (Fig. 45, no. 6). Only 23mm long. The upper bow repeats that of brooch 17 with a wing in the centre of each side. There is a marked cross-moulding running in an arc across the top and a smaller one across the bottom.. The lower bow is rounded in front and runs to the usual two-part foot-knob. There are traces of a tinned or silvered finish.

17 (+), s.f.201, Metal detected find. (Fig. 46, no. 1) Only the upper part of the upper bow survives. The head-plate is reduced to a flat surface curving in to the bow and separated from that by a cross-moulding. The bow itself has a flute down each side leaving a broad swell between. Attached to each side at the top is a wing with a boss at its end.

18 F(404), s.f.426 (Fig. 44, no. 10). The upper bow has five cross-mouldings, the one in the middle being slightly more prominent than the rest, separated by broad flutes. The lower bow is slightly rounded and tapers to an ordinary two-part foot-knob.

Hod Hills all form a large family with a bewildering variety of decorative traits, there being few set designs. This means that it can be hard to tell which are exclusively early and which run on to develop into the late first–early second century types with enamel. The Hod Hill itself arrives fully developed with the Roman army and its hangers-on. None has been shown to be from an Iron Age context, even though there is a suspicion that two from the King Harry Lane cemetery may be exceptions: one seems to have a design related to a Rosette (Stead and Rigby 1989, 286, fig. 114, g153.2) and the other is a member of the larger "Bagendon" group (ibid., 334, fig. 132, g233.3). Both are from Phase 3 burials and so could have been deposited after the conquest, but the writer favours a closing date of AD 43/5 which makes this unlikely. However, neither is what may be called a common Hod Hill.

The dating of those from Ditches for Brooches 16 and 17 is: Baldock, AD 25–50 (Stead and Rigby 1986, 120, fig. 47,114); Colchester, AD 44–60 (Niblett 1985, 116, fig. 75,35); Braughing, AD 45–55 (Potter and Trow 1988, 48, fig. 20,63); Baldock, first-third century (Stead and Rigby 1989, 120, fig. 47,118); Chichester, Flavian (Down 1981, 257, fig. 10.2,16); The Lunt, before *c.* AD 75 (Hobley 1969, 109, fig. 19,7); Dorchester, AD 75–120 (Woodward and Leach 1993, 123, fig. 62,38); Verulamium, before *c.* AD 80 (Wheeler and Wheeler 1936, 204, fig.43,7); Nettleton, late first–early second century (Wedlake 1982, 121, fig. 50,12); Fawkham, before AD 100 (Philp 1963, 69, fig. 3,1); Colchester, AD 100–150 (Crummy 1983, 10, fig. 5,32); Fishbourne, AD 100–280 (Cunliffe 1971b, 100, fig. 38,26); Chichester, second century (Down 1981, 283, fig. 10. 27,42). There is no really clear picture for the overall *floruit*, perhaps the best that can be said is that most are before AD 75/80.

As for Brooch 18, the distinctive design has produced the following dating: Fishbourne AD 43–*c*.75 (Cunliffe 1971b, 100, fig. 38,25); Verulamium mid first century (Wheeler and Wheeler 1936, 204, fig. 43,8); Verulamium 49–55 (Frere 1972, 116, fig. 30,17); Alcester first-early Antonine (Cracknell and Mahany 1994, 168, fig. 80,68); Colchester *c.* AD 50/5–AD 75/80 (Crummy 1983, 10, fig. 5,34) Caerleon AD 75–110 (Zienkiewicz 1986, 168, fig. 54,1); 9044 Nettleton later first–early second century (Wedlake 1982, 121, fig. 51, 20). The writer has noted only from a later context which should show that the bias in the dating is properly represented above. Again, a terminal date of *c.* AD 75/80 seems appropriate. It should be noted, however, that a version of this design is found amongst the enamelled series spanning the end of the first and the beginning of the second century.

Plate

19 Field-walking, Barley Slad, 1985. (Fig. 45, no. 8) The pin was hinged. The plate is flat and heavily tinned or silvered. The shape is that of a concave-sided lozenge. At each end of the long axis is a bifurcation, each arm turning out to end in a small curve. The terminals on the short axis are, as usual, poorly preserved. In the centre of the plate is a circular sunken area filled with iron corrosion products, with the remains of a rivet in the centre.

A large and eclectic family whose commonest features are found on this example: the bifurcated end and the central circular recess with a hole for a rivet. The dating given is for all varieties:

Dating: Bagendon AD 20/25–43/5 (Clifford 1961, 184, fig. 36,6); Colchester, AD 43/4–48 (Hawkes and Hull 1947, 326, pl. 98, 177,179); Hod Hill, *c.* AD 44–50 (Brailsford 1962, 13, fig. 11, F2–F5); Lockleys, Claudian (Ward-Perkins 1938, 352, fig. 2,2); Fishbourne, AD 43–*c.*75 (Cunliffe 1971b, 104, fig. 40,39); Colchester, AD 49–60/61 (Hawkes and Hull 1947, 325–6, pl. 98,165, 170, 172–3); Braughing, AD 45–150 (Potter and Trow 1988, 49, fig. 21,70); Waddon Hill, *c.* AD 50–60 (Webster 1965, 144, fig. 6,5; 1981b, 61, fig. 25,6); Longthorpe, Claudian-Neronian (Dannell and Wild 1987, 87, fig. 21,11); Silchester, AD 50/60–80 (Fulford and Timby 2000, 334 f.154,72); 11393 Colchester AD 60+; 11379 Richborough, pre-Flavian; 14729 Broxtowe *c.* AD 60–70/5; 14730, 14732 Castleford, AD 71/4–86; 11420 Wroxeter, Flavian; 14731 Castleford, AD 85/90–95/100; 11399 Colchester, before AD 100/150; 11356 Braughing, AD 100–150; 11362, 11396 Chichester, late third–early fourth century.

The writer has only four from later contexts and so it can be taken that the range above is properly representative: from the conquest to the Flavian period with a few lasting a little longer.

20 (+), s.f.173. (Fig. 45, no. 9). The pin was hinged. The main part is a small circular plate from which rise four long arms, each ending in a boss. The plate itself has a beaded border round a sunken area with a rivet hole in the middle.

This brooch may be related to the last, but there are no real parallels and the only dated one is from Baldock: 90–120 (Stead and Rigby 1986, 122, fig. 49,150).

Penannulars

21 E(262), sf.156 (Fig. 44, no. 14) Was found threaded through the catch-plate piercing of Brooch 8, the Rearhook. There are signs that the brooch had been made from rolled sheet metal. The surviving terminal was made by tapering out the wire to a point and then coiling it back to rise at right-angles to the plane of the ring.

The danger with coiled terminals is that one must distinguish between those like the ones on the present example, and those which scarcely coil at all and may only curve down to touch the ring. The former are Iron Age and run on into the early Roman period, the latter are Late Roman and are frequently found in Anglo-Saxon cemeteries. There is a danger, when terminals are either not complete, or have been carelessly made that confusion can creep in. The dating available is extensive and given below. It will be for the reader to decide where the cut-off points may fall: end of manufacture or of survival in use:

Dragonby, Iron Age (May 1996, 261 f.11.13, 141, 143) and probably Iron Age (ibid., fig. 11.13,140); West Stow, early–mid first century (West 1990, 71 166); Weekley, AD 25–mid first century (Jackson and Dix 1987, M77, fig. 23,1); Maiden Castle, AD 25–70 (Wheeler 1943, 264, fig. 86,6); Dragonby, Iron Age–Neronian/?Flavian (May 1996, 261 f.11.13,142); Wakerley, ?Iron Age (Jackson and Ambrose 1978, 220, fig. 57,9); Colchester, AD 49–61 (Hawkes and Hull 1947, 326, fig. 59,2); Hod Hill, before AD 50 (Brailsford 1962, 12, fig. 11,E8); Canterbury, AD 70/80–AD 100/110 (Blockley *et al.* 1995, 982, fig. 410,126); Gussage All Sts, mid first century (Wainwright 1979, 112, fig. 86,3044); Dragonby, early Roman? (May 1996, 261, fig. 11.13,14); Fishbourne, before AD 75 (Cunliffe 1971b, 107, fig. 40,44); Chichester, Flavian–early second century (Down 1981, 287, fig. 10.28,57); Dragonby, late first–second century (May 1996, 261, fig. 11.13,139); Castleford, AD 100–250 (Cool and Philo 1998, 56, fig. 17,148); Scole, AD 110–160 (Rogerson 1977, 134, fig. 55,12); Colchester, second–mid third century (Crummy 1983, 18, fig. 16,99); Dragonby, early–mid second century (May 1996, 261, fig. 11.13,147); Rudston, before late second century (Stead 1980, 95, fig. 62,10); Weldon, before AD 200 (Smith *et* al. 1989, 33, fig. 8,2); Stanground, late second–early third century (Dannell *et al.* 1993, 66, fig. 13,1); Wakerley, probably third century (Jackson and Ambrose 1978, 220, fig. 57,7); Baldock, third century (Stead and

Rigby 1986, 122, fig. 49,154); Ilchester, late third–early fourth century (Leach 1982, 247, fig. 117,27); Werrington, fourth century (Mackreth 1988, 92, fig. 20,4); Nettleton, mid fourth century (Wedlake 1982, 133, fig. 55,78); Chichester, mid fourth century (Down 1981, 259, fig. 10.2,23); Canterbury, AD 375–early fifth century (Blockley *et al.* 1995, 981, fig. 410,121); and the remaining eight come from Anglo Saxon cemeteries.

22 E(262), s.f.158 (Fig. 44, no. 9) Copper alloy penannular brooch (3234) too corroded to confirm the method of manufacture. Each terminal is turned back along the ring and has a groove across the centre; any other ornament has been destroyed by corrosion. The pin has a shallow hump.

Simple terminals like this have to be taken on trust: heavy wear may have destroyed a more complex design. However accepting it at face value other simple, folded terminals are dated: Hod Hill, two examples, before AD 50 (Brailsford 1962, 12, fig. 11,E11); Polden Hill Hoard, AD 50–75? (British Museum, 1846, 3–22,122); Ditches, Claudian-Neronian (Trow 1988a, 51, fig. 24,26); Halstock, before AD 60 or after AD 110/120 (Lucas 1993, 79, fig. 14,21); Bancroft villa, late first–late third century (Williams and Zeepvat 1994, 302, fig. 137,53); Dragonby, first–fourth century (May 1996, 261, fig. 11.13,150); Camerton, after AD 150 (Wedlake 1958, 234, fig. 54,64); Camerton, AD 150–200 (ibid., 234 f.54,63); Wilcote, before AD 200? (Hands 1993, 34, fig. 25,27); Wycomb, late Roman (Timby 1998, 329, fig. 138,36); and two from Anglo-Saxon cemeteries. These are clearly to be dated from latest Iron Age times into the second century.

23 E(340), s.f.184 (Fig. 44, no. 11). Both the pin and the ring are of circular section and were made from rolled sheet metal. The terminals are turned back along the ring and each has a rudimentary zoomorphic appearance with a long snout, eye-brow ridges and nicks tapering back to form the eye-sockets. The top of the head is defined by a small chisel mark on each side. The pin has a slight hump and the end is flattened to sit on the ring.

24 (+), u/s, Tr.H (Fig. 44, no. 12) Corrosion prevents the method of manufacture from being established. The terminals may have had some form of zoomorphic design; only the basic shape is left.

Both of these lie in a limbo land. They seem to have affinities with those of zoo- or near zoomorphic terminals, but not close enough to any identifiable sub-group to be put in with one. That being the case, and as none of those of the zoomorphic persuasion are Early Roman or before, the chances are that these two should be counted as being fourth century, if not late, unless the site itself provides better evidence of date.

Oddment

17 E(319) s.f. 179 (Fig. 52, no. 7) Fragment of copper alloy brooch. A complete bilateral spring without the pin. One side has been broken. There may be an axis bar. The type of brooch from which it came cannot be determined.

IRON AGE COINS

Colin Haselgrove

Catalogue

Note: Standard references in the coin list are as follows: 'Allen' = (Allen 1961); 'BMC' = (Hobbs 1996). Dating after Haselgrove (1987).

Unstratified fieldwalking find "Ditches" field

- s.f. -, Fig. 47, no. 1. Western silver unit. Allen Dobunnic A variant, cf. BMC 2950. Weight 0.69 gm, in good condition. Date *c.* 50–20 BC.

Obv. head to right, partly obscured; hair in two rows of crescents, smooth not serrated. The hair line is represented by a thin line rather than the normal pellets. Struck from a worn die. Rev. triple tailed horse left, with cock's head below and a 'dumb bell' ornament to its right. The horse has a collar or torc on its neck and a rope mane, but on this variant none of the three strands of the tail is beaded. In front of the horse is a ring and dot ornament and what may be a wheel; above it there is the usual arm with raised hand ornament.

Fill of Inner Enclosure Ditch

E(319)

- s.f. 178, Fig. 47, no. 2. Western silver unit. Allen Dobunnic G, inscribed Anted. BMC 3032. Weight 0.51 gm. Date *c.* AD 10–40, probably in the earlier part of this range.

Obv. disintegrated face to right, barely visible. Rev. stylised triple tailed horse; legend A(N) beneath the horse. Other details obscure.

Two further Iron Age coins, both Western issues inscribed Eisv, were found in the Inner Enclosure Ditch in 1982–83 (Sellwood 1988, fig 20 c, d).

Fill of Quarry pit

E(281)

- s.f. 162, Fig. 47, no. 3. Plated Western silver unit. Allen Dobunnic C – 0, BMC 2963–2968. Weight 0.82gm. Date *c.* 20 BC–AD 10, probably in the earlier part of the range.

Obv. crude head facing right with pointed nose; forehead marked with annulets, cross on chin, hair represented by groups of three pellets. Rev. triple tailed horse left, three petals on stalk beneath.

Make-up below Structure 1

F(484)

- s.f. 385, Fig. 47, no. 4. Plated Western silver unit. Probably Allen Dobunnic C, BMC 2963. Weight 0.93gm. Date as s.f. 162.

As s.f. 162, but Obv. head obscure. Rev. flower beneath horse has a central pellet and there is a crescent above the body of the horse.

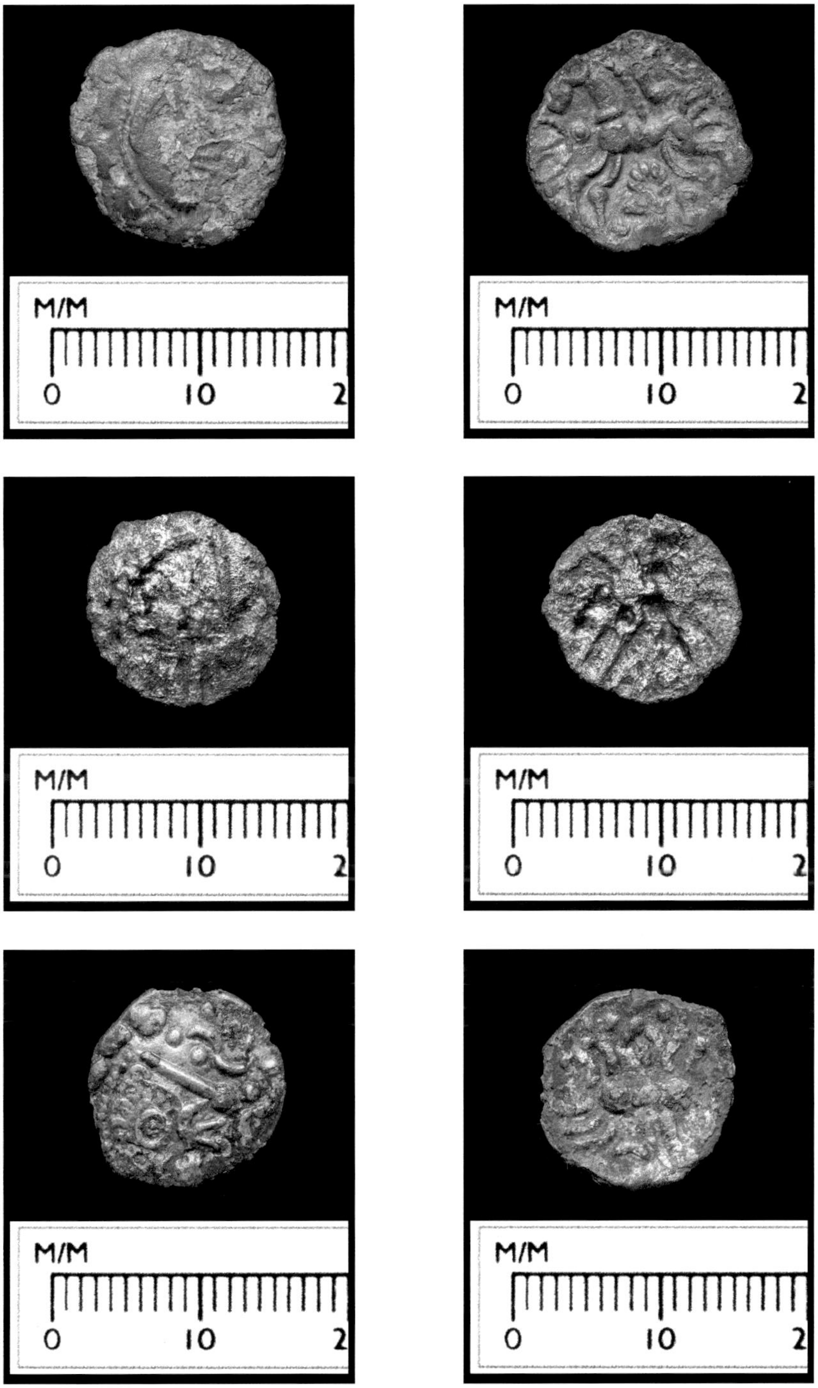

1

2

3

Fig. 47. Iron Age coins.

4

Fig. 47 continued. Iron Age coins.

Discussion

With the 1982–3 finds (Sellwood 1988), this brings to eight, the Iron Age coins found at Ditches, six of them from the excavations, the other two fieldwalking discoveries. With one exception, possibly two, the coins are local types as one would expect. The only certain import is the Tasciovanus bronze (Sellwood 1988, fig. 20 c) which originated in the Bedfordshire–Hertfordshire area of the Eastern coinage region, a facet of the outside contacts enjoyed by the wider Bagendon settlement complex of which the Ditches forms part (Moore *et al.* forthcoming; Trow 1988a). The other coin which is not certainly local is Fig. 47, no. 1. These Class A coins are certainly the prototype for the rest of the Western silver series (Allen 1961), but there are several variants and they have a wide distribution. At the time of writing, the Ditches coin is actually only the second site find in the heart of presumptive Dobunnic territory (the other is from Naunton), and three of the remaining six come from the Channel coast: at Hayling Island, Hants; Mount Batten, Devon and Bois l'Abbe, Eu, Seine Maritime. While this could reflect later secondary circulation due to their high silver content, it opens the possibility that at least some Class A variants originated outside the nascent Western coinage region and thus that the mainstream silver series starting with Class B, like the gold, has its ancestry in central southern England. Stray Class A finds show a similar pattern, with 3–4 coins from that same general area and one only from within the Western region.

The Class A coin is certainly the earliest of the Ditches finds and may date soon after the mid first century BC. It is followed chronologically by the two Class C–D coins (Fig. 47, no. 3–4) and the Tasciovanus bronze, all probably late first century BC types. The four remaining coins are all inscribed, dating to the first century AD: two of Anted (Sellwood 1988, fig. 20b) and two of Eisv (Sellwood 1988, fig. 20 c–d). None of the coins appear to have been recovered at their original place of loss and their pattern of stratification in secondary deposits is unremarkable. The latest issues, two of Eisv and one of Anted, were found associated with Claudio-Neronian material in the filling of the

Inner Enclosure Ditch (D100; E319) very much as happens with the latest coin types in south-east England (Haselgrove 1987); they could easily be post-Conquest losses. The two Class C–D issues are also both from mid first century AD or later deposits (E281; F484) but have a higher probability of being earlier losses. The other coin of Anted, from the mid to late second century AD track ditch A(29) is certainly residual. The depositional patterning thus offers little guide to the duration of the Iron Age occupation at the site.

Another way to approach this question is by comparing the Ditches finds to the larger collection from nearby Bagendon (which has 41 identifiable coins) and with the overall pattern of site finds in the Western coinage area – a total of 275 coins from 65 sites (Haselgrove 1993, 59, fig. 7). With the proviso that with such a small group, little weight can be attached to the absence of particular types and even marked trends may be misleading, the striking feature is undeniably the high proportion of inscribed issues from the excavations. At 50%, the figure is more than twice their normal incidence in the region, but one which ties in well with the other indications of the Ditches' unusual importance in the Conquest period. Less securely, the proportion of early types appears quite normal and supports what little other evidence there is for an earlier start to the occupation, principally pottery and the 'currency' bars (Trow 1988a).

The one major difficulty is the apparent contrast to Bagendon with its marked preponderance of earlier issues, which is difficult to reconcile with the later dating suggested for the latter site (Trow 1988a, 76). Unless the coins were brought there specifically for melting down, we should have to suppose that if they have any chronological significance, they were somehow transferred there with other rubbish from an earlier occupation site in the vicinity. It may therefore be worth remarking on the virtual absence of Class B coins, the earliest mainstream silver type, from the two sites, as these are the most widespread of any Western issue. This aside, however, the combined coin finds from the two sites together present a profile which *is* nearly identical to the regional mean and ought therefore to imply that the Bagendon complex as a whole has a history of occupation spanning virtually the entire currency of the Western coinage.

ROMAN COINS

Richard Reece

Note: This consolidated coin list includes coins excavated in 1982–3 (Trow 1988a, 43) marked by an asterisk.

Fill of Quarry pit/Inner Enclosure Ditch

E(310)

- s.f. 175. Claudius I, AD 41–54, RIC 94 (Ceres) provincial issue (see Kenyon below for full report).

Inner enclosure ditch

*B(13)

- s.f. 26. Marcus Aurelius, as RIC 1271 (Antoninus Pius) but a sestertius.

Outer enclosure ditch

*A(27)

- s.f. 9. House of Theodosius, AD 383–388, as CK 789.
- s.f. 8. Valentinian II, AD 388–392, as CK 162.

*A(28)

- s.f. 12. Constantine II, AD 330–345, copy as HK 49.

Rubbish deposit sealing fill of cellar

F(427)

- s.f. 232. Valerian I, AD 253–260, RIC 267 but legend 6.

Unstratified from fieldwalking (Ditches field)

Vespasian, AD 69–79, RIC 9.

Constans, AD 345–348, HK 148(?).

Third–fourth century AD illegible.

Unstratified from fieldwalking (Barley Slad field)

Carausius, AD 286–293, as RIC 98, mint mark illegible.

Barbarous radiate, AD 270–290, rev, sacrificial implements.

Barbarous radiate, AD 270–290, rev. illegible.

Barbarous radiate, AD 270–290, rev (?) Fortuna.

Constantine I, 330–335 AD, HK 55.

Constatinopolis, AD 330–345, copy as HK 52.

Constantine II, AD 330–345, copy as HK 49.

(?) House of Constantine, AD 330–345, as HK 48(?).

Constans, AD 345–348, HK 148.

House of Constantine AD 345–348, as HK 137.

Constans, AD 345–348, as HK 453(?).

Constantius II, AD 348–350, (?) CK 409.

House of Constantine, AD 350–360, copy as CK 25.

House of Constantine, AD 350–360, as CK 25.

House of Valentinian, AD 364–378, as CK 317.

Third–fourth century AD illegible.

Third–fourth century AD illegible.

Unstratified from excavation

F(+) s.f. 206. Constantine I, AD 330–335, HK 373.

F(+) s.f. 207. Barbarous radiate, AD 270–290. Rev. illegible.

CLAUDIAN PROVINCIAL COIN

Robert Kenyon

Fill of Quarry pit

E(310)

– s.f. 175. Claudius I, RIC 94 (Ceres), dupondius, 26.4 mm diam, axis 8, 7.9g, some wear.

The distinction between this provincial coin and a *dupondius* of Claudius I (AD 41–54) from the mint of Rome is clear on both stylistic grounds and in terms of size and weight, which are typically below those of its Roman counterpart. This type of *dupondius* depicting Ceres, is the second most common Claudian coin type found in this country, after the *as* which depicts Minerva. The coin is squarely struck on a round blank using competently engraved dies with accurate legends.

No die links with the series of Claudian coins from Cirencester could be positively established although a link with a slightly corroded *dupondius* can tentatively be suggested. In addition, a *dupondius* from Gloucester may have shared an obverse die with the Ditches coin and similarities in the portrait on an *as* from Wroxeter suggests that the dies used for both coins originated in the same workshop. The significance of the production of competent dies for both *dupondii* and *asses* at the same centre is indicative of a large and diverse operation. Despite the recognition of three (possibly) die-related coins in use in military centres in the western region of Britain it is not yet possible to determine the location at which they were minted, however a military origin for its circulation seems likely for this coin.

Recent analyses of two very large coin deposits, totalling in excess of 10,000 coins, found in the nineteenth and twentieth centuries in France (Besombes and Barrandon 2000) provides metallographic and stylistic evidence for 'official' minting centres operating during the reign of Claudius I in Gaul and the Iberian peninsula. These provincial mints complemented the output of the mint of Rome and were 'the source of an abundant supply of copper and brass coins issued over a very short time' (ibid.,161). In turn, those coins were supplemented in circulation by purely local strikings that were products of illicit mints.

Besombes and Barrandon's work provides a useful model against which British provenanced Claudian coins can be compared. An analysis such as this could lead to identification of which British-provenanced Claudian coins originated from outside Britain and those others that may have been struck in Britain. Comparison of the *dupondius* excavated at the Ditches with those coins illustrated in Besombes and Barrandon's study fails to provide any clear stylistic link with coins from the proposed 'official' provincial mints of Gaul or Spain. This underweight (at little more than half the weight of an official *dupondius*), undersized coin is surely a local striking from an illicit mint. Comparison with illustrations of provenanced Claudian coin-finds published in other French, Spanish and German publications also failed to identify any link with the Ditches coin. This coin is therefore likely to be a product of an illicit mint operating in Britain.

Excavations at Colchester, Essex between 1971 and 1979 produced good stratified evidence showing smaller, lighter copies of Claudian coins were produced later than full-size copies. An imitated Claudian *dupondius* of a similar size to the Ditches coin was found at Colchester (Kenyon 1987, 29) in a pre-Boudiccan destruction layer (*c.* AD 49–60/1) that would suggest a mid-Claudian – mid-Neronian date for the circulation of the Ditches coin. The degree of wear on the Ditches coin indicates some use in circulation, and so it is likely that the coin was lost within a few years of being minted.

AN IRON FINGER-RING

Martin Henig

Unstratified fieldwalking find (Fig. 48)

The ring is of simple form, flattish in section expanding markedly towards the bezel. The type (Henig 1978, 35–7, type III) is characteristic of the first and second centuries AD, but the ring is likely to be no later than *c.* 170 AD for a wider ribbon-hoop (Henig, type V) is the normal Late Antonine form. About a third of the ring remains. It was originally some 22mm in diameter and the hoop measures 2.5mm at the narrowest surviving point and 13mm across the bezel. This finger ring has also been commented on elsewhere (Henig 1990, 157 fig. 11.8; 2002, 87 illus. 37)

A red jasper intaglio with flat upper face (shape Fl Henig 1978, 35, fig. 1) is set-in the bezel. It measures 11mm in length by 9mm in breadth and is 2mm thick. The subject is a votary clad in a short tunic bending over a lighted altar as though to drop an offering onto the flame. Beyond the altar is a *tholos* with domed roof standing upon a rock. Garlands hang between the columns of the shrine of which three are shown.

The gem may be attributed to the Small Grooves Style (Maaskant-Kleibrink 1978, 251–2). Typical of this style is the patterning of thin wheel-grooves on the roof of the shrine and on the figure's tunic as well as the coarser texturing of the rocks. However, the cutting is altogether plainer and less exuberant than on a much larger red jasper cut with the same subject found at Corbridge and which I attribute to a North British workshop of the late second century (Henig 1978, 33–4, 248 and pl. xv no. 493). Also from this studio is a broken jasper intaglio from Vindolanda (Henig 1978, 292 and pl. xxvi no. App. 60) showing a similar building possibly being approached by Pan though most of the figure is missing. The more restrained and classical style of the North Cerney gem befits its earlier date and for a more-or-less contemporary comparison we cannot do

Fig. 48. Iron finger-ring.

better than cite a gem in Munich (Brandt 1972, no. 2313) depicting a putto bringing an animal offering to a comparable open shrine of containing an image of Priapus. No deity is shown within the temples on the Ditches and Corbridge gems and that on the Vindolanda stone is but roughly blocked out but there is no doubt that Priapus or similar rustic fertility god was intended.

PIPECLAY FIGURINES

Catherine Johns

Fill of cellar

F(485)

– s.f. 340, (Fig. 49, no. 12). Pipeclay figurine of Venus. The upper part of the figure is present, down to the waist, and the front and back sections, made in separate valves of the mould, have parted from each other. The height of the front half is 62mm, that of the back 68mm.

The fabric is a warm cream colour with a tinge of pink in section and on the interior surfaces. There are a few small red inclusions and tiny, very sparsely distributed, flakes of mica. The outside surface is smoothly polished. The interior surfaces bear evidence of the method of manufacture, showing deep, clear fingerprints where the artisan has pressed the clay into the deeper parts of the mould, namely the face, chest and the back of the head.

The pose is that of Venus Anadyomene, standing with her right hand raised to her hair and her left down at her side, holding a fall of drapery: the latter is of course missing in this instance. She has a rather long, narrow face whose features are so blurred as to be almost indistinguishable, a slender neck and small breasts. Her hair is dressed in a thick roll around her head with a bun low on the neck and loose tresses trailing on the shoulders. The head is tilted to the right. The general effect is of a slender figure in a slightly languid pose, but this might be modified if the whole figure were preserved.

It has not been possible to find a close parallel made from the same or a similar mould, but Rouvier-Jeanlin (1972) no. 142 is similar, though more sharply rendered. The hairstyle is well seen in Rouvier-Jeanlin no. 36.

Style and fabric indicate that the figurine was manufactured in Central Gaul: this is the usual source of pipeclay figurines found in Roman Britain. Venus was by far the most commonly represented subject, and the pose seen here was the favourite one. In the present state of knowledge, it is not possible to assign the piece to a particular manufacturer, though the names of many Gallo-Roman coroplasts are known. The figure is of second-century date.

F(426)

– s.f. 377, Not illustrated. Fragment of a second pipeclay figurine, apparently the shin of a standing figure. The cream coloured fabric is slightly coarser than that of s.f. 340, with small black and brown inclusions.

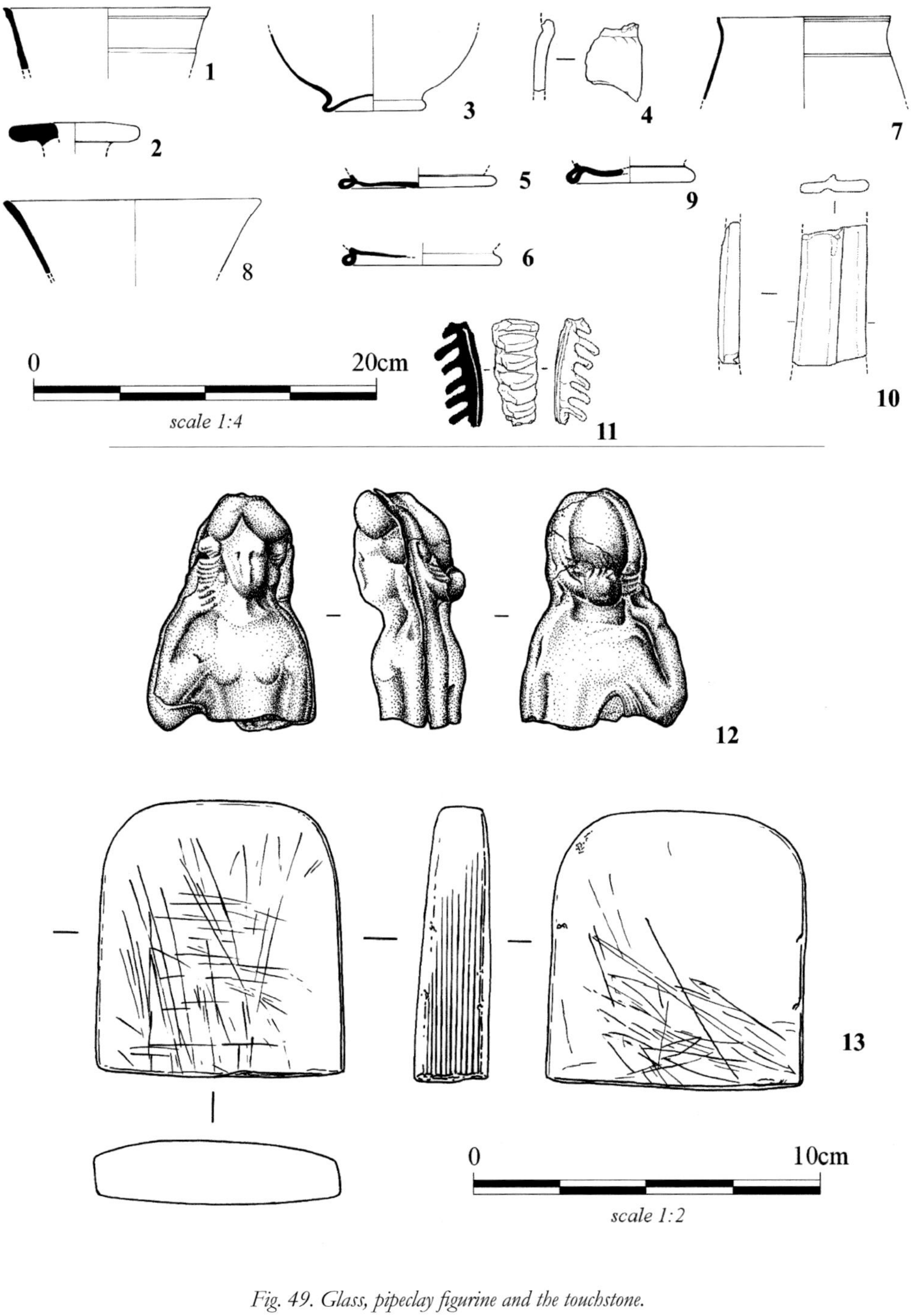

Fig. 49. Glass, pipeclay figurine and the touchstone.

THE GLASS

John Shepherd

Introduction

Seventy-eight individual pieces of glass were submitted for identification. Of these, one is modern (s.f. 222), two are Roman window glass (s.f. 318a and 318b) and three are beads (s.f. 236, 278, 283). The remainder are small fragments from a variety of well-vessel types dating form the late first to third centuries. The detailed catalogue below records thirteen identifiable fragments. The full catalogue at the end of this section itemises the body sherds which were too fragmentary to warrant more detailed description.

Discussion

Four observations can be made about the glass assemblage from Ditches villa. Firstly, as mentioned above, the forms recorded here are well-known on sites in Britain dating from the late first through to the third centuries. Secondly, the small group of beaker fragments dating from the mid to late second century from F(426) should be highlighted. Third, while common late first and second century forms are present there is an absence of recognisable late third or fourth century vessel types. Finally, the paucity of window glass on a site such as this is probably worthy of note.

These include the common forms of beakers (cat. no. 2 and 4), beakers or bowls (cat. no. 6–9) and jugs (cat. no. 10–12) of the late first century and early second century. The conical beaker, no 2, comes from a well-attested late first century group of drinking vessels and bowls, heavily decorated with facetted wheel-cutting and finished with grinding and polishing (Isings form 12). The remaining identifiable bowl and beaker fragments come from non-specific types. The jug fragments come from distinctive forms made, it would appear, in the Seine/Rhine region of the empire (Price 1978, 74). It is possible that the amber fragment, cat no.1, comes from such a vessel or the associated bulbous bodied bowl/jar (Isings 1957, form 67c).

Also recorded here are a number of prismatic or cylindrical bottle fragments (cat. no. 13 and twelve other fragments in the general catalogue) of the late first to third century. These ubiquitous vessels were used as in transit and storage containers for a variety of liquid foodstuffs, cosmetics and pharmaceutical preparations. Their presence on a site such as this is to be expected.

One significant assemblage here, however, comes from F(426) and contains fragments from a number of distinctive drinking vessels of the mid to late second century (cat. no.s 3 and 5 and fifteen other fragments in the general catalogue). These colourless cups, decorated with fine horizontal wheel cutting, can be compared to a large collection of similar vessels found in a shallow pit at Felmongers, Harlow, Essex (Price 1987) and deposited, according to the dating of the associated samian ware, to around AD 60–170. These appear to be the standard drinking vessels of the mid to late second century.

Associated with these vessels in F(426) are two fragments of window glass. One is of the common, early, cast matt/glossy variety. The second appears to be of the double glossy cylinder blown variety. Unfortunately the fragment is small so this identification is tenuous.

Finally, as mentioned above, there are no examples of the distinctive late Roman vessel types – e.g. conical beakers (Isings 1957, form 106) in natural greenish colourless tints, with or without abraded decoration and with either cracked-off or fire-rounded rims, are type fossils in Romano-British assemblages of the late third and, particularly, the fourth century. For example, see Shakenoak (Harden 1973, 103), Frocester Court (Price 1979, 41–2), Bath (Shepherd 1985, 162–3, no. 1–16) and Cirencester (Shepherd 1986, 120, nos. 625–641). Shallow bowls (Isings 1957, forms 116 and 117) in the same metal and of the same date are also absent (for example see Frocester Court, Price 1979, 42, no. 12; Shakenoak, Harden 1973, 102–3, fig. 52; Cirencester, Shepherd 1986, 121, no. 642–644).

Catalogue

Monochrome glass

1. F(426) s.f.317 Fragment from side of an indeterminate vessel, free-blow amber coloured glass. Late first–early second century AD.

Colourless glass

2. F(426) s.f.297 (Fig. 49, no.1) Fragment from rim and part of side of a conical-shaped beaker (Isings form 21). Thick colourless glass, with a faint green tint. Freeblown, ground and polished rounded rim with a fillet just below the lip, broad plain ground band above a zone of well-cut facets. Late first century AD.
3. F(426) s.f.321 (Fig. 49, no. 7) Fragment from rim and side of a beaker, freeblown colourless glass with faint green tint. Rim outsplayed and cracked off. Decorated with a horizontal wheel-cut line below the rim, on the top of the body. Mid–second century AD.
4. F(417) s.f.261 (Fig. 49, no. 8) Fragment from the rim of a beaker or bowl. Freeblown colourless glass with faint green tint. Thickened fire-rounded lip on an outsplayed rim. Late first–early second century AD.
5. F(426) s.f.316 Fragment from the lower part of a beaker, freeblown colourless glass with greenish tint. Body decorated with four horizontal wheel-cut lines. Mid-second century AD. (Not illustrated).
6. F(426) s.f.319 (Fig. 49, no. 5) Fragment from base of a beaker or bowl, freeblown colourless glass with greenish tint. Hollow tubular base ring. Second century AD.
7. F(426) s.f.293 (Fig. 49, no. 6) Fragment from base of a beaker or bowl, freeblown colourless glass with greenish tint. Hollow tubular base ring. Second century AD.
8. F(426) s.f.304 (Fig. 49, no. 3) Fragments from the lower part of a beaker or bowl, freeblown colourless glass with greenish tint. A pushed in, cut out base ring. Mid-second century AD.

Naturally-coloured glass

9. (+) s.f.152 Fragment from base of a beaker or bowl, freeblown natural greenish-blue glass. Hollow tubular base ring. Late first or second century AD. (Fig. 49, no. 9).
10. F(485) s.f.344 (Fig. 49, no. 10) Fragment from the flat strap handle of a flagon. Applied and drawn onto a blown vessel.

Dull green glass. Late first or early second century AD.

11. F(469) s.f.285 (Fig. 49, no. 4) Fragment from the lower part of the neck of a flagon or phial (Isings form 55). Mould-blown, natural greenish-blue glass. Body of vessel decorated with low-relief spiral ribs. Late first or early second century AD.
12. F(417) s.f.260 (Fig. 49, no. 11) Fragment from the pinched spur of the handle of a flagon or jug (Isings form 55). Applied and drawn natural greenish-blue glass. Late first or early second century AD.
13. F(491) s.f.359 (Fig. 49, no. 2) Fragment from the rim of a bottle (Isings form 50/51). Natural greenish-blue glass. Late first or second century AD.
14. F (491) s.f.286 Fragment from the upper part of the handle of a bottle or flagon (Isings form 50/51), applied and drawn natural greenish-blue glass. Late first or second century AD. (Not illustrated)

Miscellaneous glass fragments

Remains of glass objects too fragmentary to illustrate, by context and colour.

Key

Colours

AMB	Amber brown
BLU	Blue
COL	Colourless
NGB	Natural greenish-blue
NBG	Natural bluish-green
NG	Natural green
NB	Natural blue
WHI	white

Forms

BEAK	Beaker
BOTT	Bottle
BOTTS	Square bottle
BOWL	Bowl
CUP	Cup
JUG	Jug
PMBOWL	Pillar-moulded bowl
VESS	Vessel of indeterminate form
WIND	Window

Miscellaneous

E	Early
L	Late
Frag	Fragment
Dec	Decoration

Unstratified

- s.f.211, COL, CUP, Same vessel as in F(417) s.f.216, mid to late second century AD.
- s.f.382a, COL, VESS, Roman.
- s.f.382b, COL, VESS, Roman.
- s.f.382c, COL,VESS, Roman.
- s.f.382d, COL, VESS, Roman.
- s.f.382e, COL, VESS, Roman.
- s.f.203, NGB, BOTT, Isings form 50/51, late first or second century AD.
- s.f.383, NGB, BOTT, Isings form 50/51, late first or second century AD.
- s.f.217, NB, VESS, Roman.

Fill of Inner Enclosure Ditch

E(366)

- s.f.190, NGB, PMBOWL, Small and very abraded,, mid to late first century AD.

Phase 9a. Destruction deposits

F(416)

- s.f.221a, AMB, VESS, Different vessel to s.f.221b, late first or early second century AD.
- s.f.221b, AMB, VESS, Different vessel to s.f.221a, late first or early second century AD.

Floor Level in Room R6

F(417)

- s.f.261a, COL, VESS, Roman
- s.f.270, COL, VESS, Roman.
- s.f.261b, NGB,VESS, Roman.
- s.f.271a, NGB, VESS, Roman.
- s.f.271b, NGB, VESS, Roman.
- s.f.272, NGB, BOTTS, Isings form 50, late first or second century AD.

Fill of cellar

F(426)

- s.f.287, COL, VESS, Roman.
- s.f.295, COL, CUP, Body frag. cut linear

dec., mid to late second century AD.
- s.f.302, COL, CUP, Base frag., mid to late second century AD.
- s.f.307, COL, CUP, Body frag. Cut linear dec., mid to late second century AD.
- s.f.315a, COL, CUP, Body frag. Cut linear dec, mid to late second century AD.
- s.f.315b, COL, CUP, Body frag. Cut linear dec., mid to late second century AD.
- s.f.315c, COL, CUP, Body frag. Cut linear dec., mid to late second century AD.
- s.f.315d, COL, CUP, Body frag. Cut linear dec., mid to late second century AD.
- s.f.316a, COL, CUP, Body frag. Cut linear dec. , mid to late second century AD.
- s.f.316b, COL, CUP, Body frag. Cut linear dec., mid to late second century AD.
- s.f.316c, COL, CUP, Body frag. Cut linear dec., mid to late second century AD.
- s.f.316d, COL, CUP, Body frag. Cut linear dec., mid to late second century AD.
- s.f.316e, COL, CUP, Body frag. Cut linear dec., mid to late second century AD.
- s.f.316f, COL, CUP, Body frag. Cut linear dec., mid to late second century AD.
- s.f.327a, COL, CUP, Body frag. Cut linear dec., mid to late second century AD.
- s.f.327b, COL, CUP, Body frag. Cut linear dec., mid to late second century AD.
- s.f.292, NGB, BOTT, Isings form 50/51.,late first or second century AD.
- s.f.318a, NGB, WIND, Cast, Matt/glossy., Early Roman.
- s.f.318b, NGB, WIND, Blown, double glossy., Roman.
- s.f.318c, NGB, BOTT, Isings form 50/51., late first or second century AD.
- s.f.322, NGB, BOTTS, Isings form 50., late first or second century AD.
- s.f.331, NGB, BOTTS, Isings form 50., late first or second century AD.
- s.f.310, NG, BOWL, Rim frag., late first to third century AD.
- s.f.281, NB, BOTTS, Isings form 50., late first or second century AD.
- s.f.328, NB, BOTTS, Isings form 50., late first or second century AD.
- s.f.283, NG, BEAD, Roman.
- s.f.278, WHI, BEAD, Roman.

F(427)
- s.f.236, BLU, BEAD, Roman.

F(485)
- s.f.289, COL, BOWL, Body frag. Cut linear dec., late first or second century AD.
- s.f.355, COL, VESS, Roman.
- s.f.354, NGB, VESS, Roman.
- s.f.356, NGB, VESS, Roman.
- s.f.367a, NGB, BOTTS, Isings form 50.,late first or second century AD.
- s.f.367b,NGB, BOTT, Isings form 50/51, late first or second century AD.

F(488)
- s.f.378, COL, BOWL, Body frag. Cut linear dec., late first or second century AD.
- s.f.379, NGB, BOTTS, Isings form 50., late first or second century AD.

F(491)
- s.f.288, COL, CUP, Body frag. Cut linear dec., mid to late second century AD.
- s.f.363, BG, BOTT, Isings form 50/51, late first or second century AD.

Phase 9a, Robber Trenches

F(434)
- s.f.258, NBG, VESS, Badly distorted by fire., Roman.

Floor Level in Room R5

F(437)
- s.f.222, COL, WIND, Intrusive, Modern.

F(468)
- s.f.241a,COL, CUP, Rim frag. cut linear dec., mid to late second century AD.

– s.f.241b, COL, VESS, Roman.
– s.f.241c, COL, VESS, Roman.

Occupation layer below Structure 1
F(504)
– s.f.404a, NG, VESS, Roman.
– s.f.404b, NG, VESS, Roman.

THE TOUCHSTONE

Stephen Trow

with analysis by Andrew Middleton and petrological identification by David Moore

Fill of Inner Enclosure Ditch

E(273)

– s.f. 186 (Fig. 49, no. 13) A fragmentary sub-rectangular object in a fine grained, dense black rock considered to be a touchstone.

When viewed by eye and under a binocular microscope the stone shows fine flecks of what appears to be gold. These flecks have been analysed by energy-dispersive x-ray analysis (EDXA) in the scanning electron microscope (SEM) in an attempt to determine the composition of the metal being assayed.

The results confirm the presence of gold and suggest that the alloy being assayed was of relatively high purity, with an approximate composition Au 96%, Ag 3.5%, Cu 0.5% (the level of copper may have been somewhat reduced as a result of leaching during burial). Only a few of the numerous metal traces observed were analysed and it should be recognised that more exhaustive analysis may have revealed a range of compositions.

WORKED STONE

Fiona Roe

Rubbish deposit accumulated over cellar

F(457)

– s.f. 253. Segment from rotary quern, upper stone, probably worn, Iron Age style, traces of rings on grinding surface, smooth top surface, part of spindle hole; diam *c.* 420mm, thickness at hole 74mm, thickness at rim 65mm, 2.5kg. Drybrook sandstone (medium-grained arkosic sandstone with quartz, pinkish feldspar grains and a little mica).

Fill of Iron Age pits

F(517) Pit F[505]

– s.f. 419. Lower stone rotary quern, about three-quarters complete, thick Iron Age style, convex grinding surface, shallow socket for spindle, fairly flat base, pecked into shape round edge; diam 265mm, thickness in centre 157mm, thickness at rim 100mm, 15.5kg. Upper Old Red Sandstone, quartz conglomerate.

– s.f. 420. Fragment from rotary quern, burnt, upper stone, thick Iron Age style, part of hole for spindle, slightly concave grinding surface, top surface pecked into shape; now 132 × 125 × 121mm, 2.1kg. Upper Old Red Sandstone, sandstone.

F(541) Pit F[540]

– s.f. - Fragment from rotary quern with few diagnostic features, possibly upper stone of thick Iron Age style, small area of pecked outer surface; now 196 × 158 × 114 mm, 3kg. Upper Old Red Sandstone, sandstone, iron stained pinkish.

Discussion

Four rotary quern fragments were retrieved from the 1985 excavations. One of the querns is about three quarters complete, a lower stone with a socket for the spindle, s.f.419, while the other three are more fragmentary pieces from upper stones. All four querns are of the later Iron Age variety, being notable in particular for their relatively great thickness. Two different materials were used, deriving from in or around the Forest of Dean. Three of the querns were made from the Devonian Upper Old Red Sandstone, both quartz conglomerate s.f.419 and sandstone s.f.420 and s.f.541). These came from the phase 2 pits, giving them an approximate late Iron Age to mid first century AD date. Two fragments, representing both an upper and lower stone, were found in fill F(517) of pit F[505] and another piece came from fill F(541) of pit F[540]. The fourth fragment, s.f.253, was made from Drybrook sandstone, a Carboniferous sandstone from the same general source area. This was found in an accumulation of rubble or rubbish over a backfilled Roman cellar and looks like a residual item F(457).

These pieces demonstrate some

of the characteristics of local Iron Age rotary querns. Finds of this kind of quern are not common in Gloucestershire and they must have been in use for a relatively short period before being superseded by the altogether thinner Roman disc style of quern. Rotary querns were in use in Gloucestershire by the middle Iron Age, although the main evidence at the time of writing is from one site only. At Claydon Pike, Fairford, Upper Old Red Sandstone was used for two fragments from rotary querns (Roe in prep.). However, parts of three rotary querns made from hard, quartz sandstone, probably Upper Old Red Sandstone, were found unstratified at Uley Bury middle Iron Age hillfort (Saville 1983, fig. 15 and fiche).

Our knowledge of later Iron Age querns is often obscured by their common occurrence on sites where there is also Roman activity, as for instance at Coxwell Road, Faringdon (Shaffrey 2004, 241 and fig. 22.10). It is difficult to determine how long Iron Age style querns may have continued in use during the Roman period; some may well be of Roman date while there is always the possibility that other, disused Iron Age querns were redeposited in Roman contexts. However it is clear that Upper Old Red Sandstone was the preferred rotary quern material in the area. Two fragments occurred in late Iron Age contexts at West Hill, Uley (Roe 1993, 199). There is also the broken half of a rotary quern from Bagendon (Clifford 1961, 196 and Corinium Museum).

The choice of Drybrook sandstone to make the quern from the Ditches was less conventional, though similar finds have occasionally been recorded, such as an unstratified quern of later Iron Age type from West Drive, Cheltenham (Shaffrey 2002). A different quern material was used for a fragment of rotary quern that was found during the 1983 excavations at the Ditches (Trow 1988a, 58, fig. 28, no. 7). This is another piece of thick upper stone of the later Iron Age variety. This quern was made from May Hill sandstone, and as such is rather a rarity, since this quernstone was very much a saddle quern material and was used for very few rotary querns. The presence of May Hill sandstone at the Ditches has further significance, since it may be noted that the saddle querns found on Iron Age sites that are made from this gritstone are often associated with finds of Malvernian pottery, and especially the limestone tempered B1 variety (Roe 2007), as seen at Ditches (Trow 1988a, 64).

Consideration needs to be given to the question of whether the querns found in the late Iron Age pits might be part of structured deposits. The querns from pits here are all incomplete. However there is a possibility that querns were in fact intentionally broken up before deposition (David Heslop pers. comm.), and were perhaps intended only as token representations of corn grinding equipment. Human burials in pits, whether complete or not, are considered to be of particular significance (Cunliffe 1992, 76), and thus the two quern fragments accompanying the human bones in pit F[505] seem likely to be part of a structured deposit. The fragment of Old Red Sandstone quern from pit F[540] lacks diagnostic features and seems more likely to have been abandoned as rubbish, though it too may have had some further significance, and just possibly formed part of a closing deposit for the pit.

Details of the morphology of these local rotary querns are somewhat unclear, since no complete examples from later Iron Age contexts are known. They would appear to approximate to the 'Wessex' type described by Curwen (1937, 142 & fig. 4–13) but with grinding surfaces at comparatively shallow angles.

The upper stones in particular tend to be fragmentary, since these, with their central hole, would have tended to break more easily. For this reason there is no firm evidence as yet for the placement of handle holes on local Iron Age rotary querns but they were probably drilled into the sides of the upper stones. This is born-out by an upper stone of later Iron Age type and made from Old Red Sandstone from West Drive Cheltenham; this has a handle hole set at an angle into the upper stone (Shaffrey 2002, 99). A further detail is the method of manufacture and it can be seen that the three querns of Old Red Sandstone from the Ditches were carefully worked into shape by pecking. Similar working traces are to be found on other later Iron Age examples and on the many Roman querns made from the same stone.

This small assemblage adds to our limited knowledge of late Iron Age rotary querns. It stands out because, with inclusion of the quern from the 1982–3 excavations, no less than three different quern materials were utilised at Ditches, all imported from outside the immediate area. This site appears to stand at the transition, when May Hill sandstone, the traditional saddle quern material in the area, was found to be unsatisfactory for making rotary querns and was abandoned in favour of Old Red Sandstone. There were, perhaps, some difficulties in working the May Hill sandstone into the required shape, whereas it was possible to adopt a standardized technique of working by pecking to make the Old Red Sandstone rotary querns. The use of Drybrook sandstone may have been in the nature of an experiment, in the hope of finding the ideal quernstone, but it was the Old Red Sandstone that was to become the dominant quern material over much of southern England during the Roman period.

WORKED BONE

Stephen Trow

A large number of bone objects were recovered from the site, the majority deriving from the large deposits in the cellar. The vast majority of these finds are pins, a large number of which can be quite closely paralleled to examples found at Colchester (Crummy 1983), the Type 2 pins in particular having a probably similar date range to those found at Ditches, from the pre-Flavian to late second century AD (ibid., 21). At least one possible weaving comb was found in the cellar, which may be of Iron Age date (s.f. 366).

Floor level of room R6

F(417)

- s.f. 242. Fragmentary and burnt bone handle (not illustrated).

Fill of cellar

F(426)

- s.f. 296. (Fig. 50, no. 2) Intact slender pin with plain conical head. Crummy type 1 (Crummy 1983, 20–21). Length 76mm.
- s.f. 330. Intact slender pin with plain conical head, Crummy type 1. Length 76mm.
- s.f. 323. Repointed pin with plain conical head, Crummy type 1. Length 49mm.
- s.f. 312. (Fig. 50, no. 6) Intact pin with double groove below conical head, Crummy type 2 (Crummy 1983, 21). Length 112mm.
- s.f. 332. Broken pin with three lightly scored and incomplete grooves below conical head, Crummy type 2. Surviving length 47mm.
- s.f. 320. (Fig. 50, no. 7) Repointed pin with three grooves below conical head, Crummy type 2. Length 70mm.
- s.f. 303. Fragmentary pin with three irregularly executed grooves below low conical head, Crummy type 2. Surviving length 94mm.
- s.f. 275. Repointed sturdy bone pin with three grooves below conical head, Crummy type 2. Length 66mm.
- s.f. 333. Resharpened pin with four grooves below conical head, Crummy type 2. Length 72mm.
- s.f. 309. Intact needle with figure-of-eight eye, Crummy type 1 (Crummy 1983, 65). Length 96mm.
- s.f. 324. Resharpened needle with figure-of-eight eye, Crummy type 1. Length 66mm.
- s.f. 325. Broken bone needle with figure-of-eight eye, Crummy type 1. Surviving length 67mm.
- s.f. 329. Broken bone needle with figure-of-eight eye, Crummy type 1. Surviving length 69mm.
- s.f. 311. Broken bone needle with figure-of-eight eye, Crummy type 1. Surviving length 75mm.
- s.f.300. Green-stained (Crummy 1983, 20) needle broken through eye, Crummy type 1. Surviving length 46mm.

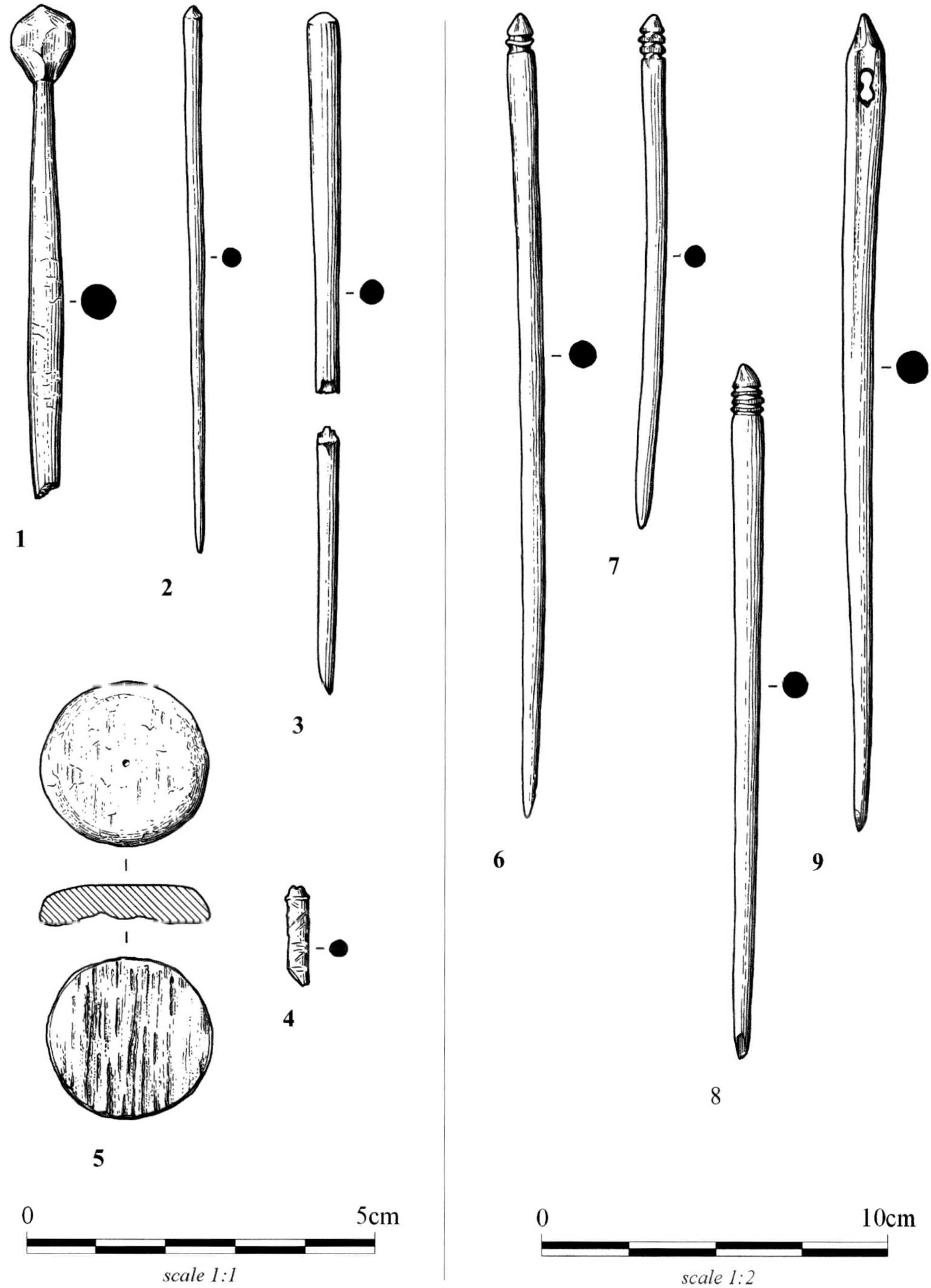

Fig. 50. Worked bone objects.

F(480)
- s.f. 269. Broken pin with two grooves below missing head, Crummy type 2. Surviving length 46mm.
- s.f. 283. Broken needle with figure-of-eight eye, Crummy type 1. Surviving length 27mm.
- s.f. 276. Fragment of green-stained needle or pin (not illustrated).

F(485)
- s.f. 357. Repointed slender pin with plain conical head, Crummy type 1. Length 49mm.
- s.f. 347. Broken pin with plain conical head, Crummy type 1. Surviving length 52mm.
- s.f. 336. Intact pin with double grooves below low conical head, Crummy type 2. Length 108mm.
- s.f. 428. Fragmentary pin with double grooves below conical head, Crummy type 2. Surviving length 46mm.
- s.f. 341. Resharpened needle with figure-of-eight eye, Crummy type 1. Length 84mm.
- s.f. 349. Broken needle fractured through eye, Crummy type 1. Surviving length 111mm.
- s.f. 339.Broken needle fractured through eye, Crummy type 1. Surviving length 71mm.

F(488)
- s.f. 369. (Fig. 50, no. 3) Fragmentary sturdy pin with low conical head, Crummy type 1. Surviving length 90mm.
- s.f. 375. Broken pin with double groove below tall conical head, Crummy type 2. Surviving length 48mm.

F(489)
- s.f. 371. (Fig. 50, no. 9) Resharpened needle with figure-of-eight eye, Crummy type 1. Length 112mm.

F(491)
- s.f. 360. (Fig. 50, no. 8) Broken sturdy pin with four grooves below conical head, Crummy type 2. Surviving length 95mm.
- s.f. 366. (Fig. 51, no. 3) Fragmentary cattle rib with shallow triangular serrated 'teeth' on surviving cut end. Small fragment of this or a similar artefact from F(514) suggests that s.f. 366 is residual and may have been originally deposited as early as phase 4. The use of this artefact is unknown. The serrations are far shallower than those on most Iron Age 'weaving combs' and a similar function seems unlikely. A possible use for s.f. 366 is for creating combed decoration on plastic materials such as unfired pottery or daub.

Rubbish deposit accumulated over cellar

F(427)
- s.f. 231. (Fig. 50, no. 1) Broken spherical-headed pin with medially swelling stem, Crummy type 3B (Crummy 1983, 21–22). Surviving length 68mm.
- s.f. 235. (Fig. 50, no. 5). Circular gaming counter.

Fill of pit F[505]

F(500)
- s.f. 388. (Fig. 50, no. 4). Phallic (?) terminal of broken pin (?). Surviving length 13mm.

Fill of pit F[564]

F(569)
- s.f. 427. Fragmentary and burnt transversely perforated ovicaprid metacarpal, possibly used as a bobbin (cf. Trow 1988a, fig. 28, no. 4 for intact example).

F(514)
- s.f. 429. Fragment of serrated cattle rib. Part of s.f 366 from context F(491) or a similar artefact. Not illustrated.

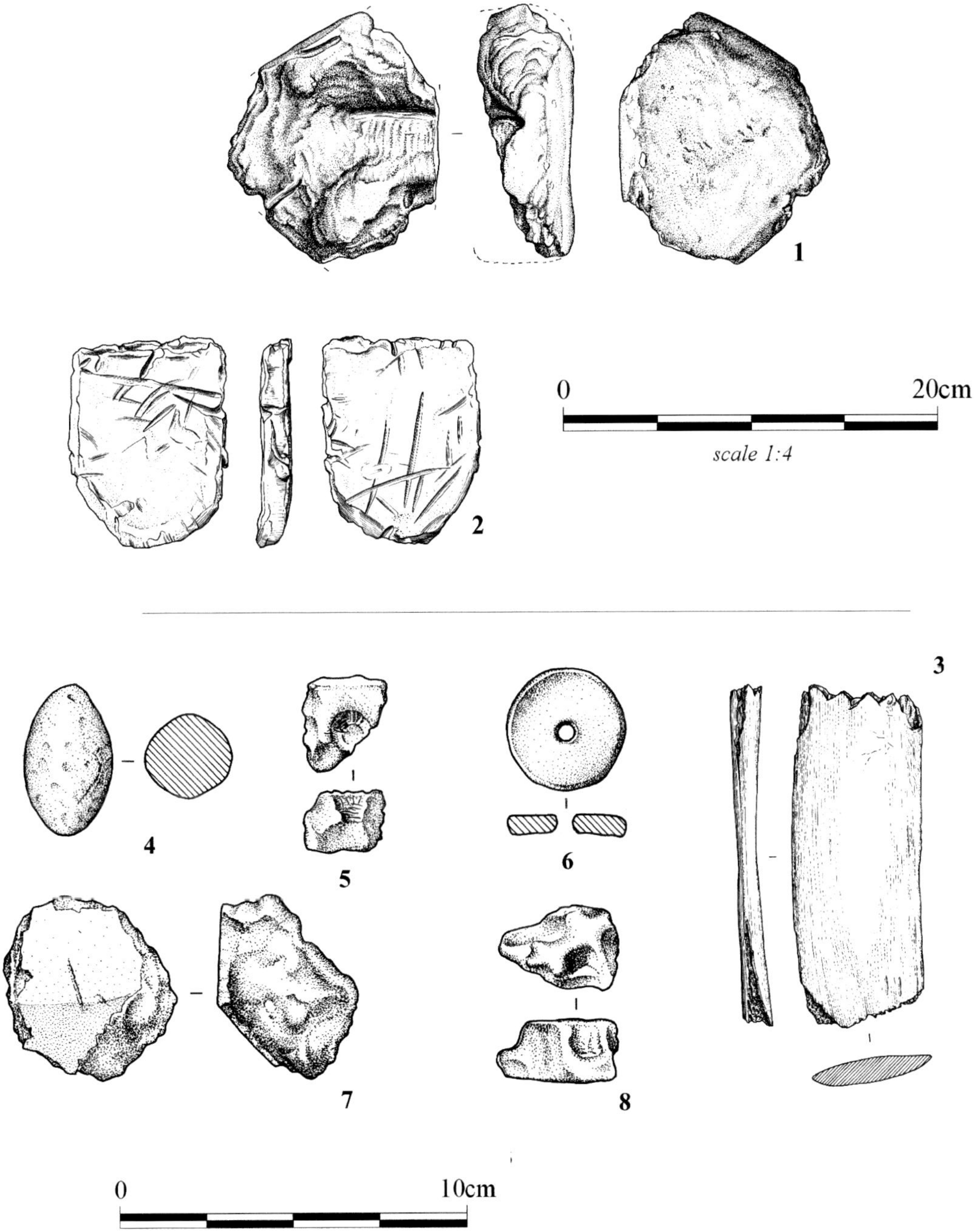

Fig. 51. Finds of clay, worked bone, plaster and lead.

LEAD/LEAD ALLOY SNAKE BRACELET

Catherine Johns

Fill of cellar
F(491)

– s.f. 365. (Fig. 52, no. 6), One terminal from a penannular snake-bracelet, 45mm long and 17mm wide. The snake-head is of the usual stylised pattern which is based on the distinctive arrangement of scales on the heads of snakes such as the Asclepian snake (*Elaphe longissima*) or the common European grass-snake (*Natrix natrix*). Behind the heads there is a ridge running along the back, but there are no engraved details, either stylised scales, often represented as a simple lattice pattern, or a purely decorative motif.

Discussion

The object belongs to an extensive series of Romano-British snake bracelets and rings in silver and base metal (for a general discussion of the typology of Roman snake jewellery, see Johns 1996, 44–47). The finest examples are probably the two from Castlethorpe, Bucks. (Marshall 1911, nos. 2782 and 8783; Way 1849, 348). The Snettisham jeweller's hoard also contains some good specimens (Johns 1997, nos 314–316). At the other end of the scale, there are numerous copper-alloy bracelets of very debased style and technique, the snake-heads simplified almost beyond recognition.

The Ditches example, which in form is an example of Johns (1996) Type Bii, is comparatively well-modelled, though it is in a simple style, and the metal of which it is made is unexpected. Lead and pewter are ill-suited for the manufacture of jewellery, and were not generally used for that purpose in Roman Britain. The usual method of simulating silver in a cheaper material was to plate bronze with silver or tin.

It is perhaps worth considering the possibility that the object was not a bracelet as such, but rather a model or archetype intended for manufacturing moulds from which bronze bracelets could be cast. In the absence of supporting evidence, however, the identification of s.f. 365 as a piece of jewellery should be preferred.

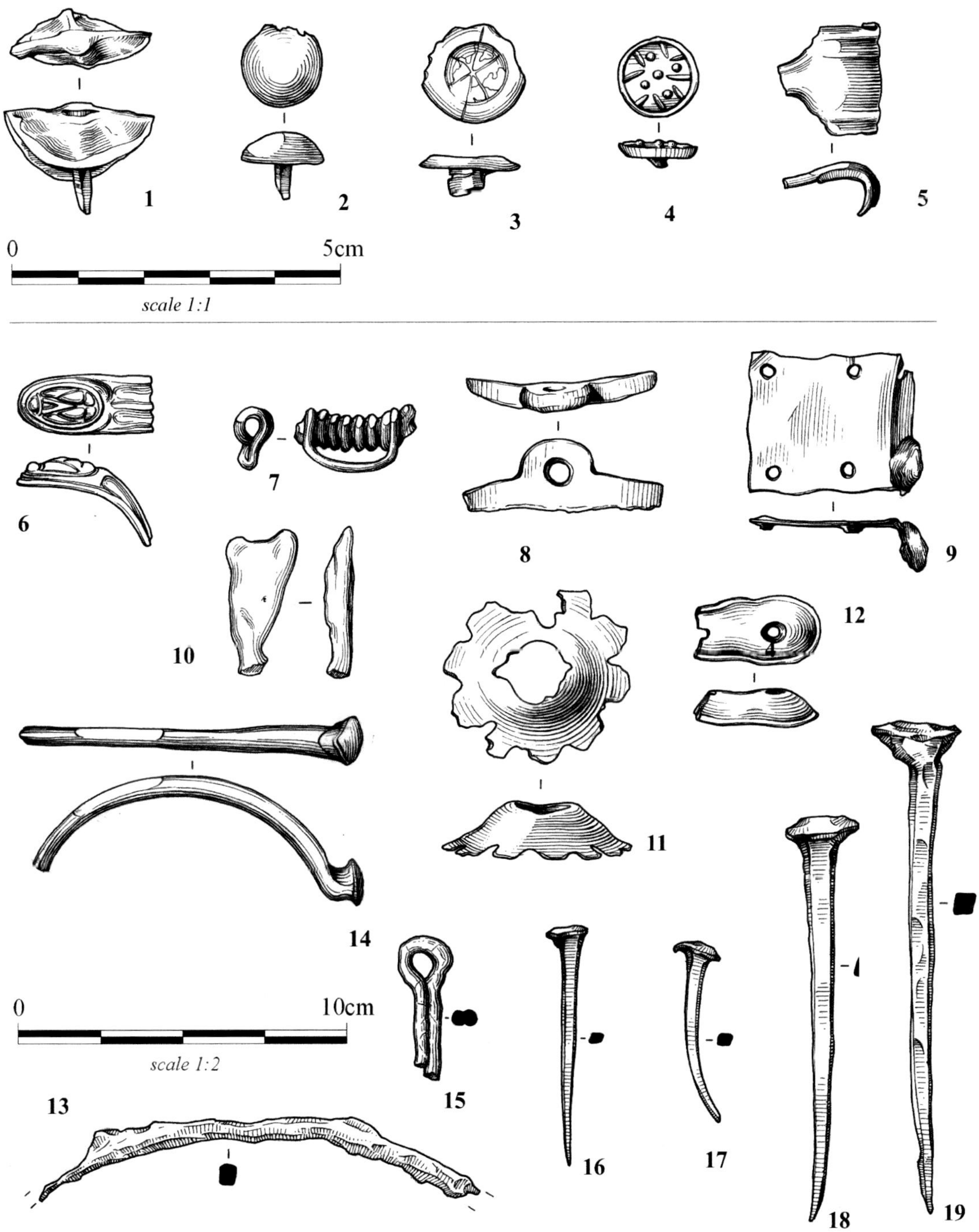

Fig. 52. Finds of copper alloy, lead snake terminal, lead and iron.

FINDS OF LEAD ALLOY

Stephen Trow

Unstratified: metal detector find from ploughsoil

F(+)

– s.f.205, (Fig. 51, no. 2) Half of a lozenge-shaped lead alloy ingot weighing 985g. Linear scars on both surfaces may have been caused by plough-action.

FINDS OF COPPER ALLOY

Stephen Trow

Unstratified from excavation

E(+)

- s.f. 153. Small pendant with White metal detail.

G(+)

- s.f. 155. (Fig. 52, no. 10) Cast boar's-head fitting with lightly-tooled details. Traces of attachment at snout (?). Decorative fitting for furniture(?) c.f. Muntham Court, Sussex plaques (Foster 1977, 17–19).

H(+)

- s.f. 189. (Fig. 46, no. 9). Fragmentary tweezers.

F(+)

- s.f. 416. Globular-headed decorative stud.

F(+)

- s.f. 208. Heat-distorted moulding with heavy transverse ribs.

Fill of Quarry pits

E(253)

- s.f. 160. Minute decorative tack.

E(273)

- s.f. 159. Angled rod, possibly broken ligula (?).
- s.f. 161. Spiral wire ring.

E(283)

- s.f. 163. (Fig. 52, no. 3) Flat-headed rivet with traces of white metal coating centrally.

E(284)

- s.f. 164. Spiral-headed pin.

E(286)

- s.f. 171. (Fig. 46, no.7). Decorative fitting with small rivet holes.
- s.f. 172. Flat-headed rivet.

Fill of Inner Enclosure Ditch

E(320)

- s.f. 181. Angled rod with broken expanded ends, possibly a ligula (?).
- s.f. 182. (Fig. 52, no. 4) Stud with applied white metal foil decorated with raised bosses and salire motif.

Layer/floor in Structure 1, room R6

F(417)

- s.f. 263. Flat-headed tack.
- s.f. 262. (Fig. 52, no. 8). Curved fitting.
- s.f. 273. Fragmentary convex stud head (not illustrated)

F(514)

- s.f. 402. Dome-headed stud.

Occupation layer below Structure 1

F(504)

- s.f. 415. (Fig. 52, no. 12).Tear-shaped convex fitting (strap-end ?) with entire and half-round rivet holes and grooved margin.
- s.f. 410. Small conical-headed decorative tacks. (five other examples not illustrated).
- s.f. 411. Flat plate with truncated rivet hole.
- s.f. 417. Convex-headed stud (not illustrated).

- A small group of scrap bronze objects including:- F(504) s.f. 400. Stud with slightly domed head (four other examples not illustrated).

F(546)
- s.f. 422. (Fig. 52, no. 5) Broken terminal fitting probably formed around a leather strap. Traces of white metal coating, margins emphasized by raised ribs.

Fill of cellar
F(426)
- s.f. 284. Flat circular-headed tack.
- s.f.306. Stud with slightly domed head.
- s.f. 308. (Fig. 46, no. 8) Globular-headed decorative tack.
- s.f. 279. (Fig. 52, no. 9). Right-angled bracket with six rivet holes, one occupied by a dome-headed rivet.
- s.f. 326. Rolled strip or "collar".

F(485)
- s.f. 348. (Fig.46, no. 4). Cosmetic scoop with angled ovate spatulate end.
- s.f. 338. (Fig. 52, no. 14). Broken drop handle.
- s.f.335. (Fig. 46, no. 6). Broken needle.

F(488)
- s.f. 368. (Fig. 52, no. 11). Fragmentary convex boss, originally with twelve "petals".
- s.f. 380. Rolled plate or "collar".

F(513)
- s.f. 401. (Fig. 52, no. 2) Concave-headed stud.

Rubble spread associated with Structure 2
F(526)
- s.f. 414. (Fig. 46, no. 3). Ligula with broken bifurcating head and angled circular spatulate end.

Fill of north–south ditch
E(264)
- s.f. -. Sub-rectangular section bar.
- s.f. -. Small dome-headed stud.

Phase 9b. Robbing of walls
F(421)
- s.f. 246. Fragmentary stud with high domed head and raised flange.

Phase 9/10. Patch of burning in south corridor
F(469)
- s.f. 251. Broken triangular-prismatic bar with raised rib on two edges.
- s.f. 250. (Fig. 46, no. 5). Cosmetic scoop with angled ovate spatulate end.

Phase 6? Slumping over Pit [540]
F(522)
- s.f. 412. (Fig. 52, no. 1) Flat-headed stud with cross motif folded double over shank.

FINDS OF IRON

Stephen Trow

Fill of Quarry pits

E(250)

- s.f. 150. (Fig. 44, no. 1). Uncertain iron object. Possibly fragment of brooch but too fragmentary for identification.

E(287)

- s.f. 510. Fragmentary split-pin.

Fill of cellar

F(426)

- s.f. 461, (Fig. 52, no. 15). Split pin.
- s.f. 237. Fragmentary collar or washer.
- s.f. 301. (Fig. 52, no. 13). Curved bar (handle?)
- s.f. 334. not illustrated. Fragmentary knife blade.
- s.f. 313. Tanged heavy knife blade.
- s.f. 290. Hook.
- s.f. 291. Long knife blade.

F(485)

- s.f. 337. Skewer.
- s.f. 346 not illustrated. Rectangular bar.

F(488)

- s.f. 376. Corrugated and flat sheet.
- s.f. 373. Spike
- s.f. 374. Bar with flared end.

F(457)

- s.f. 252. Rivetted plate.

F(427)

- s.f. 226. not illustrated. Folded bar.
- s.f. 228. Hobnails. Also s.f. 230 and 289.

F(491)

- s.f. 361. Right-angled bar.
- s.f. 364. Blade?

F(499)

- s.f. 390. Latch lifter?

Occupation layer under Structure 1

F(504)

- s.f. 405. Rectangular plate.

Fill of Iron Age pit

F(541)

- s.f. 423. Large ring

CARPENTRY NAILS

Stephen Trow

In addition to the iron finds above, a number of carpentry nails were recovered from stratified contexts with further examples recorded in fieldwalking. Four distinct types were identified:

Type 1

Square-sectioned shank off-centre to thick sub-rectangular head, usually heavily corroded. These derived principally from Claudio-Neronian contexts (see Trow 1988a, 53, fiche 1/A5). Similar types comprised the majority of the carpentry nails from Bagendon (Ruddock 1961, 189–191 and plate XLV, which also discusses method of manufacture).

Type 2

Square-sectioned shank with flat sub-square head. Shanks thinner and usually sharper-pointed than type 1 nails. Generally type 2 nails are less corroded than type 1 Type 2 nails were recovered mainly from contexts relating to the demolition/destruction of building 1. Examples from context F(488), s.f. 475 and s.f. 482. (Fig. 52, nos 16 and 17).

Type 3

Rectangular shank with thick convex head, similar to modern wire nails.

Type 4

Large bolt-like nails with square-sectioned shank and flat sub-circular or oval head. Examples are: Unstratified, s.f. 219 (Fig. 52, no. 18) and from F(480) s.f. 267 (Fig. 52, no. 19).

FINDS OF BAKED CLAY

Stephen Trow and Tom Moore

Unstratified – above context F(478)

– s.f. 431, and two others not illustrated were two small abraded fragments of 'coin mould' with vestiges of small module cups in grey fabric. A third oxidised fragment may belong to a large module mould.

Fill of Inner Enclosure Ditch

E(320)

– s.f. 194, (Fig. 51, no. 4). Dark-grey to orange-brown slingshot. Two fragmentary examples, s.f 195 and 196, not illustrated.

E(320)

– Also included a number of pieces of fired clay. Within this material one piece has finger impressions, possibly representing part of a kiln. Two larger pieces appear to be the remains of cigar-shaped firebars, also potentially from a pottery kiln (Annette Hancocks pers. comm.). These latter pieces can be compared with material from Grange Park, Northamptonshire (Hancocks 2006, fig. 70: 10–12) which also derived from transitional late Iron Age/early Roman contexts, including ditch fills. At the latter site, these appear to represent kilns and pottery manufacture, possibly taking place within the enclosure ditch itself (Hancocks 2006, 162–4; pers. comm.). Together, this material infers the presence of, at least small-scale, pottery manufacture in the vicinity. The presence of such pieces may suggest that s.f. 190 could also be a related. In addition to these pieces a small number of undiagnostic fired clay objects were recovered.

E(338)

– s.f. 190. Fragment of triangular object. ? not a loomweight.

Fill of Quarry pit

E(261)

– s.f. 191. Irregularly shaped and abraded fragment of 'coin-mould' with two small-module cups partly extant. Mid grey fabric with oxidised buff underside.

E(284)

– s.f. 197. Spherical ?slingshot.

E(286)

– s.f. 193, (Fig. 51, no. 1) Fragmentary loomweight in soft, poorly fired, open-bodied orange-buff fabric.

Fill of north–south ditch

E(264)

– s.f. 391, (Fig. 51, no. 6). Spindlewhorl cut down from potsherd in buff bodied, black surfaced fabric (fabric is probably GROGBAG).

Layer within room R9

F(478)

– s.f. 254, (Fig. 51, no. 5). Edge fragment of 'coin-mould' with single small-module cup surviving. Dark grey fabric oxidised orange on underside and edge.

- s.f. 421, (Fig. 51, no. 8). Irregular fragment of 'coin-mould' with the vestiges of five small-module cups extant. Dark grey to pale grey fabric, oxidised yellow-buff on the underside.
- s.f. 255, not illustrated. Small fragment of small-module 'coin-mould'.

WALL PLASTER

Tom Moore

The 1985 excavation recovered a substantial amount of wall plaster, primarily from the robber trenches of phase 9 associated with the abandonment of the villa. Noticeably, only a single plaster fragment was recorded as coming from the fill of the cellar (Fig. 51, no. 7), although this fragment is somewhat unusual compared to the others in being angular in shape. The absence of plaster from the cellar is in contrast to the finds from cellars such as Gorhambury, where the majority of wall plaster derived from cellar contexts (Neal *et al.* 1990, 169) and may imply that demolition material from rooms above the Ditches cellar was not incorporated in the cellar fills or that the villa was not demolished, or abandoned, until these contexts had formed. It may also support the impression from other contemporary cellars, such as Gorhambury (Neal *et al.* 1990, 171), that cellar walls were not plastered. All the plaster recovered was white-cream in colour with no clear patterns or designs apart from a single small fragment from F(434) with evidence of red paint.

Floor level in Room R6

F(417)

– 8 fragments, 76g.

Phase 9a Robber trenches of villa walls (phase 9a)

F(434)

– 6,888g; one fragment painted (s.f. 407, 1g).

F(467)

– 2 fragments, 26g.

Cellar backfill

F(426)

– s.f. 282. one fragment, angular (Fig. 51, no. 7), 20g.

MARINE MOLLUSC SHELLS

Stephen Trow and Tom Moore

(Table 22). The average meat weight of a sample of modern oysters varies enormously, from 1.2 to 35.3g. An average wet meat weight of 7.5g has been calculated for this sample based on assessments elsewhere (Winder 1980, 121). The large number from the cellar fill (approximately 2.4kg of oysters represented) in particular suggests that marine molluscs contributed a relatively significant part of the households diet by the second century AD, although the actual calories consumed with shellfish is much smaller (Murray 2002, 197). The presence of oysters in relatively early deposits, such as the inner enclosure is notable, even if only in small numbers. The presence of oysters on such sites by the mid first century AD may indicate that communities, at least on high status sites, were consuming oysters soon after the Roman conquest. The question of whether these oysters derived from the Thames or Severn estuaries cannot be confirmed but, as John Creighton (pers. comm.) notes, the transportation of oysters (presumably in water) over such long distances soon after the Roman conquest implies considerable status and cost.

	Oyster		Mussels	Scallop
	Ostrea edulis		*Mytilidae*	*Pecten sp*
Context	**Upper valve**	**Lower valve**	**valves**	
Cellar fill				
F(426)	218	175	16	1
F(455)	0	1		
F(480)	23	5		
F(485)	41	23	5	
F(488)	7	7		
F(489)	2	3	5	
F(491)	19	21	6	
F(495)	1	0		
F(497)	4	1		
F(499)	2	3		
Total	317	239		
Fill of quarry pit				
E(252)	3	0		
E(253)	20	13		
E(261)	18	13		
E(273)	9	5		
Total	50	31		
Fill of inner enclosure ditch				
E(320)	1	4		
Floor level in villa building				
F(414)	1	0		
F(417)	1	1		
Miscellaneous				
F(469)	4	1		

Table 22. Quantification of marine mollusca (minimum numbers).

HUMAN REMAINS

Kirsi Lorentz and Tom Moore

Fill F(517) of Iron Age pit F[505]

The evidence is consistent with these remains being from a single individual, although this cannot be confirmed. The bone matrix is relatively strong and the bone surfaces display light yellowish-brown discolouration. A number of fresh break surfaces are visible on the bone fragments which are likely to relate to the handling of the material after exposure by excavation. However, some break surfaces are not fresh, displaying the same discolouration as the natural surfaces of the bone. These post-mortem breaks may have occurred prior to exposure by excavation, possibly in antiquity. Macroscopic morphological observation was conducted on the fragments recovered for analysis. The scarcity of the material recovered did not allow for the application of many of the standard methods, such as sex and stature estimation. Completeness scores of bone elements have been stated following the general scheme of Buikstra & Ubelaker (1994).

Skeletal inventory

- zygomatic, right, 75% complete; temporal process missing
- maxilla, right, *c.* 100% (almost complete); superior aspect of frontal process missing
- maxilla, left, 25% complete; palate region only
- palatine, right, 50% complete; horizontal and part of perpendicular plate only
- palatine, left, 50% complete; horizontal and part of perpendicular plate only
- 2 small long-bone fragments, side cannot be assessed, <25% complete

The minimum number of individuals is one, as no bone element is duplicated.

Dentition (Table 23)

No complete teeth were recovered. Some tooth roots remained within the alveoli of the right maxilla. The tooth sockets and tooth roots remaining display recent breaks. All observable tooth root apices are closed (right maxillary second premolar, and first molar; indicates an adult age). The left side of the maxillary dental arc was not recovered, apart from the region containing the sockets for the left maxillary canine and incisors. The craniofacial region (individual bone elements listed above) had been broken into three larger, and four tiny fragments. Most of these elements come from the right craniofacial region, with the left side less well represented. The right maxillary sinus surfaces do not show any new bone growth or other kinds of pathological lesions that could be related to maxillary sinusitis. Although a very small proportion of the left maxillary sinus has been recovered, there is not enough of surface area left to be able to conduct assessment for pathology. The nasal aperture displays normal surfaces. The general morphology of the fragments recovered indicates an individual of adult age but no age diagnostic elements or regions were recovered. Not enough diagnostic features were recovered to allow sex estimation based on sexual dimorphism with confidence. However, the palate is rather shallow and narrow (female traits), rather than wide and deep (male traits). There are no cut or gnaw marks on the fragments analysed.

Discussion

The fragments of bone present in the pit are extremely fragmentary but suggest possibly an adult female. Unlike the skull fragments uncovered in the 1982–3 excavations (Brothwell 1988), there is no evidence of trauma. It is notable that, as with the earlier excavations, skull fragments occur on the site reflecting the relatively high representation of skull fragments on Iron Age sites throughout the region (Moore 2006b, 116). This may suggest that skulls, or skull fragments, were preferentially and intentionally retained for deposition after excavation of the body. The association of the skull fragments with a fragmented quern stone also indicates the deposit is likely to represent a structured association of material as seen on a range of Iron Age sites in the region and beyond (see Roe above, Brothwell 1988; Hill 1995b; Moore 2006b).

The context of this material may represent a 'closing' deposit at the end of the life of the pit. Dating evidence is inconclusive for this context although the presence of local limestone tempered pottery in later Iron Age forms, Savernake wares and other material, in contexts directly above suggests a possible early first century AD date, although an earlier date for context F(517) cannot be ruled out. If the former date is correct, it supports indications from earlier excavations and from Bagendon (Brothwell 1961) that the excarnation and deposition of human remains continued in to the first century AD, despite the otherwise apparently 'Romanized' nature of the sites.

Maxillary	left										right				
Tooth	M3	M2	M1	P2	P1	C	I2	I1	I1	I2	C	P1	P2	M1	M2	M3
Presence	-	-	-	-	-	/	/	/	/	/	/	/	Root	Root	/	/
Pathology													N	N		

Table 23. Bone elements from human remains.

Symbol	*Key*
-	Alveolus not present, no socket can be observed
/	Socket (tooth lost post-mortem)
Root	Tooth fragment retained in alveolus, crown lost post-mortem
N	None (root only)

THE CHARRED PLANT REMAINS

Jacqueline P. Huntley

Methodology

Samples were taken from three Iron Age storage pits in the form of column samples of between 0.5 and 1kg plus further bulk samples from the same pits. Bulk samples from the mid first century AD Inner Enclosure Ditch were also recovered along with material from the late Iron Age occupation layer. The ditch samples had been processed by the excavator and the flots sent to the laboratory.

The whole earth samples were air-dried in the laboratory and then either manually floated or, in the case of the two larger samples, put through a modified Siraf-style seed-machine. Flots in both cases were collected over 500μ mesh. For the assessment in 1989 the flots were simply scanned by eye for quantities of material and approximate types/quantity of remain. Some samples contained quite high amounts of charred cereal grain as well as smaller fragments. Those samples that had little visible were, nonetheless, later included in the full analyses as they were generally very small, taking little time to complete, and it was felt that any information regarding non-storage aspects of this site were worth acquiring.

For the analyses, all of the flots were examined at magnifications of up to ×50 using a Wild M3 stereomicroscope. Charred plant remains were sorted and identified by comparison with reference material belonging to the author. Nomenclature follows Clapham *et al.* (1962) for non cereal taxa and Tutin *et al.* (1964–80) for cereal taxa. Cereal grains were counted when the embryo and when what was judged as more than half of the grain were present; fragments of embryo were therefore not counted although they were noted as being present in the record. Data were standardised to seeds per 10 litres sediment as processed and to the level of context for the general discussion.

Results

24 samples from 18 contexts in total were analysed. Table 24 presents a summary table at the context level with data standardised to seeds per 10 litres; the raw data can be found in the archive. Only nine of the contexts produced seeds although concentrations varied greatly from 10 to almost 900 seeds per 10 litres sediment as processed.

Cereal grains were the most abundant and frequent remains, being dominant in all samples except F(518), in pit F[505], which produced sedge nutlets alone. Figure 53 presents the cereal grain standardised data for the remaining seven samples. In general indeterminate cereals are most common although wheat is dominant in F(570) and F(544).

	Ditch		Occup. Layer	Pit [505]	Pit [540]		Pit [564]		
Context	E(320)	E (340)	F(504)	F(518)	F(538)	F(544)	F(569)	F(577)	F(570)
Cerealia indet		25	260		60	123	40	100	276
Triticum sp	10	5	5			150		20	538
Triticum cf. spelta						8			23
Triticum cf dicoccon			1						
Hordeum hulled		15	29						
Hordeum (naked)?			1						
Hordeum undiff		3							1
Avena sp		5							
Triticum glume fragment			2			6			2
Triticum spelta glume base			3			33			16
Triticum spelta spikelet fork						2			3
Triticum brittle rachis internode			1			1			3
culm node			1			2			5
Corylus avellana shell fragment		3							
Bromus sp		5	2			14		20	3
<2mm Gramineae		5				2	20		9
Galium aparine						24			7
Rumex obtusifolius-type		8				43			
Stellaria media						3			
>4mm Gramineae						1			
Ranunculus repens-type						1			1
Polygonum convovulus			7						7
Polygonum (trigonous)			2			6			1
Polygonum persicaria			4						3
Carex (trigonous)	10		1	10		1			
2-4mm Gramineae		30							
Eleocharis palustris		13							
Juncus sp		5							
<4mm legume		3							
Rhinanthus minor agg		3							
Avena/Gram pedicel	10								
Rumex acetosella	10								

Table 24. Context level data standardised to seeds/10 litres sediment.

Most of the wheat grains remain as *Triticum* sp due to the unreliability of determining them to species (Hillman *et al.* 1996) although a few from F(544) and F(570) were tentatively identified as being from spelt from their general appearance and a few from F(504) as emmer. Spelt chaff was present in all three of these samples. No emmer chaff was recorded. Barley was generally uncommon except in

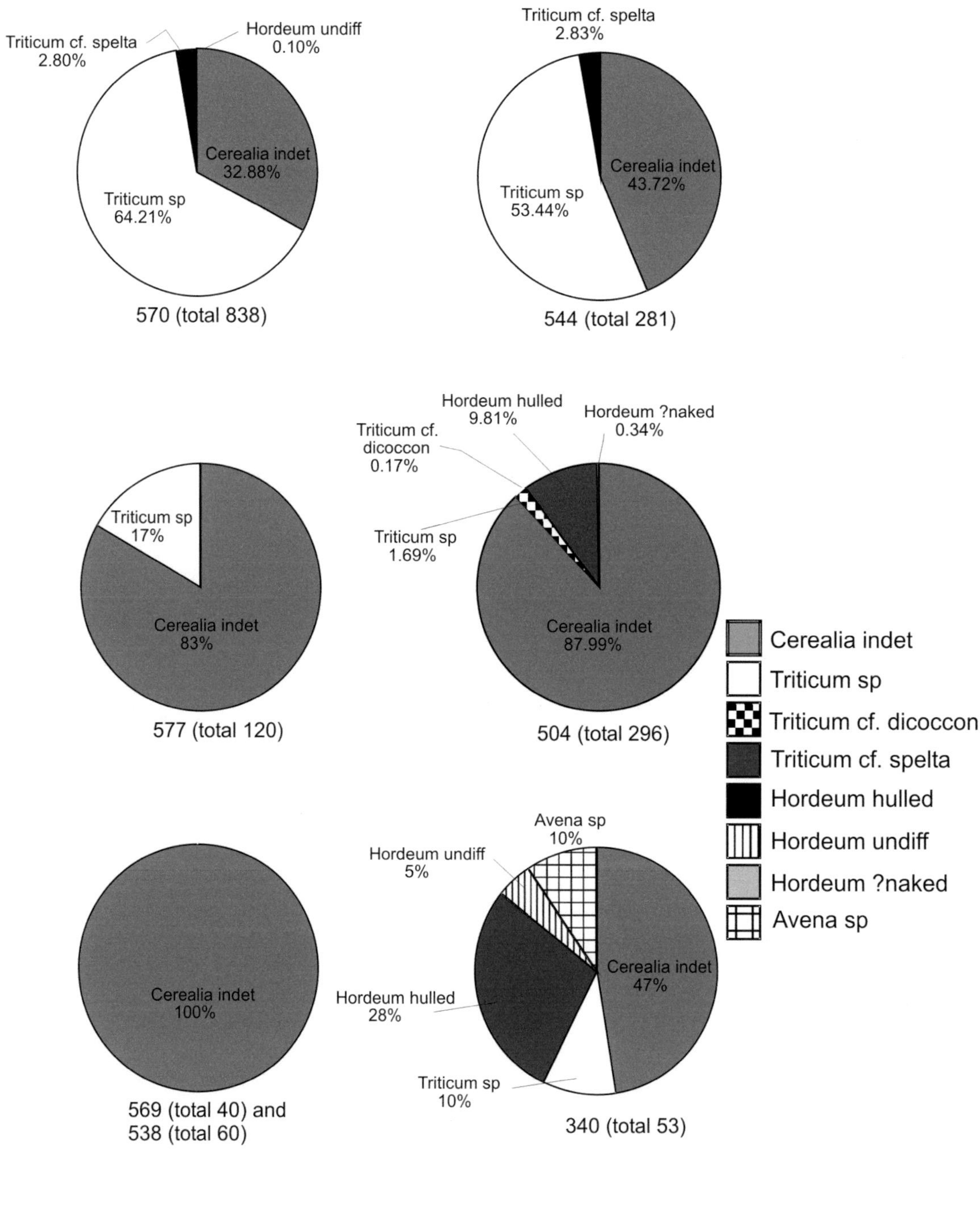

Fig. 53. Cereal grain proportions from Ditches contexts.

E(340) where the hulled variety formed 28% of the assemblage. A small amount of tentatively identified naked barley was present in F(504). No barley chaff was present. A few culm nodes were present in F(544) and F(570) – these are the remains of straw – although numbers are too few to offer specific interpretation.

Weeds seeds were recorded in most samples and suggest a variety of soil conditions. Wet ground taxa are abundant in E(340) although there are also hints of hay meadows here too from the presence of yellow rattle (*Rhinanthus minor*). Damp nutrient enriched soils are intimated for F(518) and F(570) from the various redshank (*Polygonum*) species recorded. Docks (*Rumex obtusifolius*-type) were reasonably abundant in F(544) and could indicate a longer-term fallow assemblage given that they are biennial to perennial species. Cleavers (*Galium aparine*) is also abundant in this context. It is sometimes considered to indicate autumn sowing of crops (Jones 1981) but is also a denizen of any nitrogen-enriched ground, such as manure heaps or waste ground. Brome grass (*Bromus* sp) seeds are similar in size to the cereal grains and, as a result, are often common in cereal assemblages. It seems likely that they grew amongst the cereals and were not removed during processing which is, essentially, sieving.

The proportions of grains to chaff to weed seeds are often used to indicate the various stages in such crop processing (Hillman 1981) although there are considerable discussions over the precise nature of these assemblages, see for example opposing arguments by Jones (1981) and van der Veen (1992). Plotting these values for the richer Ditches samples produces Figure 54, where it is clear that the majority of samples are fairly thoroughly processed and clean grain. E(340) is rather different with a much higher proportion of weeds. F(544) and F(569) also have rather more weeds than the remainder too.

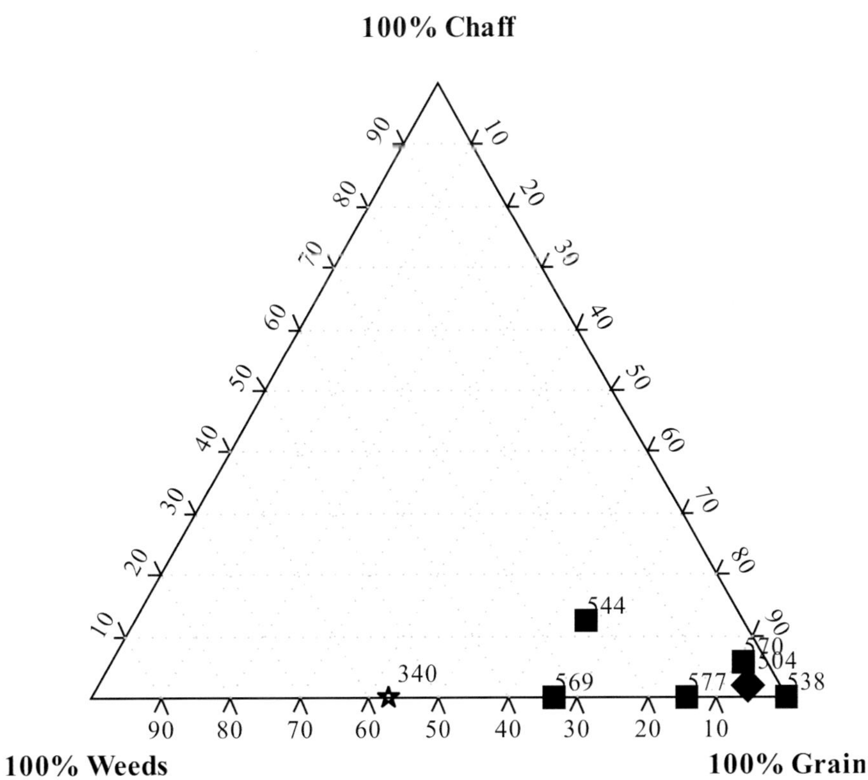

Fig. 54. Tripolo graph showing relative proportions of chaff, grain and weeds from Ditches assemblages.

Discussion

The cereals present, mainly wheat – some at least of which is spelt – but some hulled barley, are typical of the later prehistoric period for the region. The enclosure ditch seems to have received rather little in the way of cereal debris with most of its main assemblage, E(340) containing wet ground taxa. Whilst these might reflect vegetation within or on the banks of the ditch there is no obvious reason why the material should then be preserved through charring. It might therefore be more likely to reflect clearance episodes or some cereal processing debris, but without chaff. The oats (*Avena*) recorded are not necessarily cereals in their own right; they may simply be wild oats growing opportunistically. The cultivated and wild species cannot be separated when only grains are present.

Turning to the occupation layer F(504), whilst indeterminate cereal grains dominate this there is also a selection of weedy taxa and cereal chaff present. In nature it is an assemblage quite similar to that from F(570) although clearly less well preserved. This probably reflects the nature of the context rather than anything else. It is interesting to speculate why hulled barley should be the most common here (and in ditch fill E(340)) compared with its absence in the pits. Barley probably would have been eaten by humans as well as being fed to stock and it may be that it was not stored in the same way as wheat, i.e. not in pits. This apparent difference between context types for the two cereals has implications for any future sampling strategy.

The two pits F[540] and F[564] seem most likely to have been storage features. Their lowermost deposits are fairly pure wheat with indeterminate cereal grains. Clearly there are some chaff fragments and weed seeds present suggesting not totally pure grain but enough to suggest that the wheat was spelt. F(544) has rather more suggestions of a waste/ruderal assemblage which might just reflect vegetation in the immediate vicinity of the pit being burnt when the pit was, presumably, fired. The uppermost layers of these pits have very low numbers of remains in them. This very sharp contrast between the thin layer of grain rich lower fills and almost barren upper fills suggests that the material may well have been burnt *in situ* rather than reflecting rubbish being deposited within an otherwise empty pit. Pits may well have been cleansed by fire prior to a new season's storage in order to ensure that any pests were destroyed. The weed seeds present suggest cultivation on well manured and slightly damp soils with no evidence for the lighter limestone soils being used for cereal production.

ANIMAL BONE

Kevin Rielly

Introduction

The site provided a total number of 8,776 animal bones, of which 8,340 could be phased. This total has been placed into a number of bone groups, which are described in the next section (see below), but can be summarised as:

- D and Q: the fills of the major peripheral and pre-villa features of this site, namely the Inner Enclosure Ditch and the Quarry pit respectively, both dated to the mid first century AD.
- L and P: the deposits just post-dating and overlying the Quarry pit; an occupation spread and pitfills underlying the villa, again dated to the mid first century AD.
- V: villa deposits dating from the later first century AD to late second century AD, but excluding the cellar fill.
- C: the cellar fill, dated mid-late second century AD.
- R: the fill of the void over the collapsed eastern end wall, dated to the third-fourth century AD.
- Q: the mid first century AD Quarry pit provided an additional 100 fragments representing the remains of a number of partially articulated cattle skeletons.

All the bones featured in this report were recovered by hand. While recovery was notably efficient in all areas of the site, the concentration of bones within the cellar occasioned a particularly careful recovery programme. It is possible that this may have provided a biased assemblage, in comparison to those from the other site features, but obviously the better recovery would not have occurred if these fills had not shown themselves to be particularly rich in faunal material.

The general condition of the bones in terms of preservation (surface damage) and fragmentation was good. Most bones, with the exception of those from the cellar and parts of D and Q, showed some surface damage and fragmentation tended to vary depending on the depth of deposit (see Species representation).

Methodology

All the bones were fully recorded onto paper records using the system devised by Dobney and Rielly (1988). This system is divided into various headings, as follows: species, skeletal part, zones present (where each bone has been divided into discrete areas), sex, age (using tooth eruption/wear and epiphyses fusion), size and various modifications such as butchery, working and pathology. Where it was not possible to identify a bone to species or species group, as for example sheep/goat, it would be allocated to either cattle-size or sheep-size. The latter categories include most of the vertebrae (excluding atlas, axis and sacrum), all ribs and various indeterminate longbone and other fragments. Tooth eruption/wear uses the method devised by Grant (1975; 1982), while the measurements are essentially taken from von den Driesch (1976). A bone was deemed as measurable if it was a whole limb bone (bird and mammal domesticates), or if it included an epiphysis which could be classed as belonging to an adult. This includes mandibles where the adult third molar is in wear and various limb bones with fused intermediate and/or late epiphyses (see below). Identification of very young animals was undertaken by a study of the wear patterns of the teeth and otherwise by the smallness and porosity of the limbbones (following Amorosi 1989). Sexual distinctions are based on certain teeth (pig canines) and horncores (sheep and goat), as well as pelves (cattle and sheep, after Grigson (1982, 8) and Prummel and Frisch (1986, 576) respectively), and, for chicken, the presence of spurs and also of medullary bone (after Driver 1982).

The level of preservation of the bones was recorded with reference to the degree of surface damage, essentially root etching, on a scale from poor (much damage), to good (little to no damage).

Use of data

The quantification of the recorded data was undertaken on two levels, total fragment count and a weighted method involving a modified epiphysis-only count (after Grant 1975). This latter method involved the production of counts based on the number of epiphyses (whole limb bones, with the exception of phalanges, are counted twice) and the maximum occurrence of a particular zone for a selection of the remaining skeletal parts. The latter include skull, maxilla, mandible, atlas, axis and sacrum. Counts for the maxilla and mandible involved the representation of particular teeth, while the vertebrae counts were indicated by the presence of articular surfaces. The skull was quantified by counts of certain key areas as the orbit, horncore, occipital and temporal condyles, occipital crest and zygomatic. Within the final count for skull, the maximum amounts of all these parts, as well as the maxilla, were taken into account. A further consideration, when working out species abundance, was the expected frequency of particular skeletal parts. These were calculated as follows: all species, atlas and axis multiplied by two; pig, indeterminate metapodials divided by eight; first and second phalanges divided by four. The two methods were principally used to compare the representation of the major mammalian domesticates, the aim being to reduce the inherent bias within hand recovery, towards a better representation of the larger species i.e. cattle in comparison to sheep/goat and pig.

Exploitation strategies concerning the major animal and bird domesticates use the data available from the teeth and the epiphyses. All the epiphysis data has been combined into a few age groups, this following the fusion age sequence: Early (fusion of the proximal scapula, distal humerus, proximal radius, pelvis acetabulum and proximal phalange); Intermediate (includes the distal tibia and metapodials); and Late (includes the proximal humerus, proximal ulna, distal radius, proximal and distal femur, proximal tibia and proximal calcaneus). Cattle vertebrae are also used, here noting the fusion of the anterior and posterior epiphyses of the centrum. The mandibles are similarly divided into age groups, as follows: for cattle and sheep: 1. adult first molar worn and adult second molar unworn; 2. adult second molar worn and third adult molar unworn; 3. third adult molar worn corresponding to wear stages 6 to 11 (using numeric equivalents of the letters used in Grant 1975); 4. adult third molar between wear stages 12 and 13.

The mandible and epiphysis fusion data is compared with reference to certain broad age categories, which have been extrapolated from those used by O'Connor (1991, 250) specifically for mandible data, as follows: juvenile – unfused early group epiphysis; subadult – the difference between fused early and fused intermediate group epiphyses with worn second adult and unworn third adult molar; adult – fused intermediate group epiphyses with worn third mandibular molar; young adult – the difference between fused intermediate and fused late group epiphyses; older adult – fused late group epiphyses and third adult molar in full wear (corresponding to mandible wear stage 12 or 'g', see Grant (1982)). The ages applied to the various stages of tooth eruption and wear, as well as those ascribed to the epiphyses fusion are taken from a collation of information from a variety of authors described in Schmid (1972, 75 and 77), as well as additional mandible ages from Maltby (1981, 179) and Payne (1973, 293). The calculation of shoulder heights uses the factors described in von den Driesch and Boessneck (1974) and Harcourt (1974).

Finally, the level of fragmentation has been calculated using two methods: the proportion of loose teeth within the cattle, sheep/goat and pig assemblages; and the proportion of a selection of longbones, from the cattle-size and sheep-size assemblages with articular ends. The latter method employs the identified scapula, humerus, radius, ulna, femur, tibia and metapodials combined with the unidentified cattle and sheep-sized longbone fragments. The results of these analyses rely on the assumptions that an assemblage can be interpreted as showing a higher level of fragmentation if there is a higher proportion of loose teeth or a lower proportion of bones with articular ends.

This report does not include all of the tables and figures produced in the analysis stage, as the results of several of these could be best described by a sentence or two in the main text. However, all of this work is available in the archive in Cirencester Museum, as indeed are the bone records.

Trenches E and H

Phase 4

The fills of the Inner Enclosure Ditch in Trench E provided a large assemblage (D) dominated by cattle bones. This assemblage was recovered from a total of 10 fills, with the great majority arising from 'humic' layers E(320) and E(340), and the limestone rubble layer E(319). The date of the inner enclosure fills, between AD45–55, corresponds to the infilling of the adjacent Trench D section of this feature, excavated in 1982/3. Notably, the bone content of the latter fills, again largely confined to various 'humic' layers, was mainly composed of a roughly similar proportion of cattle and sheep. The similar levels of preservation of these two assemblages, as well as the dating evidence, would suggest that this difference could relate to differential deposition (see Species representation and Conclusions).

Phase 6

A number of fills were deposited into a large Quarry pit in Trench E, the cut of which partially truncated the western side of the Inner Enclosure Ditch, at a point prior to the infilling of this ditch. There is scant dating evidence, but these fills do appear to be contemporary with, or slightly later than, those of the Inner Enclosure Ditch, i.e. the mid first century

AD. The fills provided a number of moderate to large assemblages (Q), arising from what appears to be two main levels of humic spreads, essentially situated on the western half of this feature. At the lower level, most of the bones were recovered from layers E(261), E(273), E(281) and E(299), while bones from the uppermost horizon were largely derived from E(253). One of the lower layers E(273), provided a collection of semi-articulated cattle skeletons (see below), while the others, similar to the Inner Enclosure Ditch, provided an assemblage dominated by cattle bones. Notably, the Quarry pitfills provided one of the more diverse ranges of species found at this site, with the major domesticates accompanied by a relatively good representation of wild fauna, including red deer, hare and teal.

The cattle articulations within the Quarry pit, consist of three skulls (A, B and C, see Table 25 and Figure 12, five portions of articulated vertebrae (1 to 5) and seven limbs (I to VII, five with more than one bone). From the size (see Table 12) and age of the limb bones, and the age of the skulls and vertebrae, there is clearly a minimum number of six individuals. These are as follows:

1. Forelimb pair V and VI, with left hindlimb III. With fused distal tibia and unfused late epiphyses e.g. proximal femur, they can be classed as young adult, about 2–3.5yrs old. These may be associated with vertebral column 4, which is unfused.
2. Right hindlimb I and left hindlimb VII, from a young adult, with unfused vertebral column 5.
3. Left hindlimb II, with fused distal tibia and unfused later epiphyses, and is therefore from a young adult. Note that hindlimbs I and II are not from the same animal as II is clearly a larger individual. These could be associated with the unfused vertebrae within vertebral column 3.
4. Left hindlimb IV, a femur, which is fused and therefore from an old adult, aged at least 3.5yrs. This may belong to vertebral column 1, which is fused and therefore from an elderly animal at least 7–9 years old. One of the three skulls, possibly A, all of which have fully worn adult dentition and thus represent old adults, could be from the same animal.
5. Vertebral column 2, which has fused epiphyses, and is therefore from an elderly animal. Possibly associated with skulls B or C.
6. Skull B or C, from an old adult and therefore not associated with articulations 1, 2 or 3.
   This is undoubtedly a 'best fit' and some parts, in particular the vertebral columns and the skulls, may actually belong to other limb bones.

A noticeable feature of the spread of bones is that the heads are essentially at the northern end, the limbs at the southern end and the vertebrae across the middle. It can be supposed that this distribution may follow a deliberate disposal pattern. Certainly there is evidence for some portioning of these carcasses, notably the chop marks to the atlases in vertebral columns 2 and 3, suggesting decapitation. In addition, there is evidence for skinning, as shown by cut marks to the two first phalanges in hindlimb III, for jointing, related to the cut proximal tibia in hindlimb I and possibly for defleshing, shown by cut marks on the distal tibia, astragalus and calcaneus in this same hindlimb. Clearly, the proportion of butchered bones is quite small; however, the absence of cut marks on most of the bones may not be significant if the main butchery tool was the knife. It has often been quoted that a skilled butcher using a knife would tend to leave relatively few marks on the bone (see Crabtree 1989, 97). An alternative explanation, at least in part, for this level of disturbance/dismemberment is that one or more carcasses may have been pulled apart

Bone group	Skeletal parts	Age evidence	Alterations
A	Skull/maxilla	Old adult	
B	Skull/maxilla	Old adult	
C	Skull/maxilla	Old adult	
1	Axis to 5th lumbar	JF	But – kn atlas and axis
2	4th cervical to 8th thoracic, 12th thoracic to 1st caudal	JF	
	L and R pelves	Acetabulum F	
3	Atlas to 3rd cervical		But – ch and kn atlas
4	Axis to 3rd thoracic	N to JF	
5	1st to 3rd thoracic, 13th thoracic to sacrum	N	
	L and R pelves	Acetabulum F	
I	R tibia	PNDN	But – kn P and D
	R calcaneus, astragalus, navicular cuboid and cuneiform		But – kn calc and ast
	R metatarsus	PFDF	Gna – shaft
II	L tibia	PNDF	Gna – shaft
	L calcaneus, astragalus, navicular cuboid, mal lat. and cuneiform		Gna – calc P
	L metatarsus, 2 1st and 2 2nd phalanges	mt PFDF	Gna – mt shaft and both 2nd phal D
III	L femur	PNDN	
	L tibia	PJFDF	Gna – P and D
	L calcaneus, astragalus, navicular cuboid, mal lat. and cuneiform		Gna – calc P
	L metatarsus and 2 1st phalanges	mt PFDF, phal PF	But – kn both phal; Gna – phal D
IV	L femur	PJFDJF	
V	L humerus	PNDF	
	L radius/ulna	PFDN	
	L scaphoid, cuneiform, lunate, magnum and unciform		
	L metacarpus and 2 1st phalanges	mt PFDF, phal PF	Gna – both phal D
VI	R cuneiform, magnum and unciform		
	R metacarpus	PFDF	
VII	L femur	PNDN	

Age evidence and alterations: P proximal and D distal, F fused, N unfused, JF just fusing, But butchery and Gna dog gnawed, ch chop mark and kn knife mark. Vertebrae fusion refers to centrum epiphyses.

Table 25. Description of the cattle articulations from the Quarry pit E[304].

by scavengers. Indeed, several of these bones do show gnawing marks. However, the noted deposition pattern is unlikely to have been caused by scavengers, at least not entirely. Perhaps the best explanation for this accumulation of cattle bones is that these animals had been skinned, decapitated and dismembered. The flesh was then removed from the limbs, although perhaps not from the rest of the carcass, generally without any attempt to further subdivide these limbs. Deposition may have followed, or else there was a stage where these parts were openly available to scavengers. Certainly, due to the state of articulation, deposition must have occurred shortly after the culling or death of these animals. Further

Method	Trench:		E		F				
	Phase:		4	6	1–3	4	5–7	8	10
	Feature:		D	Q	L+P	V	V	C	R
	Species								
Loose teeth	Cattle	N	432	629	32	33	16	201	135
		N1	27	38	1	4	2	12	24
		%	6.2	6.0	3.1	12.1	12.5	6.0	17.8
	Sheep/Goat	N	163	322	143	84	67	169	66
		N1	6	21	8	12	13	7	25
		%	3.7	6.5	5.6	14.3	19.4	4.1	37.9
	Pig	N	110	289	51	45	38	156	13
		N1	4	20	2	16	9	14	3
		%	3.6	6.9	3.9	35.5	23.7	9.0	23.0
Art. ends	Large	N	234	389	33	54	27	258	66
		N1	60	57	7	2	4	20	17
		%	25.6	14.6	21.2	3.7	14.8	7.7	25.7
	Small	N	210	441	166	157	87	366	115
		N1	75	111	47	18	24	47	5
		%	35.7	25.1	28.3	11.4	27.6	12.8	4.3

Methods used: the proportion of loose teeth, where N number identifiable bones, N1 number of teeth and % equals N1/Nx100; the proportion of Large (cattle) and Small (sheep/goat and pig), limb bones with articular ends, including scapula, humerus, radius, ulna, femur, tibia, the metapodials and all cattle-size and sheep-size longbone shaft pieces, where N is the sum of these limb bone fragments, N1 is the number with articular ends and % equals N1/Nx100.

Table 26. State of the bones: the degree of fragmentation.

disturbance by scavengers may then have taken place, depending on the time delay between deposition and burial.

Phase 7

A small collection of bones was recovered from the cobbled surface E(252), laid over part of the uppermost Quarry pit fills. This layer is probably dated to the later first century and is therefore contemporary with the occupation of the nearby villa. However, unlike the villa deposits which feature a high count of sheep/goat bones, this assemblage is similar to the cattle dominated collections derived from the underlying quarry fills. It could perhaps be assumed that this similarity is related to redeposition/mixing, although it is perhaps significant that the phase 8 assemblage also featured a large proportion of cattle bones.

Phase 8

A rather slight north-south ditch E[255] was cut through the cobbled surface described in Phase 7 (see above). The fills of this ditch provided a moderate collection of bones, comprising just over 100 fragments (with about 50% identifiable to species). It is assumed that these fills, while obviously later than phase 7, also date to the later first century AD. The dominance of cattle bones in the ditchfill, as previously mentioned, is quite different to that derived from the contemporary villa deposits, and could perhaps relate to redeposition from the underlying strata.

Trenches F and G

Phase 1

A number of pre-villa features were discovered in Trench F, including, in temporal order, a line of stakeholes, three storage pits and an extensive occupation layer. All appear to immediately predate the Roman conquest. Animal bones were recovered from all three feature types, with a few bones from fill F(528) of stake-hole F[529] and moderate collections from the pitfills (dated to Phase 2, see below) and from the occupation layer F(504)/(546). These have been categorized as P and L respectively (see Introduction and Table 27). The occupation deposit provided a sheep/goat dominated assemblage, which is reminiscent of various Iron Age collections from the Thames Valley (Grant 1984) and beyond, as for example from the Southern By-pass excavations near Dorchester (Bullock and Allen 1997, 192), although here, unlike these other sites, there is also a reasonably good representation of pig bones.

Table 27. Species representation (hand collected total fragment counts).

Trench:	E			F					
Phase:	4	6	7+8	1	1–3	4–7	8	8–9	10
Feature:	D	Q	Over Q	L	L+P	V	C	V	R
Species									
Cattle	432	629	37	22	32	49	201	17	136
Sheep/Goat	163	322	21	111	143	151	169	31	70
Pig	110	289	14	38	51	83	156	20	14
Horse		1	2				7		13
Red deer		1							1
Roe deer					1				
Dog	1	1	1				10		4
Hare	1	14					7		5
Small rodent							13		
Chicken		6					113		
Duck	1						4		
Teal		1							
Woodcock				1	1		1		
Small passer							13		
Amphibian							3		
Fish							20		
Total iden	708	1264	75	172	228	283	717	68	243
Total uniden	792	1595	62	257	410	376	1091	95	333
Grand total	1500	2859	137	429	638	659	1808	163	576

For description of features, see text. The bones in Q do not include the cattle skeletons.

Phase 2

The three storage pits appear to have been infilled during the early to mid first century AD, which suggests they may be contemporary with the fills of the Inner Enclosure Ditch and the Quarry pit. It is therefore of some interest that the bone collections from these features are similar to those from the stratigraphically earlier occupation deposit (Phase 1), i.e. sheep dominated, compared to the cattle-dominated Trench E ditch and Quarry pit. This difference may be indicative of differential disposal (and see Species representation).

Phase 3

A small collection of bones was recovered from occupation debris, which had been compacted into the uppermost fills of the three storage pits. This layer was similar in date to the underlying fills. These bones were added to bone group P.

Phase 4

The construction phase of the villa, dated approximately to the third quarter of the first century AD, produced a small number of floor levels with bone assemblages. These include two in the most easterly part of the main block, Room 6; one composed of limestone cobbles F(484) (271 fragments, 110 identifiable) and another of limestone slabs F(514) (27,11), and one F(478) (96,41) to the south beneath the later corridor and directly over the pre-villa occupation layer F(546) (Phase 1). The species representation within these various features follows the pre-villa pattern with a high proportion of sheep/goat and a noticeable abundance of pig bones (see V[4] in Table 28).

Other, smaller collections, were taken from paving layers associated with Structure 2, a rectangular building north of the eastern part (Rooms R5 and R6) of the main block (Structure 1). It is unclear if this structure is contemporary with the main villa construction phase or is perhaps contemporary with phase 5. The paved areas with bones include F(534) (7,5), this situated between this structure and the main block and also entering the southern entrance to Structure 2, plus

Method	Period	Feature	Cattle	Sheep/Goat	Pig	N
TF	Pre-villa:	P+L	14.1	63.2	22.7	228
		D	61.3	23.1	15.6	705
		Q	50.7	26.0	23.3	1240
		D+Q	54.6	24.9	20.5	1945
	Villa:	V[4]	20.3	51.8	27.9	231
		V[5–7]	11.2	47.1	41.5	142
		V[4–7]	17.3	53.3	29.4	273
		C	38.2	32.1	29.7	526
		R	61.8	31.8	6.4	220
EO	Pre-villa:	P+L	12.5	48.9	38.6	96
		D	52.5	28.5	19.0	263
		Q	40.4	33.9	25.7	436
		D+Q	44.9	31.9	23.2	699
	Villa:	V	22.1	43.0	34.9	86
		C	27.7	35.0	37.3	177
		R	64.8	23.9	11.3	71

Data taken from Tables 1 and 2. For description of features, see text.

Table 28. Percentage abundance of major domesticates by occupation period and feature using total fragment (TF) and epiphyses only counts (EO). Hand collected data.

limestone blocks F(526) (12,6) across this entrance. These small assemblages feature seven sheep/goat and four pig fragments with no cattle.

Phase 5

This phase witnessed the construction of a timber-framed corridor or veranda along the southern side of the main block, this probably dating to the later first century AD. A small number of bones (23 fragments, 10 identified to species) were recovered from timber slots associated with this construction (fills F(561) and F(532)) within slots F(562) and F(533) respectively. In addition, bones were provided by a floor level F(417) (200,87) in room R6, which was situated directly above the phase 4 cobble surface F(484). The pattern of sheep dominance continues into this possible phase 5 floor level, but with a notable increase in pig abundance (this forms a large part of the bones in V[5–7] in Table 28).

Phase 6

A very small collection of bones, just 9 fragments (6 identifiable, all sheep/goat) were recovered from the wall footing F(436) associated with the north corridor wall F(400).

Phase 7

The southern corridor was modified to include a shallow 'wing' at each end of the main block. No bones were recovered which directly relate to these modifications, but a few were found within a limestone cobble path F(520) running at a right angle to the southern wall of the south corridor. In addition, some bones were recovered from rubble and mortar floor F(437) in room R5, comprising 16 fragments of which 7 were identifiable.

Phase 8

In this phase, cellar wall F(412) collapsed into the cellar and the space above was subsequently used for the dumping of a variety of domestic and building waste. There were a number of dumping episodes in to the cellar but the majority of a rather large bone assemblage (bone group C) was taken from one of the earlier levels F(488) and from two of the latest levels, F(485) and F(426). In sharp contrast to the previous villa phases, this assemblage shows a marked increase in cattle bones, which now appear to be the dominant species (total fragment count shown in Table 28). However, there is a continuation of the apparent rise in pig abundance with the effect that the figures show a similar proportion of sheep/goat and pig. There is the possibility that these changes may be linked with a high status diet, although the clearly excellent preservation of the bones in this feature compared to the rest of the site must also be considered (see Species Representation). The noted level of preservation and/or the perceived status of the site, may also account for the good representation of various small species, including domestic birds, game and fish, plus the local fauna, the small rodents and amphibians. Finally, there was also a small collection of non-food domesticates, including the remains of three or possibly four dogs, one of which represented the partial skeleton of a neonate puppy.

Phase 9

Much of the villa was destroyed by fire, which may have occasioned the collapse of the eastern wall F(406), which then sealed the cellar rubbish described in phase 8. There are just three deposits with bones, which are likely to date to this destruction phase. These include F(469) (75 bones, 37 identifiable), which is a patch of burning in room R6. In addition a collection was recovered from the fill F(434) (17,9) of a robber trench following the southern wall of room R6, and also from a soil layer F(497) (71,22) over the path F(520) (see phase 7). These last two deposits could, however, date to a later phase. Owing to the relatively uncertain date of these deposits, the bones were not included in the analysis. However, it is perhaps of interest that the combined assemblage follows the general pre-destruction villa pattern, discounting phase 8, with sheep in the dominant position and an abundance of pig bones.

Phase 10

The slumping of the collapsed eastern end wall provided a hollow in to which domestic material was deposited. A relatively large bone assemblage (bone group R) was recovered from each of the main levels within this dump, including general rubbish fills F(427) and F(477), as well as in rubble layer F(457). The most obvious difference between this assemblage and those from the previous deposits is the clear dominance of cattle bones. This difference, however, may relate more to the clearly high levels of fragmentation amongst these fills, rather than to any modification of food preferences or a change in status amongst the local community responsible for the deposition of this food waste (see Discussion of species representation).

Discussion of species representation

Major domesticates

The pre-villa features at the periphery of the site, including the Inner Enclosure Ditch (D) and the adjacent Quarry pit (Q, here excluding the cattle articulations), each provided large, cattle-rich assemblages (see Table 27 and Table 28). In sharp contrast, sheep/goat bones were clearly the major component of the contemporary levels directly below the villa, comprising the large occupation deposit (L) and the fills of the three storage pits (P). This difference may relate to recovery, differential preservation and/or to disposal practices. Various fragmentation processes would tend to favour the survival of cattle compared to sheep bones. It is surprising, therefore, to see that P and L actually show a higher level of fragmentation relative to both D and Q (see Table 26), suggesting that the proportion of sheep/goat in L and P may well have been greater compared to cattle at the time of deposition. A retrieval bias would have had the same result, with cattle bones more noticeable than sheep bones, thus under-representing the quantity of bones from the smaller domesticate. If preservation and retrieval can be discounted, it follows that the noted species representation patterns are more likely to be the result of differential deposition (and see Exploitation strategies).

There is a continuation of cattle-rich assemblages immediately overlying the Quarry pit (Trench E/H – phase 7 and 8), while the contemporary early villa deposits (Trench F – phase 4) were similar to those from P and L, although perhaps with a slightly greater proportion of cattle (see Table 28). It is to be wondered if these contemporary differences may again relate to disposal practices. However, the quantities of bones from the peripheral deposits is rather small and there is also a possibility that a proportion of these bones could have been redeposited from the underlying cattle-rich fills. The later villa assemblage in phases 5 to 7 appears to demonstrate a substantial increase in pig, at the expense of cattle. Again, this difference may be an artefact of the small quantity of bones. There does seem to be a rather good representation of pig throughout the villa levels up to phase 8, the cellar fills (C). This could perhaps be indicative of high status, following King (1978; 1984). Such 'affluent' sites tend to provide high counts of cattle as well as pig bones, and it is perhaps significant, in this respect, that the cellar produced the highest proportions of cattle and pig amongst the pre-destruction villa assemblages. It can perhaps be envisaged, from this evidence, that the villa reached its affluent peak just prior to its destruction.

The final assemblage (R) related to the villa, overlying the remains of the collapsed east wall, is dominated by cattle bones. However, this collection represents one of the smallest assemblages recovered from this site, plus there are clear signs that it has suffered a relatively high degree of fragmentation (see Table 26). This is particularly shown by the high proportions of sheep/goat and pig loose teeth and the low proportion of sheep-size limb bones with articular ends. It can therefore be assumed that this assemblage is biased towards cattle, although to what extent is uncertain.

Other species

The other species represented include a relatively wide array of food species, as well as non-food domesticates and local fauna. Within the first category, there are domestic birds, game and fish. It is very noticeable that the first of these, and especially chicken, is best represented in the cellar. The relative absence of such birds from other parts of the site may relate to the clearly better preservation of bones within this feature (see Introduction). Otherwise this may prefigure the obvious rise in the consumption/use of chickens by the latter part of the Roman occupation period, as for example shown at Wanborough (Rielly forthcoming a). Game species were present throughout these levels, with minor quantities of deer, woodcock and teal, and moderate concentrations of hare and small passer. The latter bones, from the cellar, are smaller than thrush and could represent one or more of a large number of species recovered from Roman sites in Britain (see Parker 1988, 212). It is known that a variety of such birds were eaten in Italy at this time (André 1961, 125), but there is the possibility that a proportion of these bones may have derived from non-food local fauna. The cellar also provided a small collection of fish bones, which, unfortunately, could not be identified to species.

The second category includes horse and dog, both of which are represented by small collections of either single bones or partial articulations. Some of the larger assemblages were recovered from the cellar, with the remains of at least two horses and three dogs, and from R, with another three horses and one dog. One of the cellar animals is a neonate, clearly showing that dogs were being bred in the vicinity, or perhaps within, the villa. It could represent an infant mortality or a deliberate attempt at population control (see Harcourt 1974 in Bullock and Allen 1997, 194).

The local fauna, comprising the small rodents and the amphibians recovered from the cellar, were clearly living in the vicinity of the villa. The small rodents could not be identified to species, other than to say they were smaller than rat. It is likely that they included a well-known Roman domestic pest, the house mouse. The amphibians were possibly chance captures, perhaps falling into, and then being trapped within, the cellar.

Discussion of exploitation strategies

Major domesticates

Each of the major periods provided a

few bones from very young individuals (see Table 29) which can be interpreted as infant mortalities. These are indications of the use of this site as a production centre, following the argument that such mortalities are likely to have been deposited in the vicinity of their place of birth. However, there is the possibility that a proportion of these may be food waste (see below). The greatest concentration of such youngsters were recovered from the cellar, with a particular abundance of piglets. It has been mentioned that this feature provided a rather high proportion of pig bones, and it can be supposed that the majority of these represent animals which were bred locally.

As pigs are principally raised for their meat, a study of their age profile will essentially suggest the intensity of exploitation for this product. Notably, the great majority of the pigs from the cellar were culled within their first year (see Table 31 and Table 32). This obviously high-intensity production is also indicative of a preference for the meat from young animals. This age group possibly included sucking pig, which could account for a proportion of the aforementioned piglets. This was a popular dish in Italy according to Roman authors (White 1970, 318–20), and as such could provide further evidence for the high-status interpretation of the waste recovered from the cellar. The pigs represented from the earlier levels at this site show a far smaller proportion of first year animals and several surviving to adulthood (adult third molar in wear, Table 30 and fused intermediate epiphyses, Table 31, and see Methodology). Most of those from the Quarry pit are either subadult or young adult (age groups 2 and 3 respectively, see Table 32), suggestive of second-year and possibly early third-year culls. Notably, the third molars from these mandibles are only slightly worn (Grant stages 'a' or 'b'). This clearly less intensive strategy could suggest a different meat preference to that represented by the cellar assemblage, or perhaps a lesser degree of Romanization/status.

Species	Feature	Mandibles	Limb bones
		N/tooth wear state	N
Cattle	D		1
	Q	2/dpm4unw and one in crypt	
	C	3/dpm4unw	
	R		1
Sheep	D		3
	P		1
	V	1/dpm4unw	
	C	1/dpm4unw	5
	R	1/dpm4jw	
Pig	D		2
	Q		2
	V	1/dpm4 in crypt	
	C		9

Table 29. Distribution of neonate/infant cattle, sheep/goat and pigs.

For description of features, see text. N equals the number of bones. Dpm4 is the fourth deciduous molar, and unw is unworn and jw is just worn (wear state 'a' after Grant 1975).

Table 30. Tooth wear/eruption data for cattle, sheep/goat and pig. Hand collected data.

Species	Feature	Age Group			
		1	2	3	4
		N	N	N	N
Cattle	P+L		5		
	D	1	5	2	
	Q	4	7	11	2
	V				2
	C	3	4	3	4
	R	1	3	5	4
Sheep/Goat	P+L				1
	D		1	1	6
	Q	2		2	6
	V		3	1	1
	C	3		1	2
	R	1		1	4
Pig	P+L			1	
	D		3	1	
	Q	3	6	8	
	C	1	1		1
	R		2	1	

For description of Age groups, see Table 8.

Table 31 (below). Cattle, sheep/goat and pig epiphysis fusion data (hand collected).

Species	Feature:	D		Q		V		C	
	Age Group	N	%F	N	%F	N	%F	N	%F
Cattle	Early	21	95.2	37	94.6	7	85.7	16	100.0
	Intermediate	28	92.8	14	85.7	0		5	80.0
	Late	26	73.0	13	38.4	2	50.0	6	66.7
	Vertebrae	20	40.0	29	31.0			6	50.0
Sheep/Goat	Early	22	95.4	37	81.1	14	92.8	15	80.0
	Intermediate	21	42.8	24	66.7	5	100.0	15	46.7
	Late	10	0.0	26	68.0	8	12.5	17	11.7
Pig	Early	12	83.3	26	73.0	8	62.5	21	38.0
	Intermediate	15	33.3	22	50.0	6	33.3	12	0.7
	Late	12	8.3	9	11.1	4	0.0	14	0.1

For description of Age groups, see Table 8. Vertebrae equal all cattle-size vertebrae

Age/fusion group	State	Cattle	Sheep	Pig
1	M1w, M2unw	0.5–1.25yrs	0.5–1yr	0.5–1yr
2	M2w, M3unw	1.25–2.25yrs	1–1.75yrs	1–1.5yrs
3	M3w, wear stage 'b' to 'f'	2.25–5yrs	2–4yrs	>1–1.5yrs
4	M3w, wear stage 'g' and greater	Greater or equal to 5yrs	Greater or equal to 4yrs	>1–1.5yrs
Early	Fused scapula P, humerus D, radius P, pelvis acetabulum A, 1st phalange P	1–1.5yrs	0.25–0.5yrs	1–1.5yrs
Intermediate	Fused tibia D and metapodial D	2–2.5yrs	1.6–2yrs	2yrs
Late	Fused humerus P, radius D, femur P and D, tibia P, calcaneus P	3.5–4yrs	3–3.5yrs	3–3.5yrs
Vertebrae	Fused epiphyses	7–9yrs		

All ages after Schmid (1972, 75 and 77), except for cattle mandible groups 3 and 4 (Maltby 1981, 179) and sheep mandible groups 3 and 4 (Payne 1973, 293).

Table 32. Ages of mandibular tooth eruption (wear stages after Grant 1975) and epiphysis fusion.

Unlike the pigs, the cattle and sheep/goat bone group assemblages are generally dominated by adult individuals. The interpretation of this data is based on decisions concerning the importance of pre-mortem as against post-mortem products, where the pre-eminence of the former is shown by a majority of adults, or more particularly, of old adults i.e. fused late group epiphyses and mandible age group 4. It is assumed that the young adult group, regarding cattle and sheep, could have still provided good quality meat, essentially prime beef and mutton respectively. Hence a large proportion of young adults would indicate a meat economy, albeit one where the animals had provided one or two clips of wool or at least one calf. Problems of interpretation arise when the mandible evidence disagrees with the epiphysis fusion evidence and where contemporary deposits appear to show different results. Certain differences may well be an artefact of the relatively small samples of age data represented in these tables. In addition, the age ranges of the mandible and epiphysis adult groups are not strictly comparable (see Table 32 and Introduction). However, there are some notable patterns within the cattle and sheep/goat age profiles. Regarding the first-century bone groups, the apparently high cull of young adult cattle in Q, shown by the difference between the fused intermediate and late age group epiphyses (Table 31), is reflected by the high proportion of age group 4 cattle mandibles (Table 30). The evidence from D, and in particular from the epiphyses data, suggest a greater survival of adults, most surviving to become old adults. This difference may suggest a greater emphasis on animals bred for their meat in Q and for secondary purposes in D. The mandible and epiphysis evidence tend to coincide regarding the sheep/goat data, at least with respect to Q, these animals following the pattern described for the cattle from D. Though the mandible data suggests that the sheep/goat from D may be similarly aged, the lesser quantity of fused intermediate epiphyses indicates a tendency towards a greater mix of meat and secondary products.

The age information from the later

Species	Site	Period	mandibles			epiphyses			
			AG 3+4	AG 4		Inter		Late	
			%	%	N	%F	N	%F	N
Cattle	Ditches 82/83	m1st c	87.0	69.5	69	78.7	80	76.7	116
	Bagendon	m1st c	68.4	44.7	38	77.1	70	71.8	71
	Wanborough	4th c	85.2	49.0	102	84.1	189	51.0	92
Sheep	Ditches 82/83	m1st c	51.2	13.1	80	69.7	86	38.2	102
	Bagendon	m1st c	36.3	17.4	132	74.6	126	48.8	123
	Wanborough	1st c	40.4	21.0	67				
		2nd/e3rd	58.1	27.9	43				
		4th c	74.3	22.7	221				
Pig	Ditches 82/83	m1st c	43.7	0.0	47	34.0	47	0.0	25
	Bagendon	m1st c	18.7	0.0	48	20.0	20	28.5	42
	Wanborough	2nd/e3rd	29.4	0.0	17				
		4th c	22.5	0.0	40				

Mandibles – AG equals mandible age group, Inter is the intermediate epiphyseal age group. N is the total number of: aged mandibles, intermediate epiphyses and late epiphyses respectively. For a description of age groups see Table 8.

Table 33. Comparison of age data from Ditches 82/83, Bagendon and Wanborough.

bone groups, specifically C and R, tends to be rather slight, but it does seem, from the mandible evidence, that the cattle from C are similar to those from Q regarding a population weighted towards meat production, while the wide age range of the sheep/goat from the same feature suggests that the animals were derived from a mixed farming economy. Both the sheep/goat and the cattle from R are indicative of an emphasis on secondary production. However, this conclusion must be viewed with caution, due to the noted high level of fragmentation within this assemblage, which may have biased the results towards a greater proportion of older mandibles.

As a rural producer site, it can obviously be assumed that the animals raised, or eventually culled, for their meat, were slaughtered and butchered within the confines/vicinity of the enclosure/villa. The presence of a wide variety of skeletal parts from each of the major domesticates and from each of the bone groups, is clearly indicative of the presence and the general deposition of processing and food waste derived from whole carcasses. Within this general representation of parts, however, it would appear that the cattle bones from D and Q include a large proportion of skull fragments, while the same species from C is largely confined to the limb bones above the carpal ('wrist') and hock joints (see Table 34). This may suggest the preferential deposition of particular types of waste, with a bias towards processing or butcher's waste in D and Q, and dressed carcass or kitchen waste in C.

The previous Ditches publication (Rielly 1988) described, in some detail, the butchery observed on the major domesticate bones. As there are clear similarities regarding the butchery patterns observed at both the earlier and later excavations at this site, it was thought appropriate to limit the present analysis to the various differences and similarities between the first century and the later villa bone groups. This analysis will essentially include the butchery

Bone group:	D			Q			C		
Skeletal part	N	N1	%	N	N1	%	N	N1	%
Skull	146	9	6.1	203	17	8.4	28		
Mandible	27	1	3.7	38	7	18.4	7	2	28.6
Atlas	3	2	66.6	5	4	80.0	1		
Axis	1	1	100	3	1	33.3			
Scapula	21	4	19.0	27	8	29.6	16	10	62.5
Humerus	14	2	7.1	21	4	19.0	11	4	36.3
Radius+ulna	12	2	16.6	37	8	21.6	15		
Metacarpus	7	4	57.1	17	2	11.8	3	1	33.3
Pelvis	23	6	26.0	31	9	29.0	6	1	16.7
Sacrum				7	2	28.5			
Femur	25	1	4.0	32	3	9.4	24	7	29.1
Tibia	66	5	7.6	47	3	6.4	39	2	5.1
Calcaneus	8			9	3	33.3	2		
Astragalus	9	1	11.1	8			2		
Metatarsus	11	2	18.2	17			5		
1st phalange	7	2	28.6	27	8	29.6	5	2	40.0

N total number of bones, N1 number of bones with cut marks, % N1/Nx100

Table 34 (above). Cattle representation of skeletal parts and frequency of parts with butchery cuts. Hand collected total fragment counts.

Table 35 (right). Use of the cleaver and the knife in cattle, sheep/goat and pig from selected bone groups. Hand collected total fragment counts.

Species:	**Cattle**		**Sheep/Goat**		**Pig**	
Bone group	chop	knife	chop	knife	chop	knife
	N	N	N	N	N	N
D	35	20	7	6	8	1
Q	64	30	17	9	20	8
C	30	7	14	1	12	3

N total number of bones with cut marks. Note the same bone may have chop and knife marks.

evidence from groups D, Q and C. In all three groups, in common with the previous Ditches butchery data, there is evidence for skinning, jointing, defleshing and marrow extraction, with each of these processes facilitated by the use of the cleaver and/or the knife. Notably, however, the proportion of bones with knife marks, including those from all three domesticates, is clearly smaller in C compared to D and Q (Table 35). The difference here is related to the clearly associated roles of the knife and the cleaver, for most aspects of the butchery process, in D and Q, and a change to a reliance on cleaver butchery to achieve the same results in C. This is well illustrated with reference to the cattle scapula butchery, this representing one of the most frequently butchered skeletal parts within these groups (see Table 34). In C, there are a number of cases with superficial chop marks parallel to the spine, which must be defleshing cuts. These are entirely absent from D or Q scapulas. This part offers further clues to a change in butchery techniques. While there are scapulae with midshaft perforations in Q and C, and chops removing part or all of the spine, both methods are clearly more common in C. In addition, several of the Q scapulae have been chopped through the midshaft, while there is no indication of this subdivision in C. The pattern of butchery to the first century scapulae is very similar to that seen from the first Ditches excavation, and also from Bagendon. This butchery may show a dual approach to scapula meat removal in the earlier period, either chopping off the meat from the blade removing the spine in the process, or just dividing the blade into two small joints, perhaps cooking the meat on the bone. Clearly, only the first of these methods survived into the second century at this site.

Other species

It can be assumed, even without any butchery marks, that most of the remaining species were culled for their meat. The few bones with cut marks include a dressing cut to a mallard metacarpus, cuts subdividing the wing in at least three chickens, and possible defleshing cuts on a lower leg bone of a hare. All of these were recovered from the cellar. Notable aspects of the cellar chickens is that almost all of the limbbones are fused (59 out of 66 i.e. 89.4%) and there are very few male birds. This clearly suggests the importance of egg production. These were undoubtedly locally kept, with the occasional younger bird killed for the pot depending on the occasion and the older birds eventually culled as they as their egg productivity declined.

The horses and dogs, as mentioned, were mainly represented by partial articulations. Here, it can be supposed that the level of disarticulation is largely related to redeposition, occasioned by lack of suitable burial, or no burial, and the action of scavengers. However, one of the horse bones, a metatarsus, from the cellar, did display a small cut mark near the distal end, which is undoubtedly a skinning cut. Obviously, some or all of these horses were skinned prior to deposition. The size of the horses (see below), indicate the presence of short to medium robust animals, perhaps indicative of general purpose farm animals rather than those used for riding purposes. All of these horses were adult, which would suggest perhaps the import of already-trained animals. In contrast, one of the dogs is very young, obviously showing some local breeding. The size and shape of the other, adult, individuals could perhaps suggest that they were used for a variety of purposes. The smallest, at about 360mm at the shoulder, could represent a small 'terrier' type suitable for chasing small game, while the larger animals may well have been guard dogs and/or deer hounds.

Size of domesticates

The size ranges for the three major domesticates are shown in Table 36, Table 37 and Table 38. Though the quantities of data are rather small, it can be suggested that there is no discernable difference between the pre-villa and villa cattle, while there do appear to be a few larger sheep in C compared to D and Q. The pig evidence is very slight but suggests, at the least, that there is no clear indication of wild boar.

The general size of these domesticates is comparable to those recovered from other sites in the locality. Notably, the D and Q sheep, in common with those from Ditches 82/83, are a little larger, in terms of mean values, than those from Bagendon (Rielly forthcoming b). However, there is no corroborative evidence from either of these bone groups for the larger sheep and cattle found at the earlier Ditches excavation. These included a sheep tibia with a distal breadth of 26.5mm, which is close to the upper range of those found in the cellar. The sheep from this feature are clearly quite similar in size (range and mean values) to those recovered from various late Roman (third and fourth centuries)

Bone group:	Skeletal part	GL(mm)	Withers/shoulder heights (mm)
I	Tibia, metatarsus		1100, 1174
II	Tibia, metatarsus		1207, 1217
III	Tibia, metatarsus		1153, 1132
IV	Femur	341.7	1185
V	Radius, metacarpus		1194, 1152
VI	Metacarpus	186	1152
VII	femur	318.2	1100

GL greatest length. Heights calculated using factors described in von den Driesch and Boessneck (1974).

Species	Period	Feature	Range	Mean	N
Cattle	mid 1st c	D+Q	1021.5–1216.9	1137.7	12
	mid 3rd c	R	1140.8–1197.1	1168.9	2
Sheep	mid 1st c	D+Q	580.9–673.7	622.5	4
	1st/2nd c	V	602.9	602.9	1
	mid 2nd c	C	575.6–590.2	582.9	2
Pig	mid 2nd c	C	767.4	767.4	1
Horse	mid 2nd c	C	1341.0	1341.0	1
	mid 3rd c	R	1303.1	1303.1	1
Dog	mid 2nd c	C	362.2	362.2	1

Shoulder heights (in millimetres) calculated from factors described for cattle, sheep, pig and horse in von den Driesch and Boessneck (1974) and for dog in Harcourt (1974).

Table 36 (top). Size of cattle skeletons from Quarry pit E[304].

Table 37 (bottom). Withers/shoulder heights of cattle, sheep, pig, horse and dog.

sites, as for example, from the villas at Frocester Court and Shakenoak (Maltby 1981, 190) and Wanborough (Rielly forthcoming a). The evidence appears to point towards a general size increase by this period within this general area and the data from the cellar may suggest that this increase took place as early as the later second century.

There is a slight indication of the 'type' of cattle and sheep from the cranial remains. Notably neither species provided hornless skulls, while the general size of the cattle horncores suggests a majority of Short Horned individuals, as described by Armitage and Clutton-Brock (1976, 331). This conclusion is based on a comparison of the range of basal diameter measurements of the Ditches examples, all from first-century deposits (notably the maximum diameter, range – 35.4–55.6mm, mean – 46.6mm and N – 6) with those of complete specimens from various Roman sites, including Wanborough (Rielly forthcoming a) and a number of London sites (using Museum of London archive material).

A few horse bones could be measured from the later levels. As well as those shown in Table 37, provided by two metapodials, it was possible to calculate approximate heights for three other limbbones, all from R, as follows: 1210, 1231 and 1119mm. Notably, the two

Species	Period	Feature	Dim	Range	Mean	N
Cattle	mid 1st c	D+Q	Tibia Bd	49.7–61.1	55.1	28
	mid 2rd c	C		60.3	60.3	1
	mid 1st c	D+Q	Metacarpal Bd	46.4–58.8	53.7	7
	mid 2nd c	C		48.4	48.4	1
	mid 3rd c	R		65.3	65.3	1
	mid 1st c	D+Q	Metatarsal Bd	44.7–56.3	50.4	6
	mid 2nd c	C		57	57	1
	mid 1st c	D+Q	Astragalus GLl	54.7–64.6	59.5	18
	mid 2nd c	C		56.4–63.1	59.5	6
	mid 3rd c	R		61.4	61.4	1
Sheep	mid 1st c	D+Q	Tibia Bd	21.5–23.9	22.8	18
	mid 2nd c	C		22.1–27.0	24.1	7
	mid 3rd c	R		21.7	21.7	1
	mid 1st c	D+Q	Metacarpal Bd	20.7–23.8	22.2	4
	mid 1st c	D+Q	Metatarsal Bd	20.4–21.5	20.9	3
	mid 2nd c	C		21.8	21.8	1
Pig	mid 1st c	D+Q	Tibia Bd	23.8–30.0	28.0	7

Dim skeletal part and dimension. Bd distal breadth, GLl greatest lateral length (after von den Driesch 1976). All measurements in millimetres.

Table 38. Selected measurements of cattle, sheep/goat and pig.

metapodials, one each from C and R, are relatively robust. A range of specimens from Roman London sites could be divided into a large robust group and a small gracile group, the former interpreted as general work animals and the latter as possible riding animals (following the information in Rackham 1995, 172). Clearly the Ditches examples fit into the former category. The overall height of the horses from this site indicates the presence of small to medium-sized ponies.

There was quite a wide range of dogs at this site, from the rather small specimen with a height of 362.5mm from C to a much larger animal, from R, with an approximate height of 585mm. In addition, further estimated heights were provided by a humerus from D, at 424mm, and a skull/mandible from C, at 520mm. Each of these dogs is within the height range for Romano-British dogs described by (Harcourt 1974, 160), while three out of the four within the upper half of this range.

Conclusions

Pre-villa occupation (mid first century AD)

The previous excavation at this site provided a mid first century cattle-rich assemblage, mainly derived from a section of the Inner Enclosure Ditch. This assemblage was interpreted as indicative of Romanizing influences (Rielly and Trow 1988, 81) following the arguments described by King (1978; 1984) and comparing the assemblage derived from the early military occupation at Cirencester (see Table 39). The latest excavation has provided two more cattle-rich collections, again mid first century AD, from the same ditch (D) and the adjacent Quarry pit (Q), both tending to reinforce the earlier interpretation. However, this site has also produced

Method	Site (Bone group)	Period	C	S/G	P	N	Reference
			%	%	%		
TF	Guiting Power	MIA	28.6	69.2	2.2	273	(Wilson 1979)
	Uley Bury	MIA	35.0	48.1	16.9	1274	(Levitan 1983)
	Ditches 82/83	m1st c	49.3	35.2	15.2	5072	(Rielly 1988)
	Ditches (D+Q)	m1st c	54.6	24.9	20.5	1945	
	Bagendon	m1st c	36.0	46.1	17.9	4911	(Rielly forthcoming b)
	Cirencester	M–l 1st c	48.4	35.8	15.8	533	(Thawley 1982b)
	Wanborough	1st c	28.1	55.8	16.1	557	(Rielly forthcoming a)
		2nd–e3rd c	43.9	44.0	12.1	560	
		4th c	59.7	31.9	8.4	4323	
	Ditches (C)	M–l 2nd c	38.2	32.1	29.7	526	
	Cirencester	4th c	47.5	28.5	23.9	953	(King 1984)
		M2nd–m3rd	80.7	13.2	6.1	975	(Thawley 1982a)
	Frocester	1st c	25.7	51.6	22.6	1034	(Noddle 1979)
		2nd–3rd	48.1	40.6	11.4	1519	
		4th	51.7	34.2	14.1	2102	
EO	Ditches 82/83	m1st c	42.3	39.1	18.6	1964	As above
	Ditches (D+Q)	m1st c	44.9	31.9	23.2	699	
	Bagendon	m1st c	32.3	46.9	20.8	2167	As above
	Wanborough	1st c	18.4	67.5	14.1	379	As above
		2nd–e3rd c	35.4	51.6	13.0	302	
		4th c	51.6	39.5	8.9	2104	
	Ditches (C)	M–l 2nd c	27.7	35.0	37.3	177	

Method: TF total fragment count and EO epiphyses only. C cattle, S/G sheep/goat and P pig. % percentage of fragments identified to each species/N x 100. N is the total number of fragments identified as cattle, sheep/goat and pig. Period: MIA mid Iron Age, e early, m mid and l late.

Table 39. Representation of major domesticates from a selection of sites. Hand collected counts.

assemblages from contemporary levels, below the villa (P and L), which are clearly dominated by sheep bones. The latter assemblage, in sharp contrast to those previously described, resembles those from Iron Age sites in this area, as Guiting Power and Uley Bury (see Table 39). One possibility is that particular species may have been preferentially disposed of in different parts of the site. There is a consistent pattern in Hampshire chalkland sites dated to the Iron Age and Romano-British periods for cattle-dominated ditch assemblages and sheep-dominated pit assemblages (Maltby 1994, 88). Various factors may have contributed to this pattern, including preferential disposal. There is a noticeably large proportion of cattle butchers waste in both D and Q, perhaps indicative of a particular disposal strategy. However, there is no obvious concentration of such parts within the cattle-rich assemblage from the previous excavation. It can perhaps be concluded, given the rather small quantities of bones from P and L, that D and Q represent the more reliable evidence for major domesticate use during this period, and that these assemblages suggest the influence of Romanization. Of interest, in this respect, is the rather lower proportion of cattle at the contemporary site at Bagendon. This is particularly significant, considering that the area around this site is clearly more suitable for cattle grazing compared to the upland farmland at the Ditches (see Rielly and Trow 1988, 81). Prior to Romanising influences, there is undoubtedly a close linkage between the proportion of cattle at various sites and the proximity of those sites to water and therefore good pasture (see Grant 1984, 109; Wilson *et al.* 1978, 136). The dominance of cattle at the Ditches is clearly an indication of the greater importance given to acculturation compared to the suitability of the surrounding area for particular husbandry regimes.

There is evidence to suggest, from the presence of very young individuals, that a proportion of the domestic stock was raised within the general vicinity of this site. Notably the quantities of such youngsters is not large, and due to possible retrieval and preservation issues, the evidence is clearly insufficient to suggest whether most or only a small proportion of the animals used within this settlement where locally bred as against imported. The great majority of the cattle and sheep were clearly culled as adults, including almost all the cattle and up to about 60% of the sheep. While there is some variation in the proportion of animals within the adult age groups between different parts of the site (see Exploitation Strategies), the overall pattern suggests that at least two thirds of the cattle and possibly as much as half the sheep survived to become old adults, here corresponding to greater than 3.5–4 years and 3–3.5 years respectively. The majority of the preadult sheep appear to have been culled as subadults, i.e. in their second year of life. Clearly, each of these two domesticates were principally raised/kept for their secondary, pre-mortem products, such as wool or milk. The good representation of sheep subadults and young adults, however, clearly suggests the importance of good quality meat as well as wool and/or milk to the local economy.

These adult mortality patterns are very similar to those derived from the previous Ditches excavations and also from Bagendon (see Table 33). In addition, each of these sites provided a relatively large proportion of subadult sheep. There are some differences in the age patterns shown by the two aging methods (see Exploitation strategies for a discussion of this problem), but essentially this data provides further evidence for a local cattle and sheep economy based on secondary products and a mixed farming strategy respectively. It was possible to sex a number of cattle bones (see below) from these two sites, which suggest a preponderance of cows. This commodity would presumably have been produced for a local market, perhaps to a large extent, for the military fort at Cirencester. Notably, cheese formed one of the principal items of food eaten by Roman troops, which is highlighted by the recovery of cheese squeezers at various military sites (Davies 1971, 127).

The cattle sex evidence was derived from a comparison of the distal breadth (Bd) of the metacarpus, which would appear to divide into female as against bull/castrate at approximately Bd=56mm. This was based on the data from several London Roman sites, where the sexual division had been initially calculated following the method described by Thomas (1988) which produced the best separation, and which was then applied to the data from Wanborough in order to assess its compatibility regarding cattle from this general area. The metacarpal measurements from the Ditches 82/83 excavation assemblage (N=10) and from Bagendon (N=6) were all smaller than

56mm and were therefore all categorized as female.

As well as the general food waste from these pre-villa features, the Quarry pit provided a large collection of cattle bones which clearly represent the partially articulated remains of six adult individuals. It was stated (see chronological narrative) that these were deposited following some attempt to skin and deflesh one or more of the carcasses and that the state of disarticulation may be the result of a combination of factors including the attention of scavengers and the aforementioned butchery activities. Clearly, the nature of these remains is very different to a number of other articulations recovered from Iron Age and/or Romano-British sites. A large quantity of sheep skeletons, dated to the third–fourth centuries AD, were recovered within a hollow at the A37 Western Link excavations near Dorchester (Rielly 1997, 271). In addition so-called 'cow burials' have been found at the Iron Age site of Guiting Power not far from Cheltenham (Marshall 1995) and also in Sussex, from an early Roman pit at Rocky Clump (John Funnell pers. comm.). However, the main difference between these animals and the Ditches examples is that they were relatively complete and showed no sign of butchery marks. It can perhaps be assumed in all of these cases, including Ditches, that these animals may have been diseased, thus precluding the use of their meat. Although, with the Ditches examples, there was clearly some use made of their postmortem products. One possible explanation is that the disease, or whatever was causing these animals to be treated differently from the normal practice, was not sufficiently onerous to warrant the abandonment of their skins. In addition, it is possible that while the meat may have been deemed unfit for human consumption, it may have been thought suitable for dogs. Obviously to go to this level of effort for one or more dogs would suggest the feeding of prized hunting/guard dogs rather than one or more of the local feral population.

The villa (late first to third century AD)

Sheep/goat were clearly the dominant food species within the early villa deposits, perhaps suggesting a continuation of the typical pre-Roman meat preferences, as described above. This pattern of sheep abundance can also be observed within the early levels at Frocester villa and in the first few decades of occupation at the town established at Wanborough (*Durocornovium*), each of which contrast with the cattle-dominated assemblage from the first century military settlement at Cirencester (see Table 39). Thornhill (Levine 2004) also has a cattle dominated assemblage which may reflect similar changes, although the poor preservation of bone at the site may have influenced species preservation. This difference clearly illustrates the link between the Romanized diet and the military, as described by King (1978; 1984), and the relatively slow transition, even within obviously Romanized settlements, from a sheep/goat to a cattle-based meat diet. The very clear difference, apparently within a rather short time span, from an obviously Romanised diet, as shown in D and Q, to one with a much greater sheep/goat component, may be indicative of a rapid decline in status. An alternative, and more likely explanation, is that the villa occupants may have differed from those in the pre-villa settlement in their readiness to accept the Romanized diet. Here of course it should be pointed out that this analysis is based on counts of bones rather than meat weights. A similar quantity of cattle and sheep bones will obviously suggest a far greater weight of beef compared to lamb/mutton. The obvious disparity between the assemblages from these deposits and the transition, in terms of bone counts, would appear to have occurred in this area by the third century, with a very obvious dependence on beef by the fourth century. The evidence from Cirencester for an earlier full transition may be related to the aforementioned early military influence.

The other species associated with the Romanized diet is the pig (see King ibid.). Several military sites have produced an abundance of pig bones, as indeed have a small selection of clearly high status civilian sites, e.g. Fishbourne villa. Notably, a high count of pig bones occurs throughout the Ditches villa deposits, and while pig abundance is demonstrably greater within these later levels, this species is also well represented within certain pre-villa features, especially in Q (see Table 28 and Table 39). The abundance of pigs dated to the villa could then indicate the high status of the occupants, but it would seem that pork was already popular and that these later occupants merely expanded an already well established production enterprise. However, most of the cellar pigs were culled prior to adulthood with an obviously good representation of juveniles, including sucking pigs, demonstrating an intensive exploitation strategy, which is in sharp contrast to the rather extensive strategy employed in the pre-villa phases. The Roman historical texts refer to a pig husbandry regime, situated near urban centres, aimed at providing young pigs to the nearby market by the simple strategy of raising two litters a year (Columella VII.9.4 in White 1970, 318). It is tempting to see a similar strategy in operation here, intended for local use as well as perhaps for the ready market at Cirencester (*Corinium*). The large proportion of chicken bones from the cellar could also be indicative of high status. This species tends to occur in larger numbers towards the latter part of the Roman period and is generally better represented in urban sites (Maltby 1994, 100).

Another indication of the level of Romanization/status is the clear difference in some butchery techniques shown by the pre-villa and cellar assemblages. The use of the cleaver as the choice butchery utensil has been described as a particularly urban phenomenon (Maltby 1989, 89). It has been suggested that an increase in cleaver butchery developed in order to meet the greater demand with an urban setting (ibid.). A similar level of cleaver work at this site may suggest an importation of urban techniques, perhaps of kitchen staff who had learnt their butchery skills in a nearby town. Of some interest here was the noted concentration of cattle kitchen waste within the cellar. This may suggest either the import of dressed carcasses, which seems unlikely, or perhaps a local two-stage butchery process. These cattle may have been slaughtered, skinned and dressed on one part of the estate, followed by the transference of the dressed carcass to the villa kitchens, where the final stages of the butchery process occurred.

It is unfortunate that the quantities of age and sex data are insufficient, with the noted exception of the pig data, to warrant a detailed analysis of either intra or inter-site comparisons. This size data is also fairly limited, although there is perhaps an indication of larger sheep from the cellar. There would appear to be an increase in sheep size by the later Roman period in this country, as demonstrated by several sites (see Maltby 1981, 190). This increase may be associated with the introduction of larger stock, perhaps of a polled variety (see Maltby 1994, 94).

BIBLIOGRAPHY

Albarella, U. (2007) The end of the Sheep age: people and animals in the Late Iron Age. In Haselgrove, C. and Moore, T. (eds) *The Later Iron Age in Britain and Beyond.* Oxbow Books, Oxford, 389–402.

Allen, D. F. (1961) A study of the Dobunnic coinage. In Clifford, E. M. (ed.) *Bagendon: a Belgic oppidum, a record of the excavations of 1954–56.* Cambridge, 75–149.

Allen, T., Miles, D. and Palmer, S. (1984) Iron Age buildings in the Upper Thames region. In Cunliffe, B. and Miles, D. (eds) *Aspects of the Iron Age in Central southern Britain.* OUCA Monograph 2, Oxford, 89–101.

Amorosi, T. (1989) *A postcranial guide to domestic neo-natal and juvenile mammals.* British Archaeological Report Int. Ser. 533, Oxford.

Anderson, A. S. (1979) *The Roman pottery industry in North Wiltshire.* Swindon Archaeological Society Report 2, Swindon.

Anderson, A. C. (1981) Some continental beakers of the first and second centuries AD. In Anderson, A. C. and Anderson, A. S. (eds) *Roman Pottery Research in Britain and North-West Europe. Part II.* British Archaeological Report Int. Ser. 123, Oxford, 321–348.

André, J. (1961) *L'alimentation et la cuisine à Rome.* Paris.

Armitage, P. L. and Clutton-Brock, J. (1976) A system for the classification and description of the horn cores of cattle from archaeological sites, *Journal of Archaeological Science* 3: 329–348.

Atkin, M. (1987) Excavation in Gloucester. An interim report, *Glevensis* 21: 5–17.

Barrett, J., Bradley, R. and Green, M. (1991) *Landscape, monuments and society.* Cambridge University Press, Cambridge.

Bayard, D. (1996) La Romanisation des Campagnes en Picardie a la lumiere des fouilles recentes: problemes d'echelle et de criteres. In Bayard, D. and Collart, J.-L. (eds) *De la Ferme Indigene a la Villa Romaine. Actes du II colloque de l'association AGER tenu a Amiens.* Revue Archeologique de Picardie 11, Chalons-sur-Marne, 157–184.

Bell, M. (1977) Excavations at Bishopstone, *Sussex Archaeological Collections* 115: 193–241.

Berry, C. A. F. (1951) The dating of Romano-British houses, *Journal Roman Studies* 41: 23–31.

Besombes, P.-A. and Barrandon, J.-N. (2000) Nouvelles properostions de classement des monnaies'bronze' de Claude 1, *Revue Numismatique* 155: 161–188, plates v–ix.

Biddulph, E. (2004). The Iron Age and Roman pottery. In Heawood, R. Iron Age and Roman activity at Watchfield Triangle, *Oxonensia* 69: 298–309.

Black, E. W. J. (1987) *The Roman villas of south-east Britain.* British Archaeological Report Brit. Ser. 171, Oxford.

Black, E. W. J. (1994) Villa-owners: Romano-British Gentleman and Officers, *Britannia* 25: 99–110.

Blagg, T. C. (1984) An examination of the connexions between military and civilian architecture in Roman Britain. In Blagg, T. C. and King, A. C. (eds) *Military and Civilian in Roman Britain: cultural relationships in a frontier province.* British Archaeological Report Brit. Ser. 136, Oxford, 249–264.

Blockley, K. (1985) *Marshfield. Ironmongers Piece. Excavations 1982–3. An Iron Age and Romano-British settlement in the south Cotswolds.* British Archaeological Report Brit. Ser. 141, Oxford.

Blockley, K. (1989) *Prestatyn 1984–5, An Iron Age Farmstead and Romano-British Industrial Settlement in North Wales.* British Archaeological Report Brit. Ser. 210, Oxford.

Blockley, K., Blockley, M., Blockley, P., Frere, S. S. and Stow, S. (1995) *Excavations in the Marlowe Car Park and Surrounding Areas.* The Archaeology of Canterbury, Volume V, Canterbury.

Boon, G. (1974) *Silchester. The Roman Town of Calleva.* 2nd edition. David and Charles, London.

Booth, P. (1999) Raleigh-Radford and the Roman villa at Ditchley: a review, *Oxonensia* 64: 39–50.

Bowden, M. and McOmish, D. (1987) The Required Barrier, *Scottish Archaeological Review* 4: 76–84.

Brailsford, J. W. (1962) *Hod Hill, volume 1. Antiquities from Hod Hill in the Durden Collection*, London.

Brandt, E. (1972) *Antike Gemmen in Deutschen Sammlungen I Stattliche Munzsammlung Munchen 3 Kaiserzeit.* Munich.

Branigan, K. (1977) *The Roman Villa in South West England.* Moonraker Press, Bradford-on-Avon.

Brodribb, A. C. C., Hands, A. R. and Walker, D. R. (1968) *Excavations at Shakenoak Farm, near Wilcote, Oxfordshire, Part I: Sites A and B.* privately printed, Oxford.

Brodribb, A. C. C., Hands, A. R. and Walker, D. R. (1971a) *Excavations at Shakenoak Farm, near Wilcote, Oxfordshire, Part 2: Sites K and B.*

Brodribb, A. C. C., Hands, A. R. and Walker, D. R. (1971b) *Excavations at Shakenoak Farm, near Wilcote, Oxfordshire, Part 3: Sites B & H.* privately printed, Oxford.

Brodribb, A. C. C., Hands, A. R. and Walker, D. R. (2005) *The Roman villa at Shakenoak Farm, Oxfordshire. Excavations 1960–1976.* British Archaeological Report Brit. Ser. 395, Oxford.

Brothwell, D. R. (1961) The human remains. In Clifford, E. (ed.) *Bagendon: A Belgic Oppidum.* Heffer and Sons, Cambridge, 268.

Brothwell, D. R. (1988) Human bone from the inner enclosure ditch, In Trow, S. D. (ed.) Excavations at Ditches hillfort, North Cerney, Gloucestershire, 1982–3, *Transactions of the Bristol and Gloucestershire Archaeological Society* 106: 77.

Buikstra, J. E. and Ubelaker, D. H. (1994) *Standards for Data Collection from Human Skeletal Remains.* Arkansas Archaeological Survey Research Series, Arkansas.

Bullock, A. E. and Allen, J. A. (1997) Animal bones. In Smith, J. C., Healy, F., Allen, M. J., Morris, E., Barnes, I. and Woodward, P. J. (eds) *Excavations along the Route of the Dorchester By-pass, Dorset, 1986–88.* Wessex Archaeology Report 11: 190–199.

Bushe-Fox, J. P. (1916) *Third report on the excavations on the site of the Roman town at Wroxeter, Shropshire, 1914.* Reports of the Research Committee of the Society of the Antiquaries of London, 4, Oxford.

Clapham, A. R., Tutin, T. G. and Warburg, E. F. (1962) *Flora of the British Isles.* 2nd edition. Cambridge University Press, Cambridge.

Clay, P. and Pollard, R. (1994) *Iron Age and Roman Occupation in the West Bridge Area, Leicester, Excavations 1962–1971.* Leicestershire Museums, Art Galleries and Records Service Archaeological Reports, Leicester.

Clifford, E. (1961) *Bagendon: A Belgic Oppidum.* Heffer and Sons, Cambridge.

Chapman, J. (2000). *Fragmentation in Archaeology: People, places and broken objects in the prehistory of south-eastern Europe.* Routledge, London.

Collart, J.-L. (1996) La naissance de la villa en Picardie: la ferme Gallo-Romaine precoce. In Bayard, D. and Collart, J.-L. (eds) *De la Ferme Indigene a la Villa Romaine. Actes du II colloque de l'association AGER tenu a Amiens.* Revue Archeologique de Picardie 11, Chalons-sur-Marne, 121–156.

Collis, J. (1996) Hillforts, enclosures and boundaries. In Collis, J. and Champion, T. (eds) *The Iron Age in Britain and Ireland: recent trends.* Sheffield University Press, Sheffield, 87–94.

Cool, H. E. M. and Philo, C. (1998) *Roman Castleford, Excavations 1974–1985, Volume I, The Small Finds,.* Yorkshire Archaeology 4, Exeter.

Cooper, N. (1998) The supply of pottery to Roman Cirencester. In Holbrook, N. (ed.) *Cirencester. The Roman town defences, public buildings and shops. Cirencester Excavations V.* Cotswold Archaeological Trust, Cirencester, 324–341.

Copeland, T. (1988) The North Oxfordshire Grim's Ditch: a fieldwork survey, *Oxonensia* 53: 277–292.

Corney, M. (1997) The origins and development of the small town of Cunetio, Mildenhall, Wiltshire, *British Numismatic Journal* 28: 337–350.

Cox, P. C. (1985) *The past in the pipeline. Archaeology of the Esso Midline.* Trust for Wessex Archaeology/ Esso.

Crabtree, P. J. (1989) *West Stow: Early Anglo-Saxon animal husbandry.* East Anglian Archaeology Report No. 47. Suffolk County Planning Department.

Cracknell, S. and Mahany, C. (1994) *Roman Alcester: Southern Extramural Area, 1964–1966 Excavations, Part 2, Finds and Discussion. Roman Alcester Series: Volume 1.* CBA Research Report 96, London.

Creighton, J. (1992) Interpreting villas, *Britannia* 23: 349–351.

Creighton, J. (2000) *Coins and power in late Iron Age Britain.* Cambridge University Press, Cambridge.

Creighton, J. (2001) The Iron Age-Roman transition. In James, S. and Millett, M. (eds) *Britons and Romans: advancing an archaeological agenda.* CBA Research report 125, York, 4–11.

Creighton, J. (2006) *Britannia: The Creation of a Roman Province.* Routledge, London & New York.

Crummy, N. (1983) *The Roman small finds from excavations in Colchester, 1971–9.* Colchester Archaeological Report 2, Colchester.

Cunliffe, B. (1971a) *Excavations at Fishbourne, 1961–1969, Volume I, The Site.* Reports of the Research Committee of the Society of Antiquaries of London, No. 27, London.

Cunliffe, B. (1971b) *Excavations at Fishbourne, 1961–1969, Volume II, The Finds.* Reports of the Research Committee of the Society of Antiquaries of London, No. 27, London.

Cunliffe, B. (1992) Pits, preconceptions and propitiation in the British Iron Age, *Oxford Journal of Archaeology,* 11(1): 69–84.

Cunliffe, B. (1998) *Fishbourne Roman Palace.* Tempus, Stroud.

Cunliffe, B. and Poole, C. (2000a) *Bury Hill, Upper Clatford, Hants, 1990. Danebury Environs programme. Vol. 2(2).* OUCA 49, Oxford.

Cunliffe, B. and Poole, C. (2000b) *Houghton Down, Stockbridge, Hants, 1994. Danebury Environs programme. Vol. 2(6).* OUCA 49, Oxford.

Cunliffe, B. and Poole, C. (2000c) *Suddern Farm, Middle Wallop, Hants, 1991 and 1996. Danebury Environs programme. Vol. 2(3).* OUCA 49, Oxford.

Curwen, E. C. (1937) Querns, *Antiquity,* 11: 133–151.

Dannell, G. B. 1988. The samian ware, in Trow, S. D. (ed.) Excavations at Ditches hillfort, North Cerney, Gloucestershire, 1982–3, *Transactions of the Bristol and Gloucestershire Archaeological Society*, 106: 59–60.

Dannell, G. B., Hartley, B. R., P., W. J. and Perrin, J. R. (1993) Excavations on a Romano-British pottery production site at Park Farm, Stanground, Peterborough, 1965–1967, *Journal of Roman Pottery Studies* 6: 51–93.

Dannell, G. B. and Wild, J. P. (1987) *Longthorpe II, The Military Works-Depot: an episode in Landscape History.* Britannia Monograph Series, No. 8, London.

Darling, M. (1985) Roman pottery. In Hurst, H. (ed.) *Kingsholm. Gloucester Archaeological reports, volume 1* Gloucester Archaeological Publications, Cambridge, 55–93.

Darlington, J. and Evans, J. (1992) Roman Sidbury, Worcester: Excavations 1959–1989, *Transactions of the Worcestershire Archaeological Society,* 13(3): 5–104.

Davies, R. W. (1971) The Roman military diet, *Britannia* 2: 122–142.

DeRoche, C. D. (1978) The Iron Age Pottery. In Parrington, M. *The excavation of an Iron Age settlement, Bronze Age ring-ditches and Roman features at Ashville Trading Estate, Abingdon. 1976–7.* CBA Res. Rep. 28. London.

Dickinson, B. M. 1996. Samian pottery. In J. May, *Dragonby. Report on Excavations at an Iron Age and Romano-British Settlement in North Lincolnshire, Vols 1 and 2*, Oxbow Monograph 61. Oxbow Books, Oxford, 591–597.

Dickinson, B. M. 1999. Samian. In C. J. Going and J. R. Hunn, *Excavations at Boxfield Farm, Chells, Stevenage, Hertfordshire*, Hertfordshire Archaeological Trust Report No. 2, Hertfordshire Archaeological Trust, Hertford, 84–7.

Dobney, K. and Rielly, K. (1988) A method for recording archaeological animal bones: the use of diagnostic zones, *Circaea* 5(2): 79–96.

Dool, J. and Wheeler, H. (1985) Roman Derby: excavations 1968–1983, *The Derbyshire Archaeological Journal* 105: 1–348.

Down, A. (1981) *Chichester Excavations V.* Chichester Excavations Committee. Philimore, Chichester.

Driver, J. C. (1982) Medullary bone as an indicator of sex in bird remains from archaeological sites. In Wilson, B., Grigson, C. and Payne, S. (eds) *Ageing and sexing animal bones from archaeological sites.* British Archaeological Report Brit. Ser. 109, Oxford, 251–254.

Drury, P. J. (1982) Form, function and the interpretation of the excavated plans of some large secular Romano-British buildings. In Drury, P. J. (ed.) *Structural Reconstruction. Approaches to the interpretation of the excavated remains of buildings.* British Archaeological Report 110, Oxford, 289–308.

Dunning, G. C. (1976) Salmonsbury, Bourton on the Water. In Harding, D. W. (ed.) *Hillforts. Later prehistoric earthworks in Britain and Ireland.* Academic Press, London, 76–118.

Ellis, P. (1999) North Leigh Roman Villa, Oxfordshire: a report on excavation and recording in the 1970s, *Britannia* 30: 199–246.

Ellis, P., Evans, J., Hanaford, H., Hughes, G. and Jones, A. 1994. Excavations in the Wroxeter hinterland 1988–1990: the archaeology of the Shrewsbury bypass, *Transactions of the Shropshire Archaeological and Historical Society* 69: 1–119.

Evans, J. 1993. Pottery function and finewares in the Roman north, *Journal of Roman Pottery Studies* 6: 95–118.

Fasham, P. J. (1987) *A banjo enclosure in Micheldever Wood, Hampshire.* Hampshire Field Club Monograph 5. Trust for Wessex Archaeology, Gloucester.

Ferdiere, A. (1988) *Les Campagnes en Gaule-Romaine. Tome 1. Les hommes et l'environment en Gaule rurale.* Collections des Hesperides. Editions Errace, Paris.

Foster, J. (1977) *Bronze boar figurines in Iron Age and Roman Britain.* British Archaeological Report Brit. Ser. 39, Oxford.

France, N. E. and Gobel, B. M. (1985) *The Romano-British Temple at Harlow.* Gloucester.

Frere, S. S. (1972) *Verulamium Excavations, Volume I.* Reports of the Research Committee of the Society of Antiquaries of London, No. 28, Oxford.

Friendship-Taylor, R. (2002) Piddington, *Current Archaeology* 182: 80.

Friendship-Taylor, R. (2006) *Iron Age and Roman Piddington. Interim report and phase descriptions of the late Iron Age settlement and Roman villa at Piddington, Northants.* The Upper Nene Archaeological Society.

Fulford, M. and Timby, J. (2000) *Late Iron Age and Roman Silchester.* Britannia Monograph Series No. 15, London.

Fulford, M. (2001) Links with the past: pervasive 'ritual' behaviour in Roman Britain, *Britannia* 32: 199–218.

Gascoigne, P. (1973) An Iron Age pit at Wood House, Guiting Power, *Transactions of the Bristol and Gloucestershire Archaeological Society,* 92: 204–207.

Giffen, A. E. van 1940–4. De Romeinsche castella in den dorpsheuvel te Valkenburg aan den Rijn (Z.N.), I, *JVT,* 25–8: 1–316.

Gosden, C. and Lock, G. (2003) Becoming Roman on the Berkshire Downs: evidence from Alfred's Castle, *Britannia* 34: 65–80.

Gould, J. (1967) Excavations at Wall, Staffs, 1964–6, on the Site of the Roman Forts, *Transactions of the Lichfield and South Staffordshire Archaeological and Historical Society* 8: 1–40.

Grant, A. (1975) The animal bones. In Cunliffe, B. (ed.) *Excavations at Portchester castle, vol 1. Roman.* Report Research Committee Society of Antiquaries London 32, London, 378–408.

Grant, A. (1982) The use of toothwear as a guide to the age of domestic ungulates. In Wilson, B., Grigson, C. and Payne, S. (eds) *Ageing and sexing animal bones from archaeological sites.* British Archaeological Report Brit. Ser. 109, Oxford, 91–108.

Grant, A. (1984) Animal husbandry in Wessex and the Thames valley. In Cunliffe, B. and Miles, D. (eds) *Aspects of the Iron Age in Central Southern Britain.* Univ of Oxford: Committee of Archaeology Monograph No. 2, 102–120.

Green, C. and Draper, J. (1978) The Mileoak Roman villa, Handley, Towcester, Northamptonshire. Report on the excavations of 1955 and 1956, *Northamptonshire Archaeology* 13: 28–66.

Greene, K. (1973) Some Romano-British material salvaged from Wanborough, Wiltshire, *Wiltshire Archaeology and Natural History Magazine* 68: 64–70.

Greene, K. (1974) A group of Roman pottery from Wanborough, Wiltshire, *Wiltshire Archaeology and Natural History Magazine* 69: 51–66.

Grigson, C. (1982) Sex and age determination of some bones and teeth of domestic cattle: a review of the literature. In Wilson, B., Grigson, C. and Payne, S. (eds) *Ageing and sexing animal bones from archaeological sites.* British Archaeological Report Brit. Ser. 109, Oxford, 7–24.

Hambleton, E. (1998) *Animal husbandry regimes in Iron Age Britain: A comparative Study of Faunal Assemblages from British Iron Age sites.* British Archaeological Report Brit. Ser. 282, Oxford.

Hampton, N. and Palmer, R. (1977) Implications of Aerial photography for archaeology, *The Archaeology Journal* 134: 157–193.

Hancocks, A. (2006) Fired clay and daub. In Jones, L., Woodward, A. and Buteux, S. (eds) *Iron Age, Roman and Saxon Occupation at Grange Park. Excavations at Courtenhall, Northamptonshire, 1999.* British Archaeological Report Brit. Ser. 425, Oxford, 157–164.

Hands, A. R. (1993) *The Romano-British roadside settlement at Wilcote, Oxfordshire, Excavations 1990–92.* British Archaeological Report Brit. Ser. 232, Oxford.

Hannan, A. (1993) Excavations at Tewkesbury 1972–74, *Transactions of the Bristol and Gloucestershire Archaeological Society* 111: 21–76.

Harcourt, R. A. (1974) The dog in prehistoric and early historic Britain, *Journal of Archaeological Science,* 1: 151–175.

Harden, D. B. (1973) Glass. In Brodribb, A. C. C., Hands, A. R. and Walker, D. (eds) *Excavations at Shakenoak farm, near Wilcote, Oxfordshire, 4.* Privately printed, Oxford, 98–107.

Harding, D. W. (1984) *Holme House, Piercebridge: excavations, 1969–70, a summary report.* University of Edinburgh Dept of Archaeology Project Paper No. 2, Edinburgh.

Harding, D. W. (2004) *The Iron Age in Northern Britain.* Routledge, London.

Haselgrove, C. (1987) *Iron Age coinage in south-east England: the archaeological context.* British Archaeological Report 174, Oxford.

Haselgrove, C. (1993) The development of British Iron Age coinage, *British Numismatic Journal* 153: 18–62.

Haselgrove, C. (1995) Social and symbolic order in the origins and layout of Roman villas in Northern Gaul. In Metzler, J., Millett, M., Roymans, N. and Slofstra, J. (eds) *Integration in the Early Roman West.* Dossiers d'Archeologie du Musee National d'Histoire et d'Art IV, Luxembourg, 65–76.

Hassall, M. and Rhodes, J. (1975) Excavations at the New Market Hall, Gloucester, 1966–7, *Transactions of the Bristol and Gloucestershire Archaeological Society* 93: 15–100.

Hawkes, C. F. C. and Hull, M. R. (1947) *Camulodunum, first report on the excavations at Colchester 1930–1939.* Reports of the Research Committee of the Society of Antiquaries of London, 14, Oxford.

Hencken, T. C. (1938) The excavation of the Iron Age camp on Bredon Hill, Gloucestershire, 1935–1937, *The Archaeological Journal* 95: 1–111.

Henig, M. (1978) *A Corpus of Roman Engraved Gemstones from British sites.* British Archaeological Report Brit. Ser. 8, second edition, Oxford.

Henig, M. (1990) A house for Minerva: temples, aedicula shrines and signet rings. In Henig, M. (ed.) *Architecture and Architectural sculpture in the Roman Empire.* OUCA Monograph 29, 152–160.

Henig, M. (2002) *The Heirs of King Verica. Culture and Politics in Roman Britain.* Tempus, Stroud.

Hill, J. D. (1995a) The Pre Roman Iron Age in Britain and Ireland: An overview, *Journal of World Prehistory* 9: 47–98.

Hill, J. D. (1995b) *Ritual and Rubbish in the Iron Age of Wessex.* British Archaeological Report Brit. Ser. 242, Oxford.

Hill, J. D. (2002) Just about the potters wheel? Using, making and depositing middle and later Iron Age pots in East Anglia. In Woodward, A. and Hill, J. D. (eds) *Prehistoric Britain: the ceramic basis.* Prehistoric Ceramics Research Group Occasional Publication 3. Oxbow Books, Oxford, 143–161.

Hillman, G. (1981) Reconstructing crop husbandry practices from charred remains of crops. In Mercer, R. (ed.) *Farming Practice in British Prehistory.* Edinburgh University Press, Edinburgh, 123–162.

Hillman, G., Mason, S., de Moulins, D. and Nesbitt, M. (1996) Identification of archaeological remains of wheat: the 1992 London workshop, *Circaea,* 12: 195–209.

Hingley, R. (1989) *Rural settlement in Roman Britain.* Seaby, London.

Hingley, R. (1990) Iron Age currency bars: the archaeological and social context, *The Archaeological Journal* 147: 91–117.

Hingley, R. (2005) Iron Age 'Currency bars' in Britain: items of exchange in liminal contexts? In Haselgrove, C. and Wigg, D. (eds) *Ritual and coinage.* Gebruder Mann Verlag, Mainz, 183–206.

Hingley, R. (2006) The deposition of iron objects in Britain during the later prehistoric and Roman periods: Contextual analysis and the significance of iron, *Britannia* 37: 213–57.

Hirst, K. (n.d.) *An evaluation of archaeological remains at Waltham Roman villa, Gloucestershire.* Time Team unpublished report.

Hobbs, R. (1996) *British Iron Age coins in The British Museum.* British Museum Press, London.

Hobley, B. (1969) Neronian-Vespasianic military site at The Lunt, Baginton, Warwickshire, *Transactions and proceedings of the Birmingham Archaeological society 1966–67,* 83: 65–129.

Hofmann, B. 1985. *Catalogue des Estampilles sur Vaisselle Sigilllée,* Revue Archéologique Sites, Hors-série No. 27, Gonfaron.

Holbrook, H. and Bidwell, P. T. (1991) *Roman Finds from Exeter.* Exeter Archaeological Reports: Volume 4, Exeter.

Holbrook, N. (1994). Corinium Dobunnorum: Roman Civitas Capital and Roman Provincial Capital. In Darvill, T. and Gerrard, C. (eds) *Cirencester: Town and Landscape: an urban archaeological assessment.* Cotswold Archaeological Trust, Cirencester, 57–86.

Holbrook, N. (2006) The Roman Period. In Holbrook, N. and Jurica, J. (eds) *Twenty-five years on. The Archaeology of Gloucestershire.* Cotswold Archaeology, Cheltenham, 97–132.

Hurst, H. R. (1986) *Gloucester, The Roman and Later Defences, Excavations on the E. Defences and a reassessment of the defensive sequence.* Gloucester Archaeological Reports, Vol. 2, Gloucester.

Isings, C. (1957) *Roman Glass from Dated Finds. Archaeologica Traiectina 2.* J. B. Wolters, Groningen.

Jackson, D. and Dix, B. (1987) Late Iron Aqe and Roman settlement at Weekly, Northants, *Northamptonshire Archaeology* 21: 41–93.

Jackson, D. A. and Ambrose, T. M. (1978) Excavations at Wakerley, Northants, 1972–75, *Britannia* 9: 115–242.

James, S. (1988) Possible Roman military metalwork. In Trow, S. (ed.) Excavations at Ditches hillfort, North Cerney, Gloucestershire, 1982–3, *Transactions of the Bristol and Gloucestershire Archaeological Society,* 106: 51.

James, S. (2001) Romanization and the peoples of Britain. In Terrenato, N. (ed.) *Italy and the West: Comparative Issues in Romanization.* Oxbow Books, Oxford, 77–89.

Jarrett, M. J. and Wrathmell, S. (1981) *Whitton, An Iron Age and Roman Farmstead in South Glamorgan.* University of Wales Press, Cardiff.

Johns, C. (1996) *The jewellery of Roman Britain.* UCL Press, London.

Johns, C. (1997) *The Snettisham Roman Jeweller's hoard.* British Museum Press, London.

Jones, M. K. J. (1981) The development of crop husbandry. In Jones, M. K. J. and Dimbleby, F. (eds) *Environment and Man: Iron-Age to Anglo-Saxon periods.* British Archaeological Report 87: 95–127.

Kenyon, R. F. (1987) The Claudian coinage. In Crummy, N. (ed.) *The Coins from Excavations in Colchester 1971–9.* Colchester Archaeological report 4: 24–41.

King, A. C. (1978) A comparative survey of bone assemblages from Roman sites in Britain, *University of London, Institute of Archaeology Bullettin* 15: 207–232.

King, A. C. (1984) Animal bones and the dietary identity of

military and civilian groups in Roman Britain, Germany and Gaul. In Blagg, T. C. and King, A. C. (eds) *Military and civilian in Roman Britain: cultural relationships in a frontier province*. British Archaeological Reports Brit. Ser. 136, Oxford, 187–218.

Knorr, R. 1919. *Töpfer und Fabriken verzierter Terra-sigillata des ersten Jahrhunderts*, Stuttgart.

Lawes, J. (2006) Delusions of grandeur in Somerset?, *Current Archaeology* 201: 498–501.

Leach, P. (1982) *Ilchester. Vol. 1, Excavations 1974–5*. Western Archaeological Trust Monography 3. Bristol.

Leach, P. (1993) The pottery. In Woodward, A. and Leach, P. *The Uley Shrines. Excavation of a ritual complex on West Hill, Uley, Gloucestershire: 1977–9*. English Heritage Archaeological Report 17, London, 219–249.

Leech, R. and Leach, F. (1982) Roman town and countryside 43– 450AD. In Aston, M. and Burrow, I (ed.) *The archaeology of Somerset*. Bridgewater, 63–82.

Levine, M. (2004) The faunal remains. In Jennings, D., Muir, J., Palmer, S. and Smith, A. (eds) *Thornhill Farm, Fairford, Gloucestershire: An Iron Age and Roman pastoral site in the Upper Thames Valley. Thames Valley Landscapes Monograph 23*. Oxford Archaeology, Oxford, 109–132.

Lucas, R. N. (1993) *The Romano-British villa at Halstock, Dorset, Excavations, 1967–1985*. Dorset Natural History and Archaeological Society, Monograph Series, No. 13.

Maaskant-Kleibrink, M. (1978) *Catalogue of the Engraved Gems in the Royal Coin Cabinet, The Hague. The greek, Etruscan and roman collections*, The Hague.

Mackreth, D. F. (1988) Excavation of an Iron Age and Roman Enclosure at Werrington, Cambridgeshire, *Britannia* 19: 59–151.

MacRobert, E. (1993). The pottery. In Hannan, A. Excavations at Tewkesbury 1972–3, *Transactions of the Bristol and Gloucestershire Archaeological Society* 111: 55–63.

Maltby, M. (1981) Iron Age, Romano-British and Anglo-Saxon animal husbandry – a review of the faunal evidence. In Jones, M. and Dimbleby, G. (eds) *The environment of man: the Iron Age to the Anglo-Saxon period*. British Archaeological Report Brit. Ser. 87, Oxford, 155–203.

Maltby, M. (1989) Urban rural variations in the butchering of cattle in Romano-British Hampshire. In Serjeantson, D. and Waldron, T. (eds) *Diet and Craft in Towns*. British Archaeological Report Brit. Ser. 199, Oxford, 75–106.

Maltby, M. (1994) The meat supply to Roman Dorchester and Winchester. In Hall, A. R. and Kenward, H. R. (eds) *Urban-rural connexions: perspectives from environmental archaeology*. Symposia of the Association for Environmental Archaeology 12: 85–102.

Manley, J. and Rudkin, D. (2003) *Facing the palace : excavations in front of the Roman palace at Fishbourne (Sussex, UK) 1995–99*. Sussex Archaeological Society, Lewes.

Marshall, A. (1991) *A defensively ditched, trapezoidal enclosure of later Iron Age date and Roman farmsteading area at The Bowsings, Guiting Power, Glos*. Cotswold Archaeological research group research report 6.

Marshall, A. (1995) From Iron Age to Roman: The Park and Bowsings sites at Guiting Power, *Glevensis* 28: 13–19.

Marshall, A. (1999) Wharton's Furlong, Cold Aston, in Wills, J. and Rawes, J. (eds) Archaeological Review No. 23 (1998), *Transactions of the Bristol and Gloucestershire Archaeological Society* 117: 167–188.

Marshall, A. (2001) Functional analysis of settlement areas: Prospection over a defended enclosure of Iron Age date at the Bowsings, Guiting power, Glos. UK, *Archaeological Prospection* 8(2): 79–106.

Marshall, F. H. (1911) *Catalogue of jewellery in the British Museum, Greek, Roman and Etruscan, in the Department of Antiquities*. British Museum, London.

Martins, C. (2005) *Becoming Consumers: Looking beyond Wealth as an Explanations of Villa Variability*. British Archaeological Report Brit. Ser. 403, Oxford.

Martin, T. S. (2007) Techniques for exploring context, deposition and chronology. In R. Hingley and S. H. Willis (eds) *Roman Finds: Context and Theory; Proceedings of a conference held at the University of Durham*. Oxbow Books, Oxford, 86–99.

Massy, J.-L. (1989) Fontoy, Moselle, *Gallia Information. Prehistoire et Histoire,* 1989(2): 107.

May, J. (1996) *Dragonby, Report on Excavations at an Iron Age and Romano-British Settlement in North Lincolnshire*. Oxbow Monograph No. 61, Oxford.

McSloy, E. (2006) The Pottery. In Coleman, L., Hancocks, A. and Watts, M. *Excavations on the Wormington to Tirely Pipeline, 2000. Four sites by the Carrant Brook and River Isbourne, Gloucestershire and Worcestershire*. Cotswold Archaeology Monograph 3. Cirencester, 37–56.

McWhirr, A. (1986) *Houses in Roman Cirencester*. Cirencester Excavations 3, Cirencester.

Meadows, I. D. (1992) Three Roman Sites in Northamptonshire: Excavations by E. Greenfield at Bozeat, Higham Ferrers, and Great Oakley between 1961 and 1966, *Northamptonshire Archaeology* 24: 77–94.

Meates, G. W. (1979) *The Roman villa at Lullingstone, Kent. Volume 1: the site*. Monograph series of the Kent Archaeological Society I, Maidstone.

Meates, G. W. (1987) *The Roman Villa at Lullingstone, Kent, Volume II: The Wall Paintings and Finds*. Monograph Series of the Kent Archaeological Society, No. 3, Maidstone.

Miles, D. (1986) *Archaeology at Barton Court Farm, Abingdon,*

Oxfordshire. OAU Report 3. CBA Research Report 50, Oxford.

Millett, M. (1990) *The Romanization of Britain*. Cambridge University Press, Cambridge.

Moore, T. (2001) Hailey Wood Camp: a Roman Temple complex in the Cotswolds?, *Transactions of the Bristol and Gloucestershire Archaeological Society* 119: 83–93.

Moore, T. (2006a) The Iron Age. In Holbrook, N. and Juřica, J. (eds) *Twenty-five years on. The Archaeology of Gloucestershire*. Cotswold Archaeology BAGAR 3, Cheltenham, 61–96.

Moore, T. (2006b) *Iron Age societies in the Severn-Cotswolds: developing narratives of social and landscape change*. British Archaeological Report Brit. Ser. 421, Oxford.

Moore, T. (2007) Life on the edge? Exchange, community, and identity in the later Iron Age of the Severn-Cotswolds. In Haselgrove, C. and Moore, T. (eds) *The Later Iron Age in Britain and Beyond*. Oxbow Books, Oxford, 41–61.

Moore, T., Reece, R. and Trow, S. (forthcoming) Excavations at Bagendon, Gloucestershire, 1979–1981.

Moore, T., James, S., Reece, R. and Trow, S. (in prep.) Ditches and Bagendon in context.

Morris, E. (2005) Pottery and briquetage. In Thomas, N. (ed) *Conderton Camp, Worcestershire: a small middle Iron Age hillfort on Bredon Hill*. CBA Res. Rep. 143, London, 117–146.

Mudd, A., Williams, R. and Lupton, A. (1999) *Excavations alongside Roman Ermin Street, Gloucestershire and Wiltshire. The archaeology of the A419/A417 Swindon to Gloucester Road scheme*. Oxford Archaeological Unit, Oxford.

Murray, E. (2002) Marine molluscan remains from Rathgurren ringfort. In Comber, M. M. V. Duigan's excavations at the Ringfort of Rathgureen, Co. Galway, 1948–9, *Proceedings of the Royal Irish Academy* 102: 194–197.

Neal, D. S. (1974) *The excavation of the Roman villa in Gadebridge park, Hemel Hempstead 1963–8*. London, Soc. Antiq. Res. Rep. XXXI.

Neal, D. S., Wardle, A. and Hunn, J. (1990) *Excavation of the Iron Age, Roman and medieval settlement at Gorhambury, St. Albans*. English Heritage. Archaeological Report 14, London.

Niblett, R. (1985) *Sheepen: an early Roman industrial site at Camulodunum*. Council for British Archaeology Research Report No. 57, London.

O'Connor, T. P. (1991) Bones from 46–54 Fishergate. In *The Archaeology of York 15(4)*. Council for British Archaeology, London, 209–298.

Oswald, A. (1997) A doorway on the past: practical and mystic concerns in the orientation of roundhouse doorways. In Gwilt, A. and Haselgrove, C. (eds) *Reconstructing Iron Age societies*. Oxbow Monograph 71, Oxford, 87–95.

Oswald, F. 1936–7. *Index of Figure-Types on Terra Sigillata ('Samian Ware')*, University Press of Liverpool, Liverpool.

Parker, A. J. (1988) The birds of Roman Britain, *Oxford Journal of Archaeology*, 7(2): 197–226.

Parker-Pearson, M. (1996) Food, fertility and front doors in the first Millennium BC. In Champion, T. and Collis, J. (eds) *The Iron Age in Britain and Ireland: Recent Trends*. Sheffield University Press, Sheffield, 117–132.

Parry, C. (1998) Excavations near Birdlip, Cowley, Gloucestershire 1987–88, *Transactions of the Bristol and Gloucestershire Archaeological Society* 116: 25–92.

Partridge, C. (1981) *Skeleton Green, a Late Iron Age and Romano-British Site*. Britannia Monograph Series, No. 2.

Payne, S. (1973) Kill-off patterns in sheep and goats: the mandibles from Asvan Kale, *Anatolian Studies* 23: 281–303.

Perring, D. (1989) Cellars and Cults in Roman Britain, *The Archaeological Journal* 146: 279–301.

Perring, D. (2002) *The Roman House in Britain*. Routledge, London.

Philp, B. J. (1963) The Romano-British farmstead at Eastwood, Fawkham, *Archaeologia Cantiana* 78: 55–73.

Philp. B., Parfitt, K., Willson, J., Dutto, M. and Williams, W. (1991). *The Roman villa at Keston, Kent. First Report (Excavations 1968–1978)*. Kent Monograph Series 6, Dover.

Potter, T. W. (1979) *Romans in North-West England, Excavations at the Roman forts of Ravenglass, Watercrook and Bowness-on-Solway*. Cumberland and Westmorland Antiquarian and Archaeological Society, Research Series, Volume I, Kendal.

Potter , T. W. and Trow, S. D. (1988) Puckeridge-Braughing, Herts.: The Ermin Street Excavations, 1971–1972, The Late Iron Age and Roman Settlement, *Hertfordshire Archaeology*, 10.

Price, E. (2000) *Frocester, A Romano-British settlement, its antecedents and successors. Volume 1: The Sites*. Gloucester and District Archaeological Group, Stonehouse.

Price, J. (1978) Trade in Glass. In du Plat Taylor, J. and Cleere, H. (eds) *Roman shipping and trade: Britain and the Rhine Provinces*. CBA Research Report 24, London, 70–78.

Price, J. (1979) The Glass. In Gracie, H. S. and Price, E. G. Frocester Court Roman villa: second report 1968–77: the courtyard, *Transactions of the Bristol and Gloucestershire Archaeological Society* 97: 37–46.

Price, J. (1987) Glass from Felmongers, Harlow in Essex. A dated deposit of vessel glass found in an Antonine pit, *Annales du 10e Congres de l'Association Internationale pour l'Histoire du Verre: Madrid-Segovie 23–23 Septembre 1985*, 185–206.

Prummel, W. and Frisch, H. J. (1986) A Guide for the

distinction of Species, Sex and Body Side in Bones of Sheep and Goat, *Journal of Archaeological Science* 13: 567–577.

Rackham, D. J. (1995) Appendix: skeletal evidence of medieval horses from London sites. In Clark, J. (ed.) *The medieval horse and its equipment c 1150–1450. Medieval finds from excavations in London* 5: 169–174.

Raleigh-Radford, C. A. (1936) The Roman Villa at Ditchley, Oxon, *Oxoniensia* 1: 24–69.

RCHME (1976) *Iron Age and Romano-British monuments in the Gloucestershire Cotswolds. County of Gloucester Vol. 1* HMSO, London.

Reece, R. (2003) The siting of Roman Corinium, *Britannia* 34: 276–280.

Richardson, K. M. (1951) The excavation of Iron Age villages on Boscombe Down West, *Wiltshire Archaeology and Natural History Magazine* 54: 123–168.

Rielly, K. (1988) The animal bone. In Trow, S. D. (ed.) Excavations at Ditches Hillfort, North Cerney, Gloucestershire, 1982–3, *Transactions of the Bristol and Gloucestershire Archaeological Society* 106: 77–79, fiche 71/ B13 – 72/C77.

Rielly, K. (1997) Animal bone. In Smith, J. C., Healy, F., Allen, E. L., Morris, E., Barnes, I. and Woodward, P. J. (eds) *Excavations along the Route of the Dorchester By-pass, Dorset, 1986–88.* Wessex Archaeology Report No. 11: 270–273.

Rielly, K. (forthcoming a) The animal bones, in Fitzpatrick, A, The Roman town of Wanborough. Wessex Archaeological Trust.

Rielly, K. (forthcoming b) The animal bones. In Moore, T., Reece, R. and Trow, S. *Excavations at Bagendon, Gloucestershire, 1979–1981.*

Rielly, K. and Trow, S. (1988) The Ditches animal bone assemblage in its regional context. In Trow, S. (ed.) Excavations at Ditches Hillfort, North Cerney, Gloucestershire, 1982–3, *Transactions of the Bristol and Gloucestershire Archaeological Society* 106: 79–82.

Rigby, V. (1982) The Coarse Pottery. In Wacher, J. and McWhirr, A. (eds) *Early Roman occupation at Cirencester. Cirencester Excavations I.* Cirencester Excavations Committee, Cirencester, 153–197.

Rigby, V. (1988) The Gallo-Belgic wares. In Trow, S. D. (ed.) Excavations at Ditches hillfort, North Cerney, Gloucestershire. 1982–3, *Transactions of the Bristol and Gloucestershire Archaeological Society,* 106: 60–62.

Rivet, A. L. F. (1969) The Social and Economic aspects. In Rivet, A. L. F. (ed.) *The Roman villa in Britain.* Routledge and Kegan Paul, London, 173–216.

Rodwell, W. J. and Rodwell, K. A. (1985) *Rivenhall: investigations of a villa, church and village 1950–1977.* CBA Research Report 55, Chelmsford Archaeological Trust Report 4, London.

Rodwell, W. J. 1988. Samian ware. In Wickenden, N. P., Excavations at Great Dunmow, Essex: a Romano-British Small Town in the Trinovantian Civitas, *East Anglian Archaeology*, Report 41, Chelmsford Archaeological Trust Report 7, Essex County Council, 76–9.

Roe, F. (1993) Worked stone. In Woodward, A. and Leach, P. (eds) *The Uley Shrines. Excavation of a ritual complex on West Hill Uley, Gloucestershire 1977–9.* English Heritage Arch. Report 17, London, 197–201.

Roe, F. (2007) Worked stone. In Miles, D., Palmer, S., Smith, A. and Jones, G. (eds) *Iron Age and Roman Settlement in the Upper Thames Valley: Excavations at Claydon Pike and other sites within the Cotswold Water Park.* Thames Valley Landscapes Monograph 26. Oxford Archaeology: 51–53.

Rogers, G. B. 1974. *Poteries Sigillées de la Gaule Centrale*, 28th supplement to *Gallia*, Paris.

Rogerson, A. (1977) Excavations at Scole, 1973. *East Anglian Archaeology* Report 5, 97–224.

Rouvier-Jeanlin, M. (1972) *Les Figures Gallo-romaines en terre cuits au Musee des Antiquites Nationales.* Gallia suppl.XXIV, Paris.

Ruddock, F. A. 1961. Metal-working at Bagendon and finds of metal, clay, stone, flint and glass. In Clifford, E. (ed.) *Bagendon: A Belgic Oppidum.* Heffer and Sons, Cambridge, 186–201.

Saville, A. (1979) *Excavations at Guiting Power, Gloucestershire 1974.* CRAAGS Occasional Paper 7, Bristol.

Saville, A. (1980) *Archaeological sites in the Avon and Gloucestershire Cotswolds: an extensive survey of a rural archaeological resource with specific reference to plough damage.* CRAAGS Survey 5, Bristol.

Saville, A. (1983) *Uley Bury & Norbury Hillforts. Rescue excavations at two Gloucestershire Iron Age sites.* Western Archaeological Trust. Excavation Monograph No. 5.

Schmid, E. (1972) *Atlas of animal bones.* Elsevier, New York.

Sellwood, L. C. (1988) The British coins. In Trow, S. D. (ed.) Excavations at Ditches hillfort, North Cerney, Gloucestershire, 1982–3. *Transactions of the Bristol and Gloucestershire Archaeological Society* 106: 40–43.

Shaffrey, R. (2002) Catalogue of worked stone. In Catchpole, T., Excavations at West Drive, Cheltenham, Gloucestershire 1997–9, *Transactions of the Bristol and Gloucestershire Archaeological Society* 120: 99.

Shaffrey, R. (2004) The worked stone objects. In Cook, J. Guttmann, E. B. A. and Mudd, A. Excavations of an Iron Age site at Coxwell Road, Faringdon, *Oxoniensia* 69: 241–249.

Shepherd, J. (1985) Roman glass. In Cunliffe, B. a. D., P. (ed.) *The Temple of Sulis Minerva at Bath.* Oxford University Committee for Archaeology Monograph 7, Oxford, 161–164.

Shepherd, J. D. (1986) The Glass. In McWhirr, A. (ed.) *Houses in Roman Cirencester.* Cirencester Excavations 3, Cirencester, 117–121.

Smith, D. J. (1978) Regional aspects of the winged corridor villa in Britain. In Todd, M. (ed.) *Studies in the Romano-British villa.* Leicester University Press, Leicester, 117–148.

Smith, D. Hird, L. and Dix, B. (1989) The Roman villa at Great Weldon, Northants. *Northamptonshire Archeology* 22: 23–67.

Smith, J. T. (1997) *Roman Villas: a study in social structure.* Routledge, London.

Stanfield, J. A. and Simpson, G. 1958. *Central Gaulish Potters.* London, Oxford University Press.

Stanfield, J. A. and Simpson, G. 1990. *Les Potiers de la Gaule Centrale,* Revue Archéologiques Sites, Hors-série 37, Gonfaron.

Stanford, S. C. (1974) *Croft Ambrey.* Adams and Sons, Hereford.

Stead, I. M. (1976) *Excavations at Winterton Roman Villa, and other Roman sites in north Lincolnshire, 1958–1969.* Department of the Environment Archaeological Report, No. 9, London.

Stead, I. M. and Rigby, V. (1986) *Baldock. The excavation of a Roman and Pre-Roman settlement 1968–72.* Britannia Monograph Series 7, London.

Stead, I. M. and Rigby, V. (1989) *Verulamium: the King Harry Lane site.* English Heritage Archaeological Report No. 12, London.

Stevens, C. (1996) *Iron Age and Roman agriculture in the upper Thames Valley: archaeological and social perspectives.* PhD thesis. University of Cambridge.

Swan, V. (1975) Oare reconsidered and the origins of Savernake ware, *Britannia* 6: 37–61.

Thomas, N. (2005) *Conderton Camp, Worcestershire: A small middle Iron Age hillfort on Bredon Hill.* CBA Research Report 143, London.

Thomas, R. N. W. (1988) A statistical evaluation of criteria used in sexing cattle metapodials, *Archaezoologia,* 2 (1.2): 83–92.

Timby, J. (1990) Severn valley ware: a reassessment, *Britannia* 21: 243–251.

Timby, J. (1998) *Excavations at Kingscote and Wycomb, Gloucestershire.* Cotswold Archaeological Trust, Cirencester.

Timby, J. (1999a) Later Prehistoric and Roman pottery. In Mudd, A., Williams, R. and Lupton, A. (eds) *Excavations alongside Roman Ermin Street, Gloucestershire and Wiltshire. The archaeology of the A419/A417 Swindon to Gloucester Road scheme. Volume 2.* Oxford Archaeological Unit, Oxford, 320–338.

Timby, J. (1999b) Pottery supply to Gloucester colonia. In Hurst, H. (ed.) The Coloniae of Roman Britain: new studies and a review. Papers held at Gloucester on 5–6 July 1997 *Journal of Roman Archaeology (Supplementary series)* 36, Portsmouth, Rhode Island, 37–44.

Timby, J. (2000) The pottery. In Price, E. (ed.) *Frocester, A Romano-British settlement, its antecedents and successors. Volume 2: The Finds.* Gloucester and District Archaeological Group, Stonehouse, 125–148.

Timby, J. (2004) Pottery. In Jennings, D. Muir, J. Plamer, S. Smith, A. and Hayden, C. *Thornhill Farm, Fairford, Gloucestershire: An Iron Age and Roman pastoral site in the Upper Thames Valley.* Thames Valley Landscapes Monograph 23. Oxford Archaeological Unit, Oxford.

Todd, M. (1978) Villas and Romano-British society. In Todd, M. (ed.) *Studies in the Romano-British Villa.* Leicester University Press, Leicester, 197–208.

Tomber, R. and Dore, J. (1998) *The National Roman fabric reference collection. A handbook.* MOLAS monograph 2/ English Heritage, London.

Trow, S. (1982) An early intaglio found near Cirencester, Gloucestershire, *Britannia* 13: 322–323.

Trow, S. (1988a) Excavations at Ditches hillfort, North Cerney, Gloucestershire, 1982–3, *Transactions of the Bristol and Gloucestershire Archaeological Society* 106: 19–85.

Trow, S. (1988b) The Coarse pottery. In Trow, S. Excavations at Ditches hillfort, North Cerney, Gloucestershire, 1982–3, *Transactions of the Bristol and Gloucestershire Archaeological Society* 106: 64–76.

Trow, S. (1990) By the northern shores of Ocean. Some observations on acculturation processes at the edge of the Roman world. In Blagg, T. and Millett, M. (eds) *The Early Roman Empire in the West.* Oxbow Books, Oxford, 103–108.

Trow, S. and James, S. (1988) Ditches Villa, North Cerney: an example of locational conservatism in the Early Roman Cotswolds. In Branigan, K. and Miles, D. (eds) *The Economies of Romano-British Villas.* J.R. Collis Publications, Sheffield, 83–87.

Tutin, T. G., Heywood, V. H., Burges, N. A., Moore, D. M., Valentine, D. H., Walters, S. M. and Webb, D. A. (1964–80) *Flora Europaea vols 1–5.* Cambridge University Press, Cambridge.

Tyers, P. (1996) *Roman pottery in Britain.* Batsford, London.

van der Veen, M. (1992) *Crop husbandry regimes: an archaeobotanical study of farming in northern England 1000 BC – AD 500.* J.R. Collis publications, Department of Archaeology and Prehistory, Sheffield.

von den Driesch, A. (1976) *A guide to the measurement of animal bones from archaeological sites.* Peabody Museum Bulletin 1, Cambridge, Massachusetts.

von den Driesch, A. and Boessneck, J. A. (1974) Kritische Anmerkungen zur Widerristhöhenberechnung aus Längenmaßen vor- und frühgeschichtlicher Tierknochen, *Saugetierkundliche Mitteilungen* 22: 325–348.

Wainwright, G. J. (1979) *Gussage All Saints: an Iron Age settlement in Dorset.* Department of the Environment Archaeological Reports, No. 10, London.

Walthew, C. V. (1975) The town house and the villa house in Roman Britain, *Britannia* 6: 189–205.

Ward-Perkins, J. B. (1938) The Roman Villa at Lockleys, Welwyn, *The Antiquaries Journal* 18: 339–376.

Way, A. (1849) Account of the discovery of an Armilla of pure gold in clearing a coppice near Wendover in Buckinghamshire in 1847, *Archaeologia* 33: 347–349.

Webster, G. (1965) Further Investigations on the Site of the Roman Fort at Waddon Hill, Stoke Abbott, 1960–62, *Proceedings of the Dorset Natural History and Archaeological Society,* 86: 135–149.

Webster, G. (1981a) The Excavation of a Romano-British rural establishment at Barnsley Park: Part 1, *Transactions of the Bristol and Gloucestershire Archaeological Society* 99: 21–78.

Webster, G. (1981b) Final Report on the Excavations of the Roman Fort at Waddon Hill, Stoke Abbott, 1963–69, *Proceedings of the Dorset Natural History and Archaeological Society,* 101: 51–90.

Webster, G. (1982) The Excavation of a Romano-British rural establishment at Barnsley Park: Part 2, *Transactions of the Bristol and Gloucestershire Archaeological Society,* 100: 56–89.

Webster, G. (2002) Excavations by Graham Webster, 1955–85. In Chadderton, J. (ed.) *The Legionary Fortress at Wroxeter.* English Heritage Archaeological Report No. 19, London.

Webster, J. (2001) Creolizing the Roman Provinces, *American Journal of Archaeology,* 105: 209–225.

Webster, J. (2005) Archaeologies of slavery and servitude: bringing 'New World' perspectives to Roman Britain, *Journal of Roman Archaeology* 18: 161–179.

Webster, P. (1976) Severn Valley ware: a preliminary study, *Transactions of the Bristol and Gloucestershire Archaeological Society* 94: 18–46.

Webster, P. (1993). The post-fortress Coarsewares. In Manning, W. H. (ed.) *Report on the Excavations at Usk 1965–1976. The Roman pottery.* Cardiff University Press, Cardiff, 227–357.

Wedlake, W. (1958) *Excavations at Camerton, Somerset.* Camerton Excavation club, Bath.

Wedlake, W. J. (1982) *The excavation of the shrine of Apollo at Nettleton, Wiltshire 1956–71.* Reports of the Research Committee of the Society of Antiquaries of London 40, Dorking.

West, S. (1990) *West Stow, The Prehistoric and Romano-British Occupations.* East Anglian Archaeology, Report No. 48, Bury St. Edmunds.

Wheeler, R. E. M. (1943) *Maiden Castle, Dorset. Reports of the Research Committee of the Society of Antiquaries of London 12,* Oxford.

Wheeler, R. E. M. and Wheeler, T. V. (1936) *Verulamium, a Belgic and two Roman Cities.* Reports of the Research Committee of the Society of Antiquaries of London, No. 11, Oxford.

White, K. D. (1970) *Roman farming.* Thames and Hudson, London.

Williams, R. J. and Zeepvat, R. J. (1994) *Bancroft, A Late Bronze Age/Iron Age Settlement, Roman Villa and Temple-Mausoleum.* Buckinghamshire Archaeological Society Monograph Series, No. 7, Buckingham.

Willis, S. H. 1998a. Samian pottery in Britain: exploring its distribution and archaeological potential, *The Archaeological Journal* 155: 82–133.

Willis, S. H. 1998b. The Iron Age and Roman pottery, in L. Main, Excavation of a timber round-house and broch at the Fairy Knowe, Buchlyvie, Stirlingshire, *Proceedings of the Society of Antiquaries of Scotland* 128, for 1998, (293–417): 321–31.

Willis, S. H. (2000a) The pottery. In Jackson, R. (ed.) *The Roman settlement of Ariconium, near Weston-under-Penyard, Herefordshire: an assessment and synthesis of the evidence.* Archaeological service. Worcestershire County Council/ English Heritage. Worcestershire County Council Archaeology Society Report 833.

Willis, S. H. (2000b). The samian pottery, in Ferris, I. M., Bevan, L. and Cuttler, R., *The Excavation of a Romano-British Shrine at Orton's Pasture, Rocester, Staffordshire,* British Archaeological Report Brit. Ser. 314, Oxford, 38–45.

Willis, S. H. 2005. *An E-monograph: Samian pottery, a resource for the study of Roman Britain and beyond. The results of the English Heritage funded Samian Project,* in *Internet Archaeology,* 17. http://intarch.ac.uk/journal/issue17/willis_toc.html

Willis, S. H. In press. *The samian pottery, in R. White and M. van Leusen, The Wroxeter Hinterland Survey,* Birmingham University and English Heritage Monograph.

Wilson, B., Hamilton, J., Bramwell, B. and Armitage, P. (1978) The animal bones. In Parrington, M. (ed.) *The excavation of an Iron Age settlement, Bronze Age ring ditchs and Roman features at Ashville trading estate, Abingdon (Oxfordshire), 1974–76.* Council for British Archaeology Research Report 28, London, 110–139.

Wilson, D. R. (1974) Romano-British villas from the air, *Britannia* 5: 251–261.

Winder, J. 1980. The marine molluscs. In Holdsworth, P. *Excavations at Melbourne Street, Southampton 1971–76.* Southampton Archaeological research committee report 1, Council for British Archaeology Research Report 33, London, 121–127.

Woodward, A. and Leach, P. (1993) *The Uley Shrines. Excavation of a ritual complex on West Hill, Uley, Gloucestershire: 1977–9.* English Heritage. Archaeological Report No. 17, London.

Woodward, P., Davies, S. and Graham, A. (1992). *Excavations at the Old Methodist Chapel and Greyhound Yard, Dorchester, 1981–1984.* Dorset Natural History and Archaeological Society Monograph 12, Dorchester.

Woolf, G. (1998) *Becoming Roman: The origins of provincial civilization in Gaul.* Cambridge University Press, Cambridge.

Wrathmell, S. and Nicholson, A. (1990) *Dalton Parlours Iron Age settlement and Roman Villa.* West Yorkshire Archaeology Services, Wakefield.

Wymark, C. (2003) *Thames Water repairs to public sewers, Cirencester, Gloucestershire. Programme of archaeological recording.* Cotswold Archaeology CA 03140.

Young, C. (1977) *The Roman pottery industry of the Oxford region.* British Archaeological Report Brit. Ser. 43, Oxford.

Zienkiewicz, J. D. (1986) *The Legionary Fortress Baths at Caerleon.* CADW, Cardiff.

INDEX